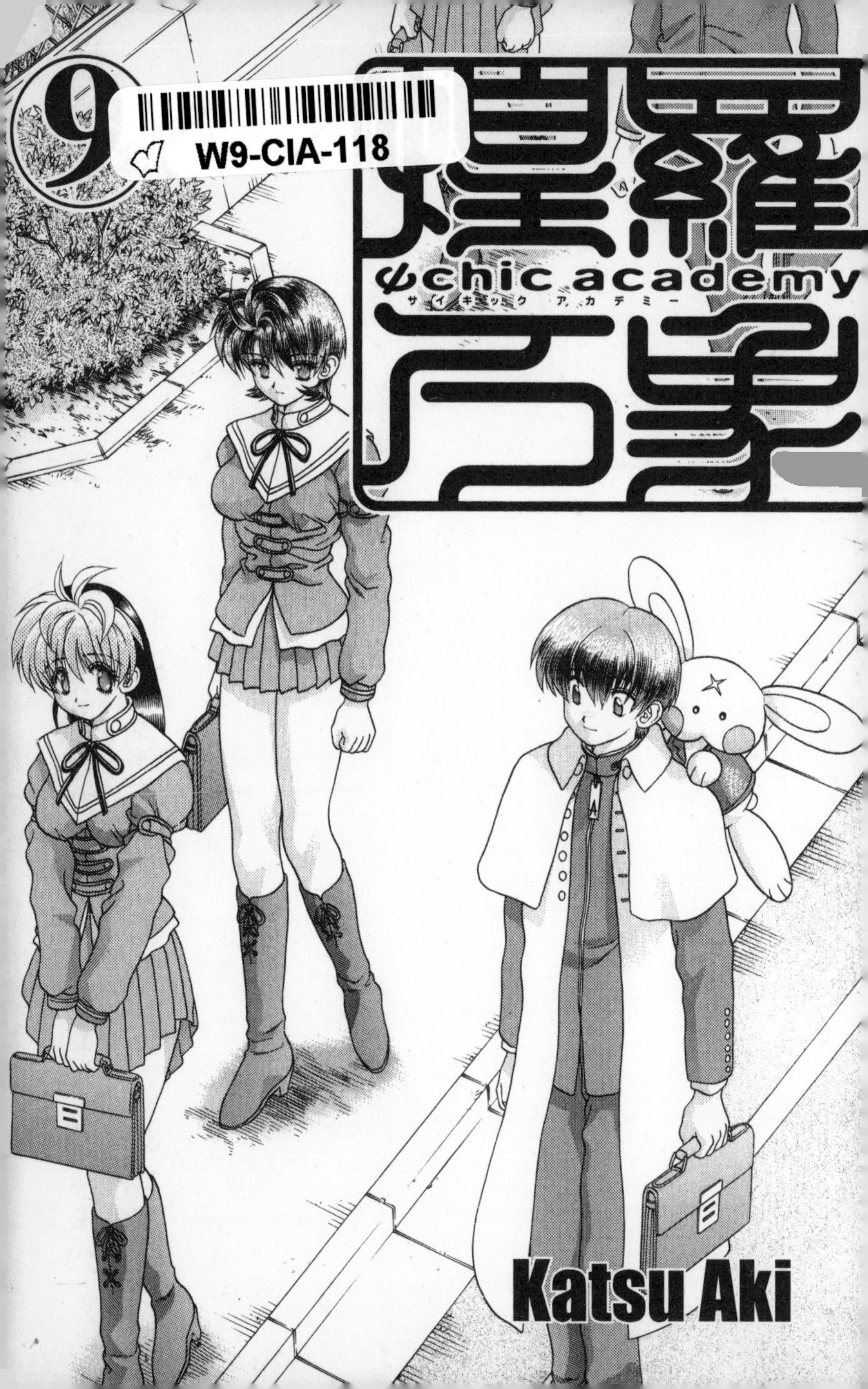
9
ψchic academy
サイキック アカデミー
Katsu Aki

Psychic Academy

Volume 9

By
Katsu Aki

TOKYOPOP®

HAMBURG // LONDON // LOS ANGELES // TOKYO

Psychic Academy Vol. 9

Created by Katsu Aki

Translation - Yuki N. Johnson
English Adaptation - Nathan Johnson
Retouch and Lettering - Lucas Rivera
Production Artist - Rafael Najarian
Cover Design - Seth Cable

Editor - Aaron Suhr
Digital Imaging Manager - Chris Buford
Production Managers - Jennifer Miller and Mutsumi Miyazaki
Managing Editor - Jill Freshney
VP of Production - Ron Klamert
Publisher and Editor-in-Chief - Mike Kiley
President and C.O.O. - John Parker
C.E.O. - Stuart Levy

A  Manga

TOKYOPOP Inc.
5900 Wilshire Blvd. Suite 2000
Los Angeles, CA 90036

E-mail: info@TOKYOPOP.com
Come visit us online at www.TOKYOPOP.com

ISBN: 1-59532-428-3

First TOKYOPOP printing: September 2005
10 9 8 7 6 5 4 3 2 1
Printed in Canada

Story Thus Far...

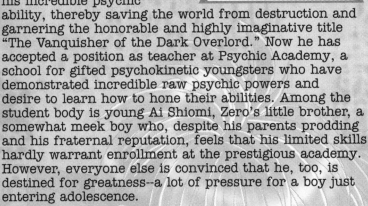

Zerodyme Kyupura Pa Azalraku Vairu Rua Darogu (a.k.a. Zero) stopped the evil demon lord with his incredible psychic ability, thereby saving the world from destruction and garnering the honorable and highly imaginative title "The Vanquisher of the Dark Overlord." Now he has accepted a position as teacher at Psychic Academy, a school for gifted psychokinetic youngsters who have demonstrated incredible raw psychic powers and desire to learn how to hone their abilities. Among the student body is young Ai Shiomi, Zero's little brother, a somewhat meek boy who, despite his parents prodding and his fraternal reputation, feels that his limited skills hardly warrant enrollment at the prestigious academy. However, everyone else is convinced that he, too, is destined for greatness--a lot of pressure for a boy just entering adolescence.

As Ai and Mew struggle with the emotional implications of their Para Dream, an unknown aura attacks the Academy. Mew is injured in the fray and although the intent of this mysterious assailant is unclear, one thing is--the power of this aura could rival even Zerodyme's. However, the intrigue doesn't end there, as Mew falls into the hands of the enigmatic Dr. Watabe--creating a whole new puzzle that Ai must solve.

CONTENTS

psychic academy

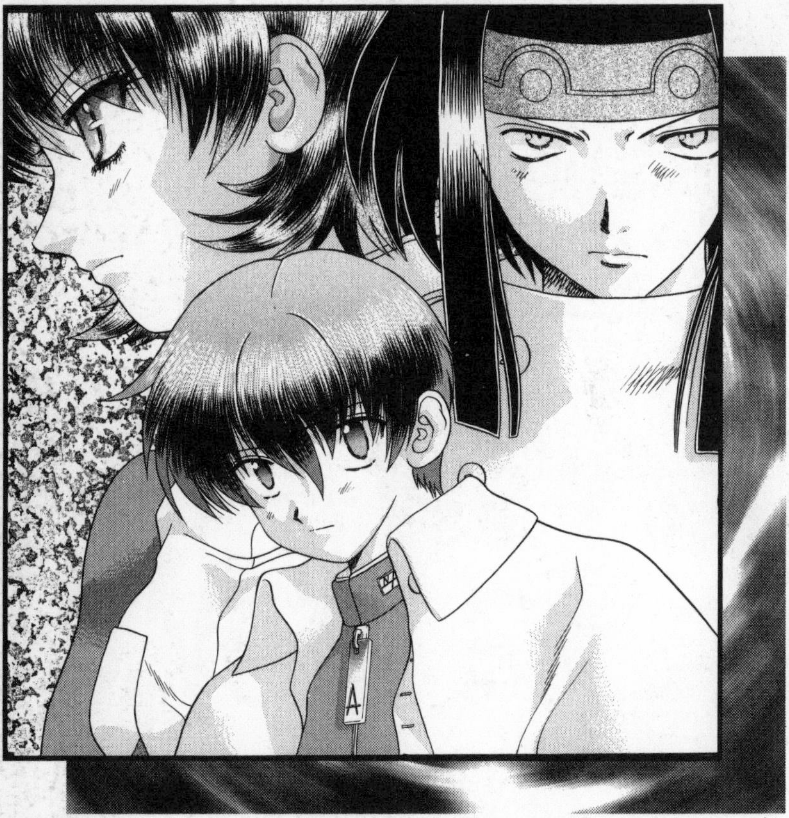

Chapter 28: The Normal School Routine

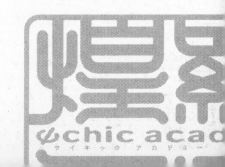

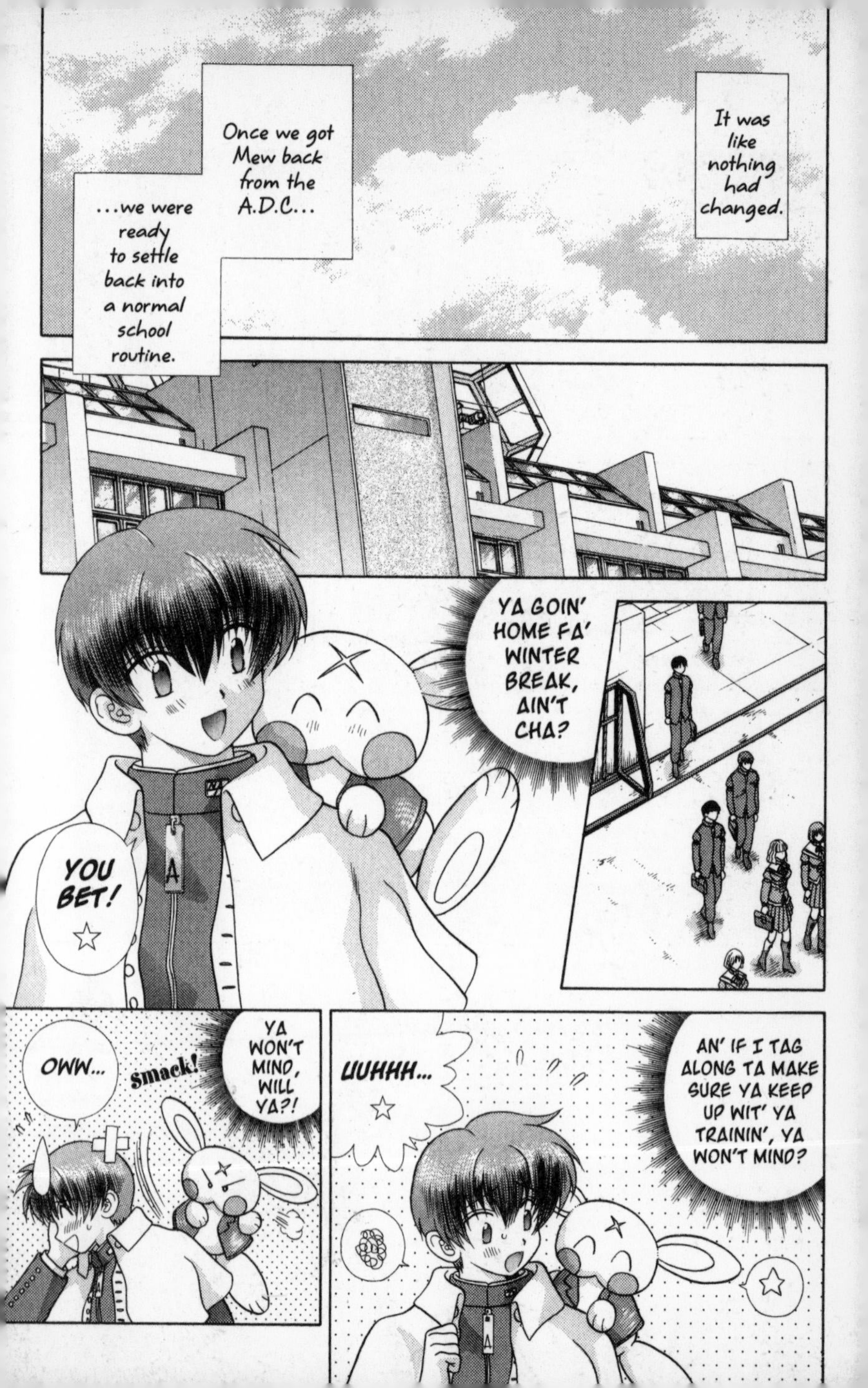

It was like nothing had changed.
Once we got Mew back from the A.D.C...
...we were ready to settle back into a normal school routine.
YA GOIN' HOME FA' WINTER BREAK, AIN'T CHA?
YOU BET! ☆
AN' IF I TAG ALONG TA MAKE SURE YA KEEP UP WIT' YA TRAININ', YA WON'T MIND?
UUHHH... ☆
YA WON'T MIND, WILL YA?!
Smack!
OWW...

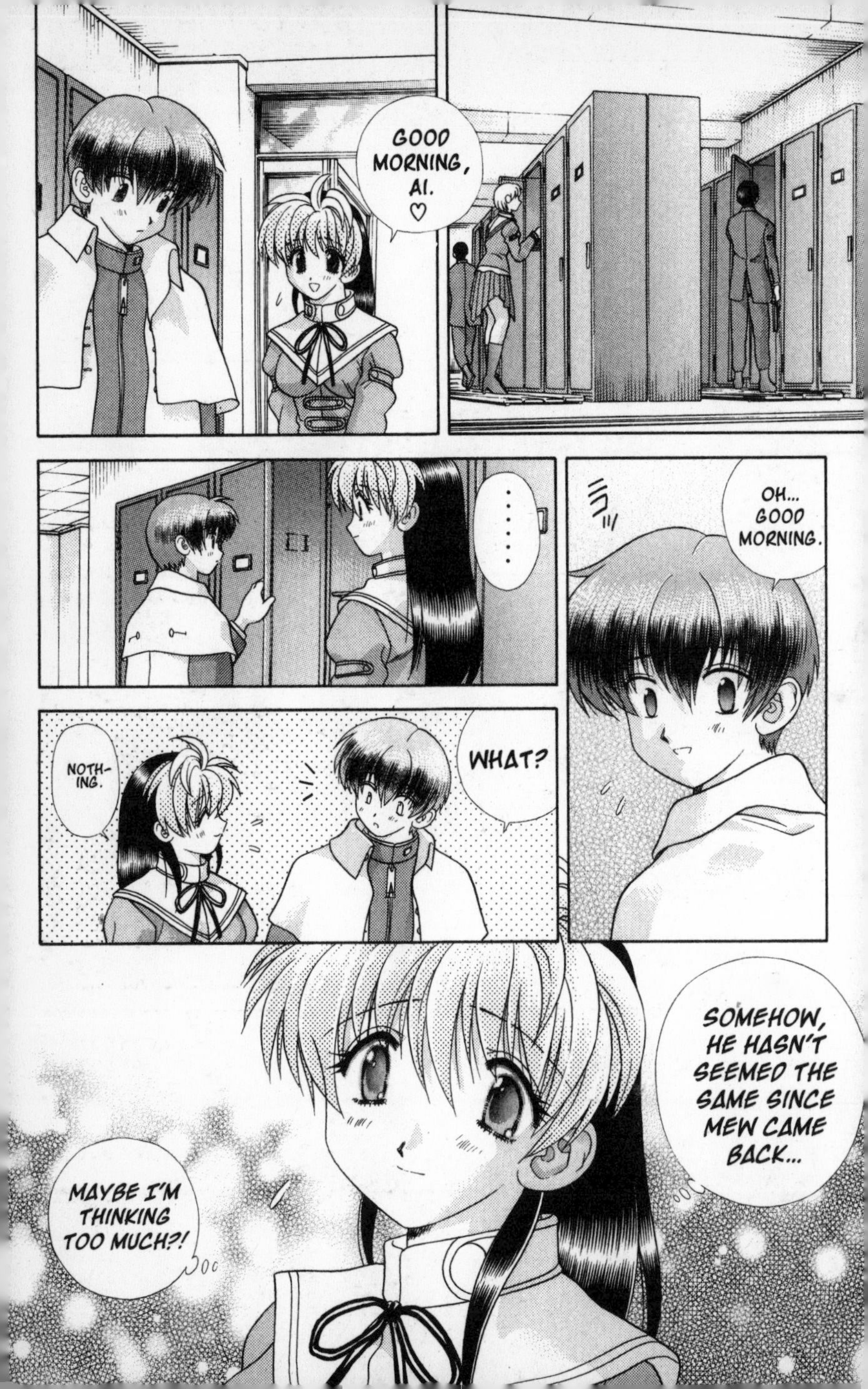
GOOD MORNING, AI. ♡
OH... GOOD MORNING.
......
WHAT?
NOTH-ING.
SOMEHOW, HE HASN'T SEEMED THE SAME SINCE MEW CAME BACK...
MAYBE I'M THINKING TOO MUCH?!

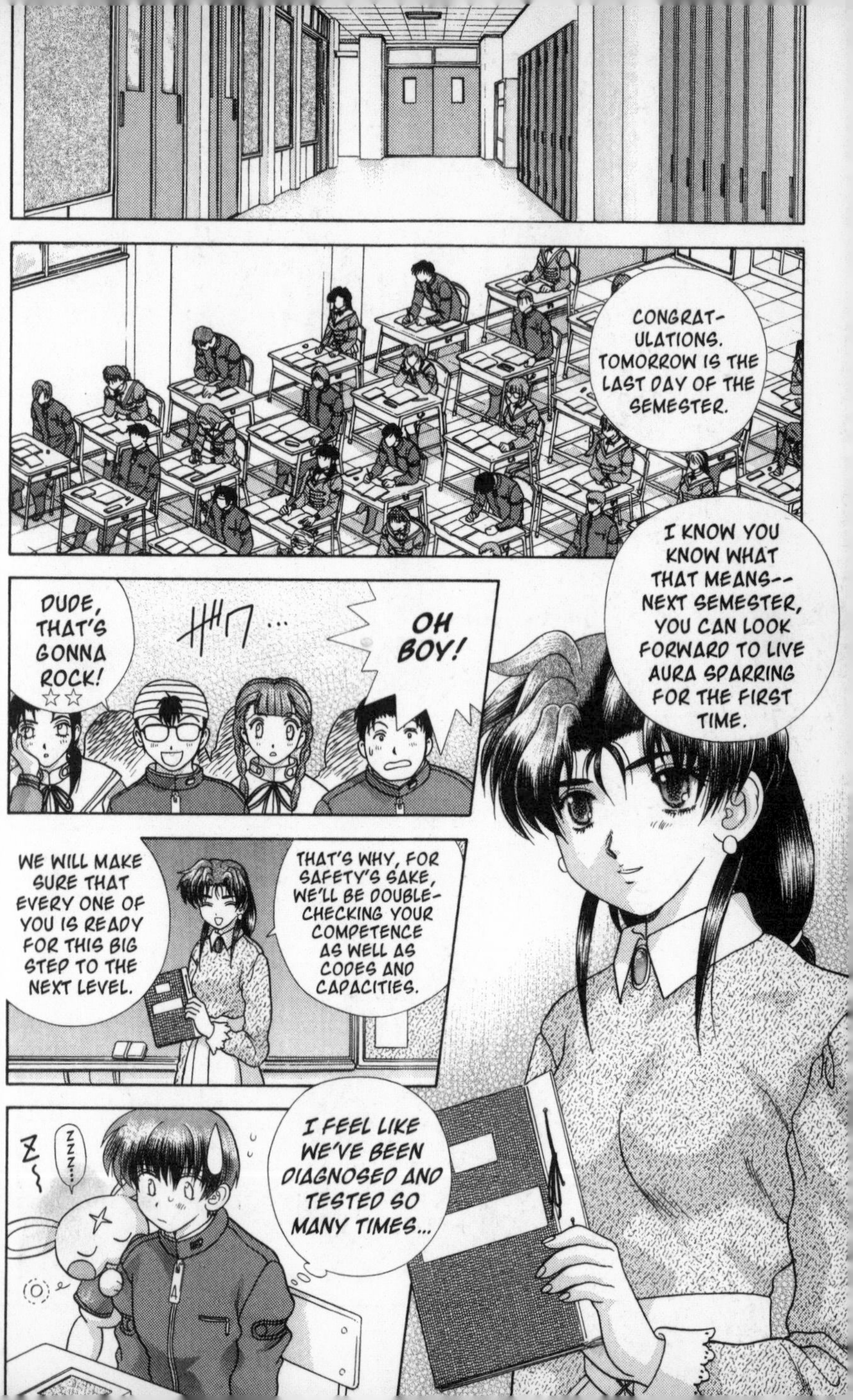
CONGRAT-ULATIONS. TOMORROW IS THE LAST DAY OF THE SEMESTER.
I KNOW YOU KNOW WHAT THAT MEANS-- NEXT SEMESTER, YOU CAN LOOK FORWARD TO LIVE AURA SPARRING FOR THE FIRST TIME.
OH BOY!
DUDE, THAT'S GONNA ROCK!
WE WILL MAKE SURE THAT EVERY ONE OF YOU IS READY FOR THIS BIG STEP TO THE NEXT LEVEL.
THAT'S WHY, FOR SAFETY'S SAKE, WE'LL BE DOUBLE-CHECKING YOUR COMPETENCE AS WELL AS CODES AND CAPACITIES.
I FEEL LIKE WE'VE BEEN DIAGNOSED AND TESTED SO MANY TIMES...
ZZZ...

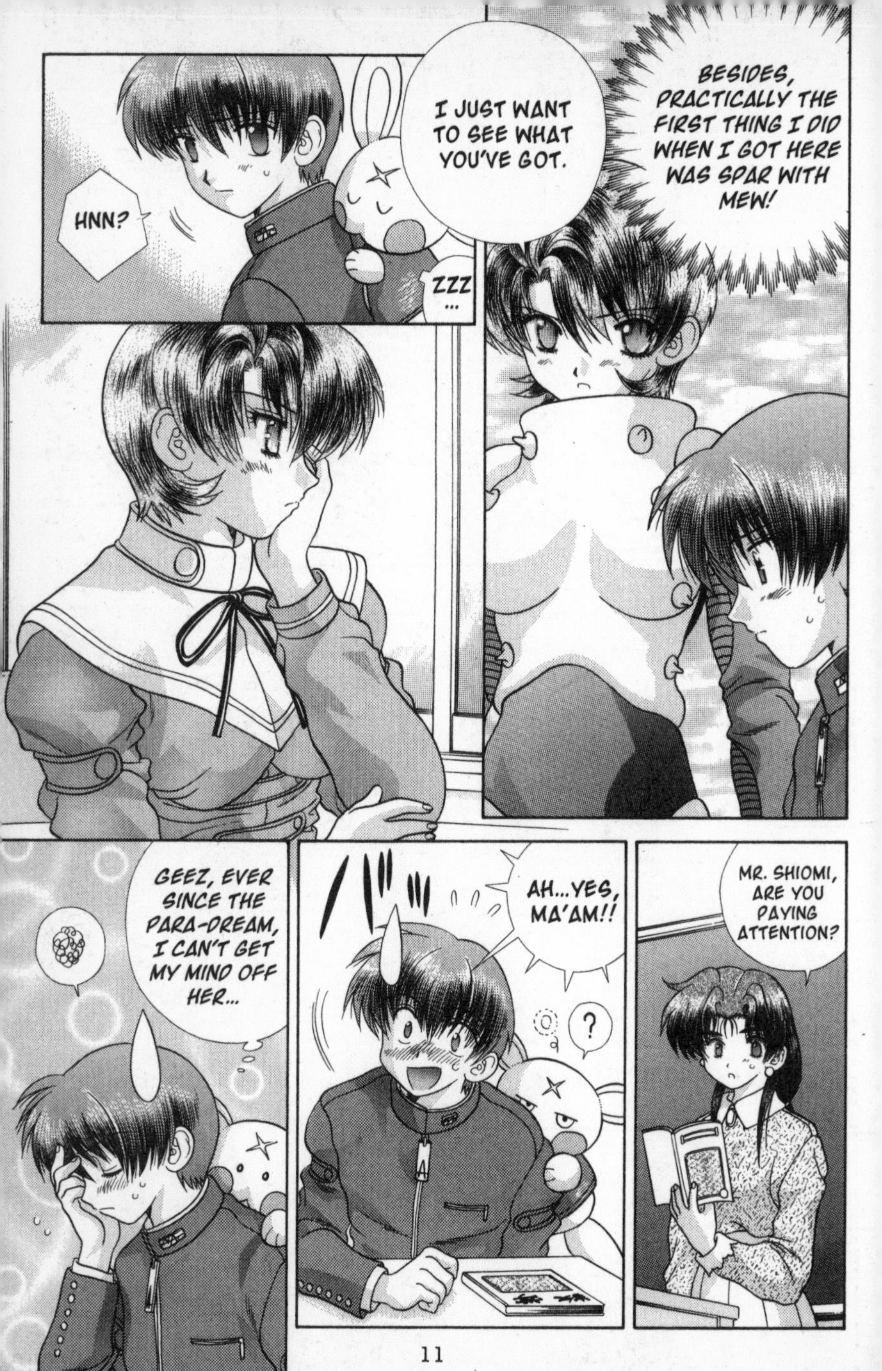

I JUST WANT TO SEE WHAT YOU'VE GOT.
BESIDES, PRACTICALLY THE FIRST THING I DID WHEN I GOT HERE WAS SPAR WITH MEW!
HNN?
ZZZ...
MR. SHIOMI, ARE YOU PAYING ATTENTION?
AH...YES, MA'AM!!
?
GEEZ, EVER SINCE THE PARA-DREAM, I CAN'T GET MY MIND OFF HER...

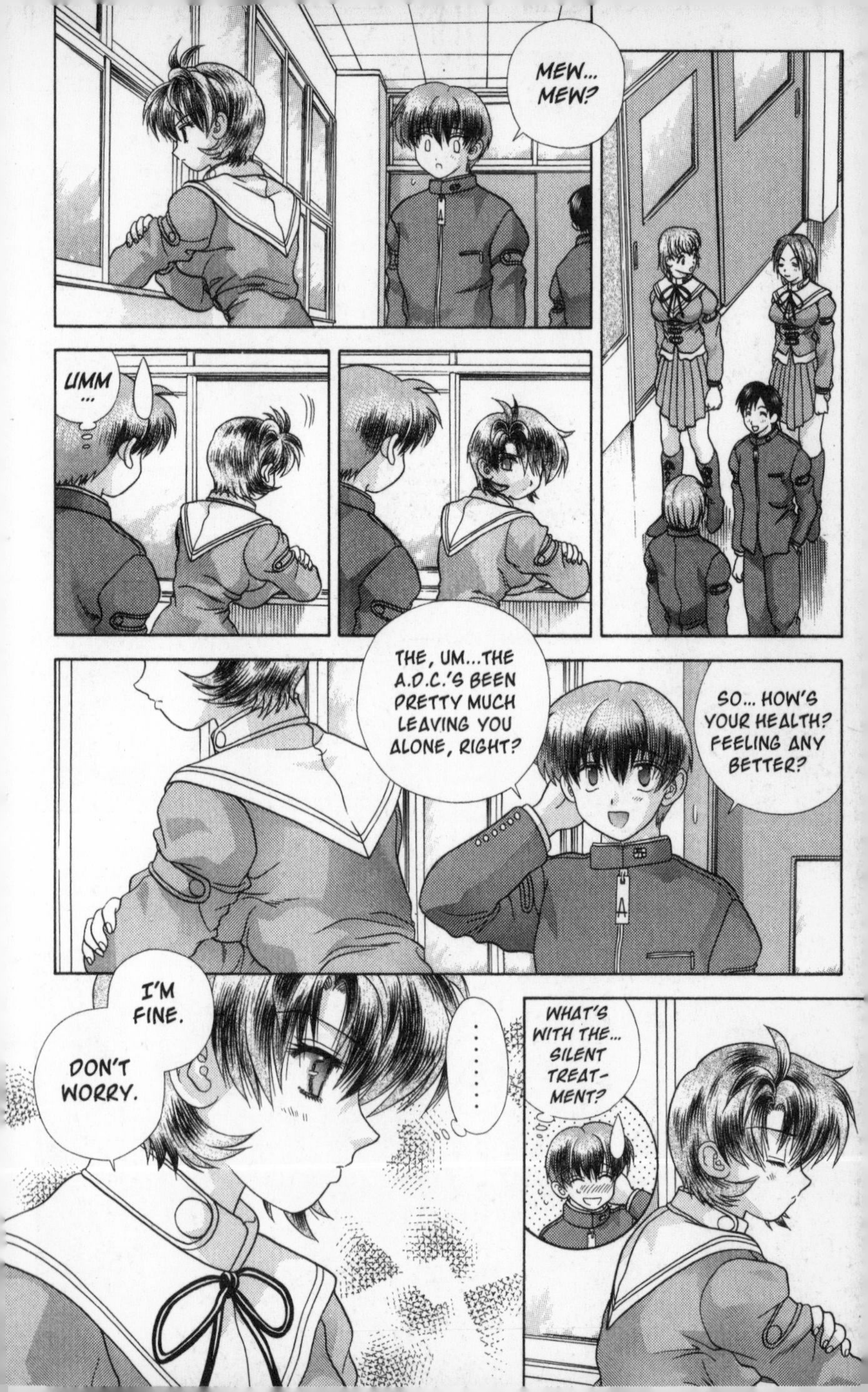
MEW... MEW?
UMM ...
THE, UM...THE A.D.C.'S BEEN PRETTY MUCH LEAVING YOU ALONE, RIGHT?
SO... HOW'S YOUR HEALTH? FEELING ANY BETTER?
I'M FINE.
DON'T WORRY.
....
WHAT'S WITH THE... SILENT TREATMENT?

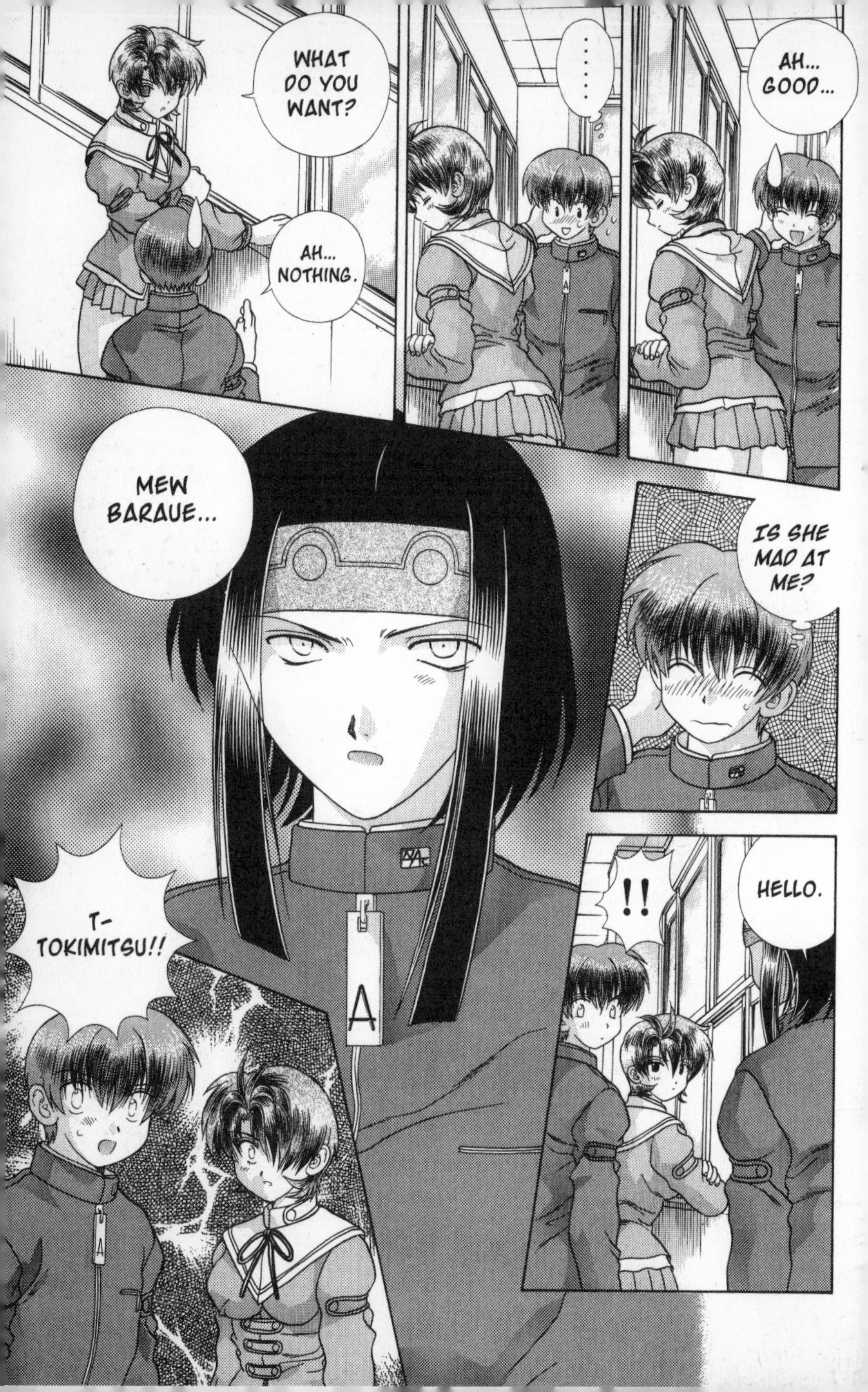
WHAT DO YOU WANT?
AH... NOTHING.
......
AH... GOOD...
IS SHE MAD AT ME?
HELLO.
!!
T-TOKIMITSU!!
MEW BARAUE...

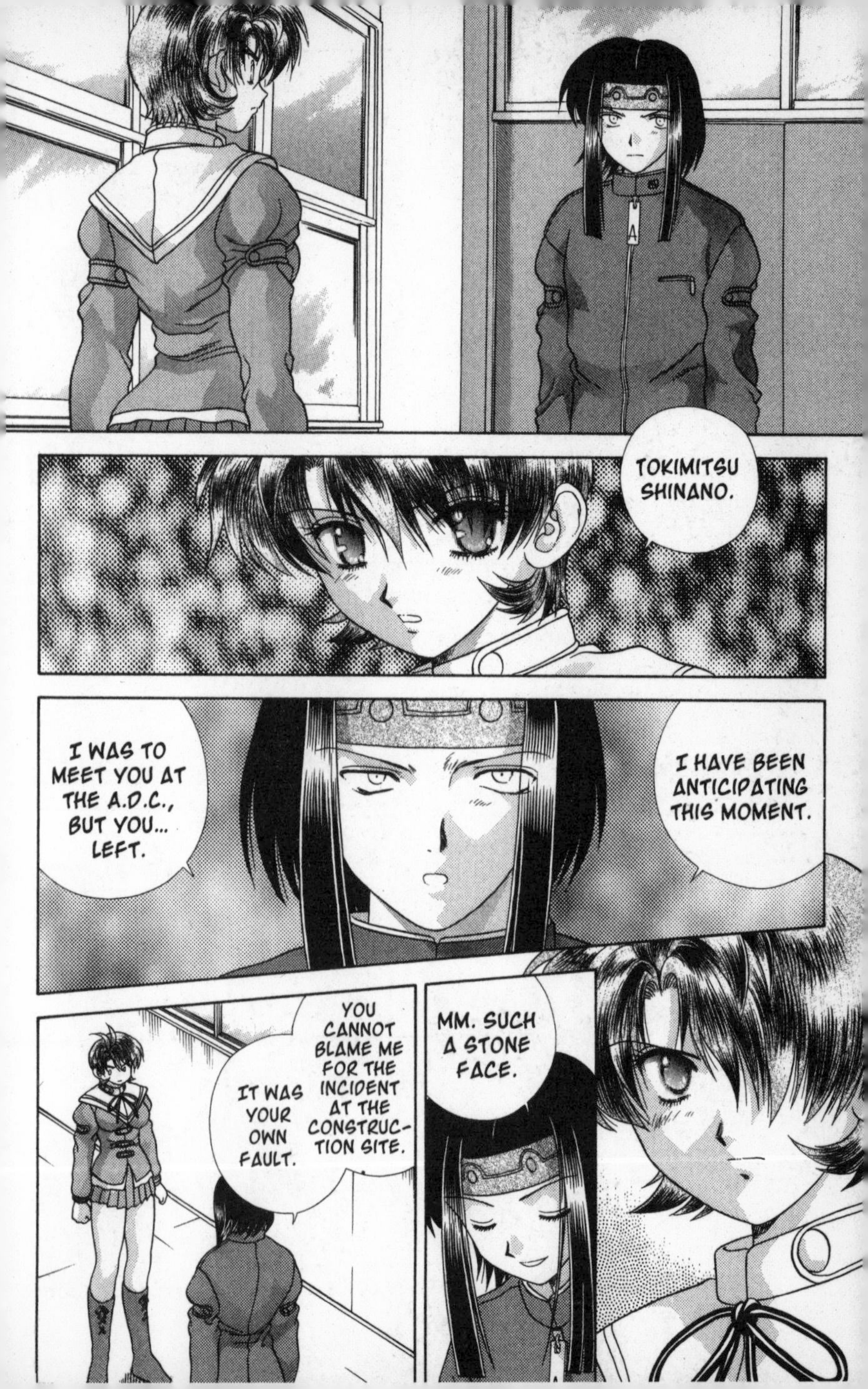
TOKIMITSU SHINANO.
I HAVE BEEN ANTICIPATING THIS MOMENT.
I WAS TO MEET YOU AT THE A.D.C., BUT YOU... LEFT.
MM. SUCH A STONE FACE.
YOU CANNOT BLAME ME FOR THE INCIDENT AT THE CONSTRUCTION SITE.
IT WAS YOUR OWN FAULT.

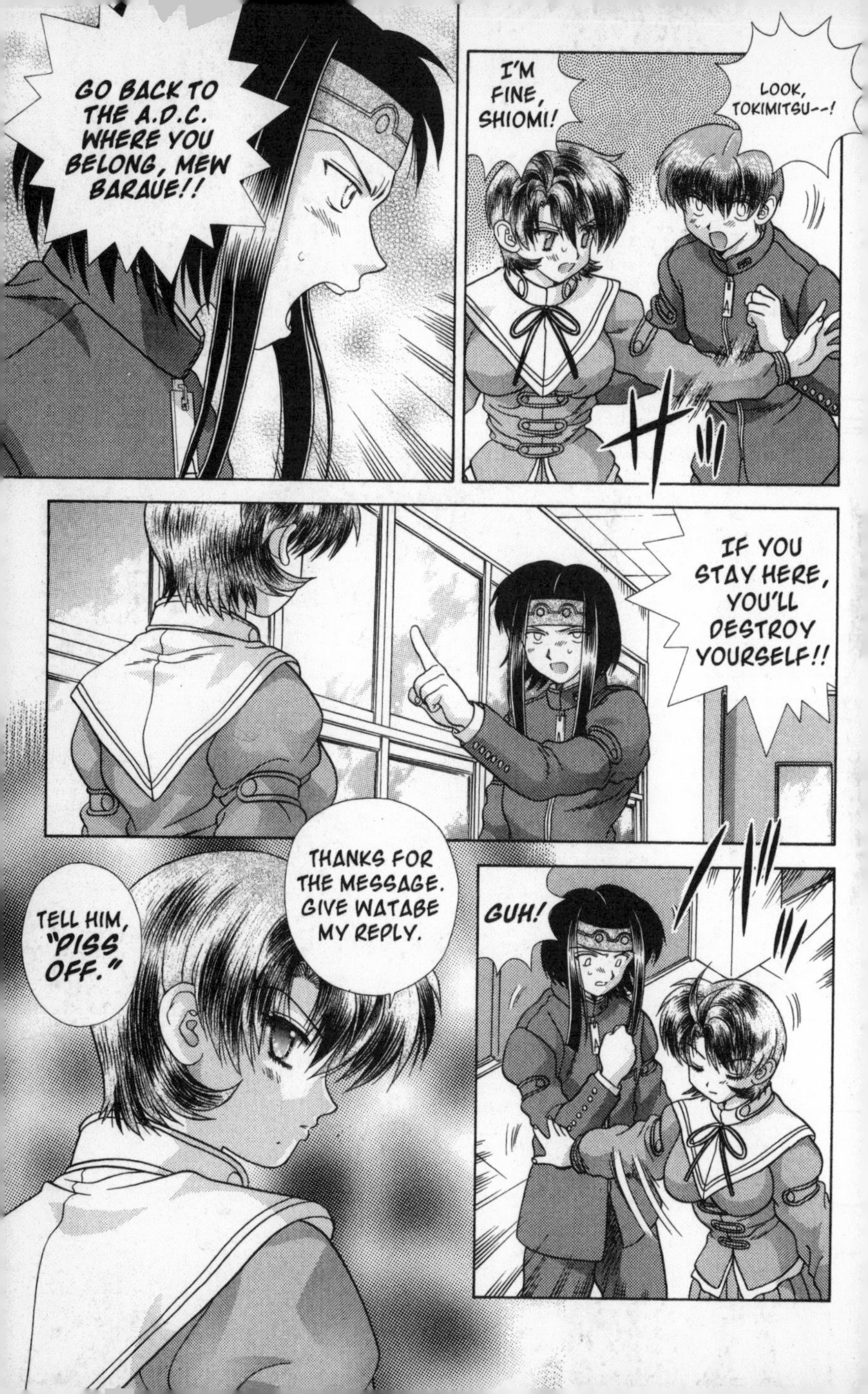

GO BACK TO THE A.D.C. WHERE YOU BELONG, MEW BARAUE!!
I'M FINE, SHIOMI!
LOOK, TOKIMITSU--!
IF YOU STAY HERE, YOU'LL DESTROY YOURSELF!!
THANKS FOR THE MESSAGE. GIVE WATABE MY REPLY.
TELL HIM, "PISS OFF."
GUH!

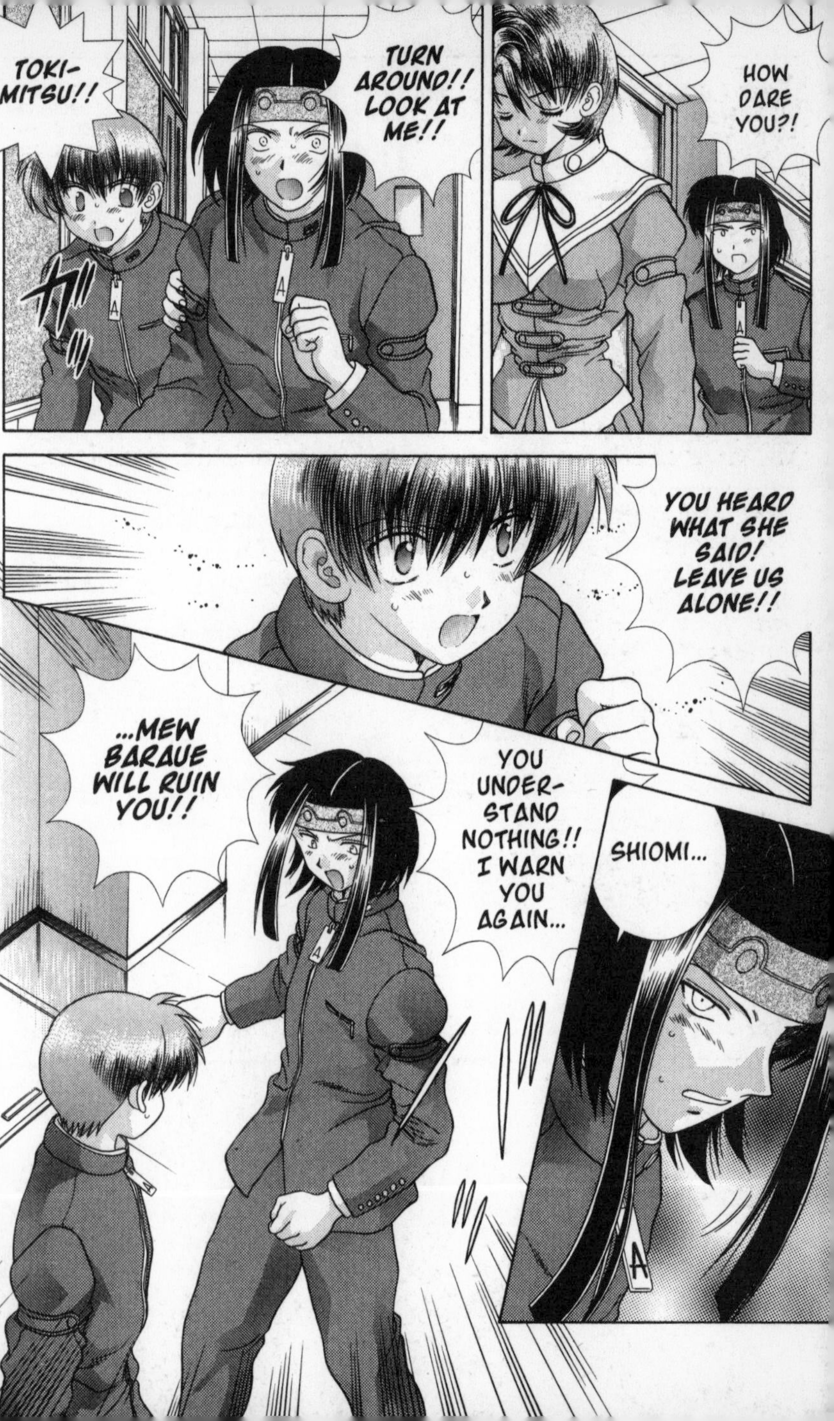
HOW DARE YOU?!
TURN AROUND!! LOOK AT ME!!
TOKI-MITSU!!
YOU HEARD WHAT SHE SAID! LEAVE US ALONE!!
SHIOMI...
YOU UNDER-STAND NOTHING!! I WARN YOU AGAIN...
...MEW BARAUE WILL RUIN YOU!!

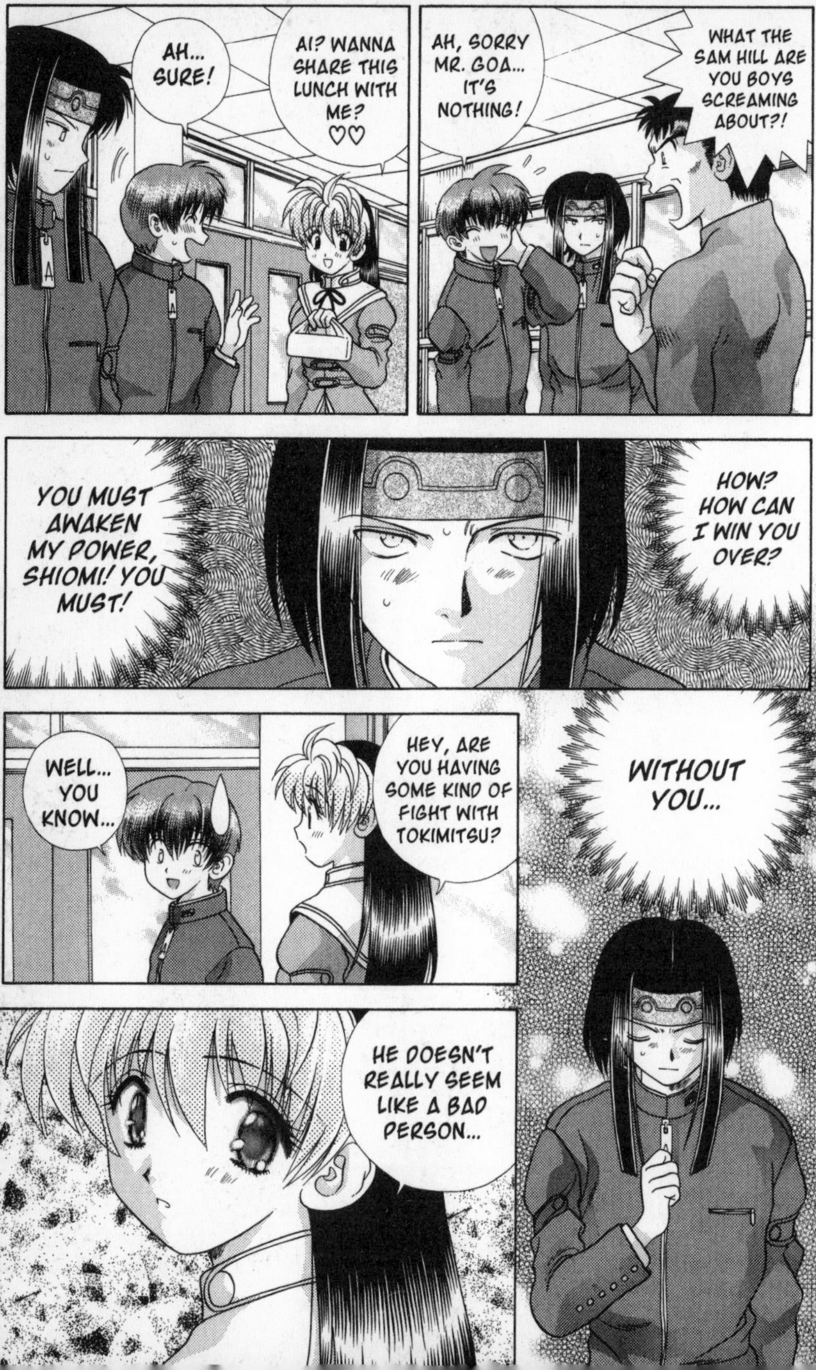
AI? WANNA SHARE THIS LUNCH WITH ME? ♡♡
AH... SURE!
WHAT THE SAM HILL ARE YOU BOYS SCREAMING ABOUT?!
AH, SORRY MR. GOA... IT'S NOTHING!
YOU MUST AWAKEN MY POWER, SHIOMI! YOU MUST!
HOW? HOW CAN I WIN YOU OVER?
WITHOUT YOU...
HEY, ARE YOU HAVING SOME KIND OF FIGHT WITH TOKIMITSU?
WELL... YOU KNOW...
HE DOESN'T REALLY SEEM LIKE A BAD PERSON...

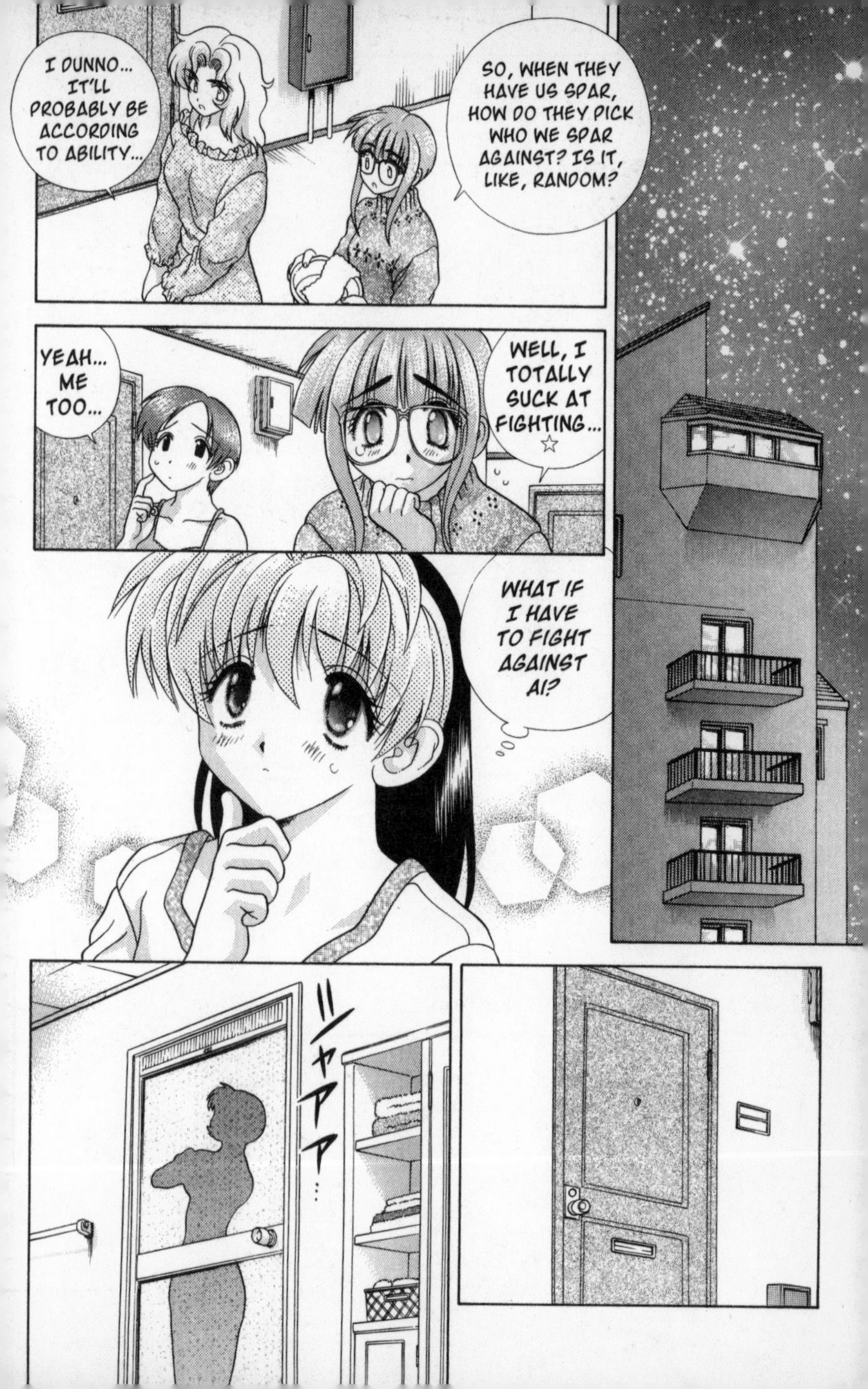
SO, WHEN THEY HAVE US SPAR, HOW DO THEY PICK WHO WE SPAR AGAINST? IS IT, LIKE, RANDOM?
I DUNNO... IT'LL PROBABLY BE ACCORDING TO ABILITY...
WELL, I TOTALLY SUCK AT FIGHTING...☆
YEAH... ME TOO...
WHAT IF I HAVE TO FIGHT AGAINST AI?
シャアア...

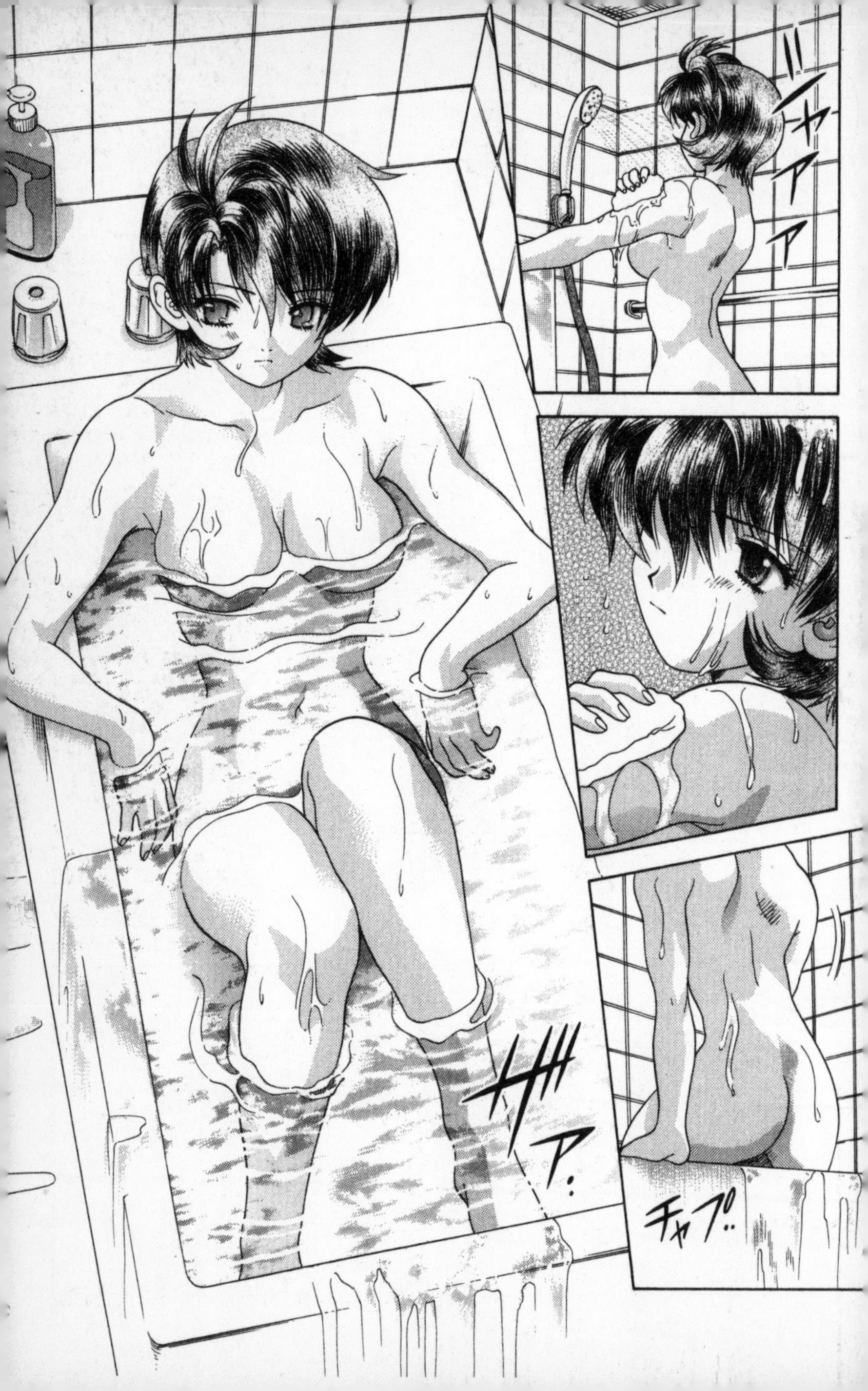
シャアアア
チャプ‥
ザザァ‥

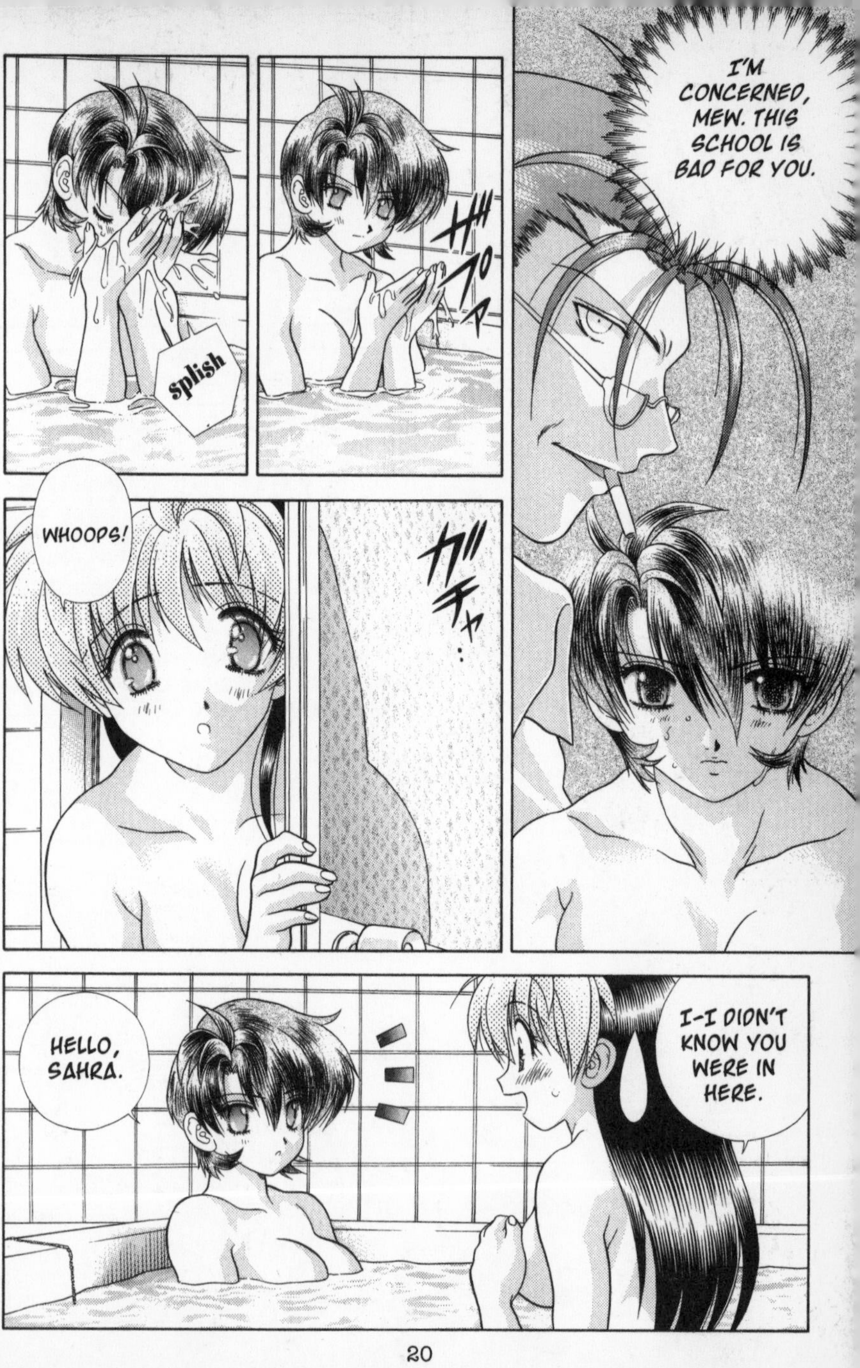
I'M CONCERNED, MEW. THIS SCHOOL IS BAD FOR YOU.
splish
WHOOPS!
ガチャ
I-I DIDN'T KNOW YOU WERE IN HERE.
HELLO, SAHRA.

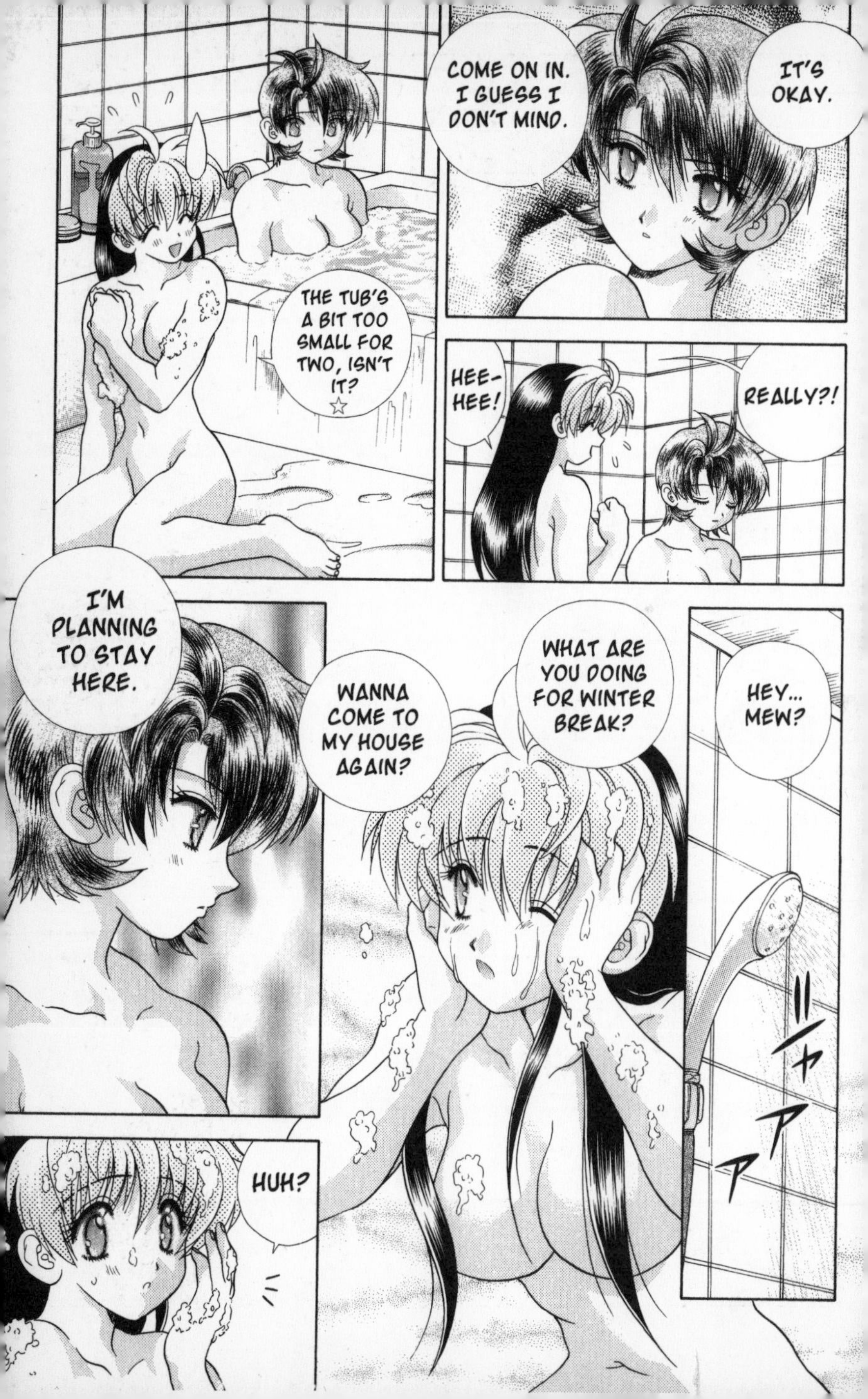
IT'S OKAY.
COME ON IN. I GUESS I DON'T MIND.
THE TUB'S A BIT TOO SMALL FOR TWO, ISN'T IT? ☆
REALLY?!
HEE-HEE!
HEY... MEW?
WHAT ARE YOU DOING FOR WINTER BREAK?
WANNA COME TO MY HOUSE AGAIN?
I'M PLANNING TO STAY HERE.
シャアア
HUH?

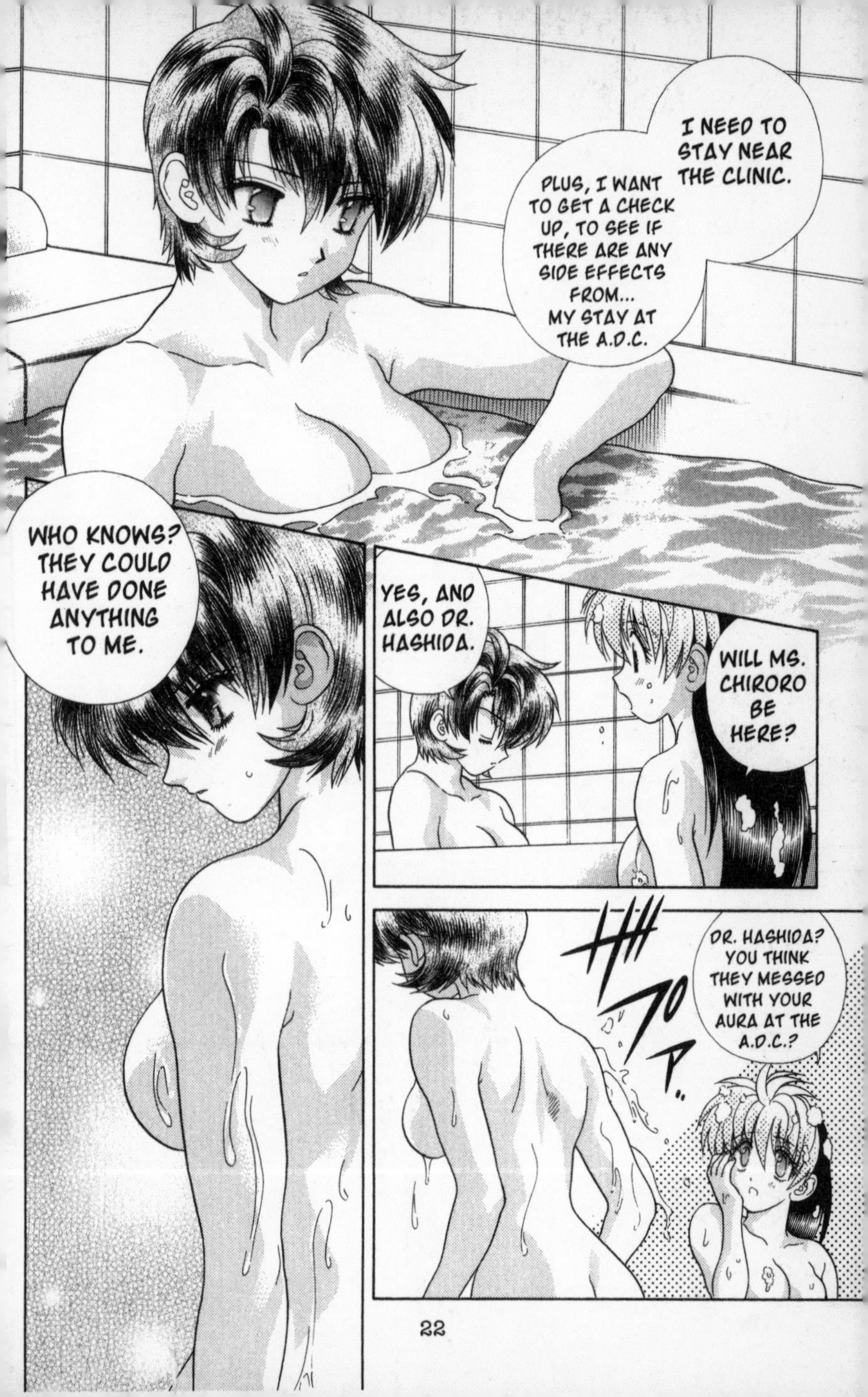

I NEED TO STAY NEAR THE CLINIC.
PLUS, I WANT TO GET A CHECK UP, TO SEE IF THERE ARE ANY SIDE EFFECTS FROM... MY STAY AT THE A.D.C.
WHO KNOWS? THEY COULD HAVE DONE ANYTHING TO ME.
WILL MS. CHIRORO BE HERE?
YES, AND ALSO DR. HASHIDA.
DR. HASHIDA? YOU THINK THEY MESSED WITH YOUR AURA AT THE A.D.C.?

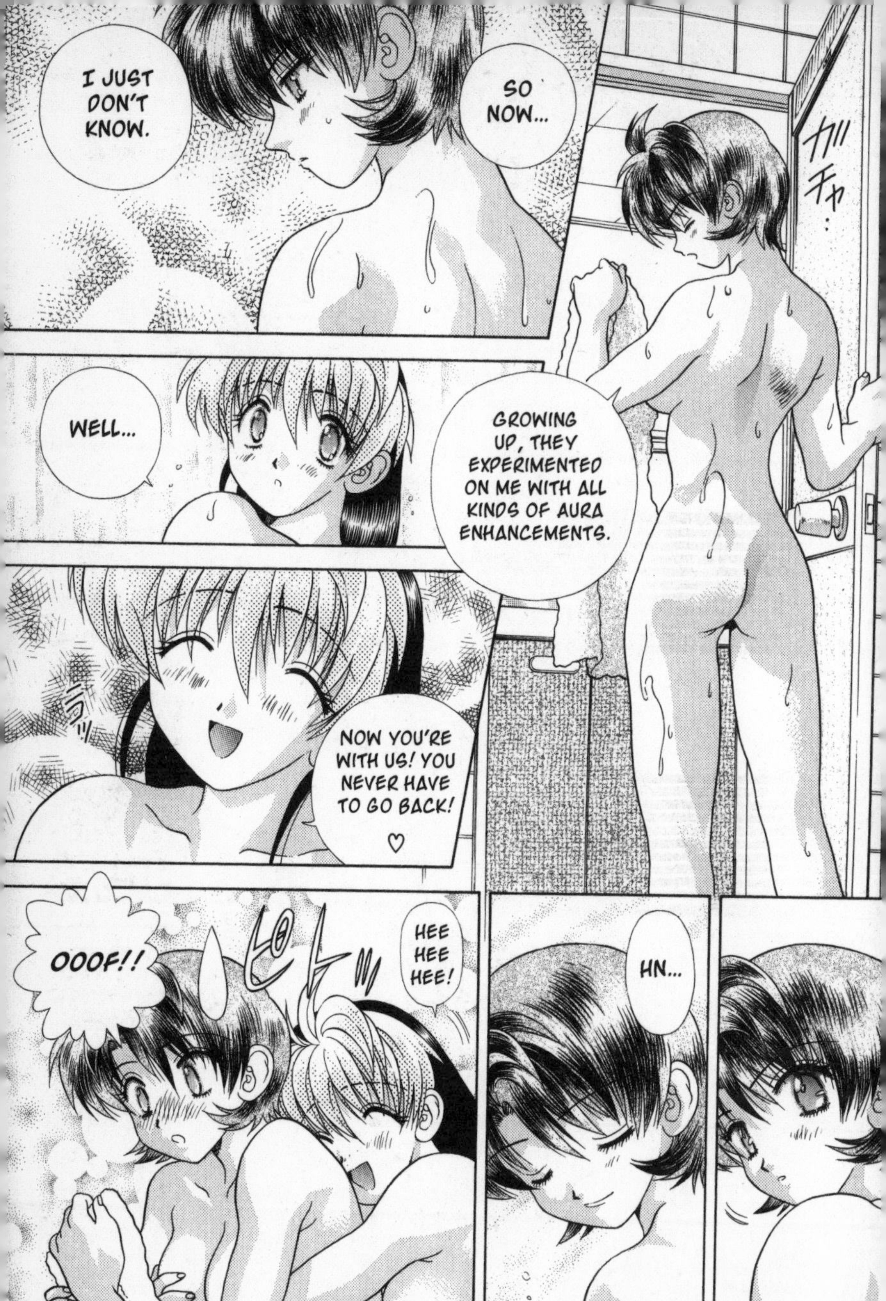
SO NOW...
I JUST DON'T KNOW.
ガチャ
GROWING UP, THEY EXPERIMENTED ON ME WITH ALL KINDS OF AURA ENHANCEMENTS.
WELL...
NOW YOU'RE WITH US! YOU NEVER HAVE TO GO BACK! ♡
HN...
HEE HEE HEE!
OOOF!!

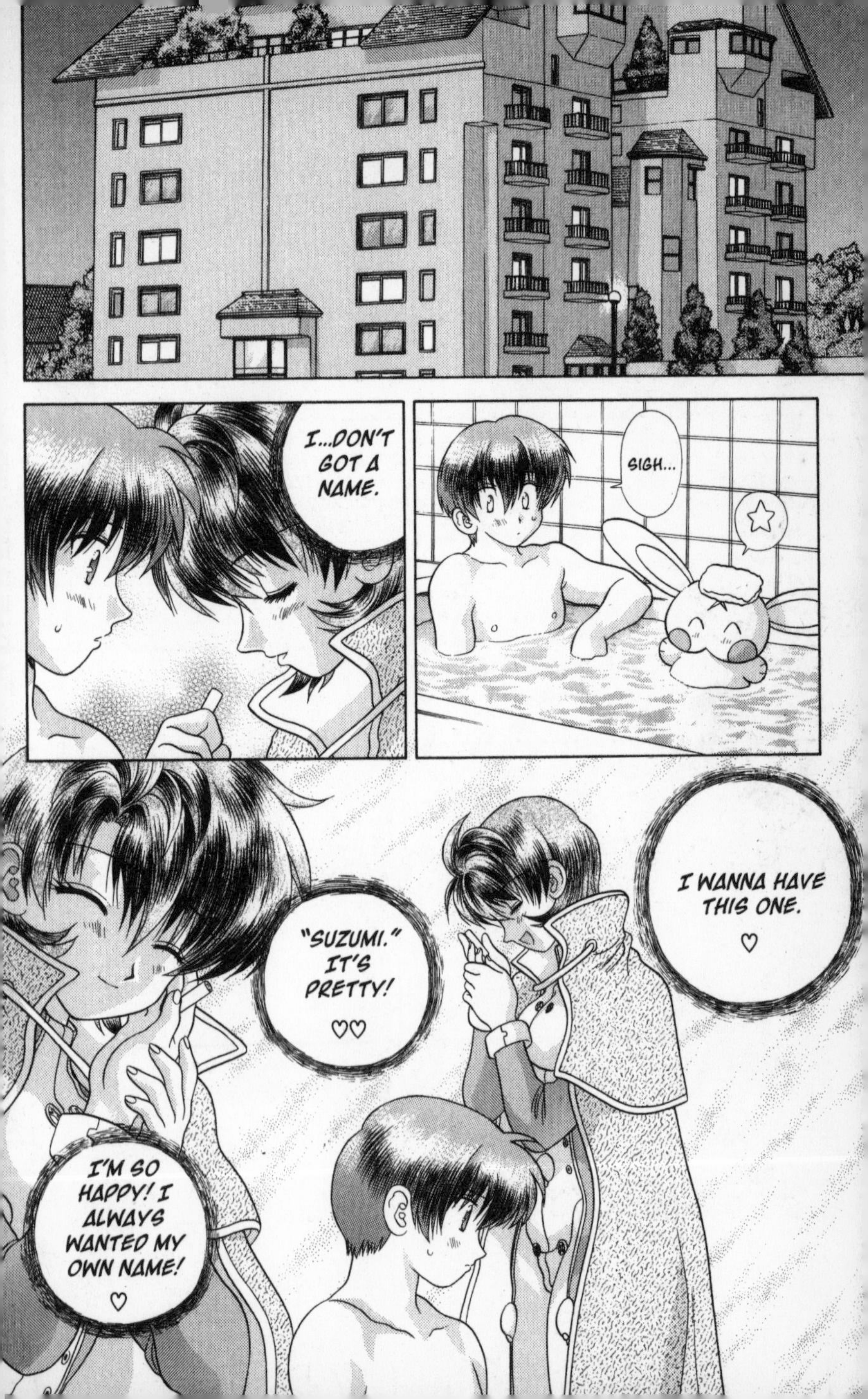
SIGH...
☆
I...DON'T GOT A NAME.
I WANNA HAVE THIS ONE. ♡
"SUZUMI." IT'S PRETTY! ♡♡
I'M SO HAPPY! I ALWAYS WANTED MY OWN NAME! ♡

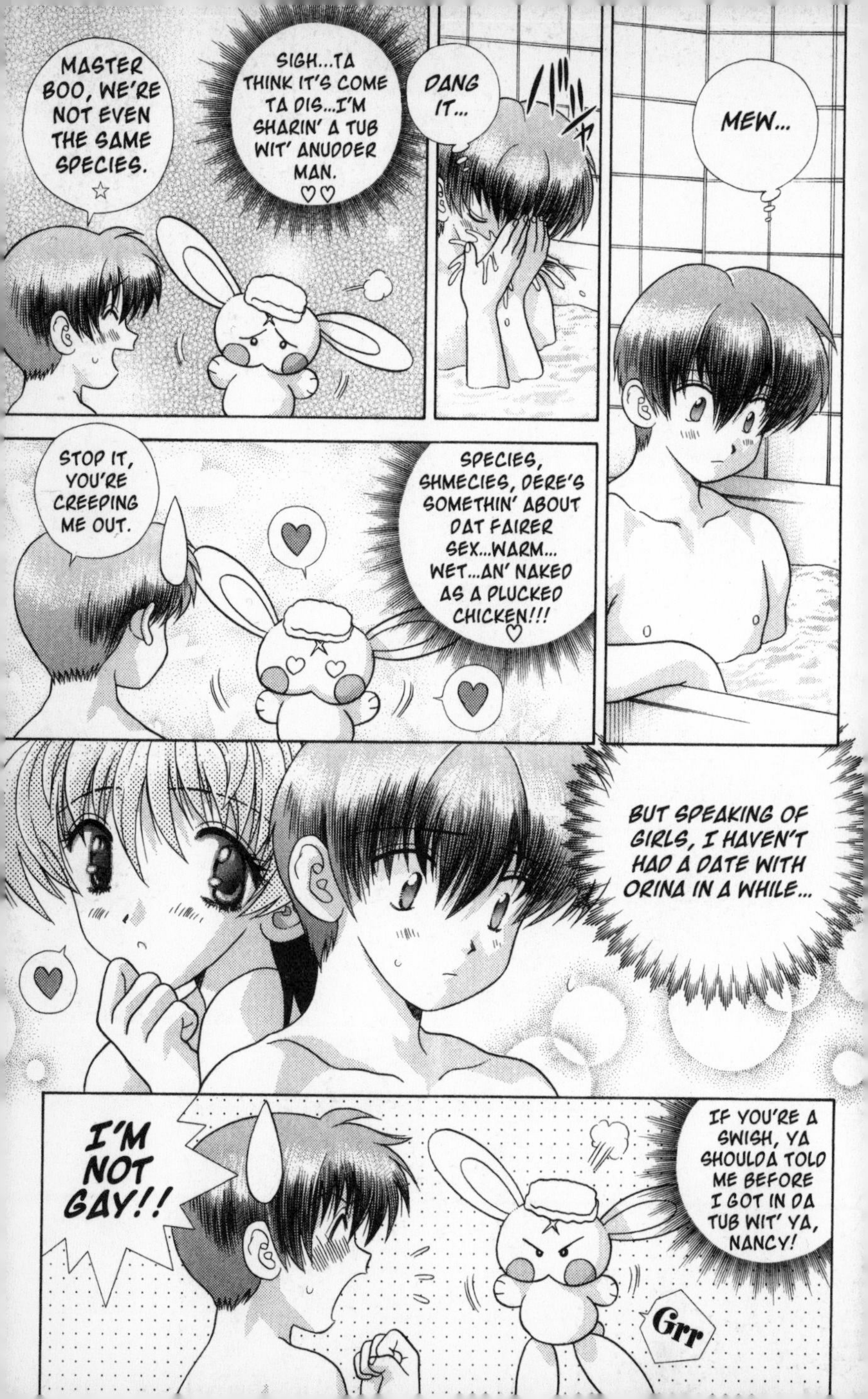
MASTER BOO, WE'RE NOT EVEN THE SAME SPECIES. ☆
SIGH...TA THINK IT'S COME TA DIS...I'M SHARIN' A TUB WIT' ANUDDER MAN. ♡♡
DANG IT...
MEW...
STOP IT, YOU'RE CREEPING ME OUT.
SPECIES, SHMECIES, DERE'S SOMETHIN' ABOUT DAT FAIRER SEX...WARM... WET...AN' NAKED AS A PLUCKED CHICKEN!!! ♡
BUT SPEAKING OF GIRLS, I HAVEN'T HAD A DATE WITH ORINA IN A WHILE...
I'M NOT GAY!!
IF YOU'RE A SWISH, YA SHOULDA TOLD ME BEFORE I GOT IN DA TUB WIT' YA, NANCY!
Grr

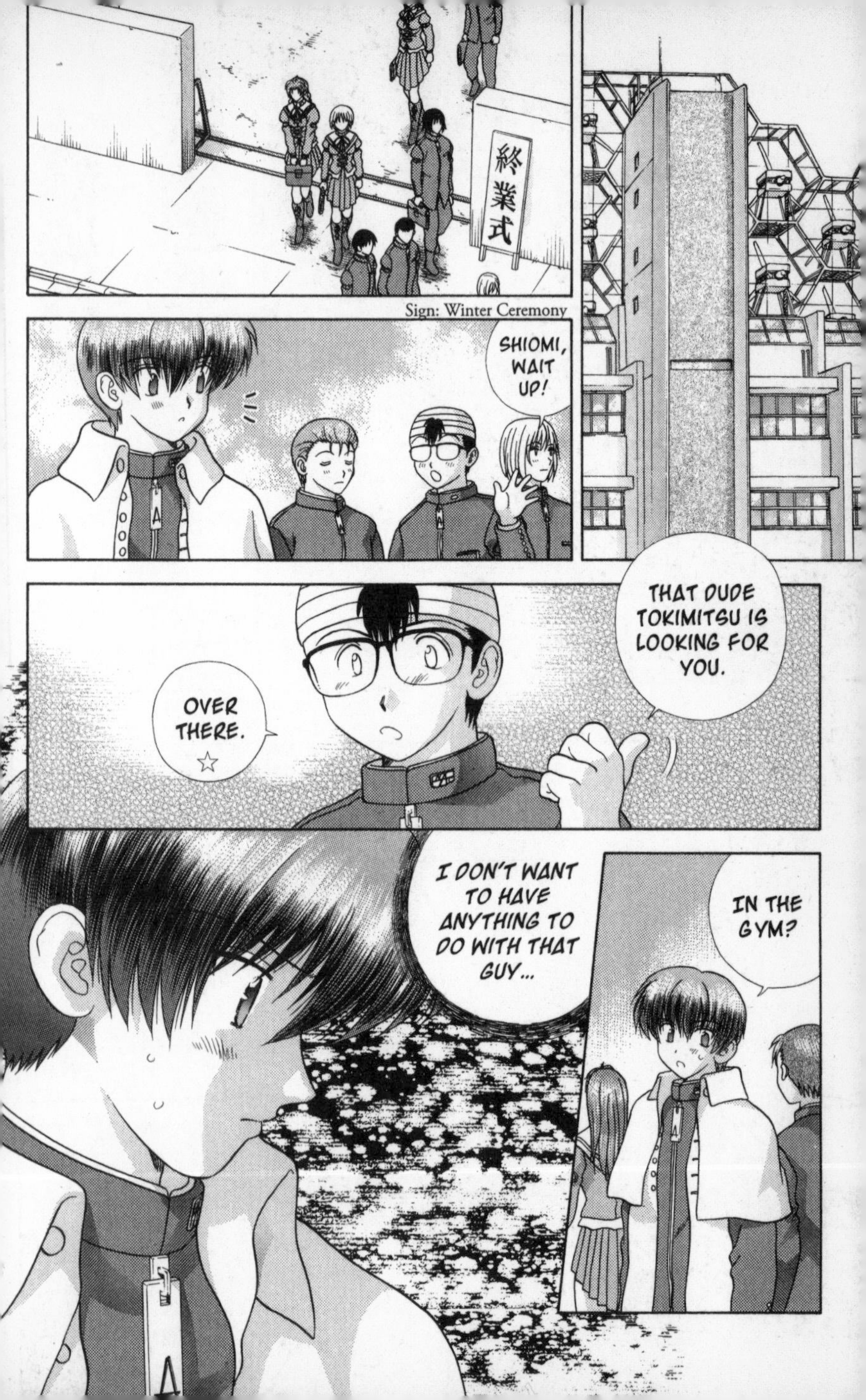
終業式
Sign: Winter Ceremony
SHIOMI, WAIT UP!
THAT DUDE TOKIMITSU IS LOOKING FOR YOU.
OVER THERE. ☆
IN THE GYM?
I DON'T WANT TO HAVE ANYTHING TO DO WITH THAT GUY...

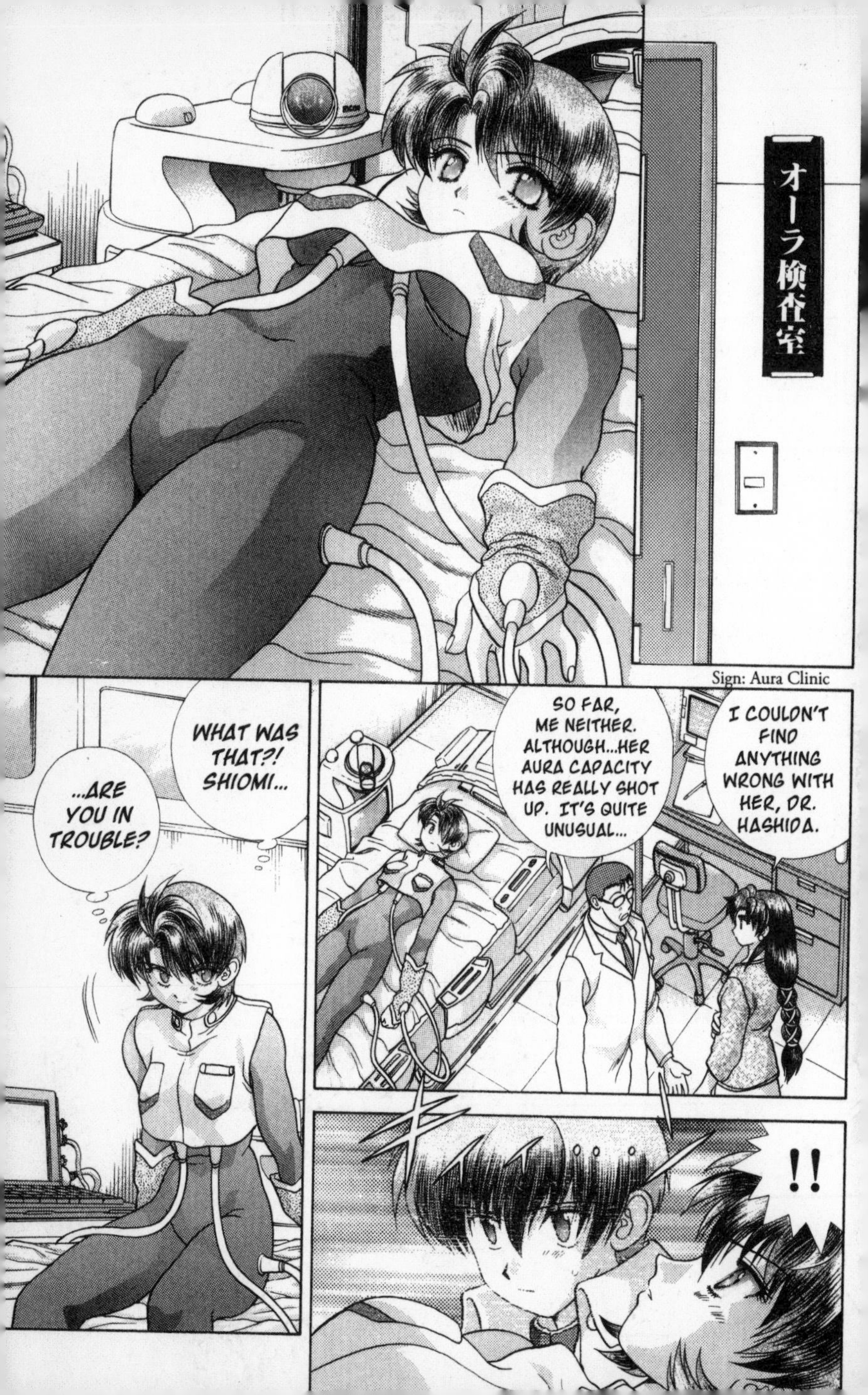
オーラ検査室
I COULDN'T FIND ANYTHING WRONG WITH HER, DR. HASHIDA.
SO FAR, ME NEITHER. ALTHOUGH...HER AURA CAPACITY HAS REALLY SHOT UP. IT'S QUITE UNUSUAL...
WHAT WAS THAT?! SHIOMI...
...ARE YOU IN TROUBLE?
!!
Sign: Aura Clinic

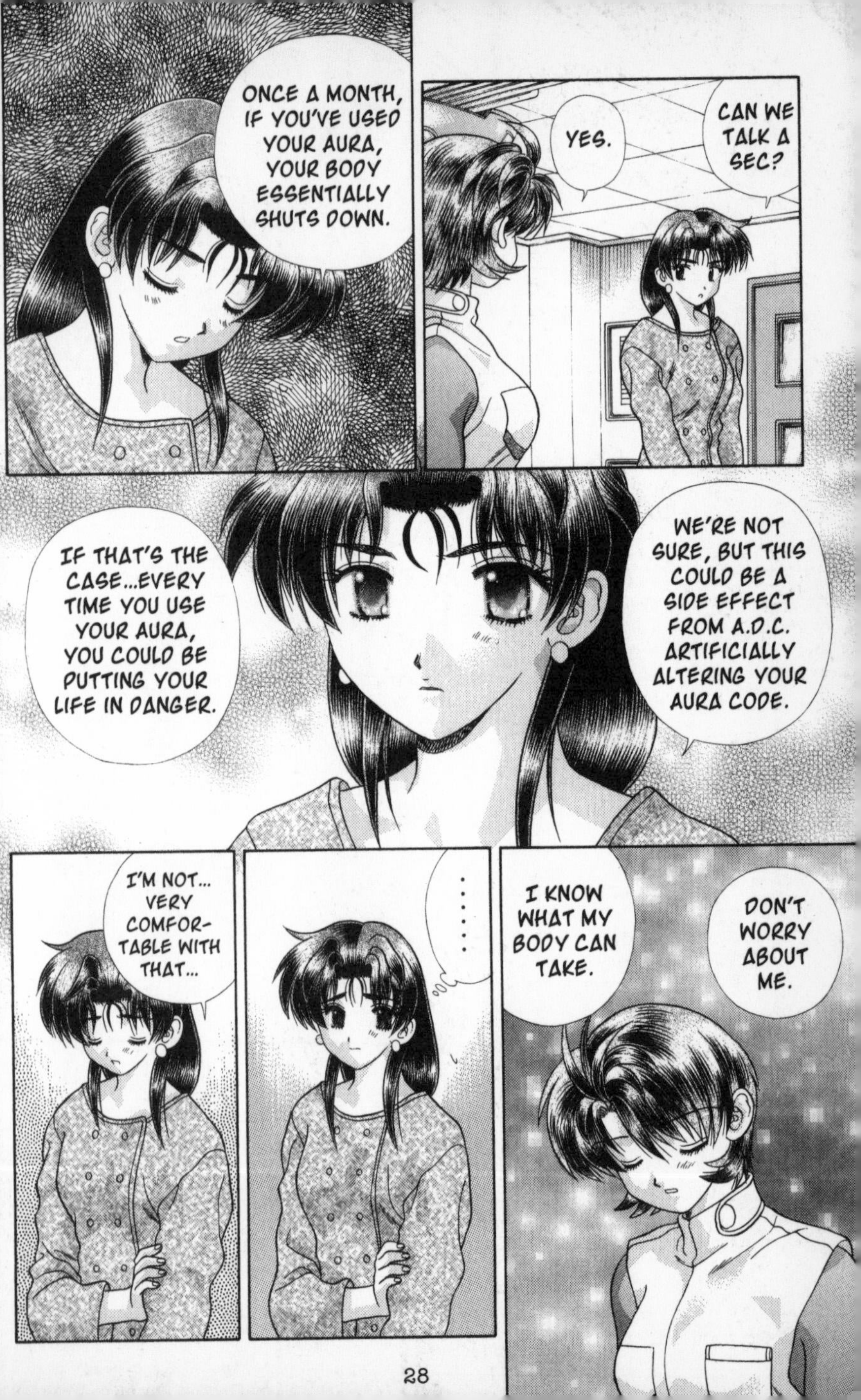
CAN WE TALK A SEC?
YES.
ONCE A MONTH, IF YOU'VE USED YOUR AURA, YOUR BODY ESSENTIALLY SHUTS DOWN.
WE'RE NOT SURE, BUT THIS COULD BE A SIDE EFFECT FROM A.D.C. ARTIFICIALLY ALTERING YOUR AURA CODE.
IF THAT'S THE CASE...EVERY TIME YOU USE YOUR AURA, YOU COULD BE PUTTING YOUR LIFE IN DANGER.
DON'T WORRY ABOUT ME.
I KNOW WHAT MY BODY CAN TAKE.
......
I'M NOT... VERY COMFOR-TABLE WITH THAT...

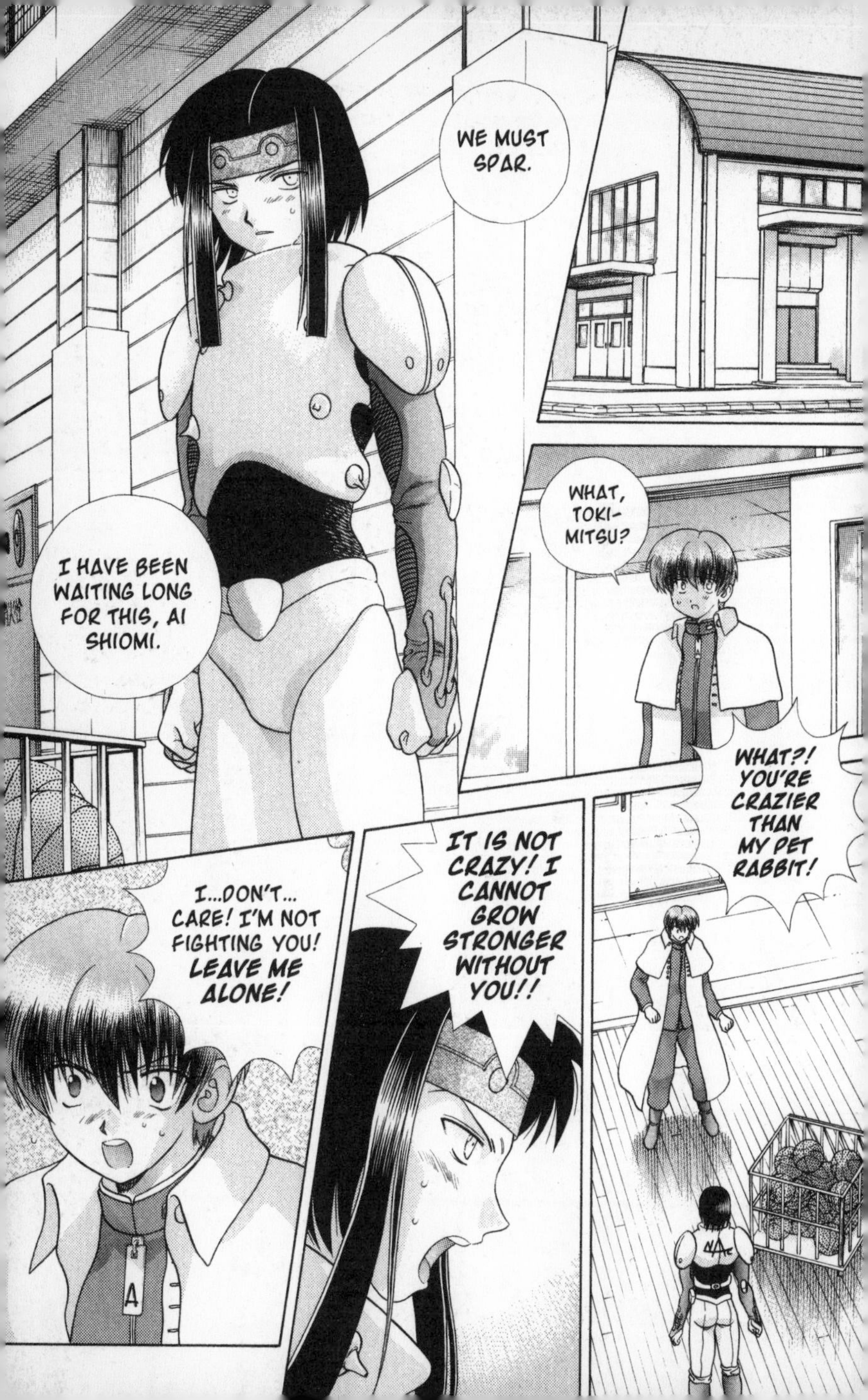

WHAT, TOKI-MITSU?
I HAVE BEEN WAITING LONG FOR THIS, AI SHIOMI.
WE MUST SPAR.
WHAT?! YOU'RE CRAZIER THAN MY PET RABBIT!
IT IS NOT CRAZY! I CANNOT GROW STRONGER WITHOUT YOU!!
I...DON'T... CARE! I'M NOT FIGHTING YOU! LEAVE ME ALONE!

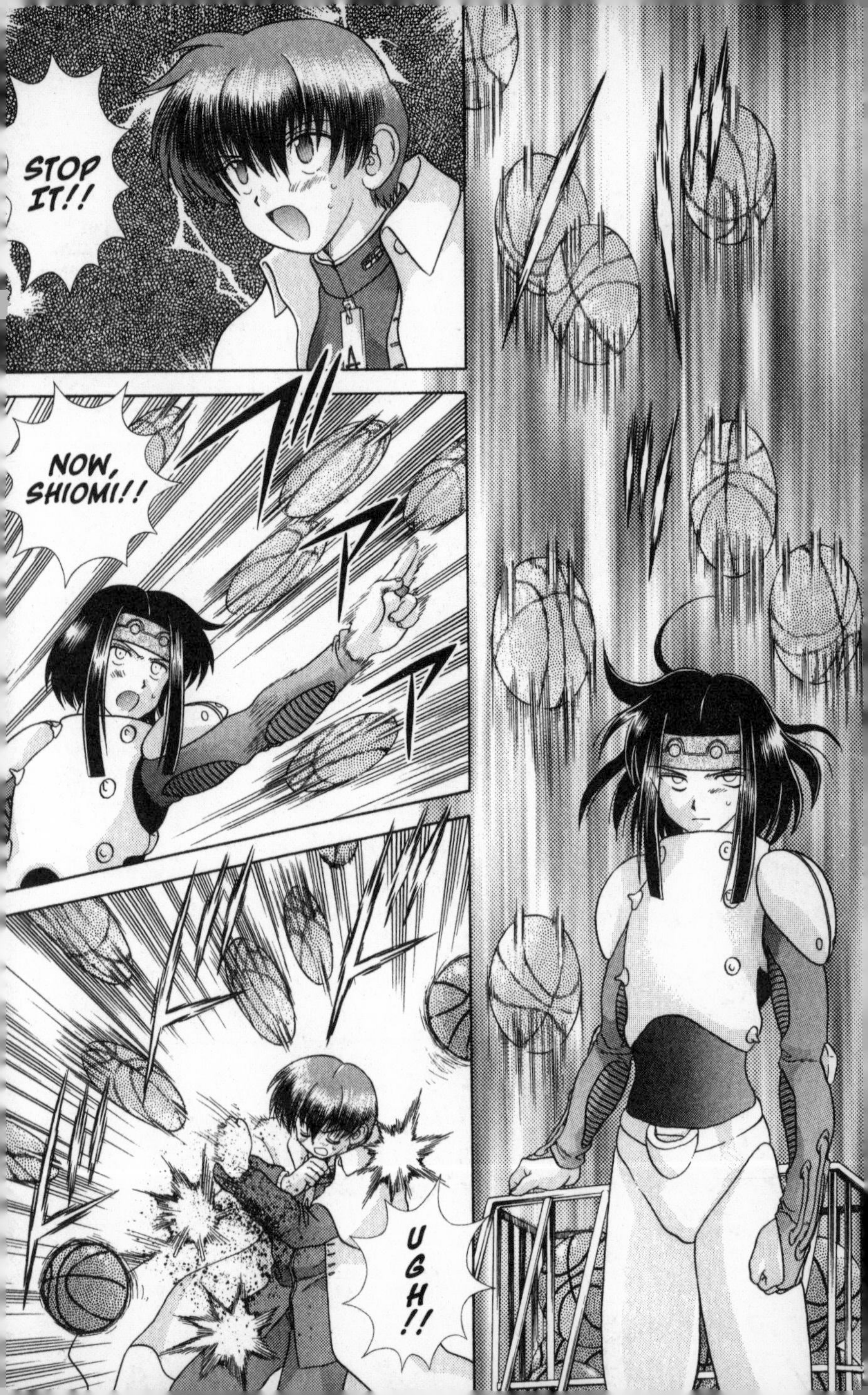
STOP IT!!
NOW, SHIOMI!!
UGH!!

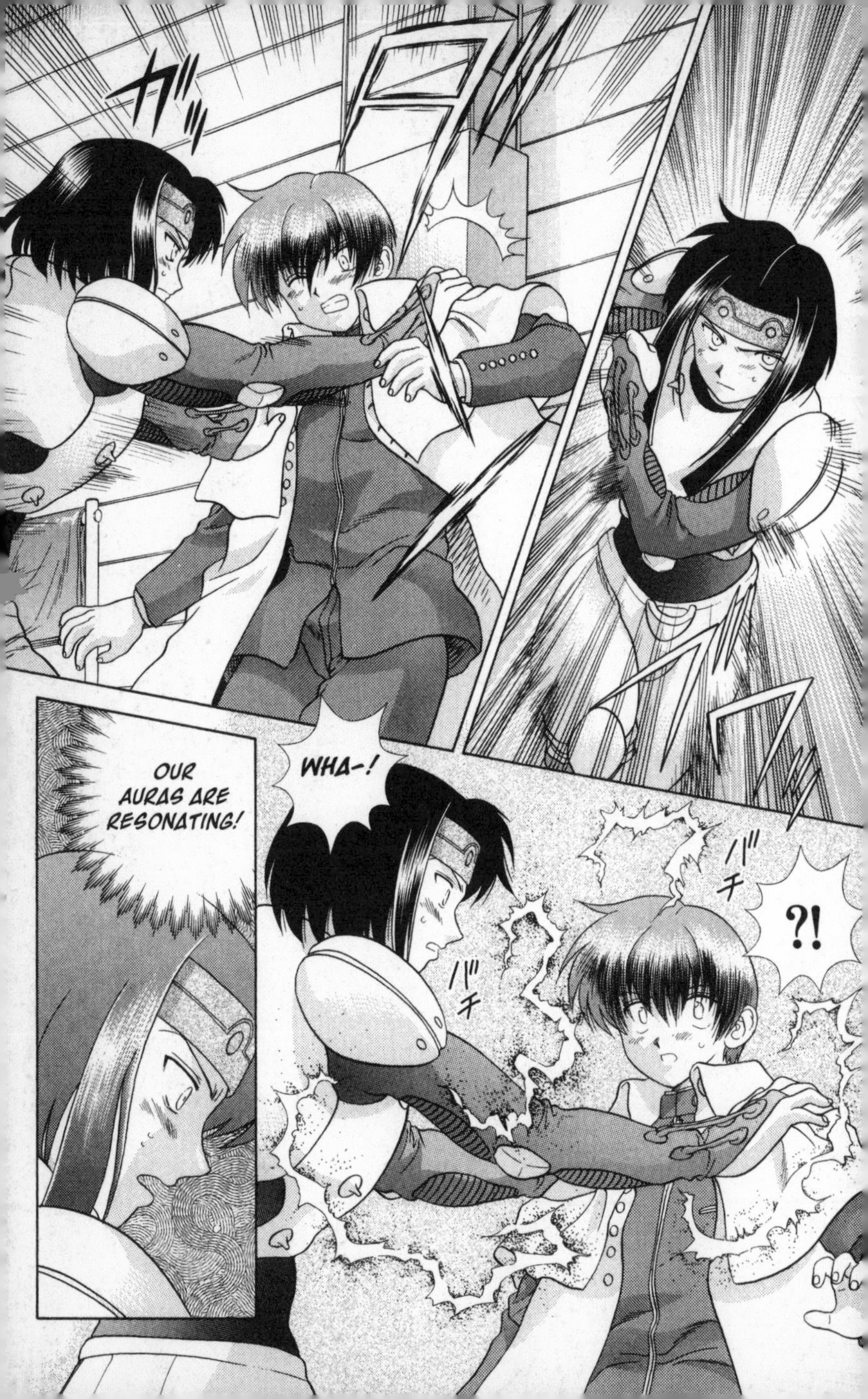
?!
WHA-!
OUR AURAS ARE RESONATING!

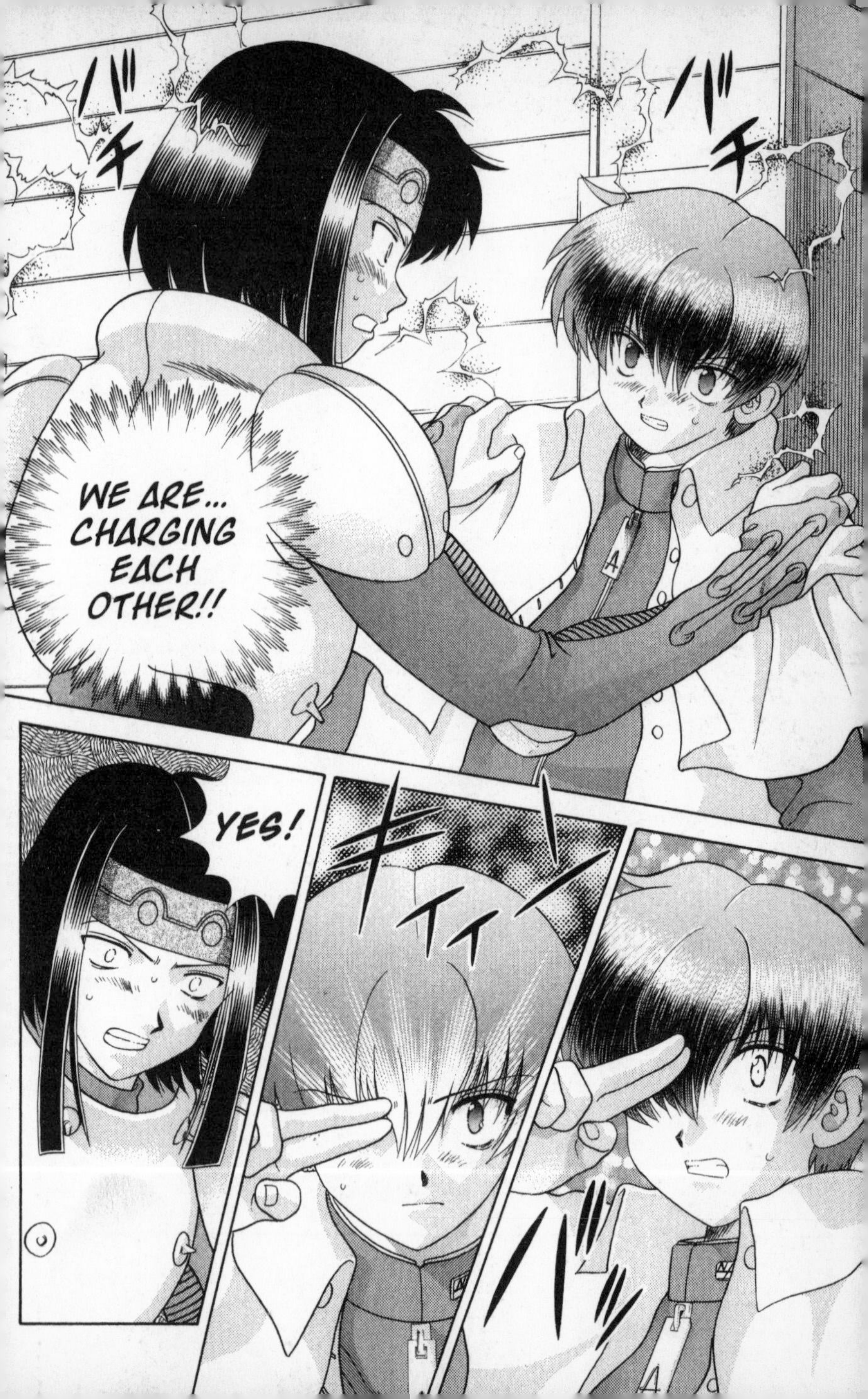

バチ
バチ
WE ARE... CHARGING EACH OTHER!!
YES!
キイイィー

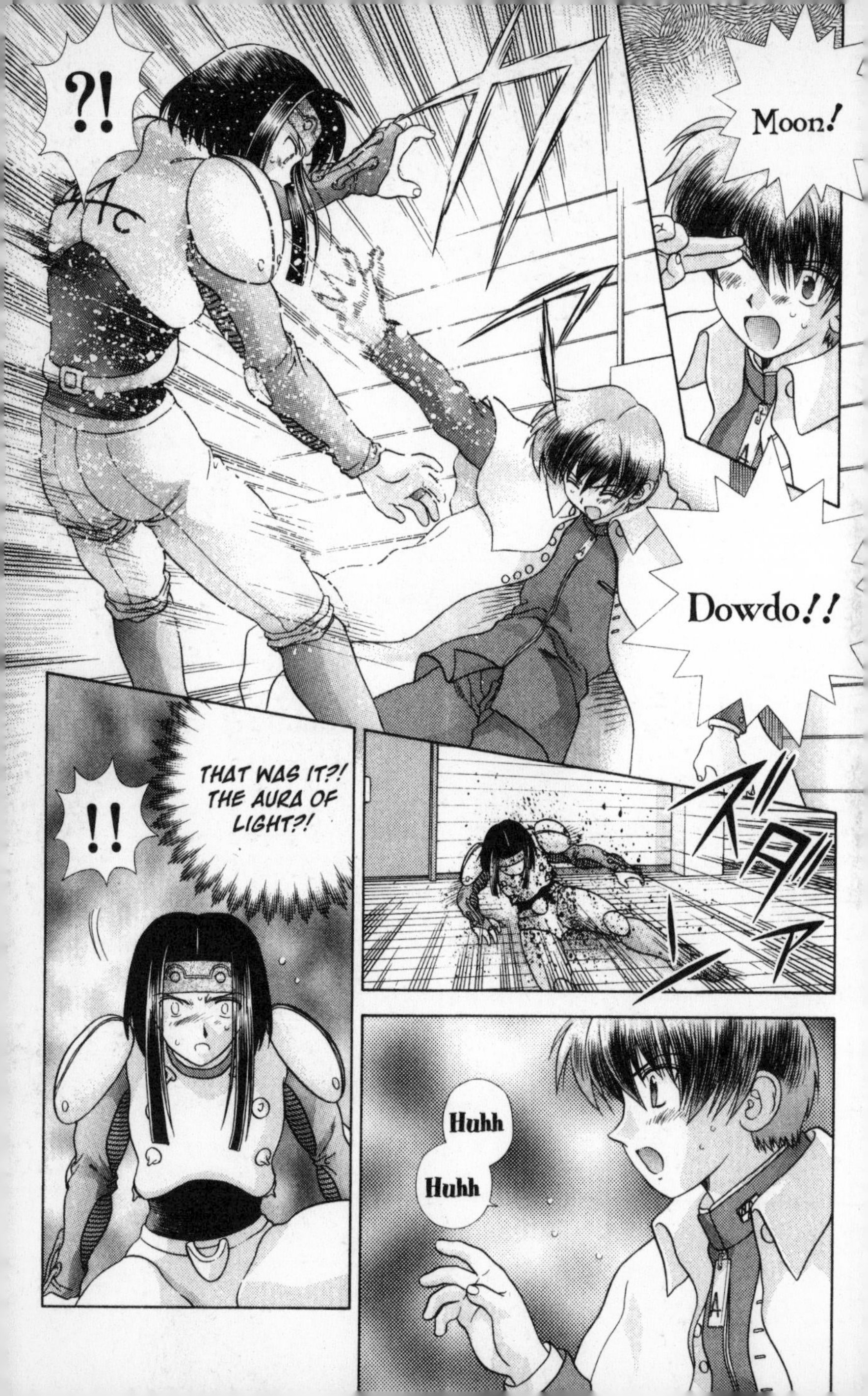
Moon!
?!
Dowdo!!
THAT WAS IT?! THE AURA OF LIGHT?!
!!
Huhh
Huhh

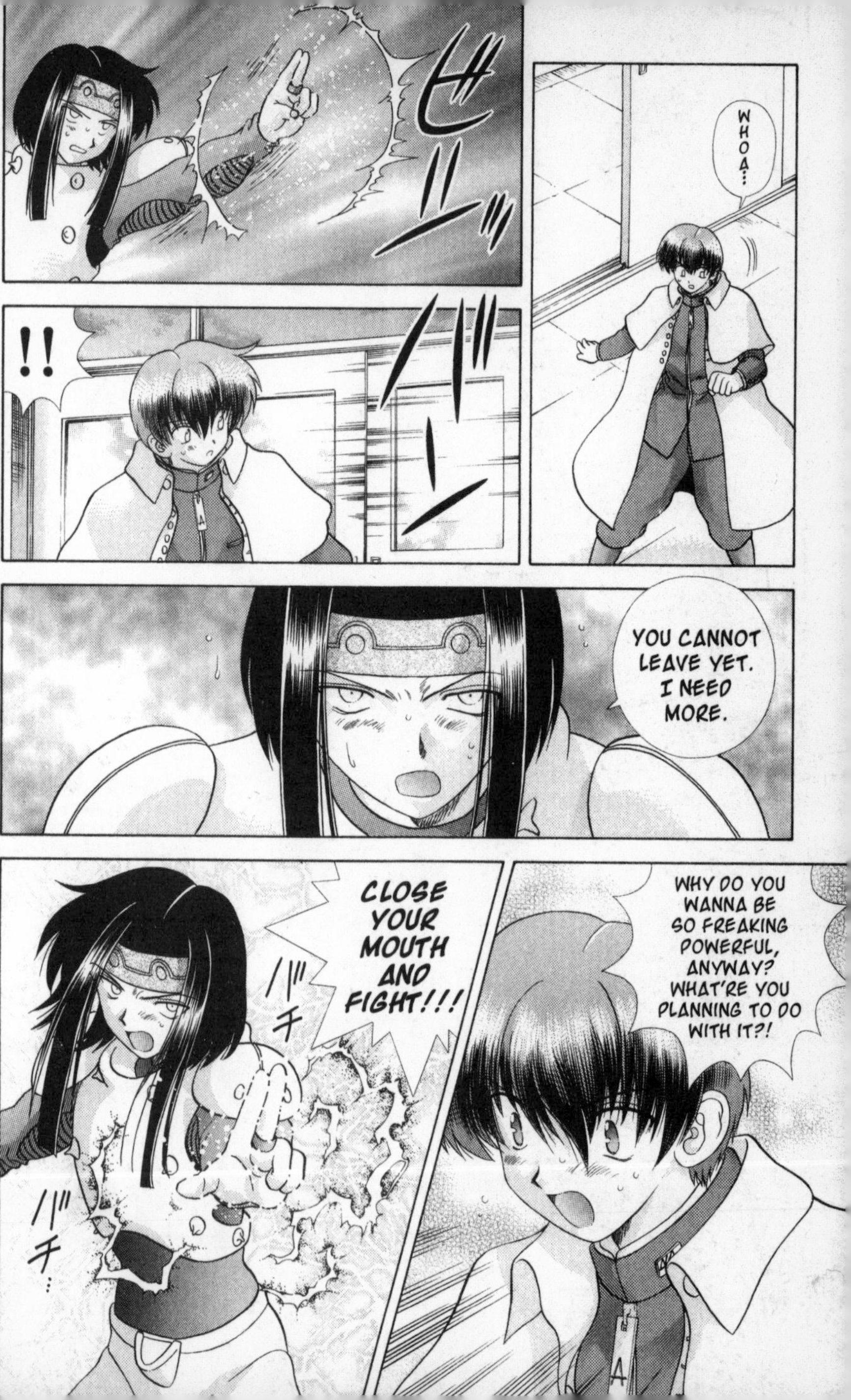
WHOA...
!!
YOU CANNOT LEAVE YET. I NEED MORE.
WHY DO YOU WANNA BE SO FREAKING POWERFUL, ANYWAY? WHAT'RE YOU PLANNING TO DO WITH IT?!
CLOSE YOUR MOUTH AND FIGHT!!!
バチ
バチ...

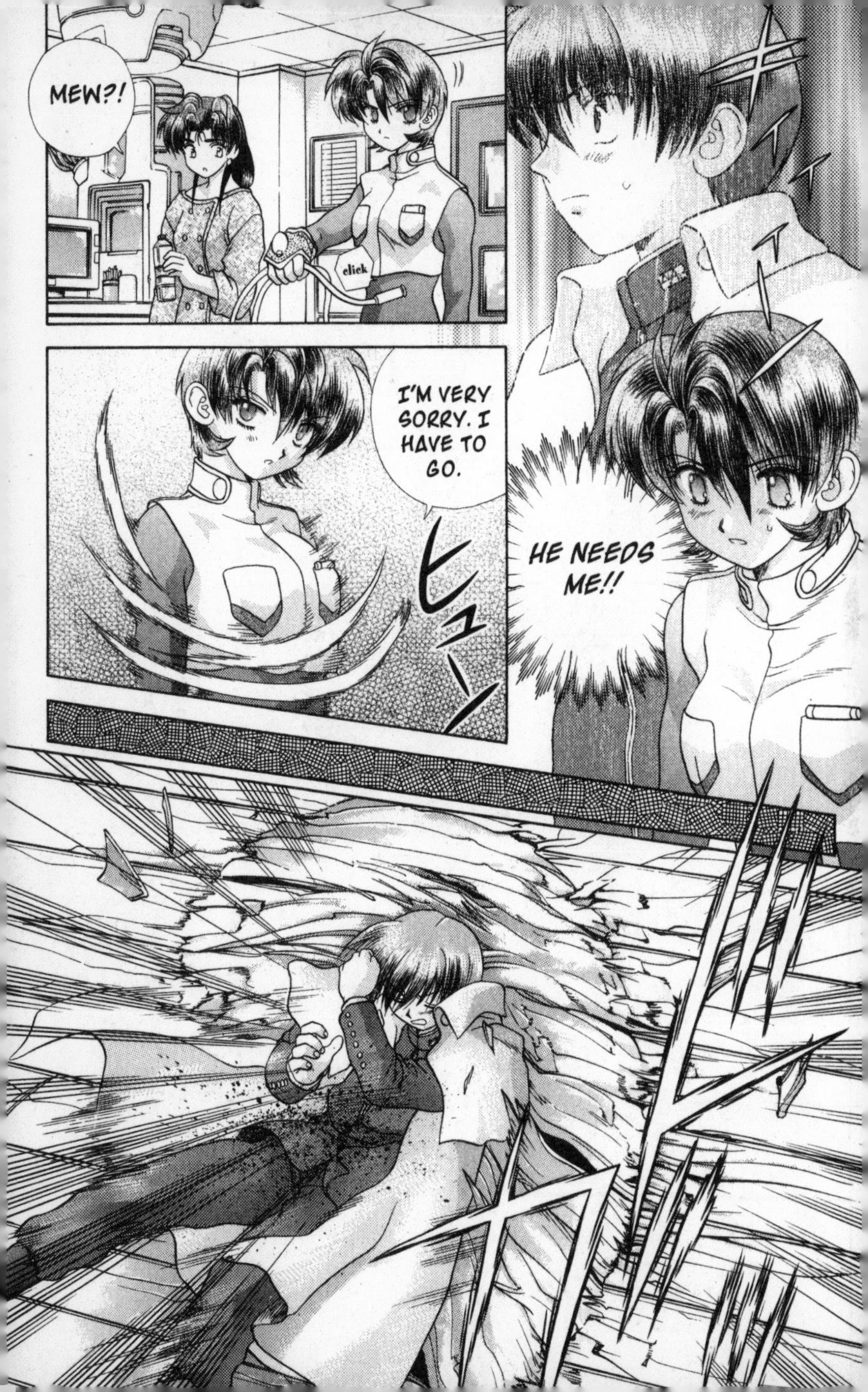
MEW?!
click
I'M VERY SORRY. I HAVE TO GO.
HE NEEDS ME!!

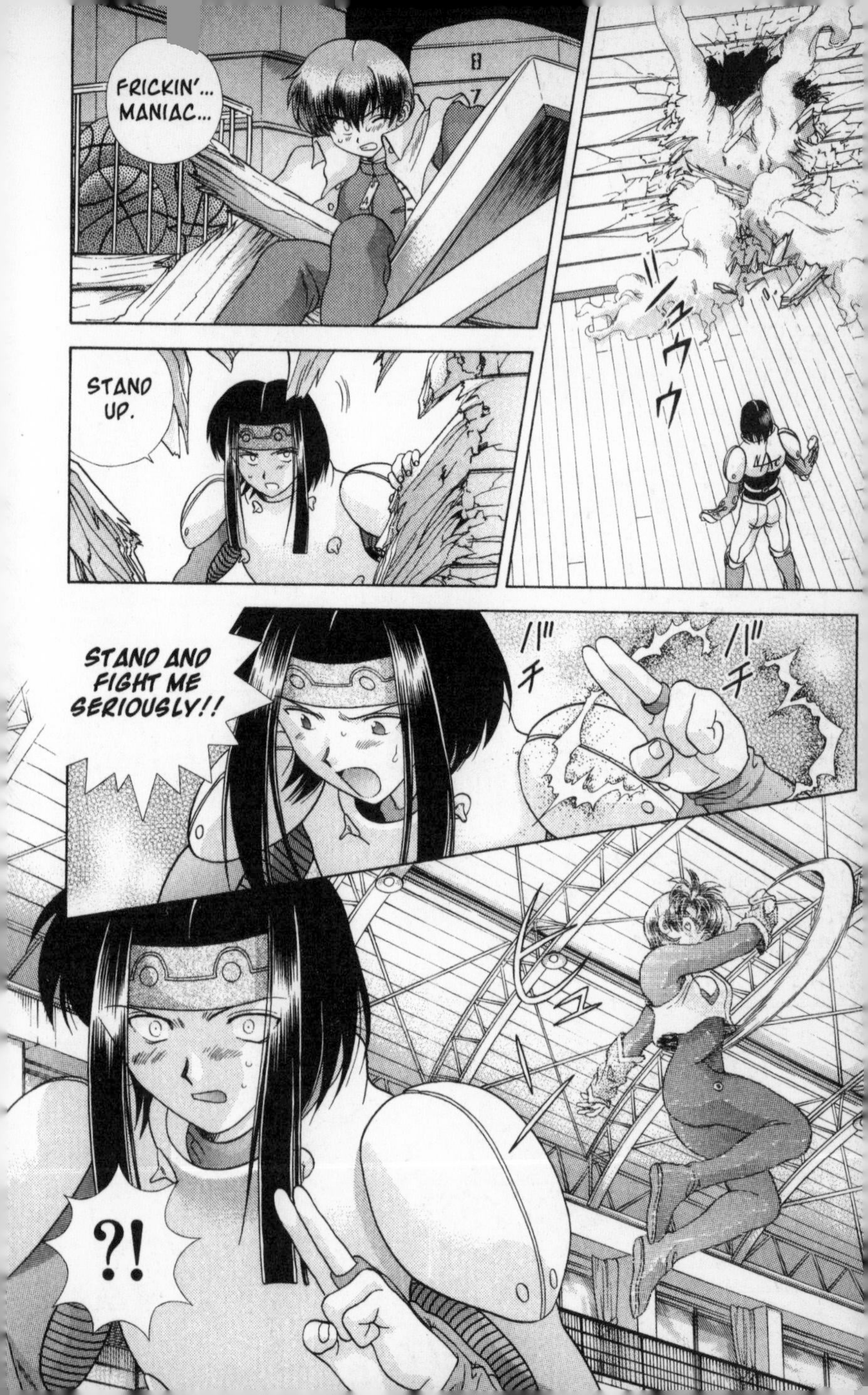

ジュウウ
FRICKIN'... MANIAC...
STAND UP.
バチ
バチ
STAND AND FIGHT ME SERIOUSLY!!
?!

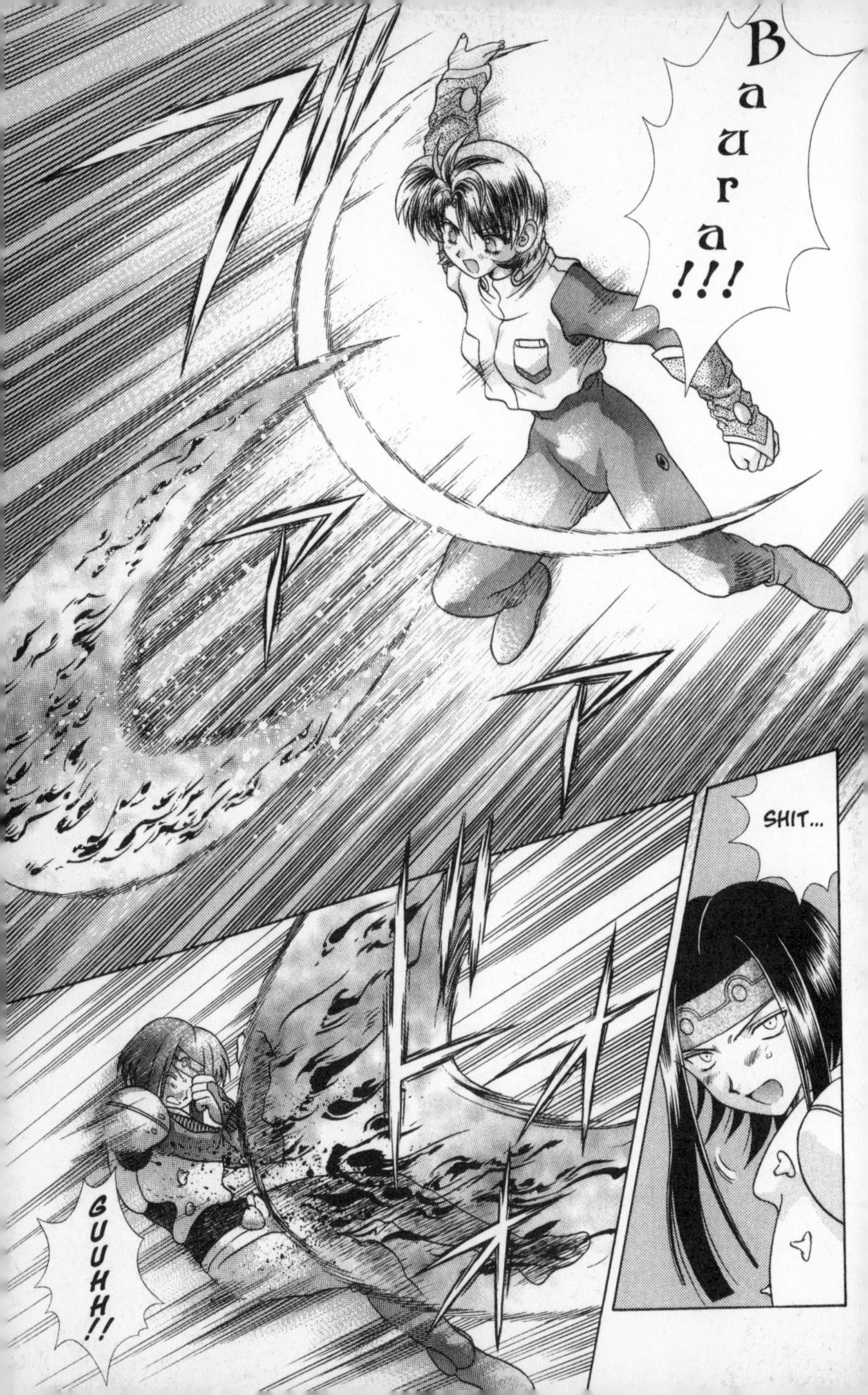
Baura!!!
SHIT...
GUUHH!!

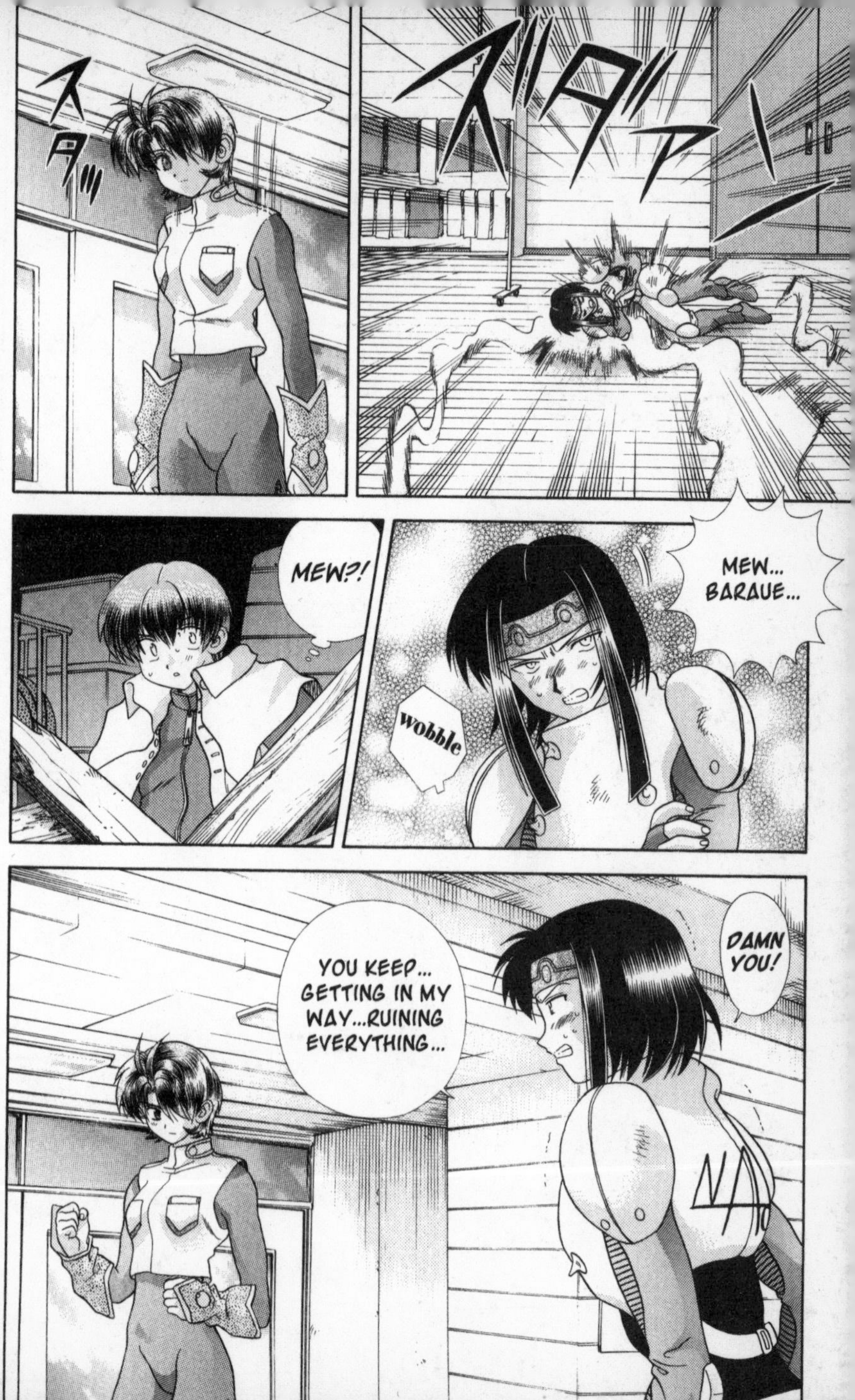
スタッ
MEW... BARAUE...
wobble
MEW?!
DAMN YOU!
YOU KEEP... GETTING IN MY WAY...RUINING EVERYTHING...

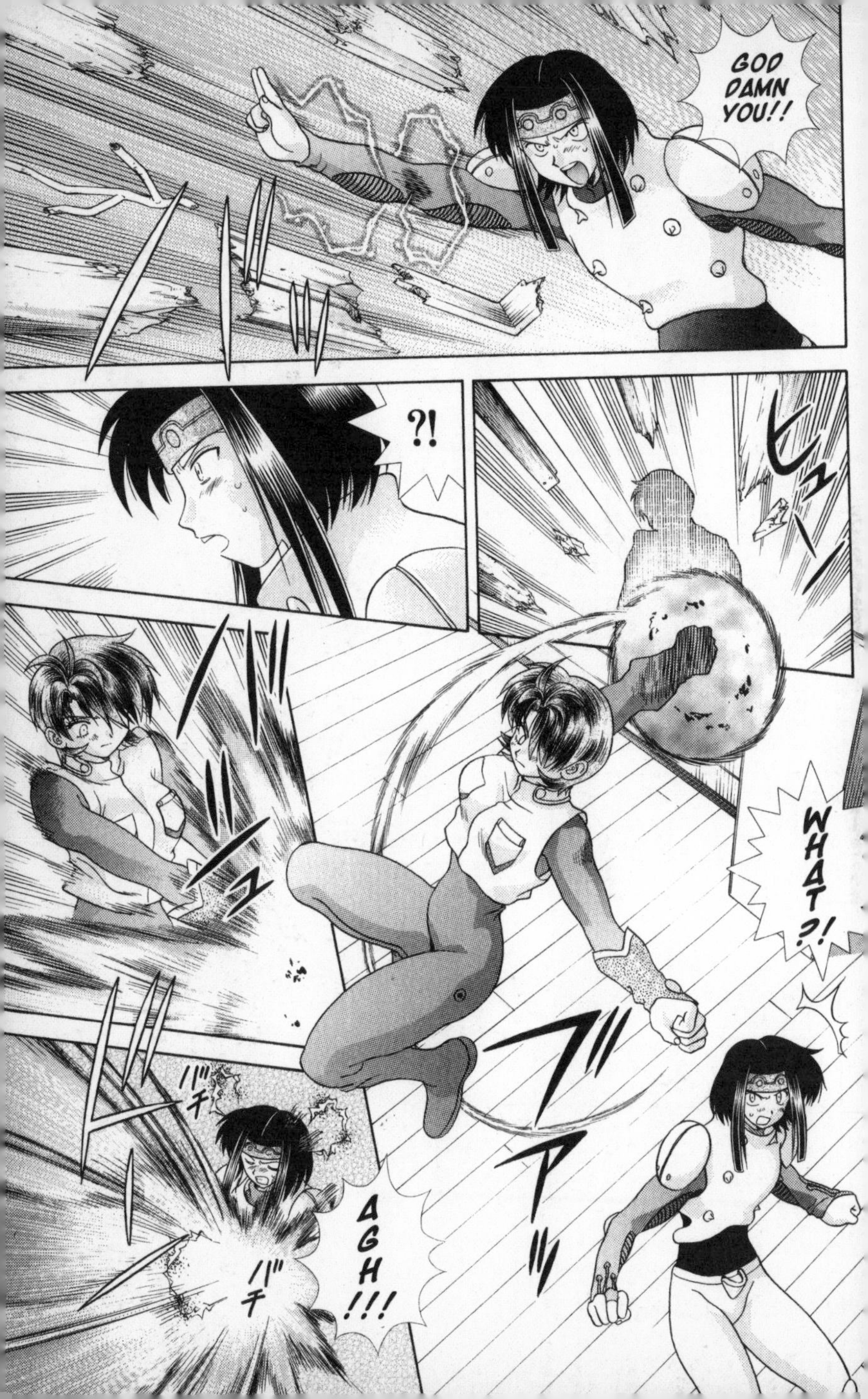
GOD DAMN YOU!!
ヒュ
?!
WHAT?!
ブア
AGH!!!
バチ
バチ

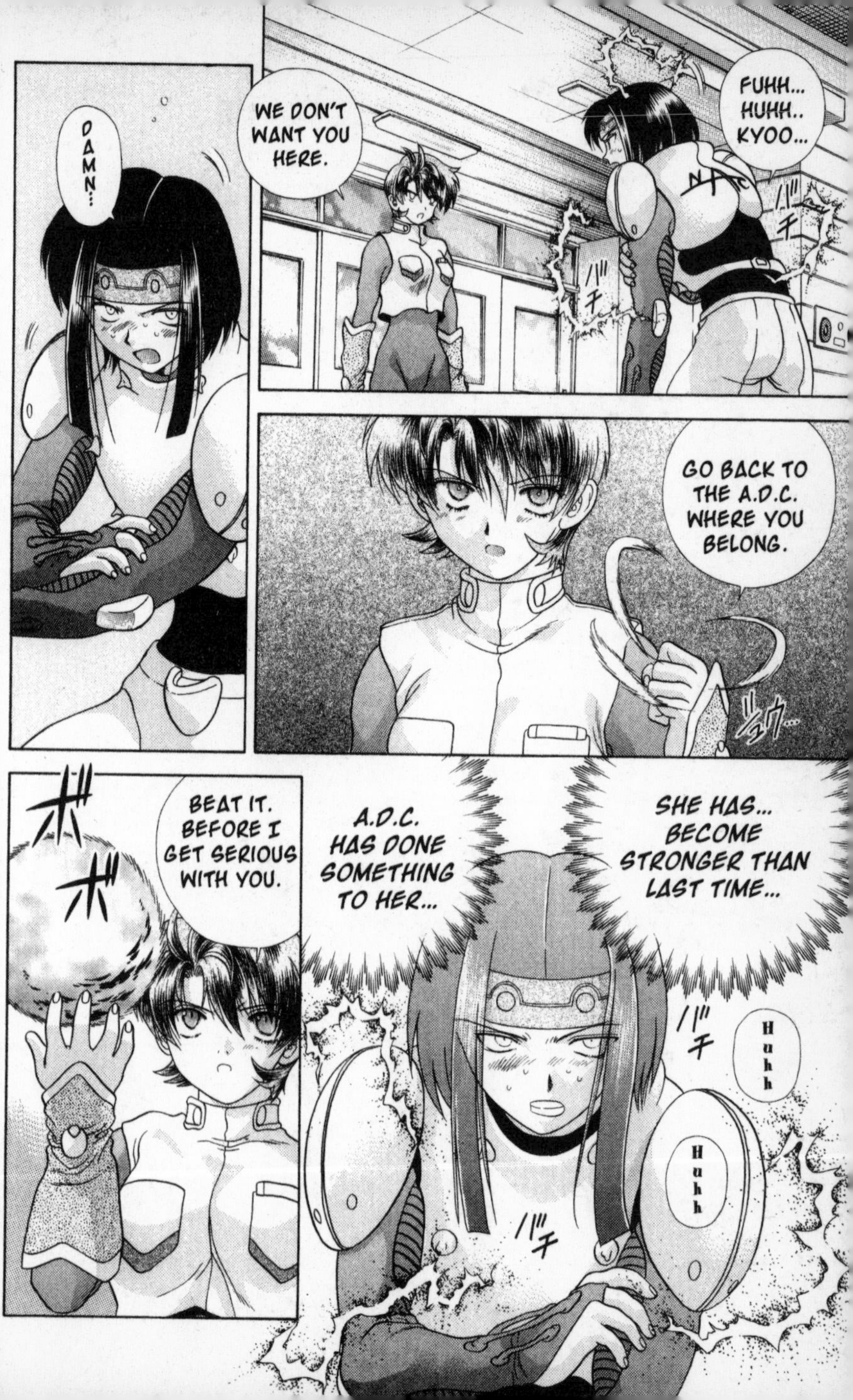
FUHH... HUHH.. KYOO...
WE DON'T WANT YOU HERE.
GO BACK TO THE A.D.C. WHERE YOU BELONG.
DAMN...
SHE HAS... BECOME STRONGER THAN LAST TIME...
A.D.C. HAS DONE SOMETHING TO HER...
Huhh
Huhh
BEAT IT. BEFORE I GET SERIOUS WITH YOU.

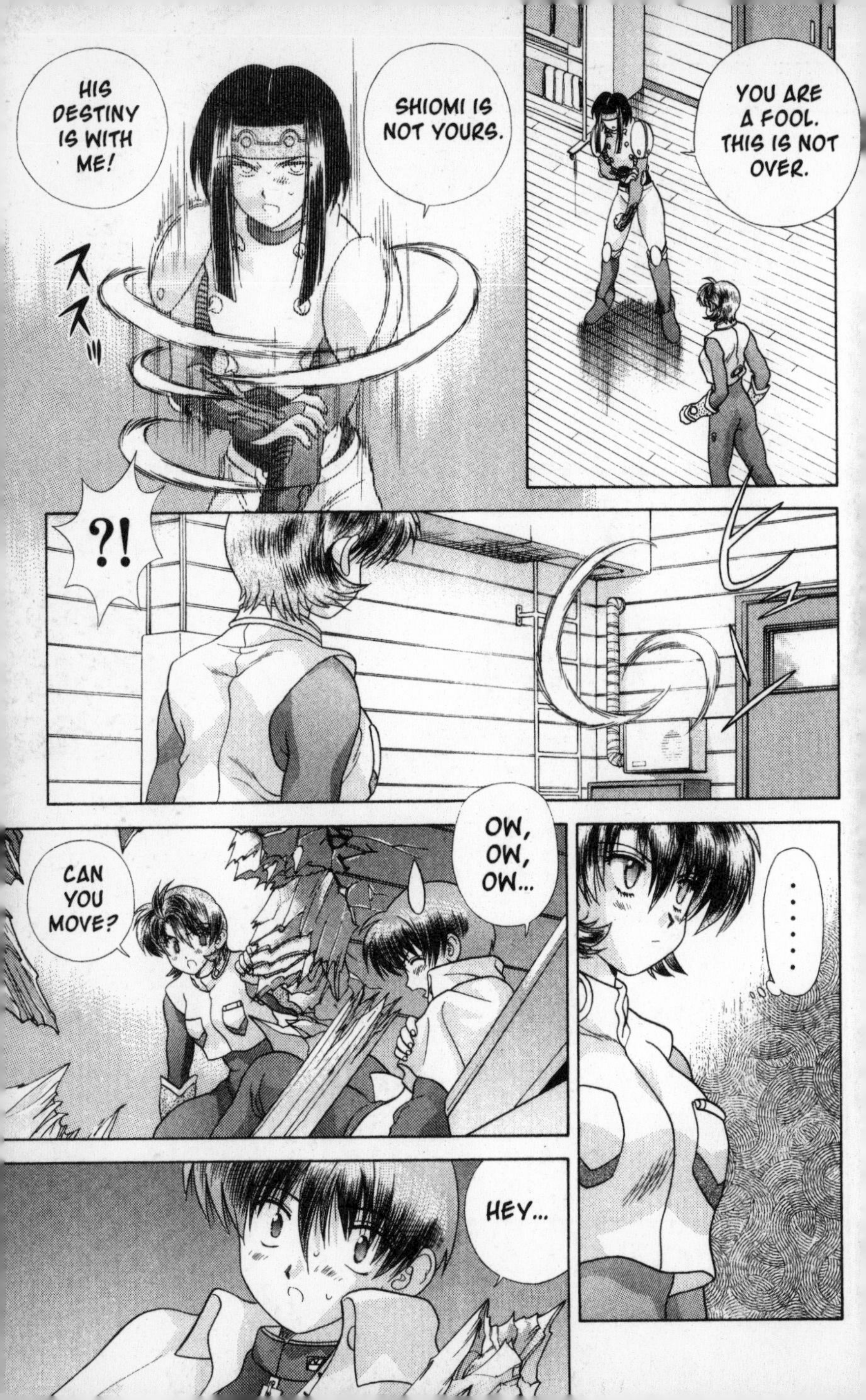
YOU ARE A FOOL. THIS IS NOT OVER.
SHIOMI IS NOT YOURS.
HIS DESTINY IS WITH ME!
?!
.....
OW, OW, OW...
CAN YOU MOVE?
HEY...

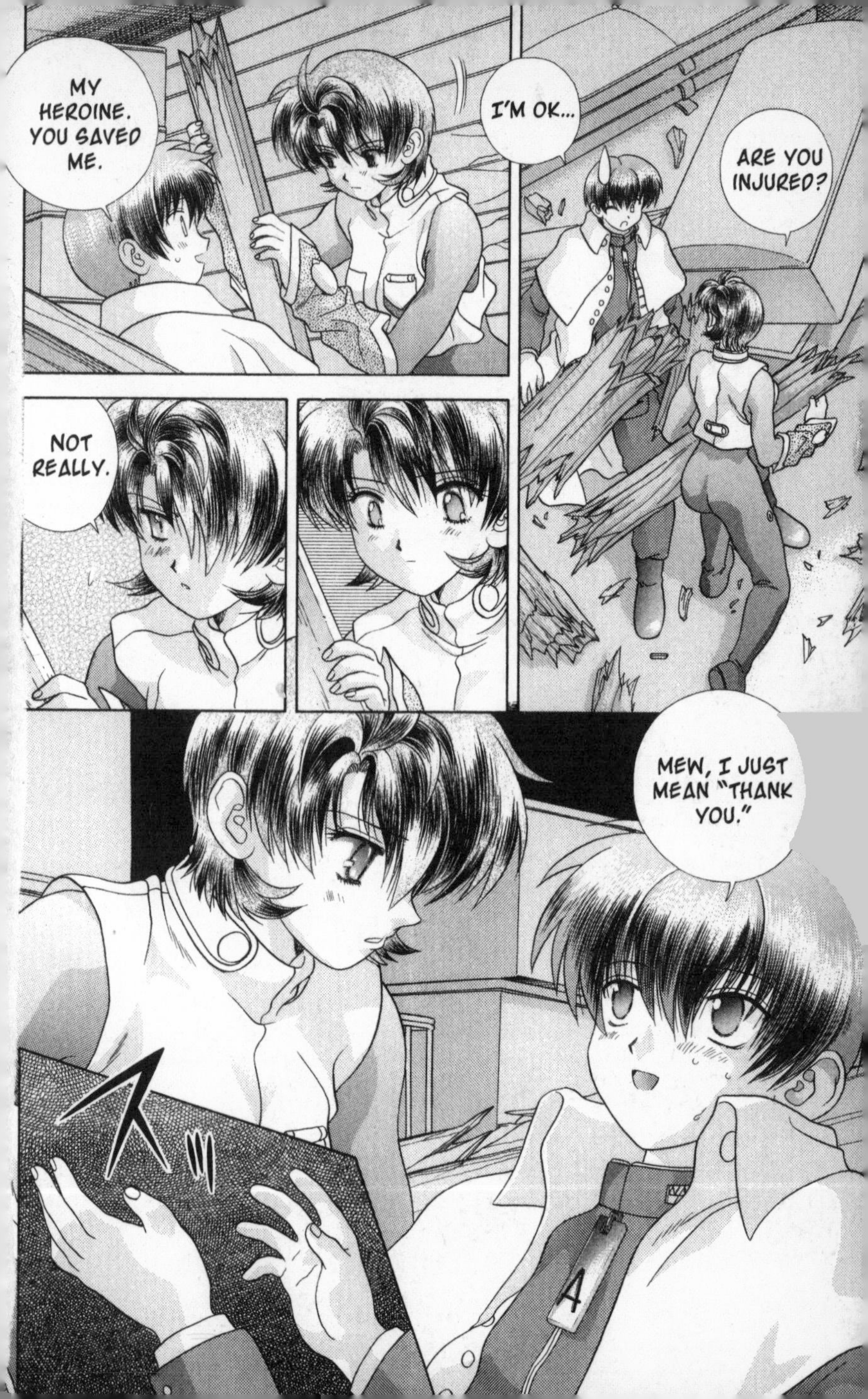
ARE YOU INJURED?
I'M OK...
MY HEROINE. YOU SAVED ME.
NOT REALLY.
MEW, I JUST MEAN "THANK YOU."

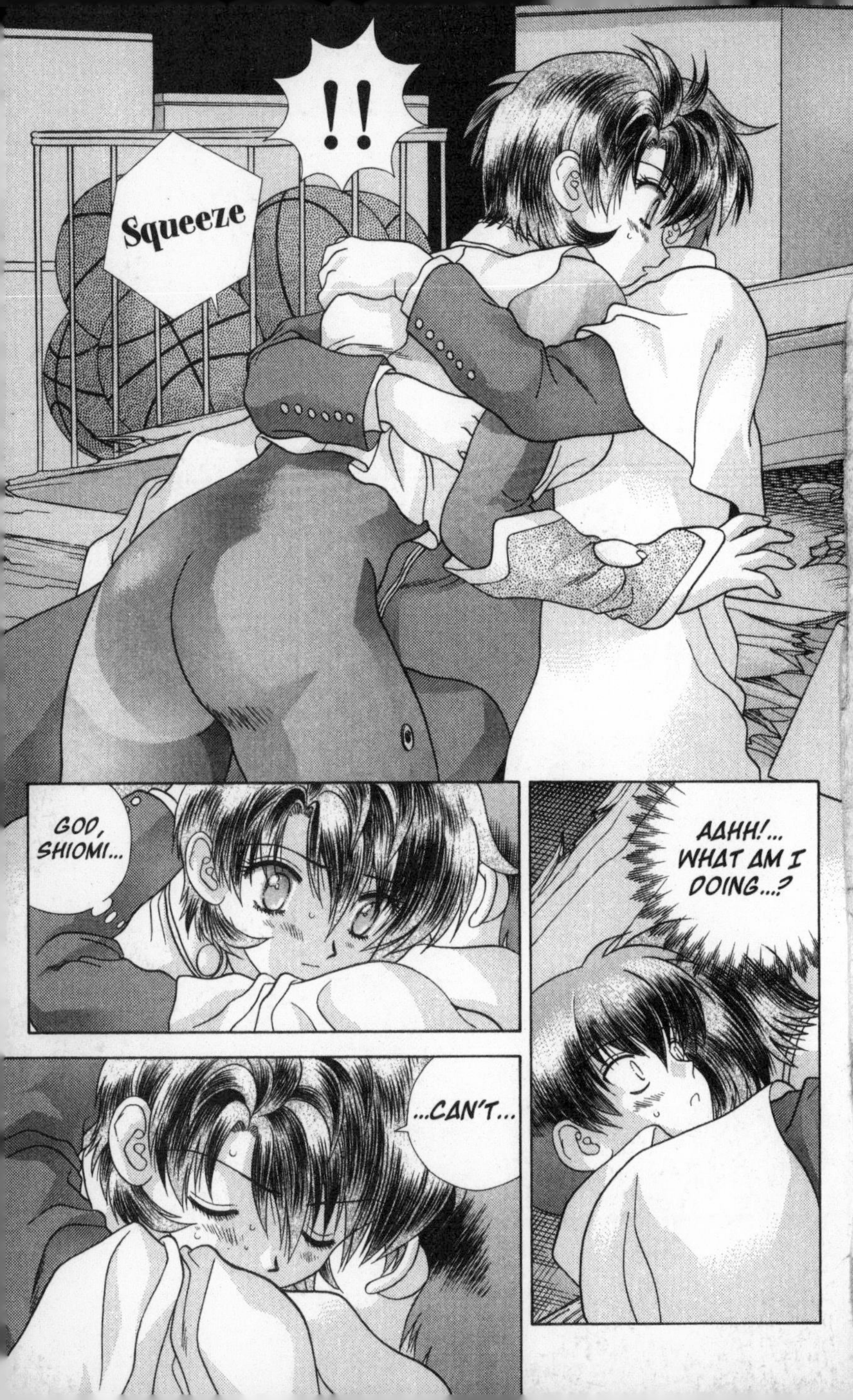
!!
Squeeze
AAHH!... WHAT AM I DOING...?
GOD, SHIOMI...
...CAN'T...

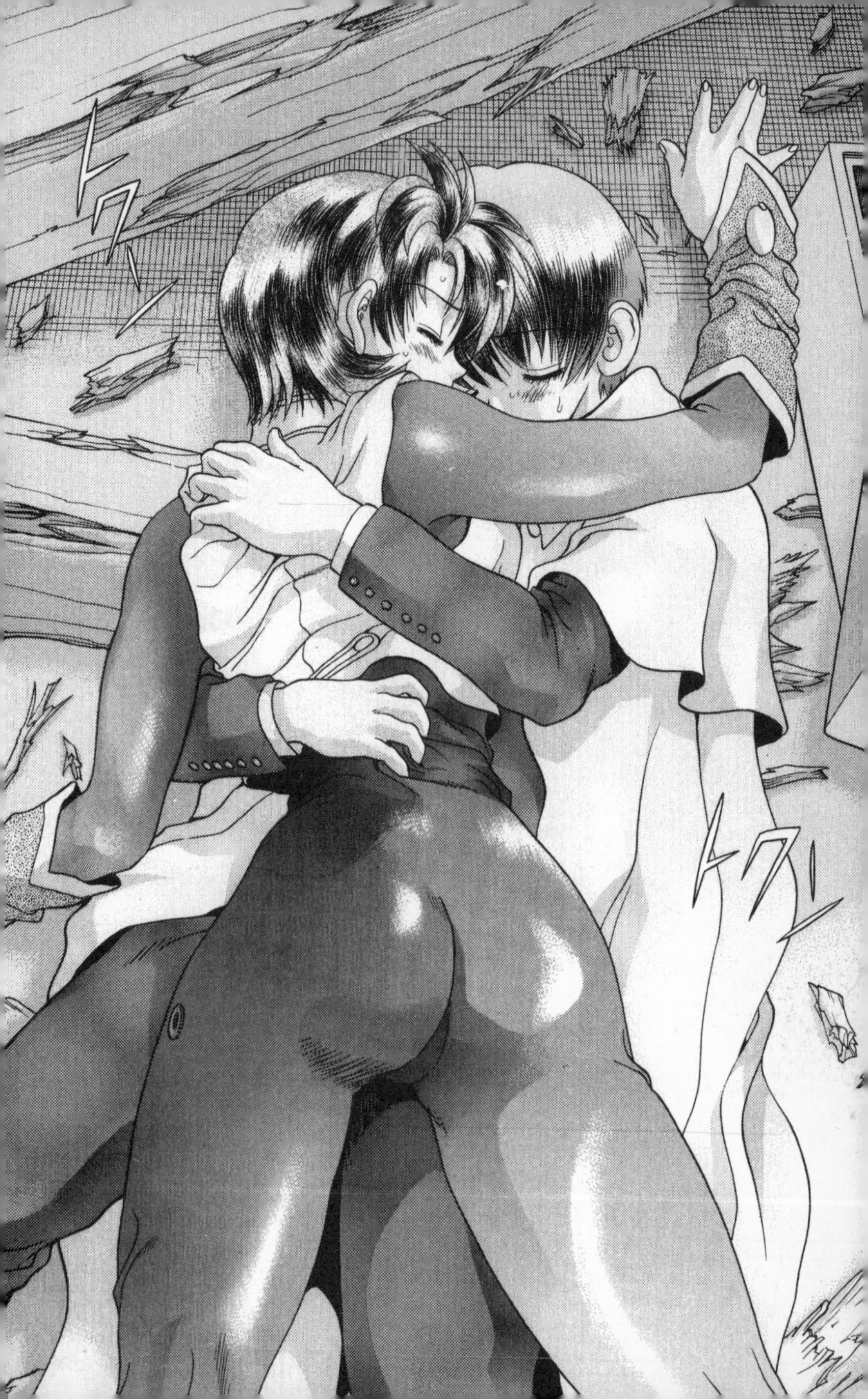
トクン
トクン

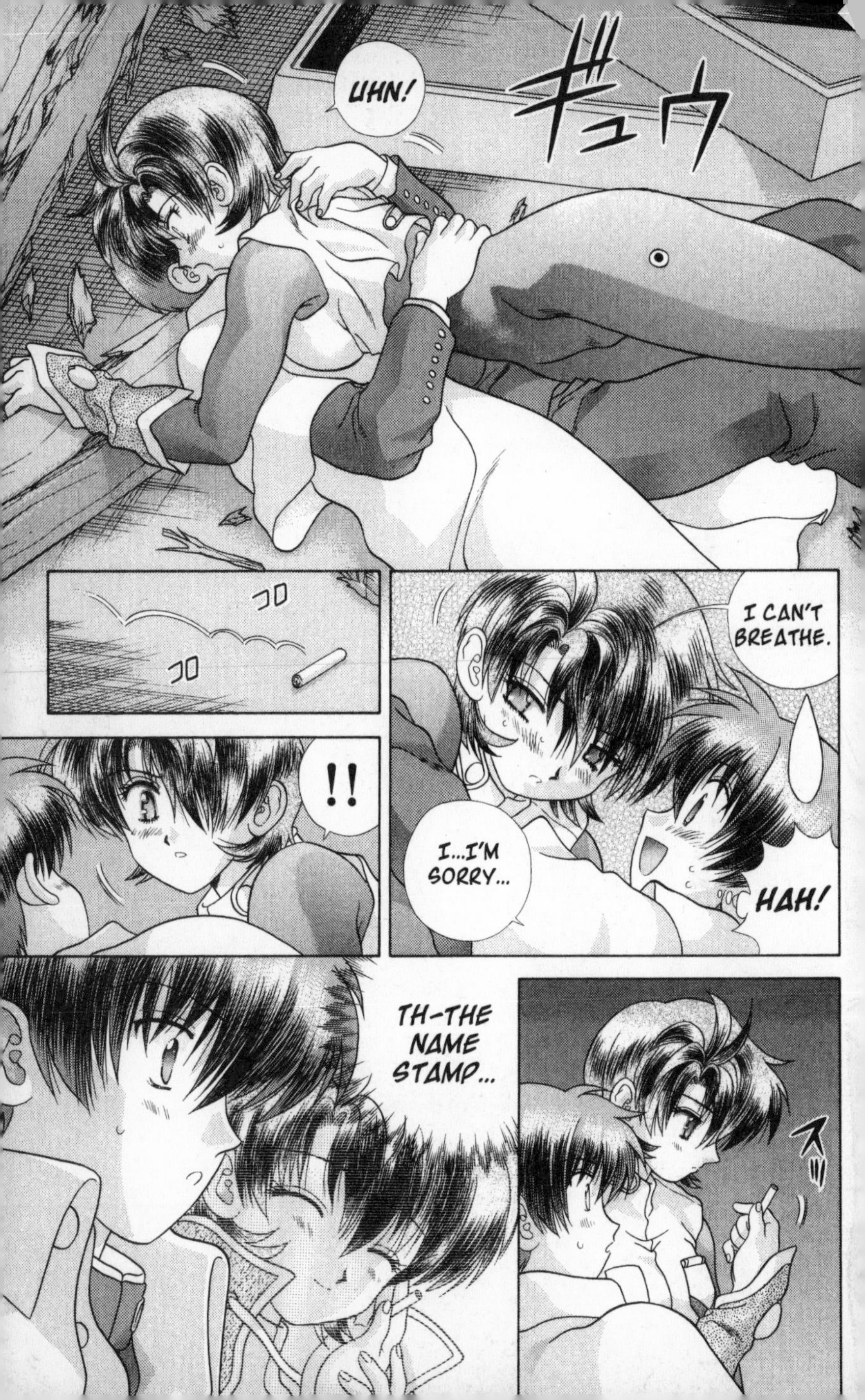
ギュウ
UHN!
I CAN'T BREATHE.
HAH!
I...I'M SORRY...
コロ
コロ
!!
スッ
TH-THE NAME STAMP...

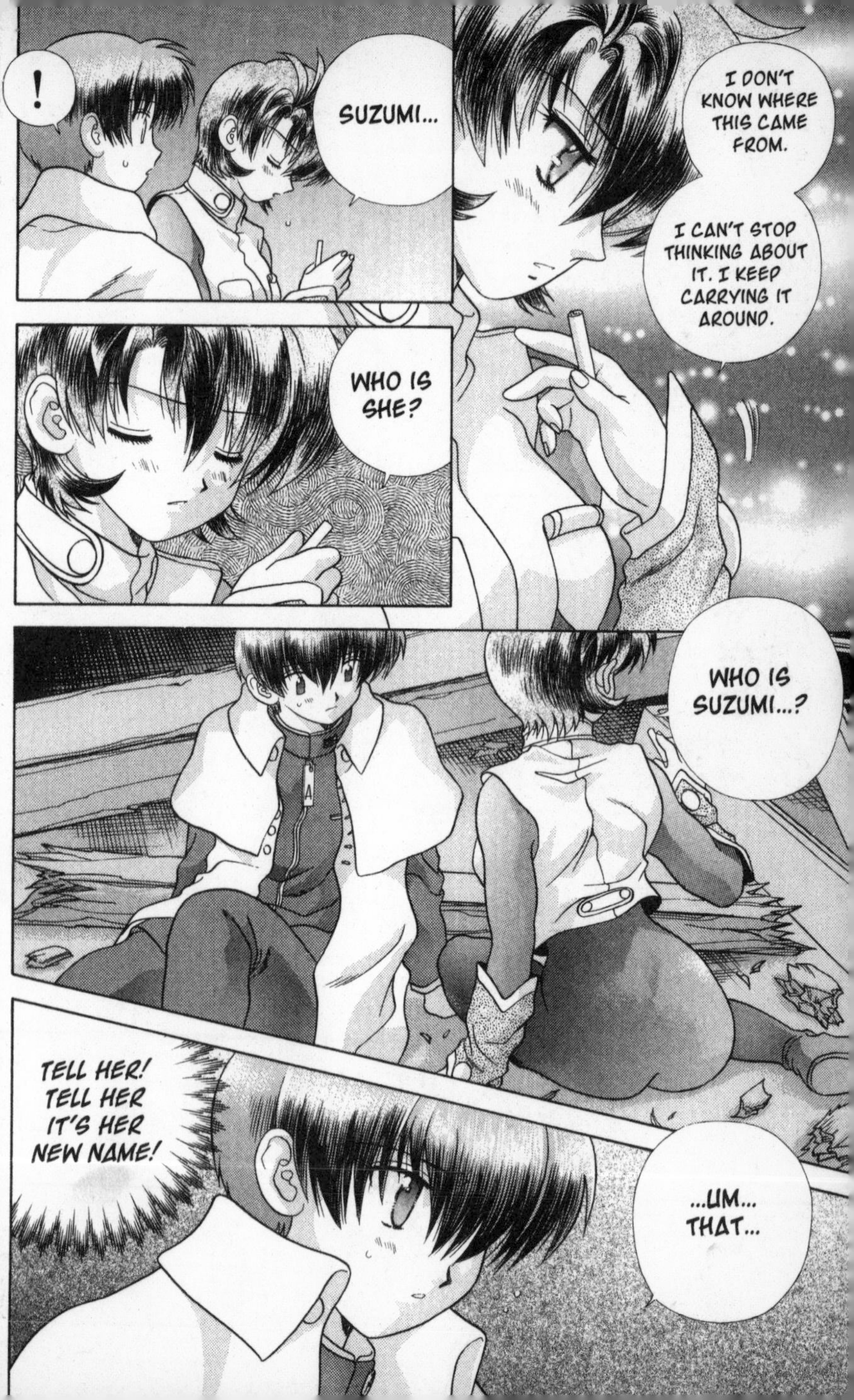
I DON'T KNOW WHERE THIS CAME FROM.
I CAN'T STOP THINKING ABOUT IT. I KEEP CARRYING IT AROUND.
SUZUMI...
!
WHO IS SHE?
WHO IS SUZUMI...?
...UM... THAT...
TELL HER! TELL HER IT'S HER NEW NAME!

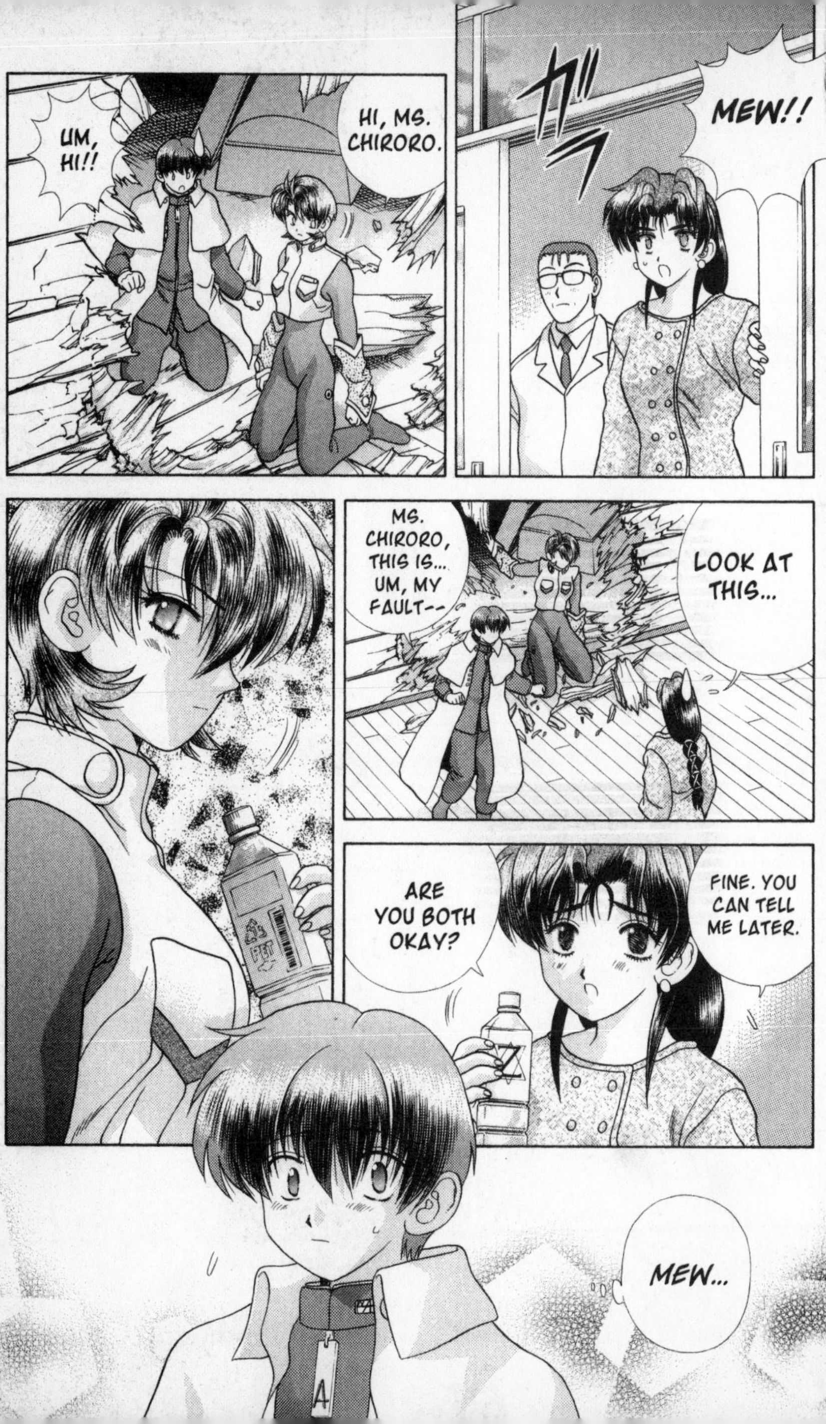
MEW!!
HI, MS. CHIRORO.
UM, HI!!
LOOK AT THIS...
MS. CHIRORO, THIS IS... UM, MY FAULT--
FINE. YOU CAN TELL ME LATER.
ARE YOU BOTH OKAY?
MEW...

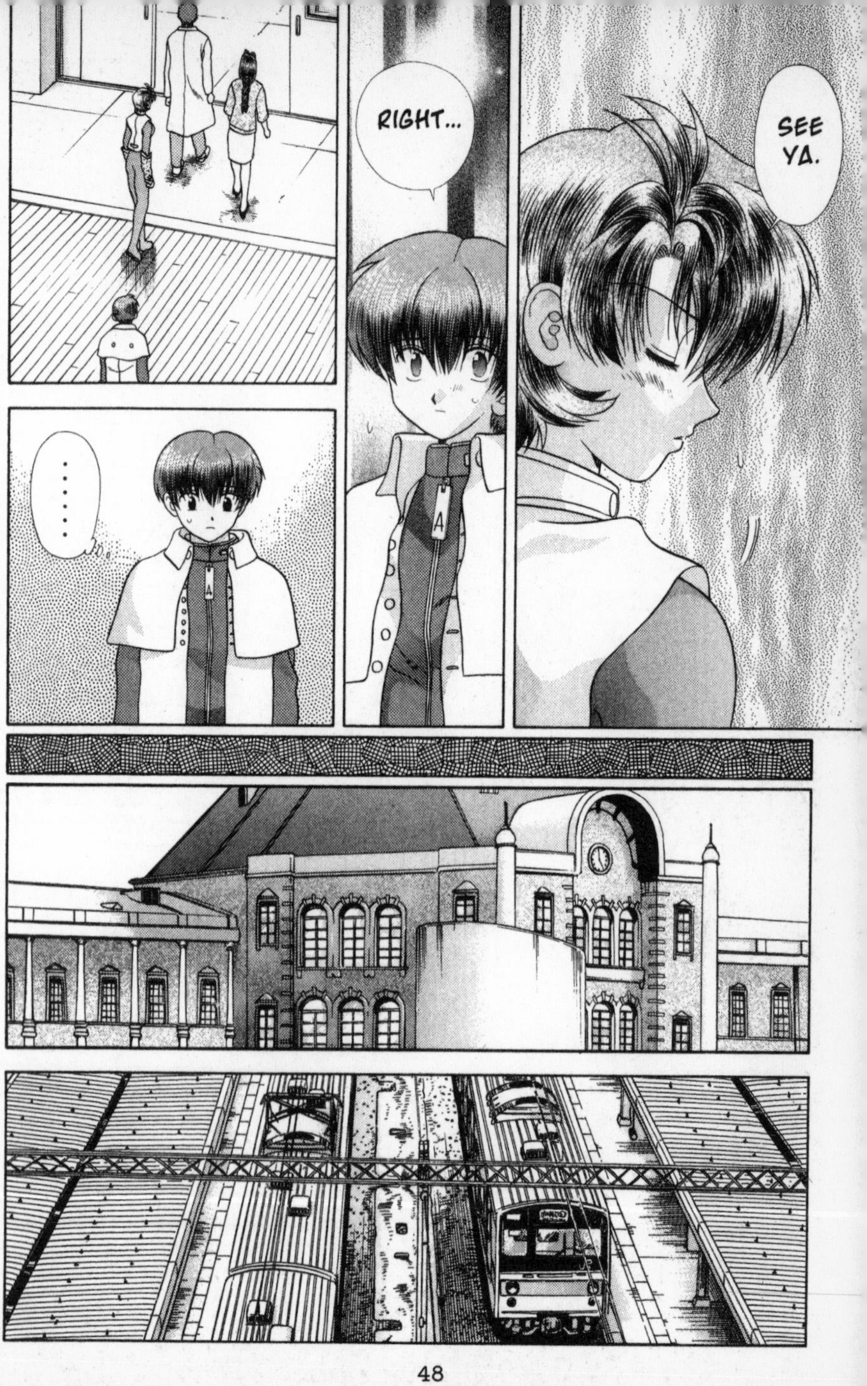
SEE YA.
RIGHT...
......

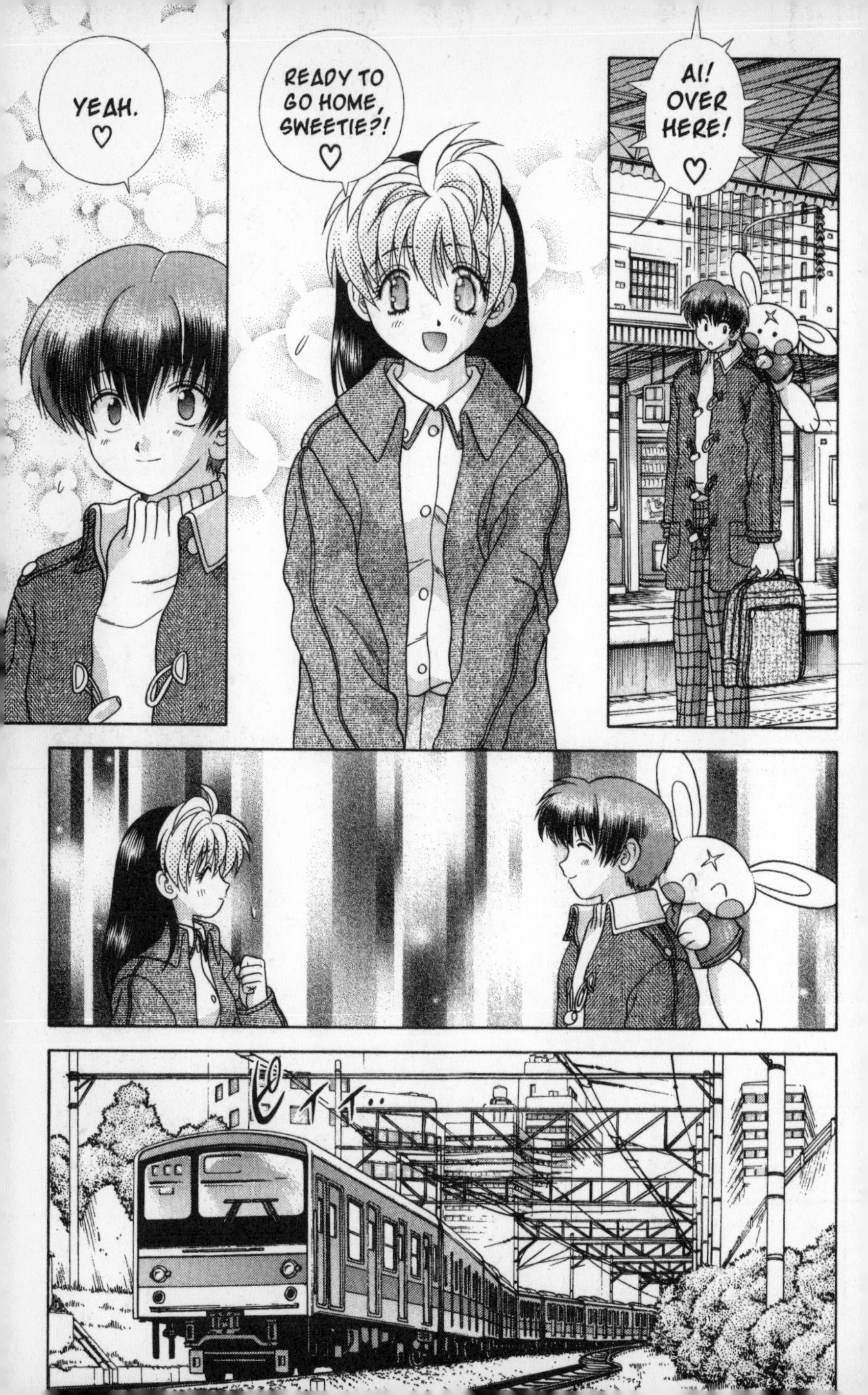
AI! OVER HERE! ♥
READY TO GO HOME, SWEETIE?! ♥
YEAH. ♥

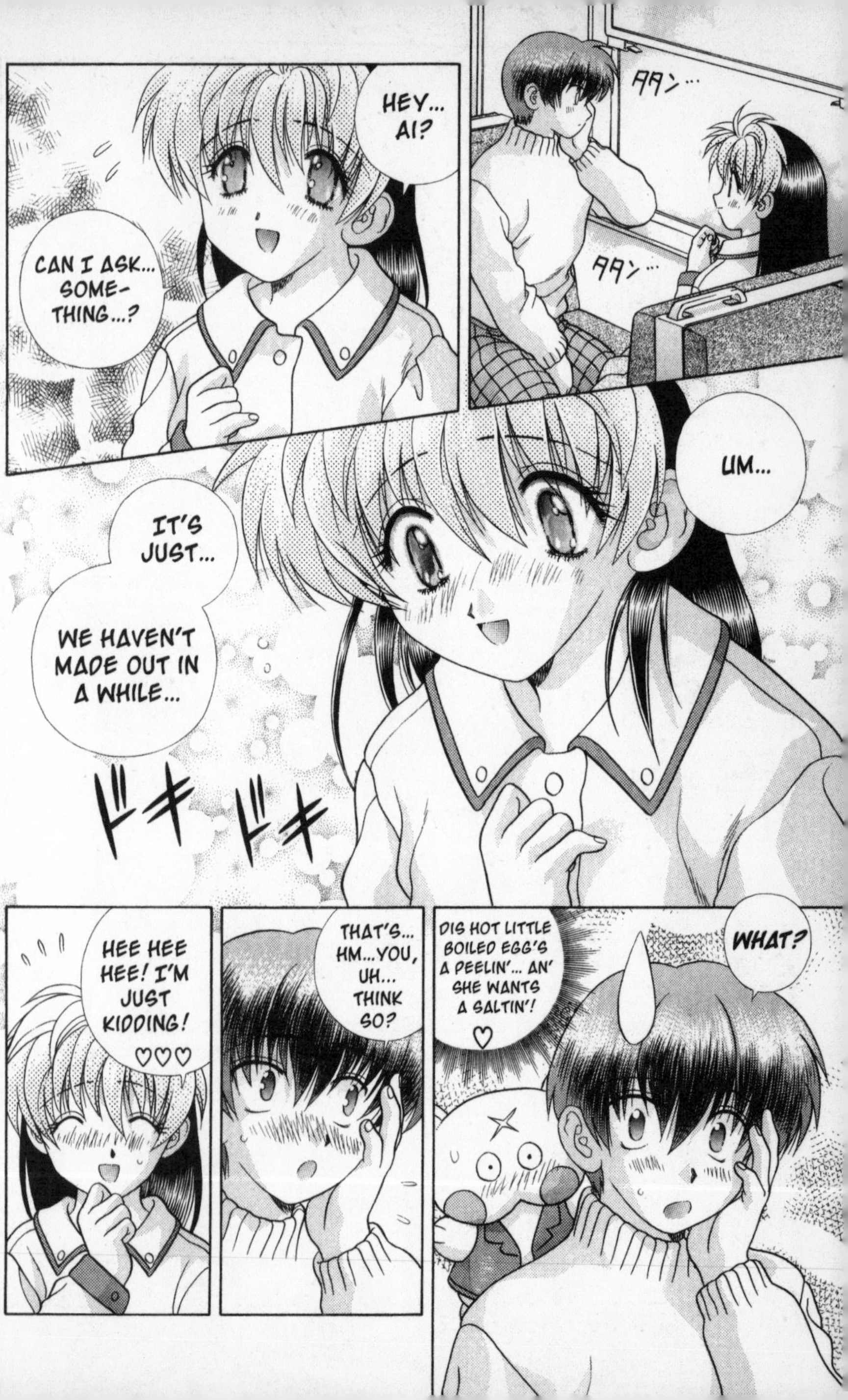
タタン…
タタン…
HEY... AI?
CAN I ASK... SOME-THING...?
UM...
IT'S JUST...
WE HAVEN'T MADE OUT IN A WHILE...
ドキ ドキ
WHAT?
DIS HOT LITTLE BOILED EGG'S A PEELIN'... AN' SHE WANTS A SALTIN'! ♡
THAT'S... HM...YOU, UH... THINK SO?
HEE HEE HEE! I'M JUST KIDDING! ♡♡♡

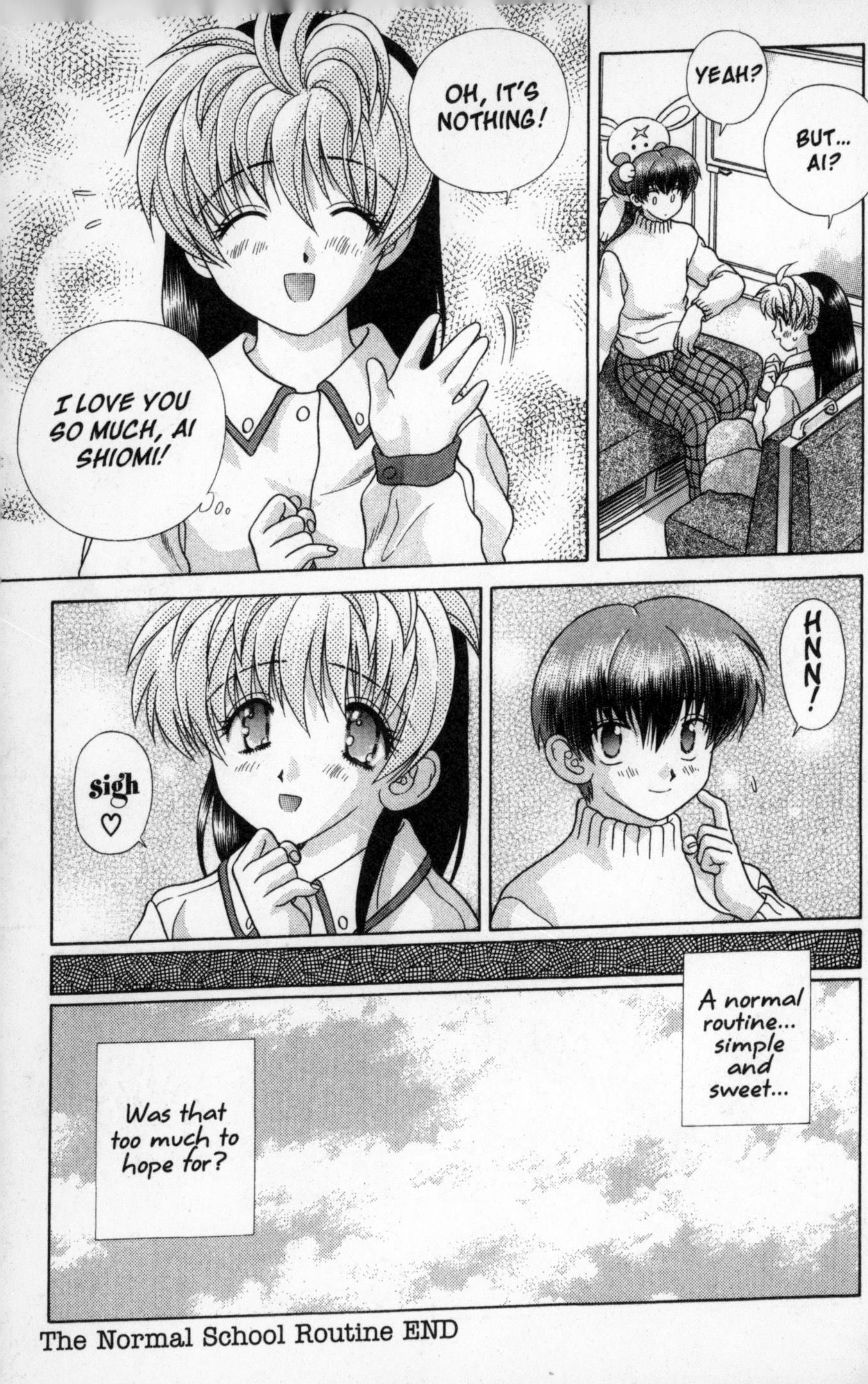
YEAH?
BUT... AI?
OH, IT'S NOTHING!
I LOVE YOU SO MUCH, AI SHIOMI!
HNN!
sigh ♡
A normal routine... simple and sweet...
Was that too much to hope for?

The Normal School Routine END

Chapter 29 Chocoholism

A

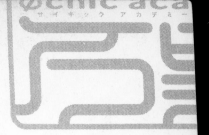

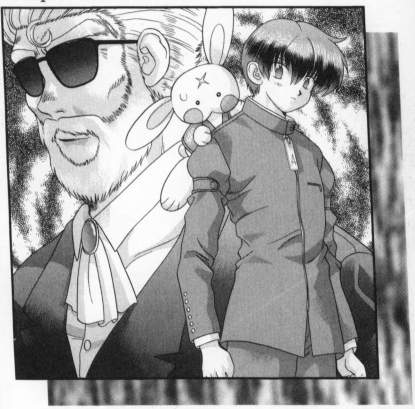

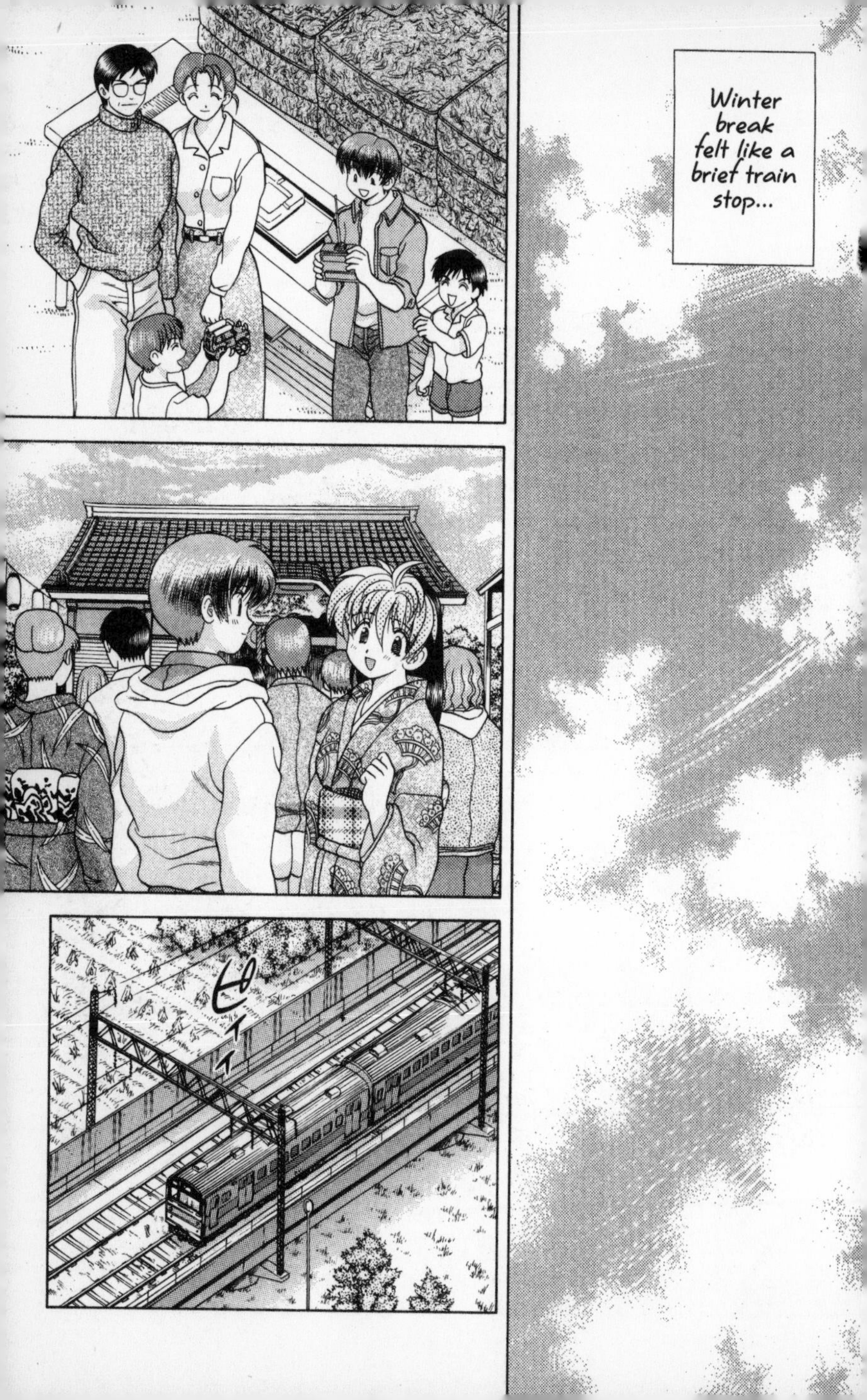
Winter break felt like a brief train stop...
ピイイ

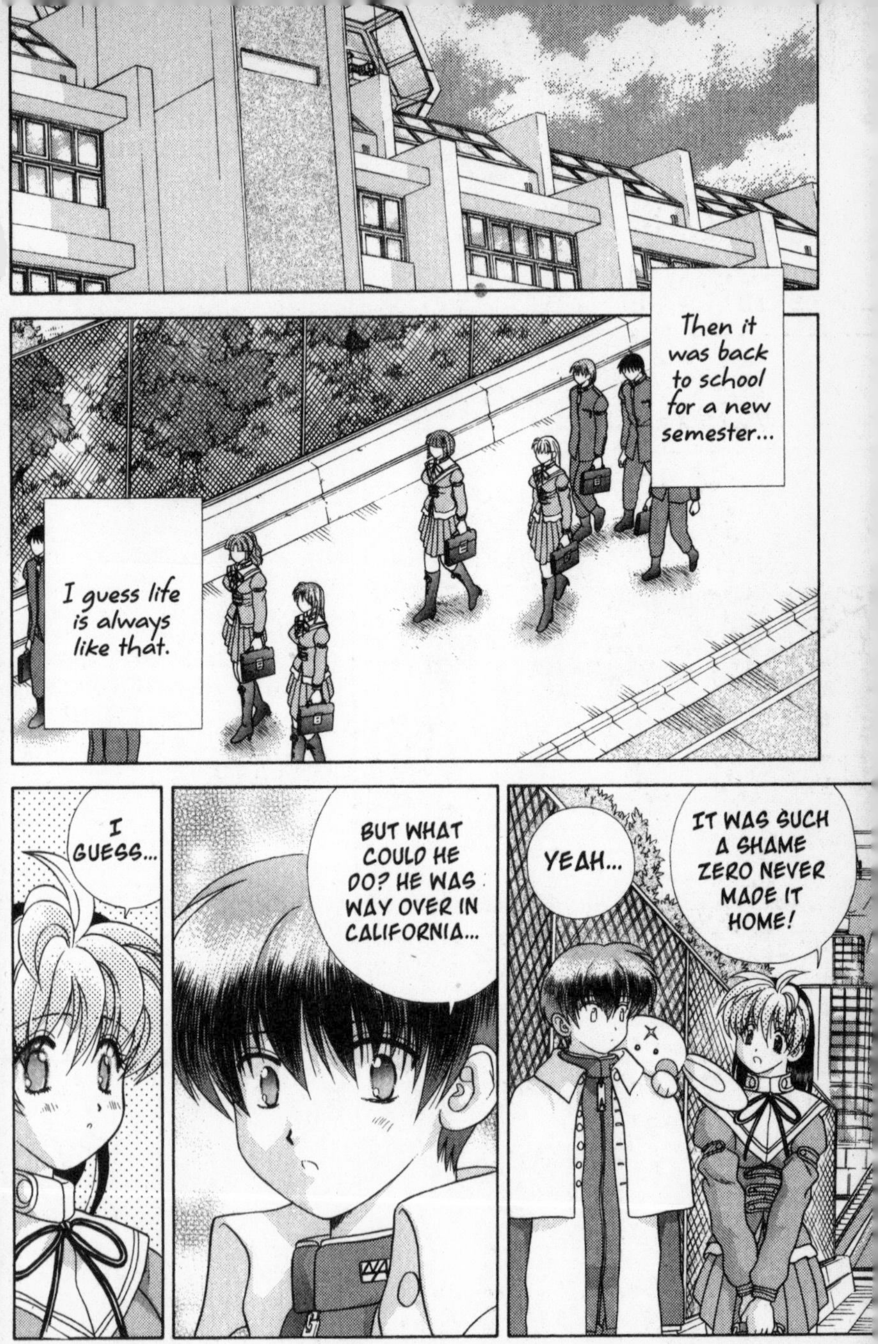
Then it was back to school for a new semester...
I guess life is always like that.
IT WAS SUCH A SHAME ZERO NEVER MADE IT HOME!
YEAH...
BUT WHAT COULD HE DO? HE WAS WAY OVER IN CALIFORNIA...
I GUESS...

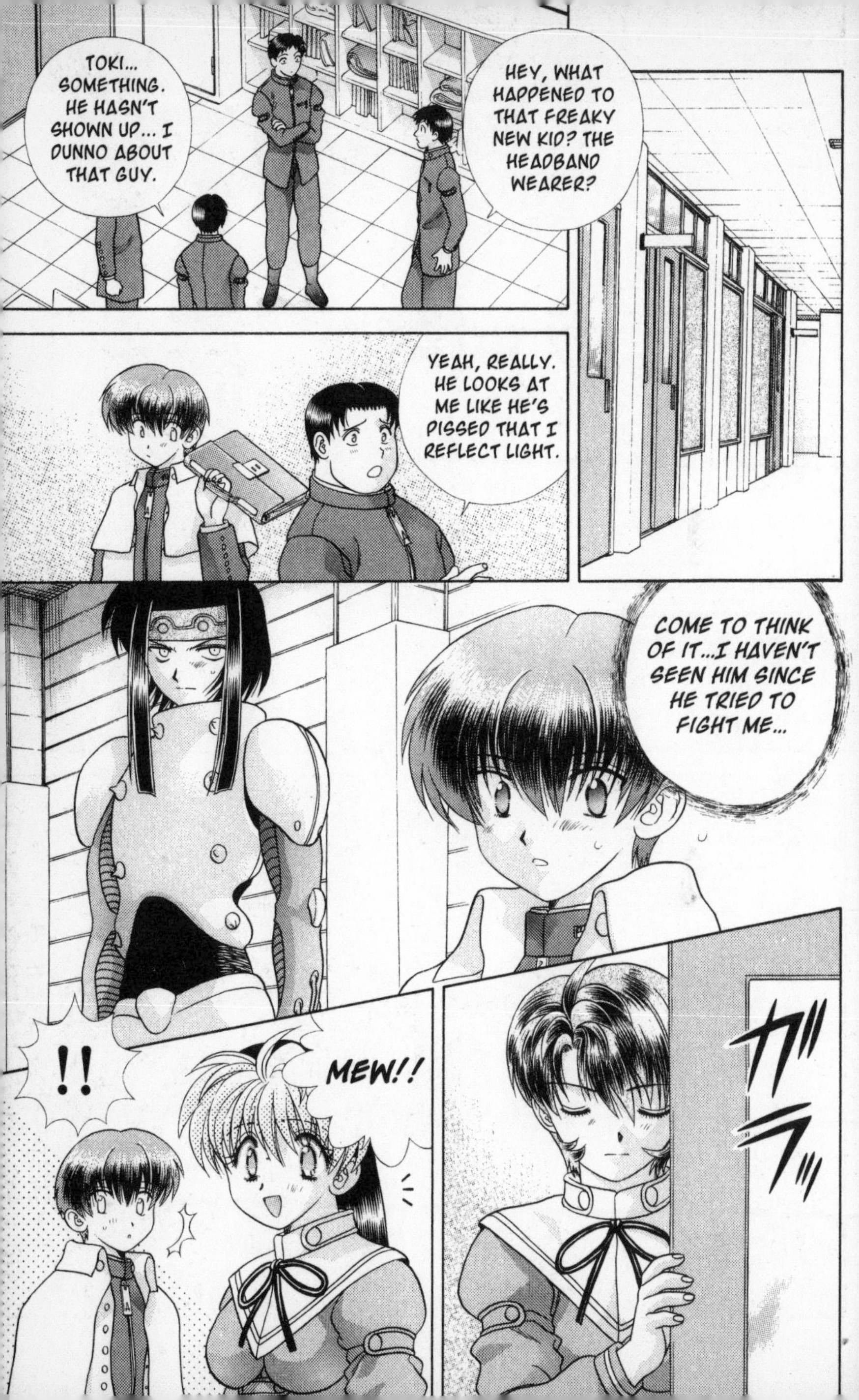
HEY, WHAT HAPPENED TO THAT FREAKY NEW KID? THE HEADBAND WEARER?
TOKI... SOMETHING. HE HASN'T SHOWN UP... I DUNNO ABOUT THAT GUY.
YEAH, REALLY. HE LOOKS AT ME LIKE HE'S PISSED THAT I REFLECT LIGHT.
COME TO THINK OF IT...I HAVEN'T SEEN HIM SINCE HE TRIED TO FIGHT ME...
ガララ
MEW!!
!!

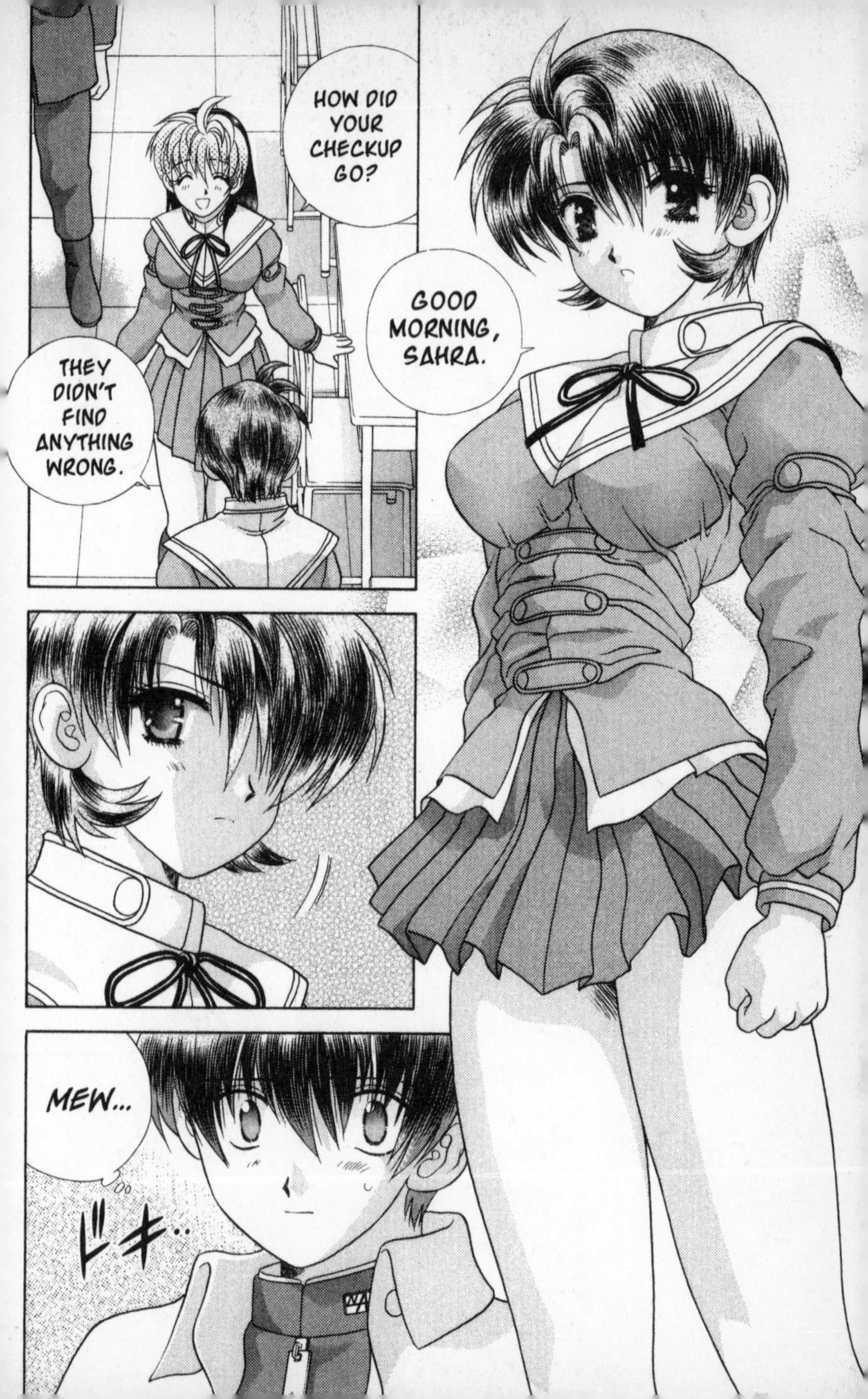
GOOD MORNING, SAHRA.
HOW DID YOUR CHECKUP GO?
THEY DIDN'T FIND ANYTHING WRONG.
MEW...
ドキ..

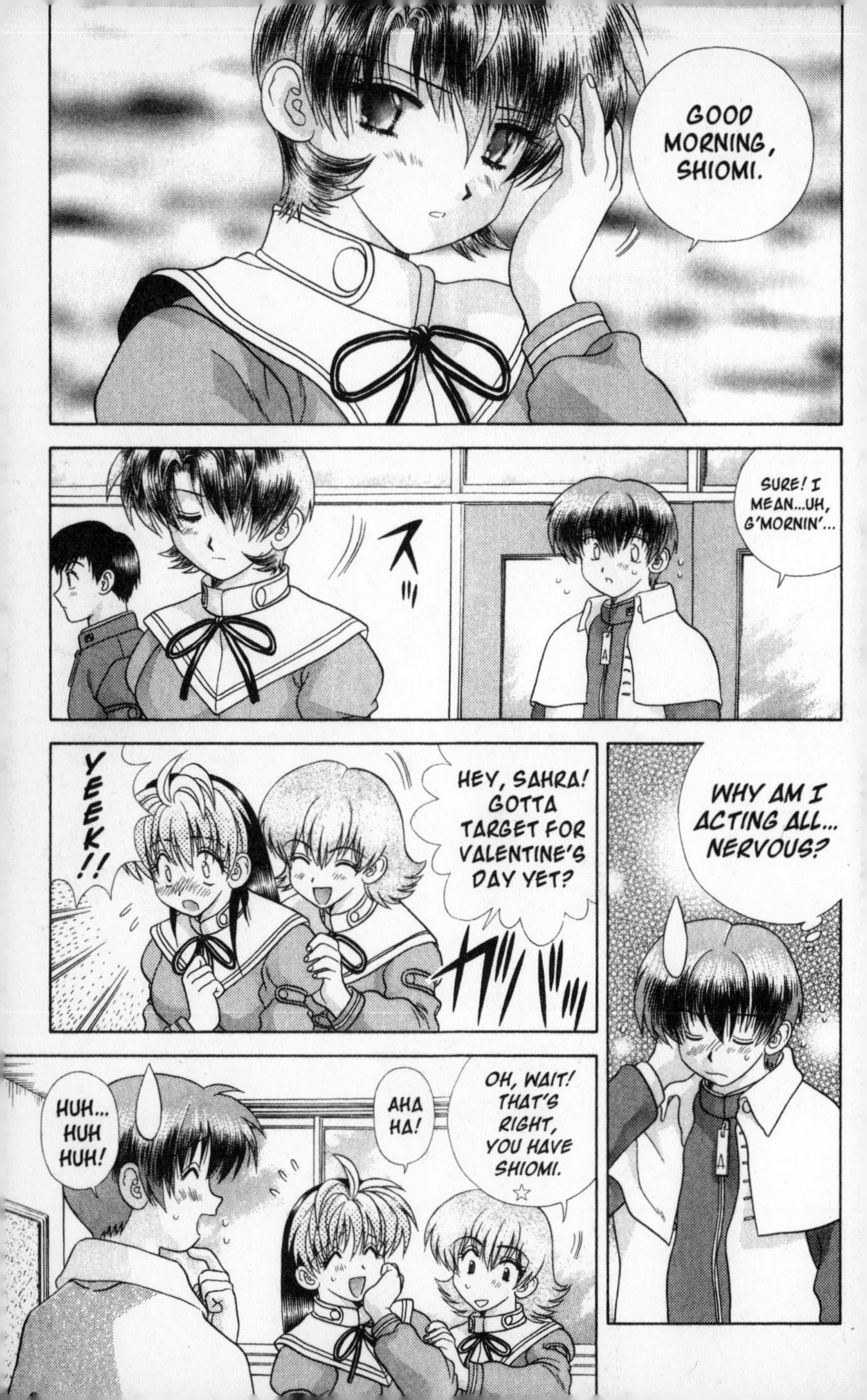
GOOD MORNING, SHIOMI.
SURE! I MEAN...UH, G'MORNIN'...
WHY AM I ACTING ALL... NERVOUS?
HEY, SAHRA! GOTTA TARGET FOR VALENTINE'S DAY YET?
YEEK!!
OH, WAIT! THAT'S RIGHT, YOU HAVE SHIOMI. ☆
AHA HA!
HUH... HUH HUH!

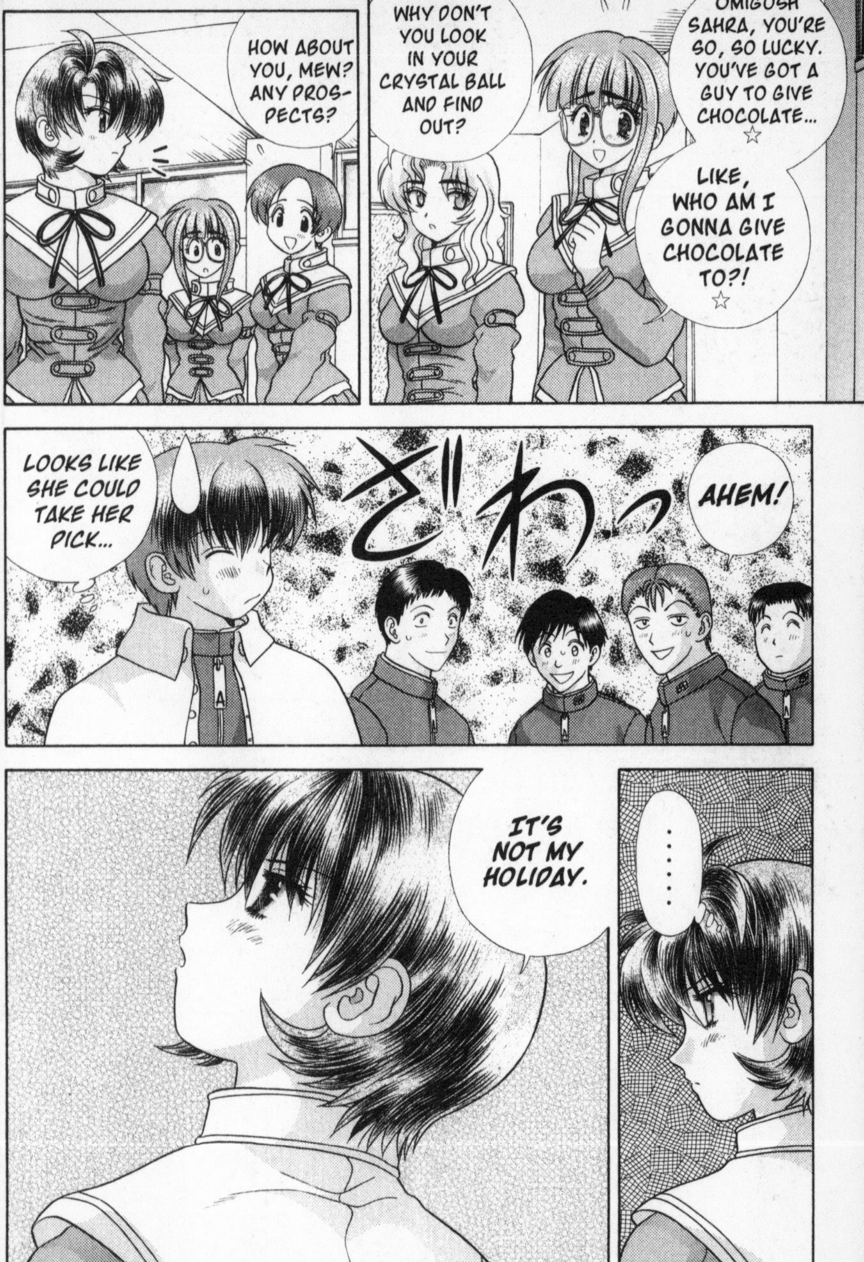
OMIGOSH SAHRA, YOU'RE SO, SO LUCKY. YOU'VE GOT A GUY TO GIVE CHOCOLATE...☆
LIKE, WHO AM I GONNA GIVE CHOCOLATE TO?! ☆
WHY DON'T YOU LOOK IN YOUR CRYSTAL BALL AND FIND OUT?
HOW ABOUT YOU, MEW? ANY PROS-PECTS?
AHEM!
ざわっ
LOOKS LIKE SHE COULD TAKE HER PICK...
......
IT'S NOT MY HOLIDAY.

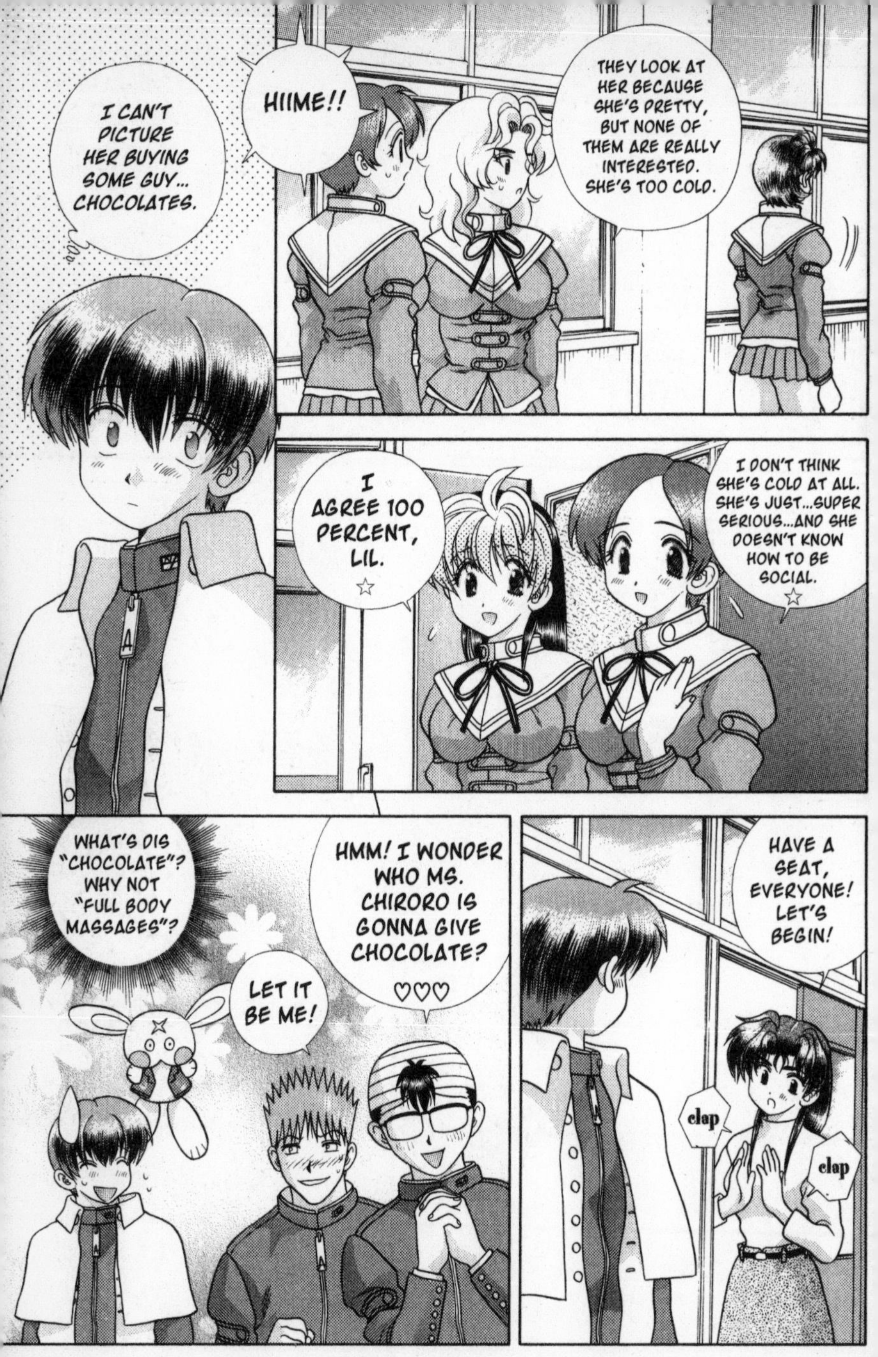
I CAN'T PICTURE HER BUYING SOME GUY... CHOCOLATES.
HIIME!!
THEY LOOK AT HER BECAUSE SHE'S PRETTY, BUT NONE OF THEM ARE REALLY INTERESTED. SHE'S TOO COLD.
I DON'T THINK SHE'S COLD AT ALL. SHE'S JUST...SUPER SERIOUS...AND SHE DOESN'T KNOW HOW TO BE SOCIAL. ☆
I AGREE 100 PERCENT, LIL. ☆
WHAT'S DIS "CHOCOLATE"? WHY NOT "FULL BODY MASSAGES"?
HMM! I WONDER WHO MS. CHIRORO IS GONNA GIVE CHOCOLATE? ♡♡♡
LET IT BE ME!
HAVE A SEAT, EVERYONE! LET'S BEGIN!
clap
clap

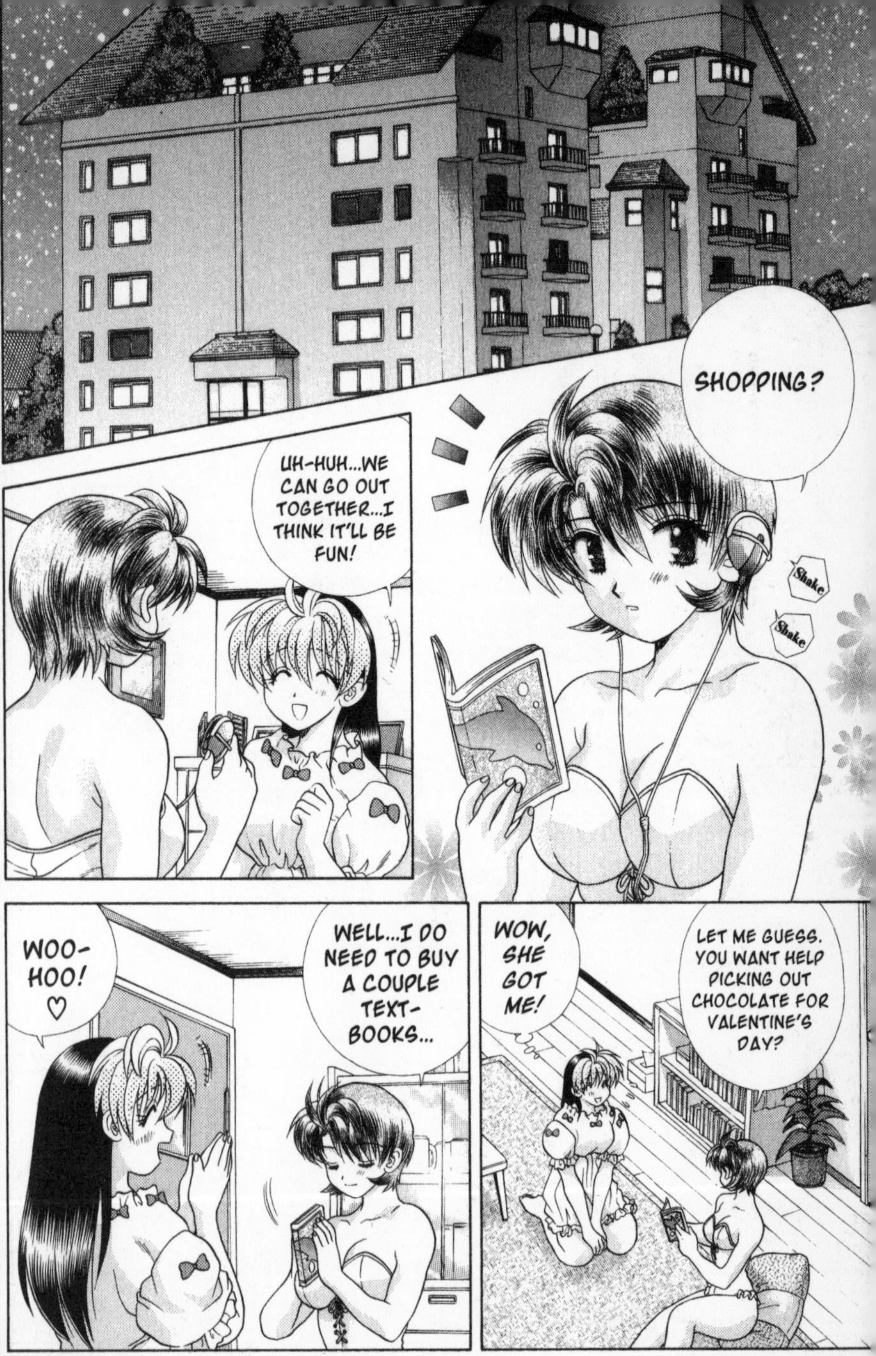
SHOPPING?
Shake
Shake
UH-HUH...WE CAN GO OUT TOGETHER...I THINK IT'LL BE FUN!
LET ME GUESS. YOU WANT HELP PICKING OUT CHOCOLATE FOR VALENTINE'S DAY?
WOW, SHE GOT ME!
WELL...I DO NEED TO BUY A COUPLE TEXT-BOOKS...
WOO-HOO! ♡

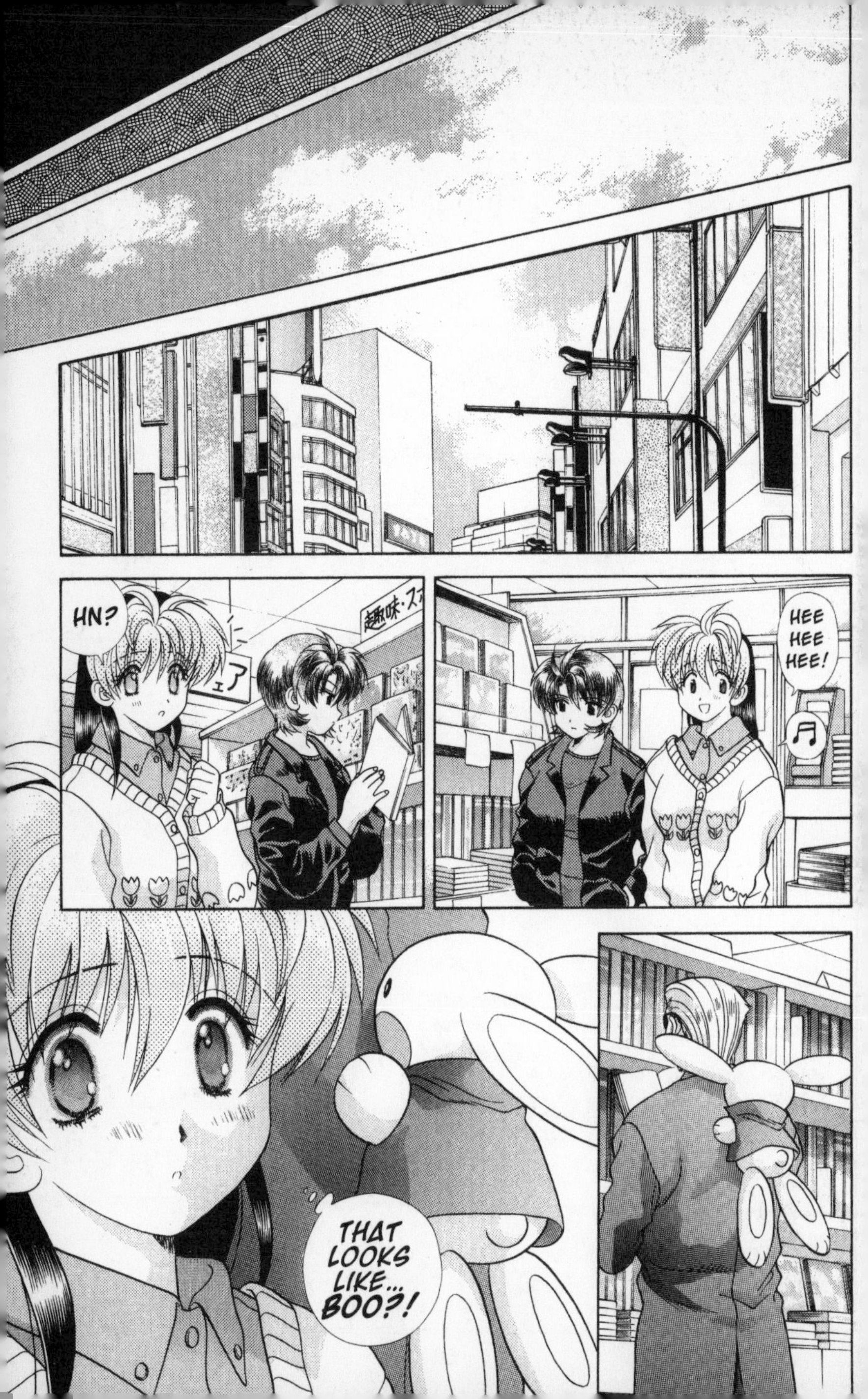
HEE HEE HEE!
♫
HN?
THAT LOOKS LIKE... BOO?!

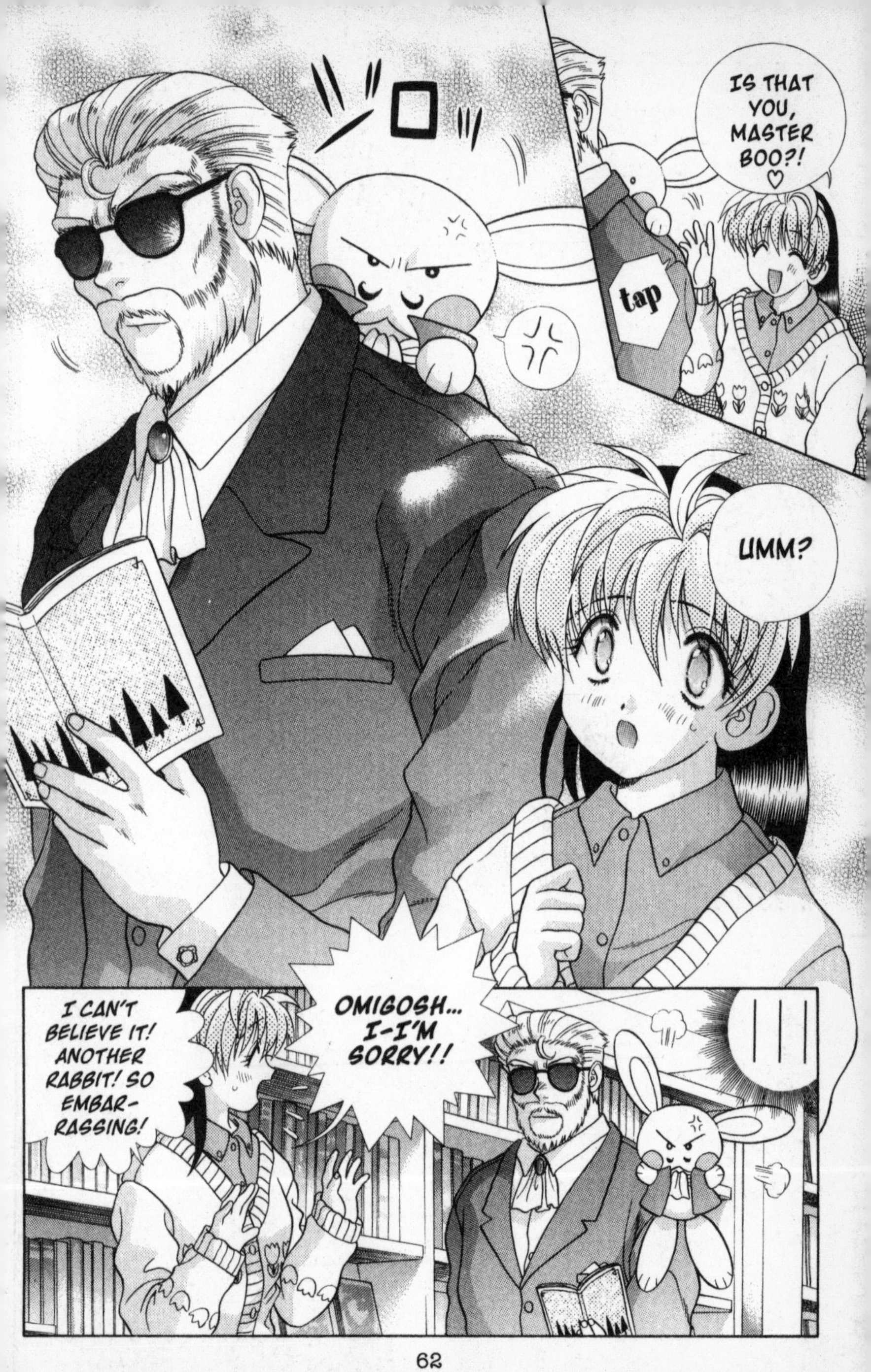
IS THAT YOU, MASTER BOO?! ♡
tap
UMM?
OMIGOSH... I-I'M SORRY!!
I CAN'T BELIEVE IT! ANOTHER RABBIT! SO EMBAR-RASSING!

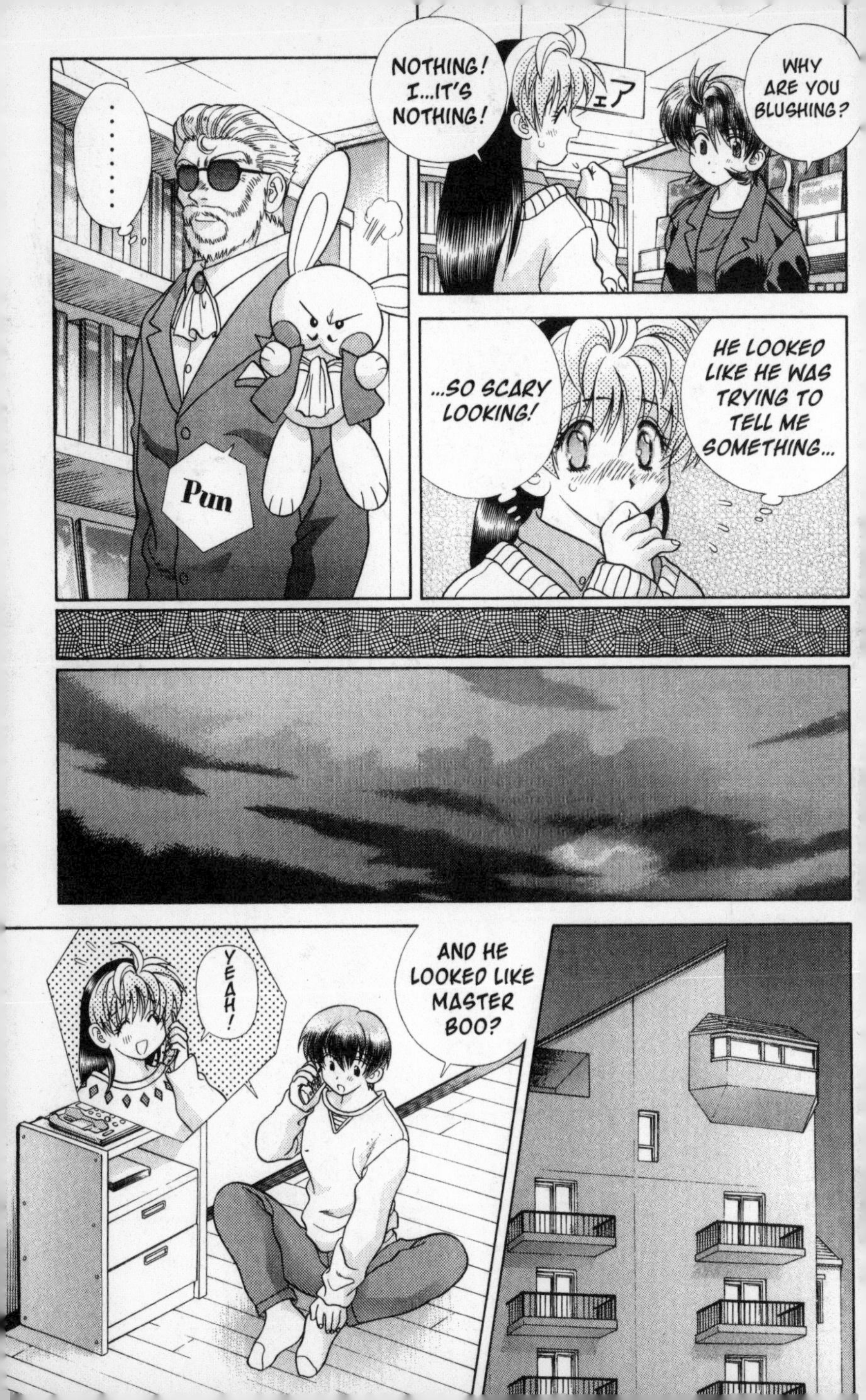
WHY ARE YOU BLUSHING?
NOTHING! I...IT'S NOTHING!
ェア
HE LOOKED LIKE HE WAS TRYING TO TELL ME SOMETHING...
...SO SCARY LOOKING!
......
Pun
AND HE LOOKED LIKE MASTER BOO?
YEAH!

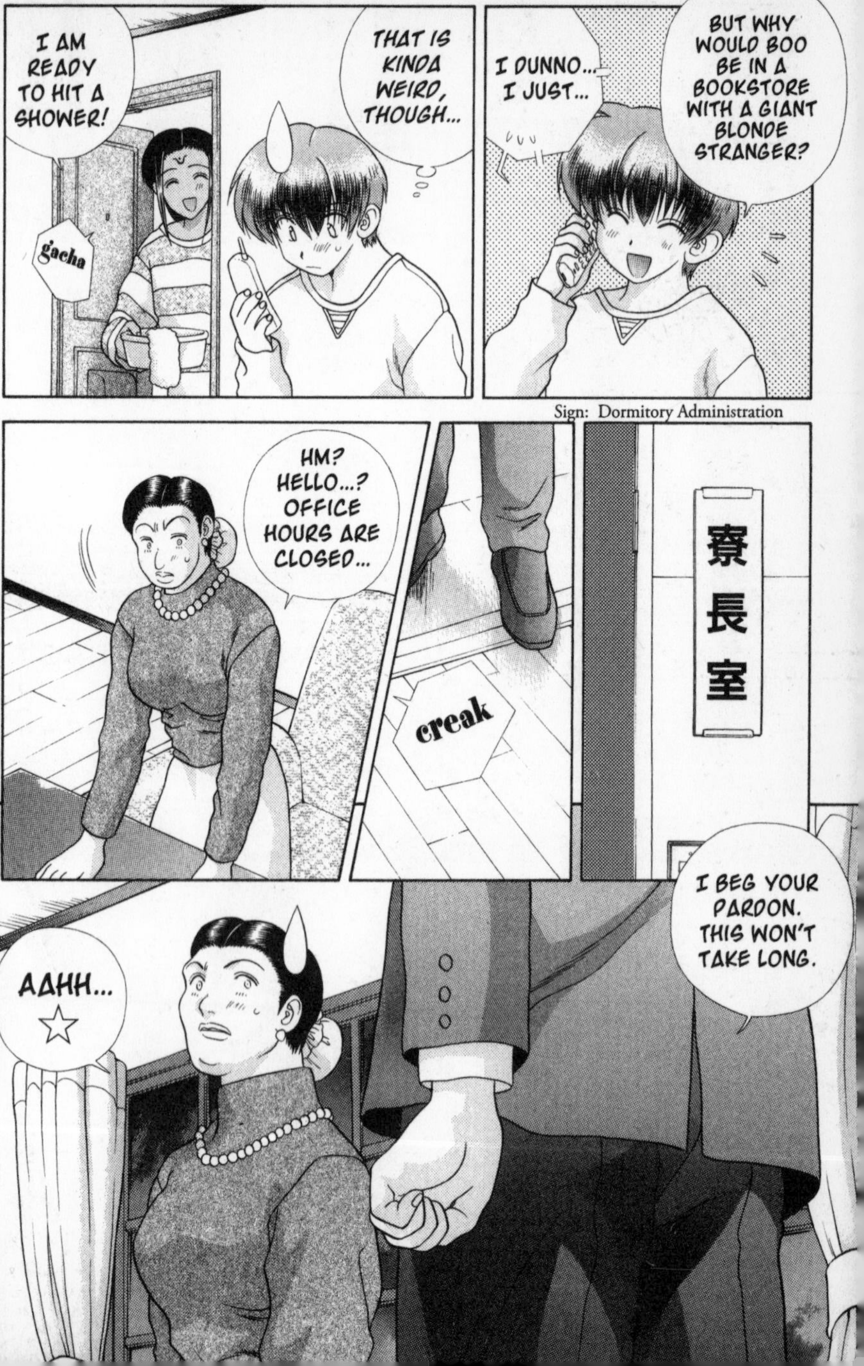
BUT WHY WOULD BOO BE IN A BOOKSTORE WITH A GIANT BLONDE STRANGER?
I DUNNO... I JUST...
THAT IS KINDA WEIRD, THOUGH...
I AM READY TO HIT A SHOWER!
gacha
Sign: Dormitory Administration
寮長室
creak
HM? HELLO...? OFFICE HOURS ARE CLOSED...
I BEG YOUR PARDON. THIS WON'T TAKE LONG.
AAHH... ☆

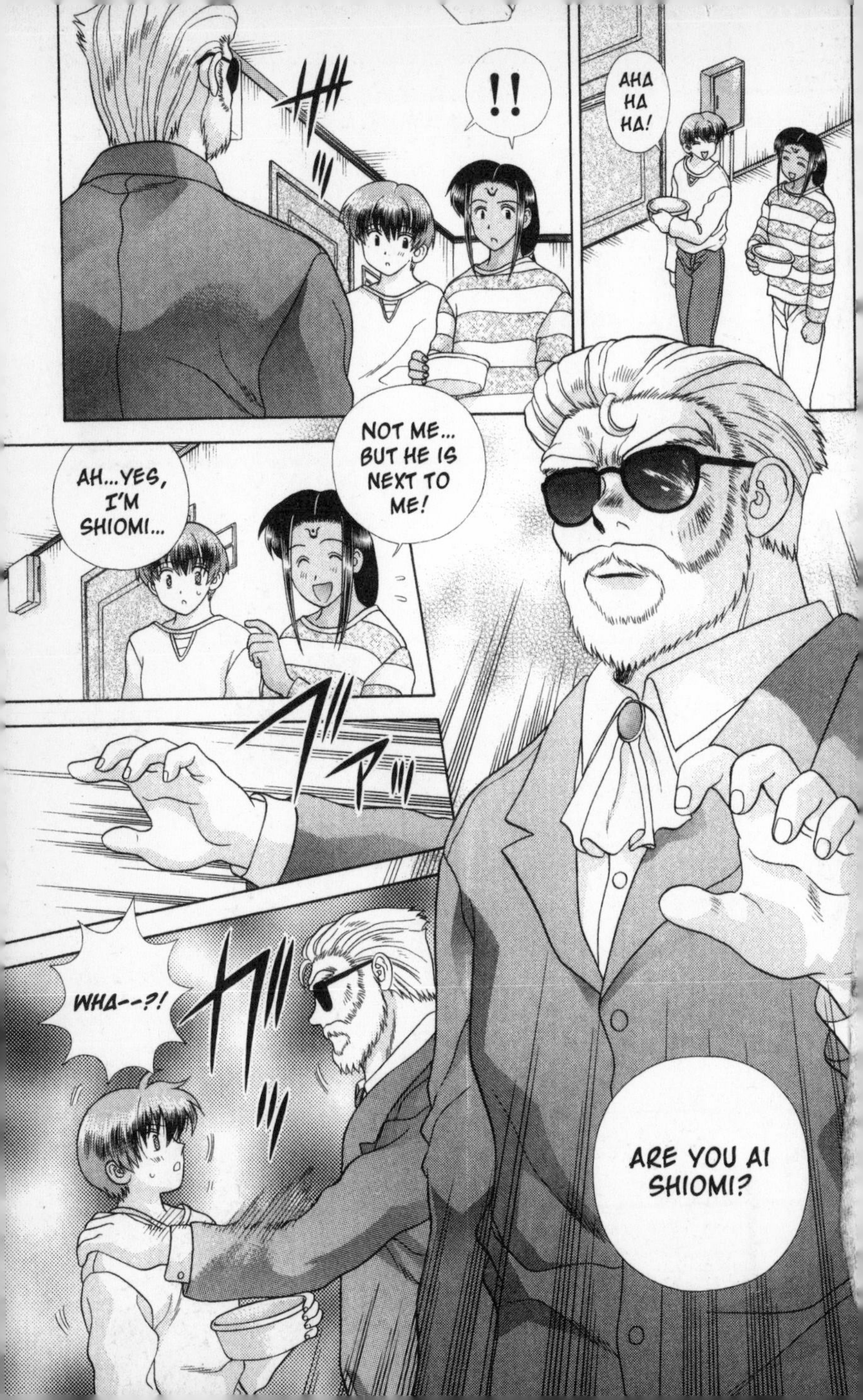
AHA HA HA!
!!
ARE YOU AI SHIOMI?
NOT ME... BUT HE IS NEXT TO ME!
AH...YES, I'M SHIOMI...
WHA--?!

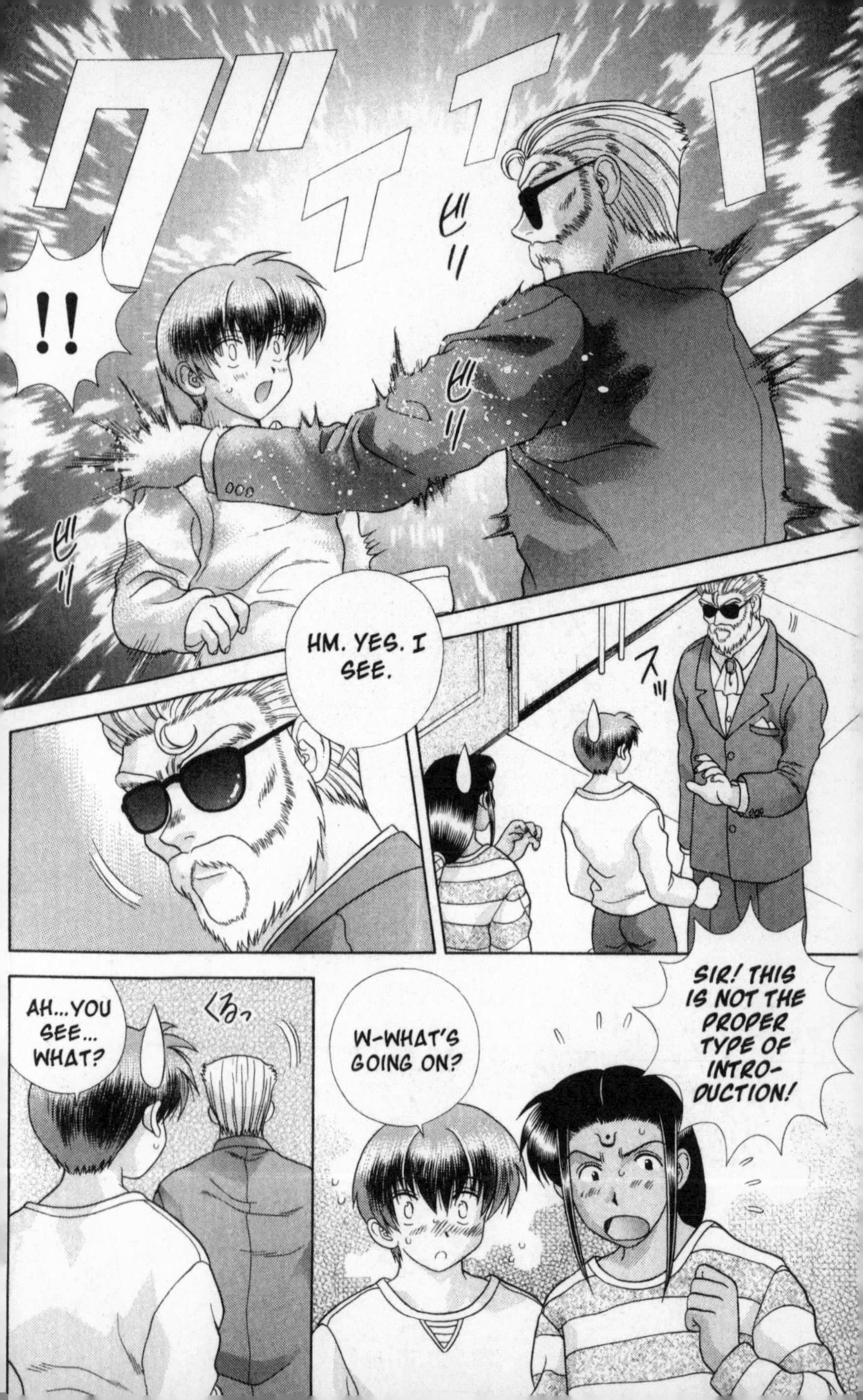
!!
HM. YES. I SEE.
SIR! THIS IS NOT THE PROPER TYPE OF INTRO-DUCTION!
W-WHAT'S GOING ON?
AH...YOU SEE... WHAT?

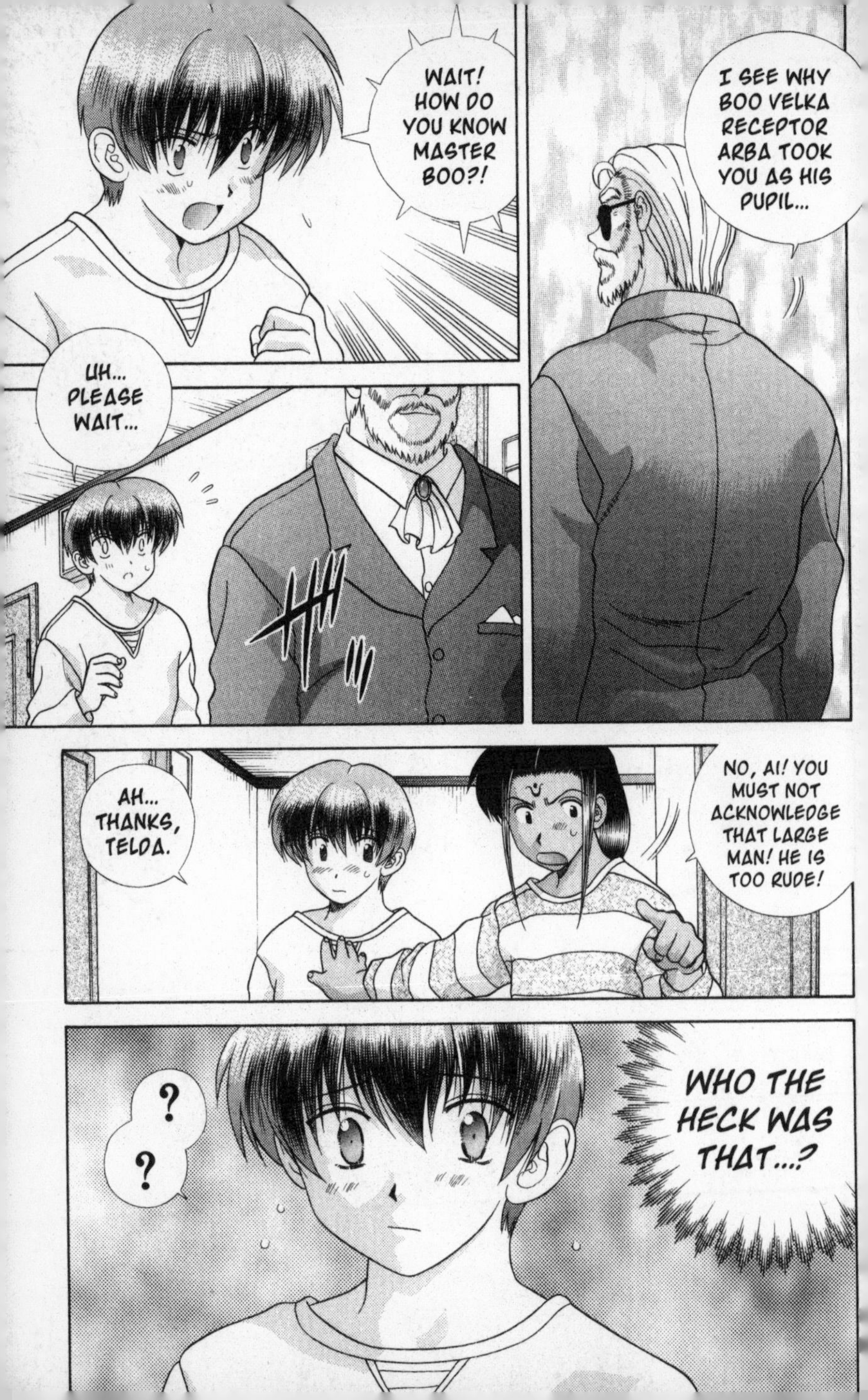
I SEE WHY BOO VELKA RECEPTOR ARBA TOOK YOU AS HIS PUPIL...
WAIT! HOW DO YOU KNOW MASTER BOO?!
UH... PLEASE WAIT...
NO, AI! YOU MUST NOT ACKNOWLEDGE THAT LARGE MAN! HE IS TOO RUDE!
AH... THANKS, TELDA.
? ?
WHO THE HECK WAS THAT...?

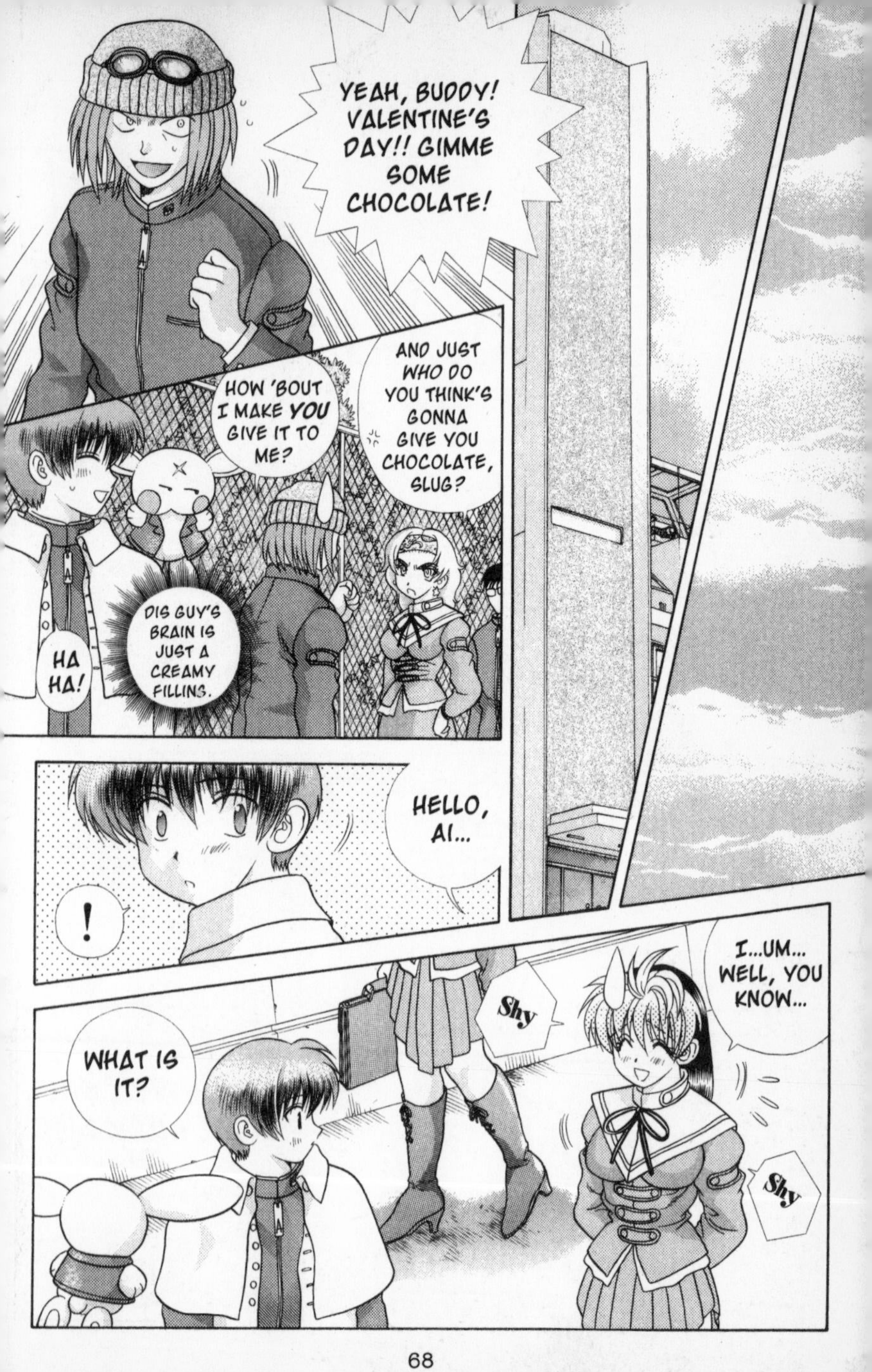

YEAH, BUDDY! VALENTINE'S DAY!! GIMME SOME CHOCOLATE!
HOW 'BOUT I MAKE *YOU* GIVE IT TO ME?
AND JUST WHO DO YOU THINK'S GONNA GIVE YOU CHOCOLATE, SLUG?
DIS GUY'S BRAIN IS JUST A CREAMY FILLINS.
HA HA!
HELLO, AI...
!
WHAT IS IT?
Shy
I...UM... WELL, YOU KNOW...
Shy

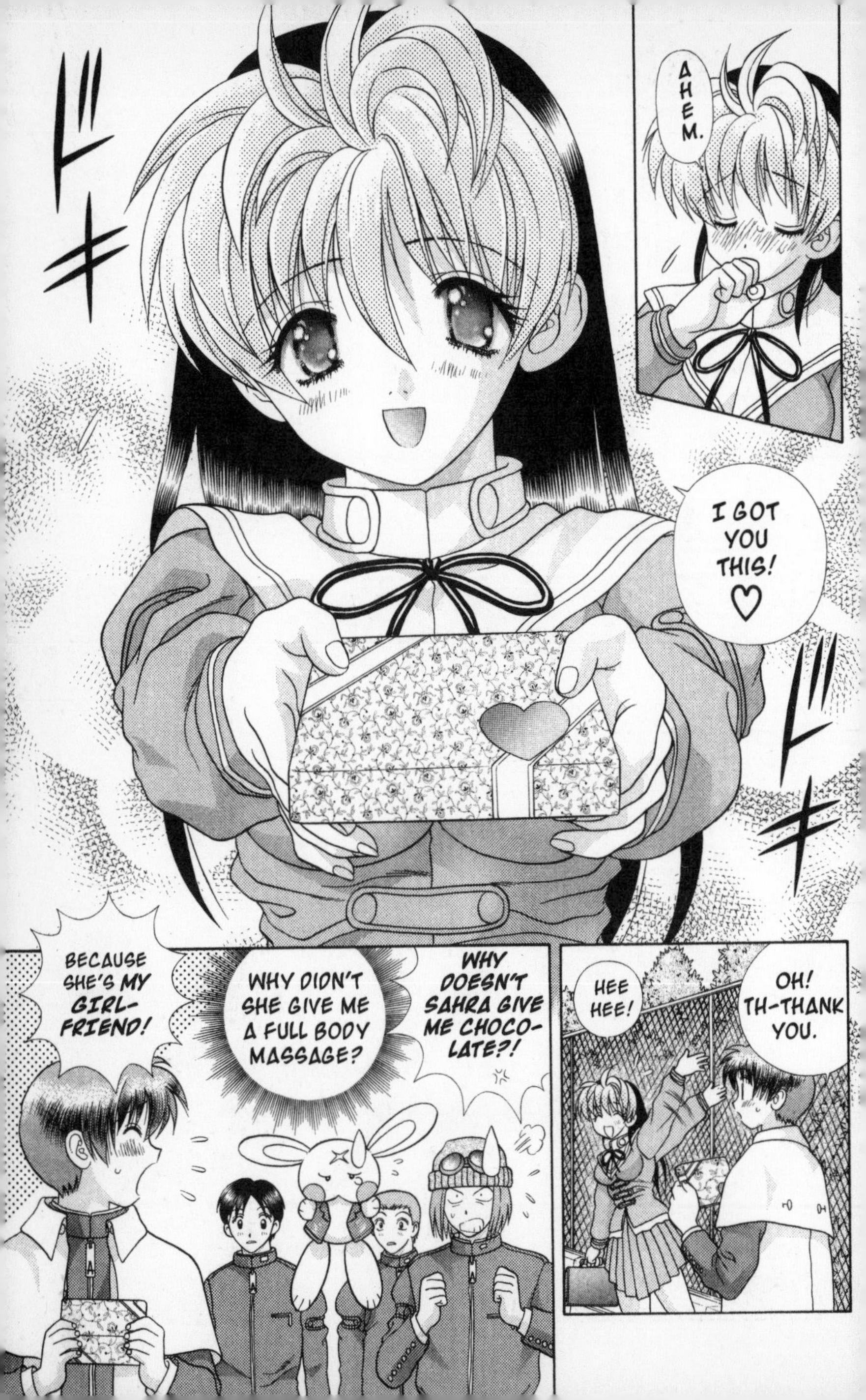
AHEM.
ドキ
I GOT YOU THIS! ♡
ドキ
OH! TH-THANK YOU.
HEE HEE!
WHY DOESN'T SAHRA GIVE ME CHOCOLATE?!
WHY DIDN'T SHE GIVE ME A FULL BODY MASSAGE?
BECAUSE SHE'S MY GIRL-FRIEND!

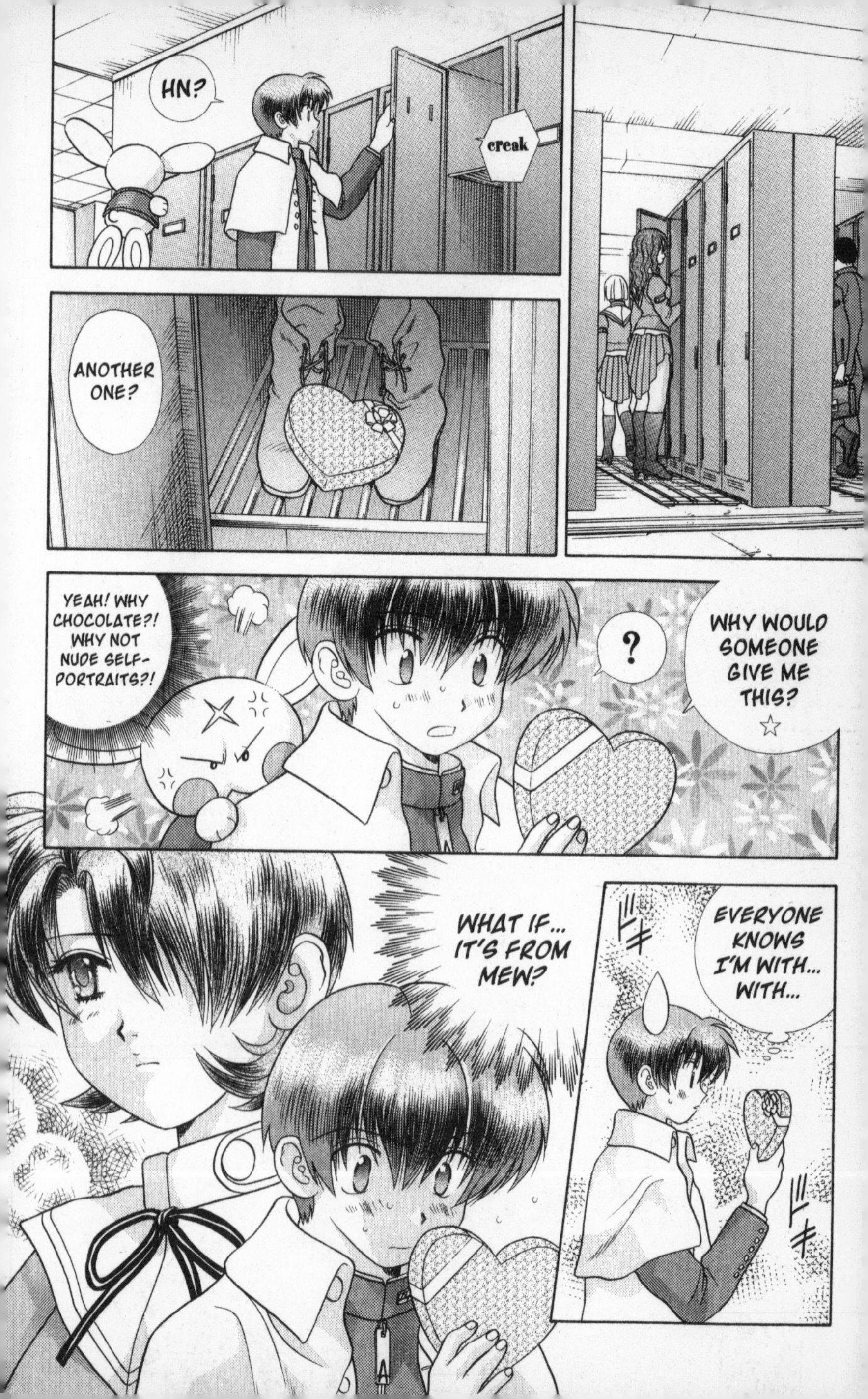
HN?
creak
ANOTHER ONE?
?
WHY WOULD SOMEONE GIVE ME THIS? ☆
YEAH! WHY CHOCOLATE?! WHY NOT NUDE SELF-PORTRAITS?!
EVERYONE KNOWS I'M WITH... WITH...
ドキ
ドキ
WHAT IF... IT'S FROM MEW?

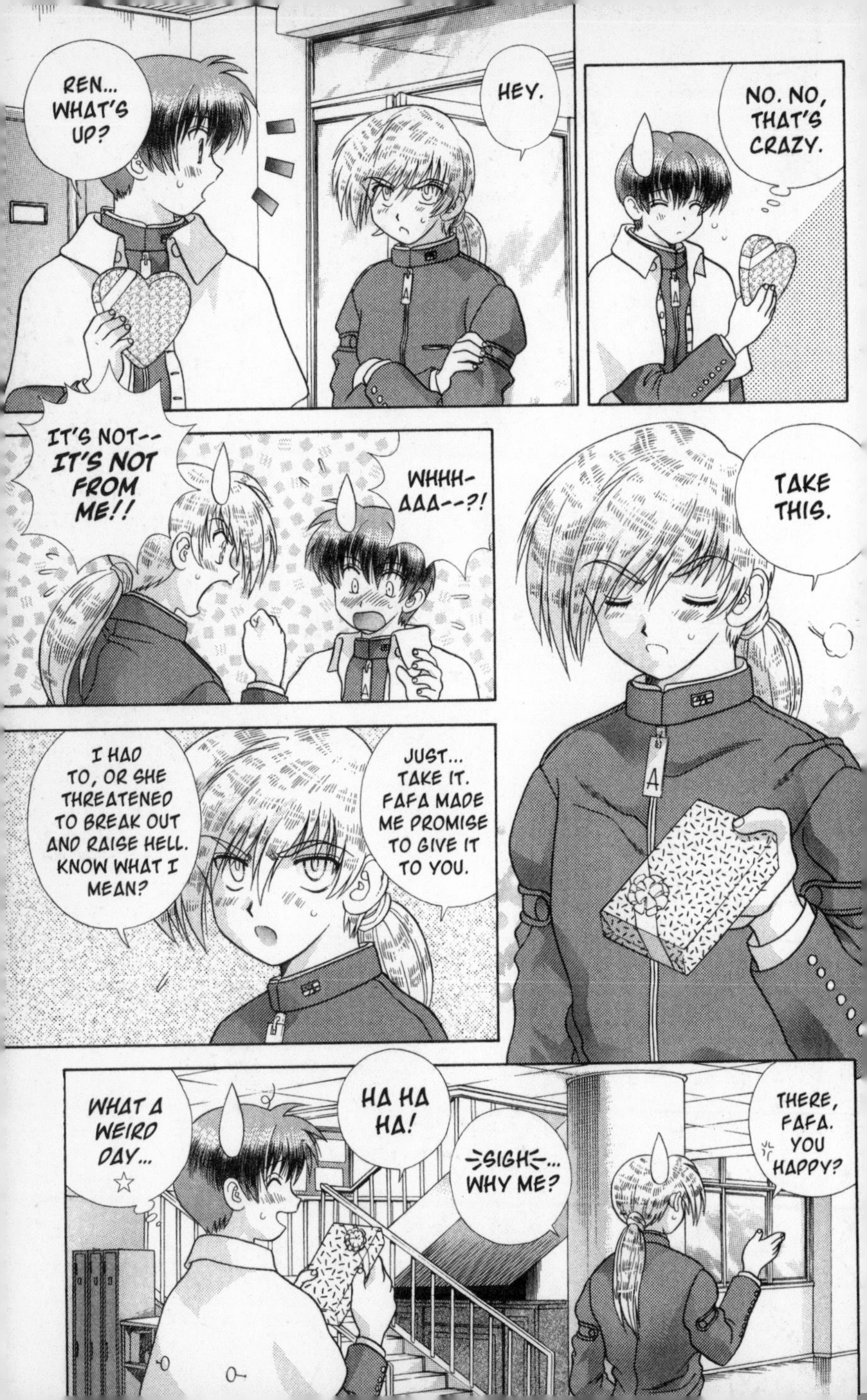
NO. NO, THAT'S CRAZY.
HEY.
REN... WHAT'S UP?
TAKE THIS.
WHHH-AAA--?!
IT'S NOT-- IT'S NOT FROM ME!!
JUST... TAKE IT. FAFA MADE ME PROMISE TO GIVE IT TO YOU.
I HAD TO, OR SHE THREATENED TO BREAK OUT AND RAISE HELL. KNOW WHAT I MEAN?
THERE, FAFA. YOU HAPPY?
=SIGH=... WHY ME?
HA HA HA!
WHAT A WEIRD DAY... ☆

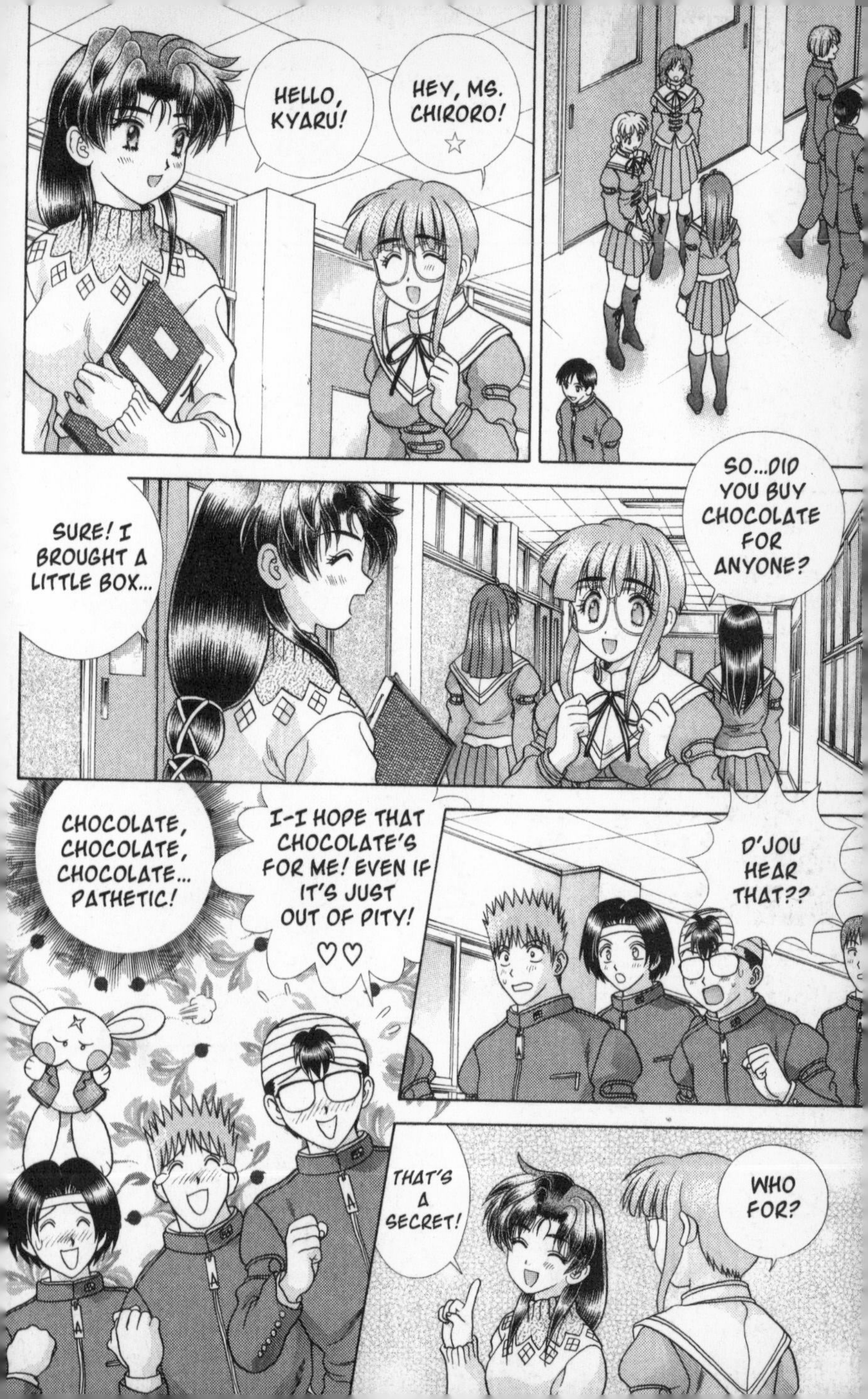
HELLO, KYARU!
HEY, MS. CHIRORO! ☆
SO...DID YOU BUY CHOCOLATE FOR ANYONE?
SURE! I BROUGHT A LITTLE BOX...
D'JOU HEAR THAT??
I-I HOPE THAT CHOCOLATE'S FOR ME! EVEN IF IT'S JUST OUT OF PITY! ♡♡
CHOCOLATE, CHOCOLATE, CHOCOLATE... PATHETIC!
WHO FOR?
THAT'S A SECRET!

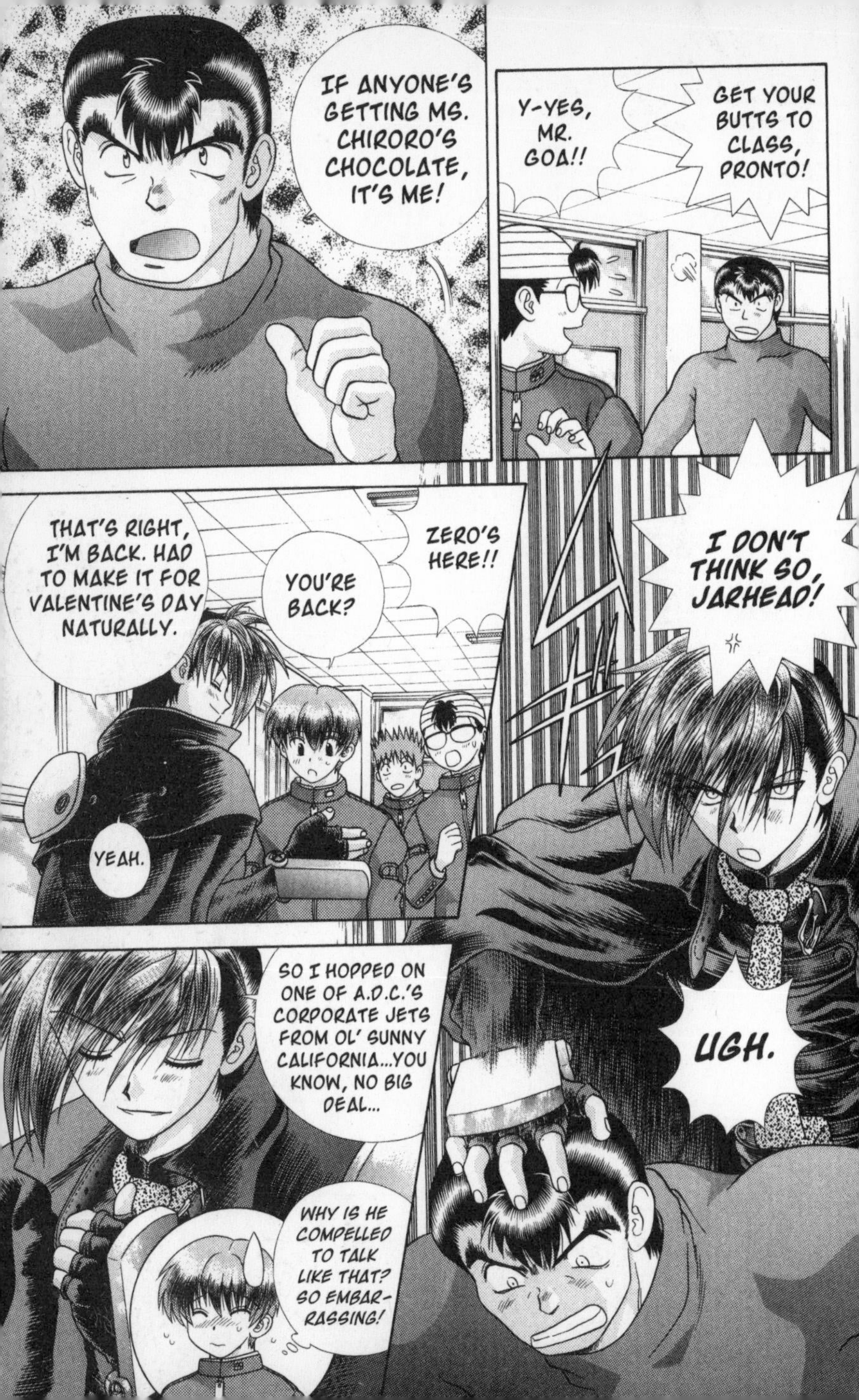
GET YOUR BUTTS TO CLASS, PRONTO!
Y-YES, MR. GOA!!
IF ANYONE'S GETTING MS. CHIRORO'S CHOCOLATE, IT'S ME!
I DON'T THINK SO, JARHEAD!
ZERO'S HERE!!
YOU'RE BACK?
THAT'S RIGHT, I'M BACK. HAD TO MAKE IT FOR VALENTINE'S DAY NATURALLY.
YEAH.
UGH.
SO I HOPPED ON ONE OF A.D.C.'S CORPORATE JETS FROM OL' SUNNY CALIFORNIA...YOU KNOW, NO BIG DEAL...
WHY IS HE COMPELLED TO TALK LIKE THAT? SO EMBAR-RASSING!

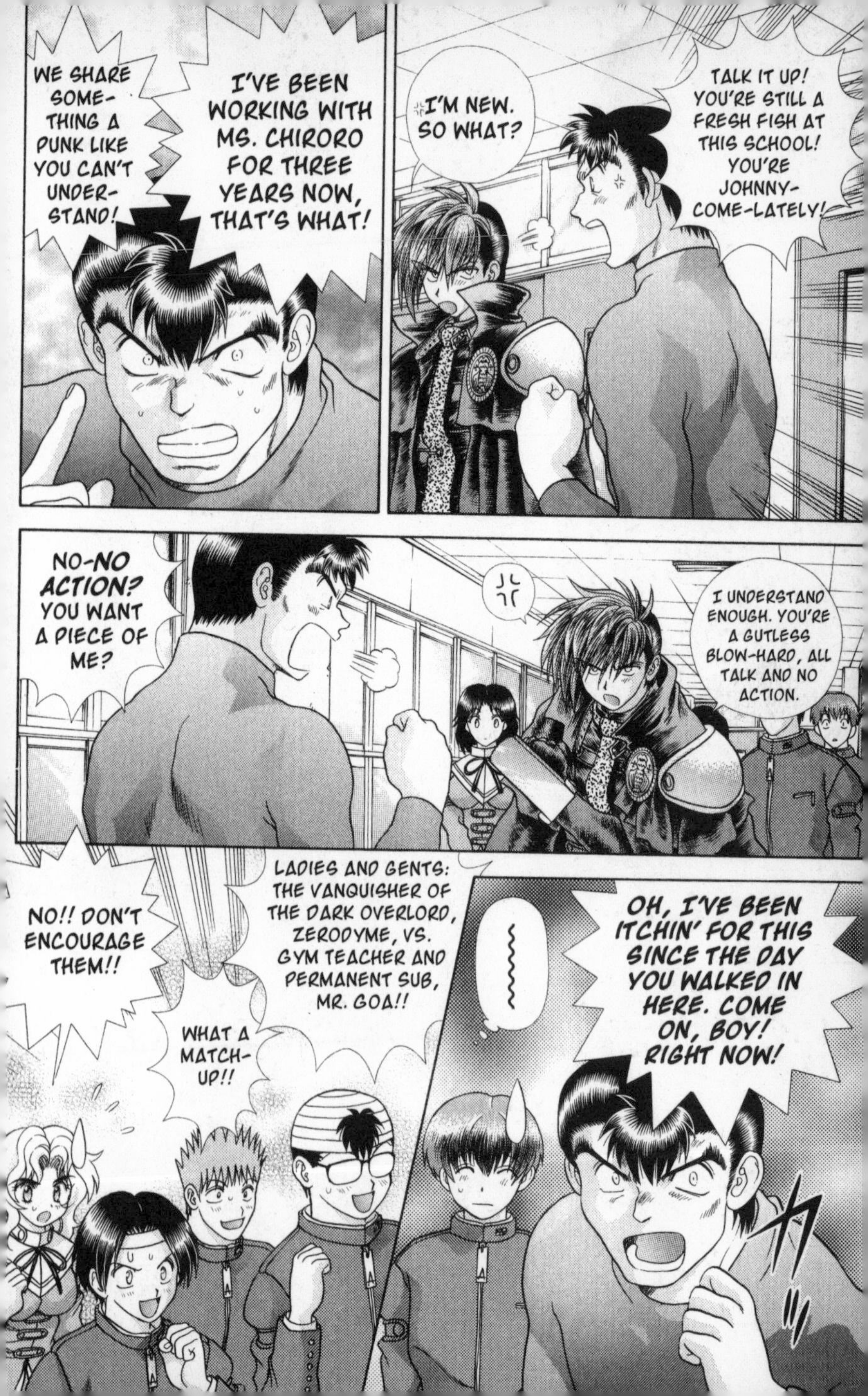
TALK IT UP! YOU'RE STILL A FRESH FISH AT THIS SCHOOL! YOU'RE JOHNNY-COME-LATELY!
I'M NEW. SO WHAT?
I'VE BEEN WORKING WITH MS. CHIRORO FOR THREE YEARS NOW, THAT'S WHAT!
WE SHARE SOMETHING A PUNK LIKE YOU CAN'T UNDERSTAND!
I UNDERSTAND ENOUGH. YOU'RE A GUTLESS BLOW-HARD, ALL TALK AND NO ACTION.
NO-NO ACTION? YOU WANT A PIECE OF ME?
OH, I'VE BEEN ITCHIN' FOR THIS SINCE THE DAY YOU WALKED IN HERE. COME ON, BOY! RIGHT NOW!
LADIES AND GENTS: THE VANQUISHER OF THE DARK OVERLORD, ZERODYME, VS. GYM TEACHER AND PERMANENT SUB, MR. GOA!!
WHAT A MATCH-UP!!
NO!! DON'T ENCOURAGE THEM!!

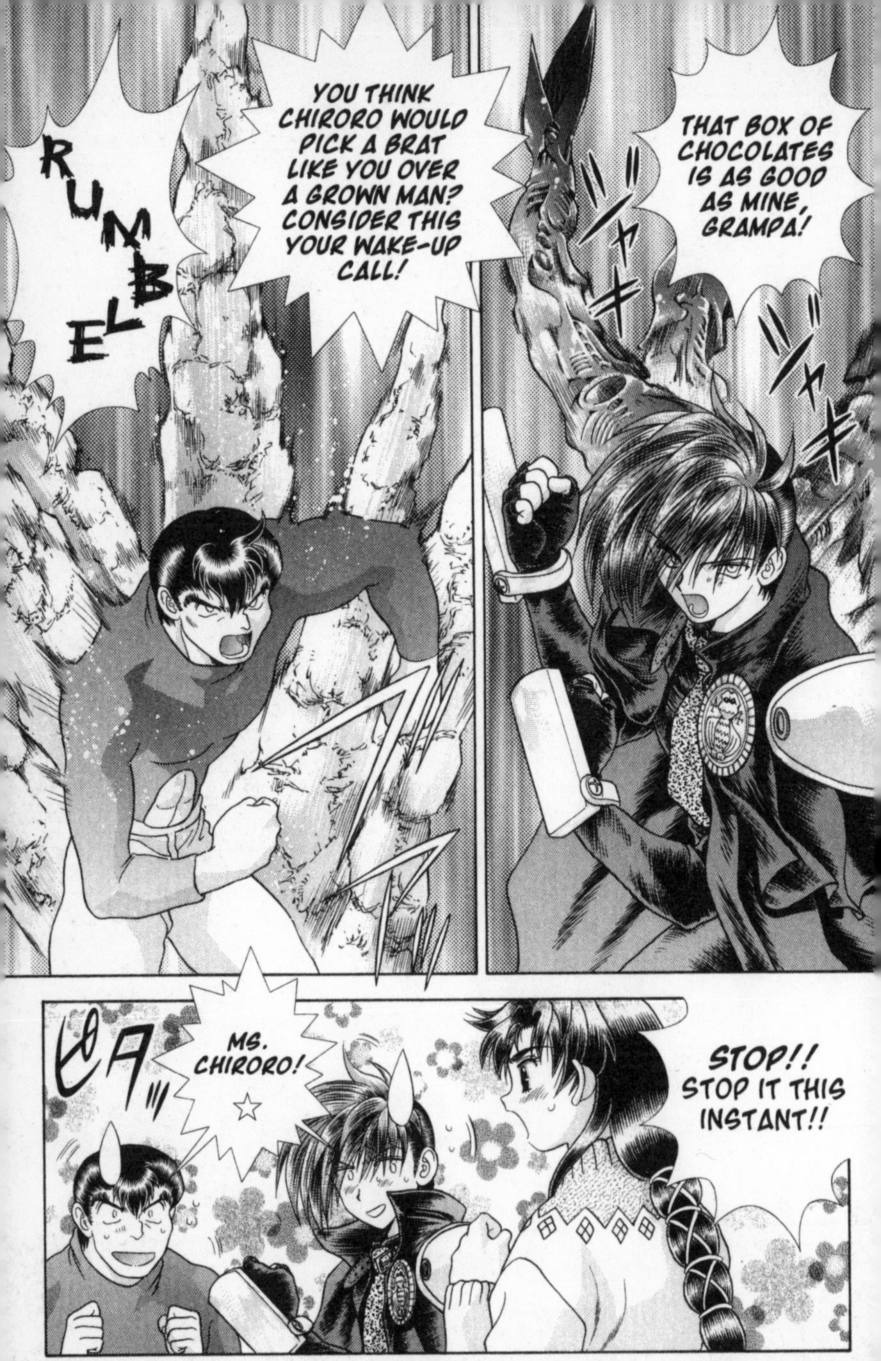
THAT BOX OF CHOCOLATES IS AS GOOD AS MINE, GRAMPA!
ジャキ
ジャキ
YOU THINK CHIRORO WOULD PICK A BRAT LIKE YOU OVER A GROWN MAN? CONSIDER THIS YOUR WAKE-UP CALL!
RUMBLE
STOP!! STOP IT THIS INSTANT!!
MS. CHIRORO! ☆
ピタ

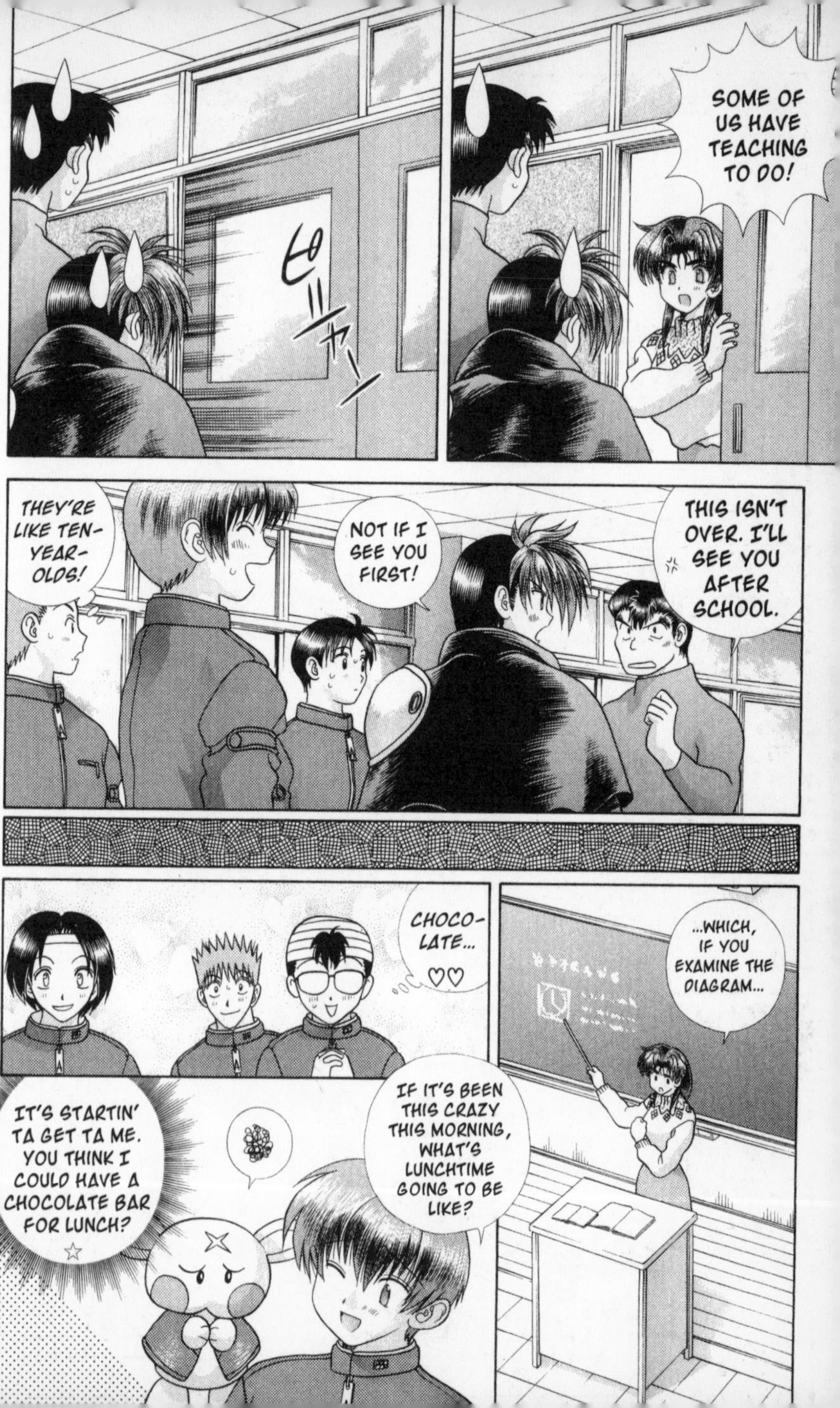
SOME OF US HAVE TEACHING TO DO!
ピシャーン
THIS ISN'T OVER. I'LL SEE YOU AFTER SCHOOL.
NOT IF I SEE YOU FIRST!
THEY'RE LIKE TEN-YEAR-OLDS!
...WHICH, IF YOU EXAMINE THE DIAGRAM...
CHOCOLATE... ♡♡
IF IT'S BEEN THIS CRAZY THIS MORNING, WHAT'S LUNCHTIME GOING TO BE LIKE?
IT'S STARTIN' TA GET TA ME. YOU THINK I COULD HAVE A CHOCOLATE BAR FOR LUNCH? ☆

MMMMM...

THAT HEART SHAPED BOX... MAYBE IT IS FROM MEW...I MEAN, WHO ELSE?

OH MAN... I CAN'T EVEN LOOK AT HER!

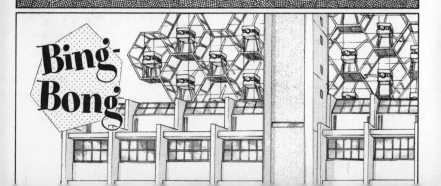

Bing-
Bong

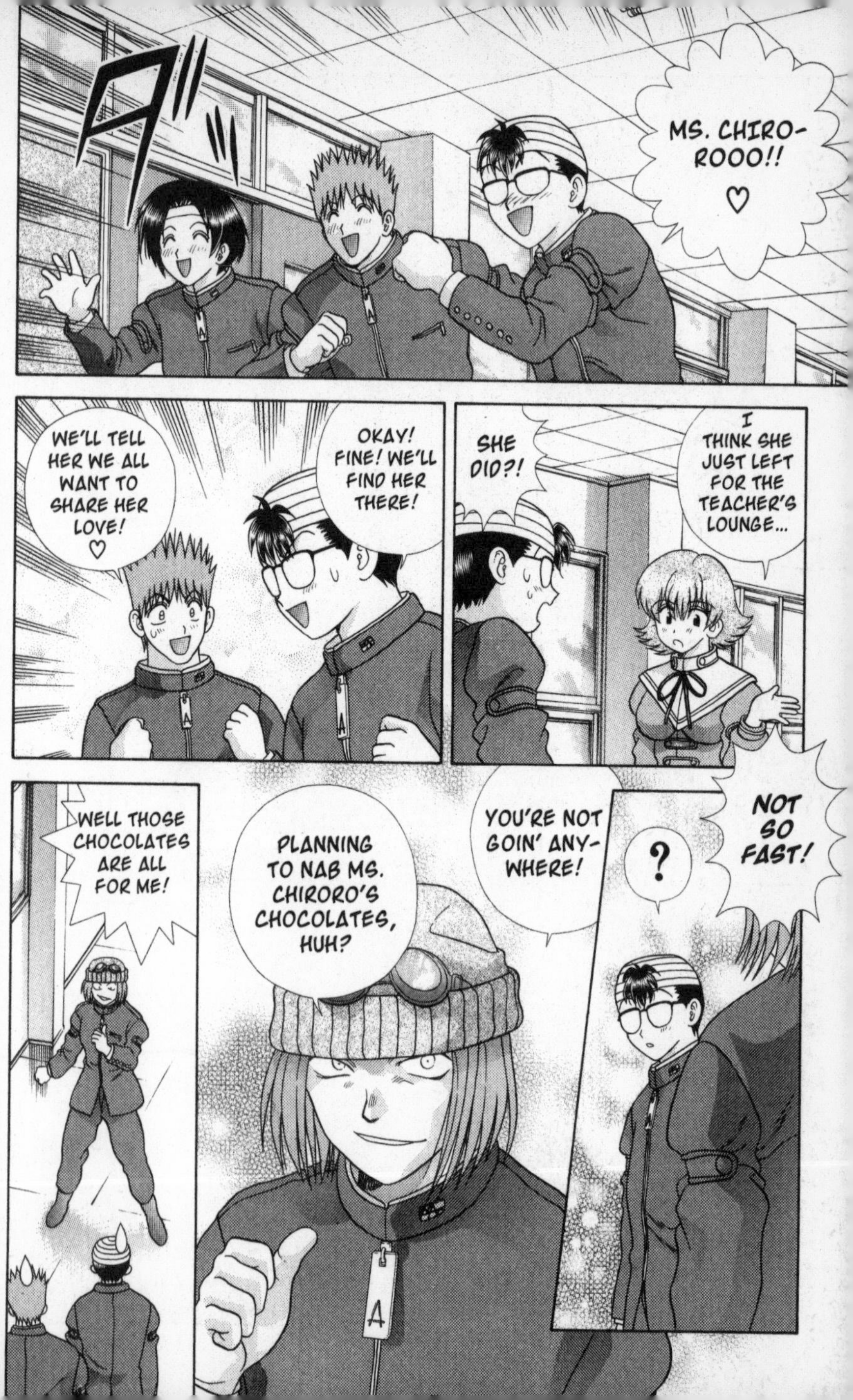
MS. CHIRO-ROOO!! ♡
I THINK SHE JUST LEFT FOR THE TEACHER'S LOUNGE...
SHE DID?!
OKAY! FINE! WE'LL FIND HER THERE!
WE'LL TELL HER WE ALL WANT TO SHARE HER LOVE! ♡
NOT SO FAST!
?
YOU'RE NOT GOIN' ANY-WHERE!
PLANNING TO NAB MS. CHIRORO'S CHOCOLATES, HUH?
WELL THOSE CHOCOLATES ARE ALL FOR ME!

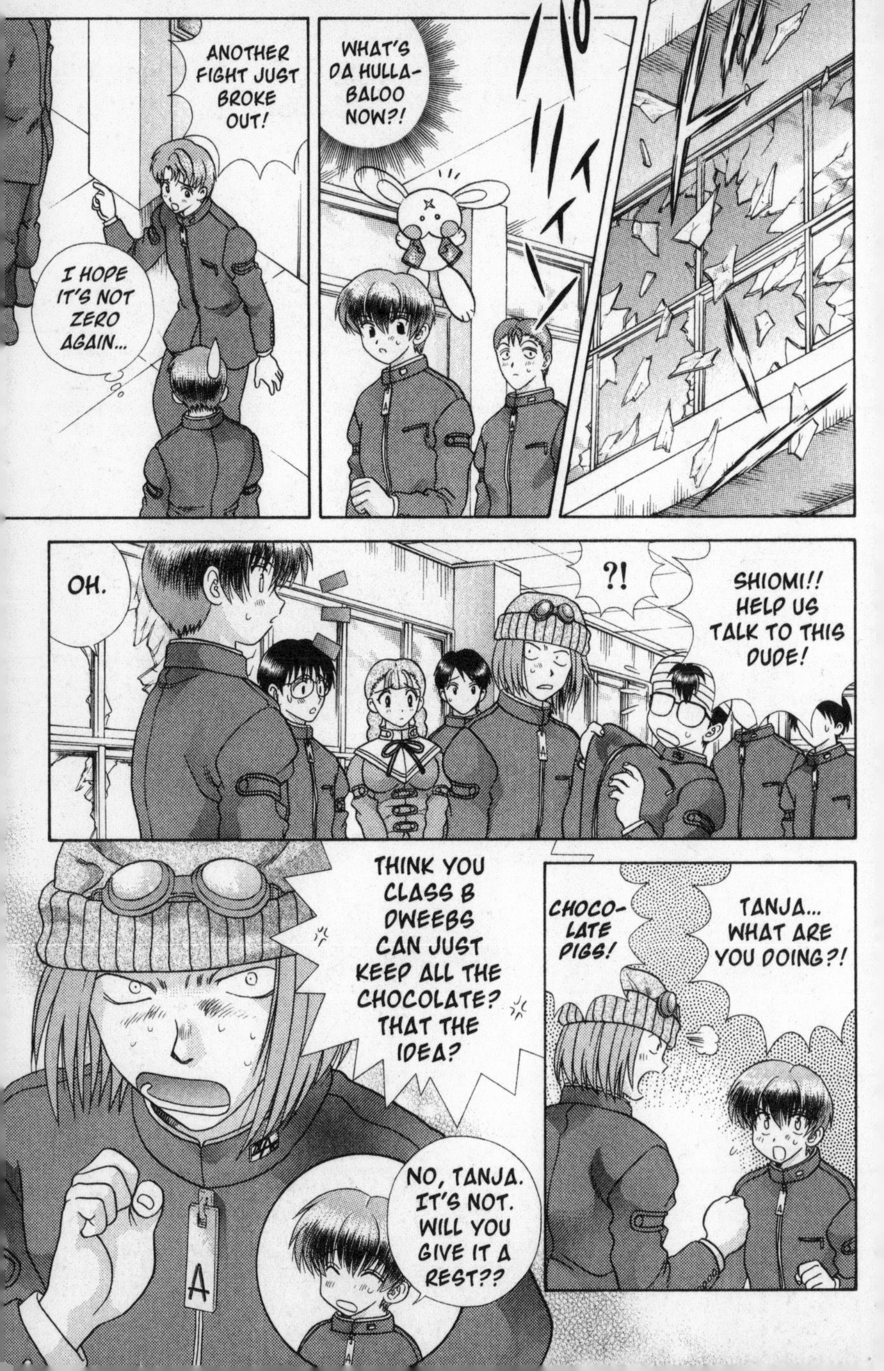
WHAT'S DA HULLA-BALOO NOW?!
ANOTHER FIGHT JUST BROKE OUT!
I HOPE IT'S NOT ZERO AGAIN...
SHIOMI!! HELP US TALK TO THIS DUDE!
?!
OH.
TANJA... WHAT ARE YOU DOING?!
CHOCO-LATE PIGS!
THINK YOU CLASS B DWEEBS CAN JUST KEEP ALL THE CHOCOLATE? THAT THE IDEA?
NO, TANJA. IT'S NOT. WILL YOU GIVE IT A REST??

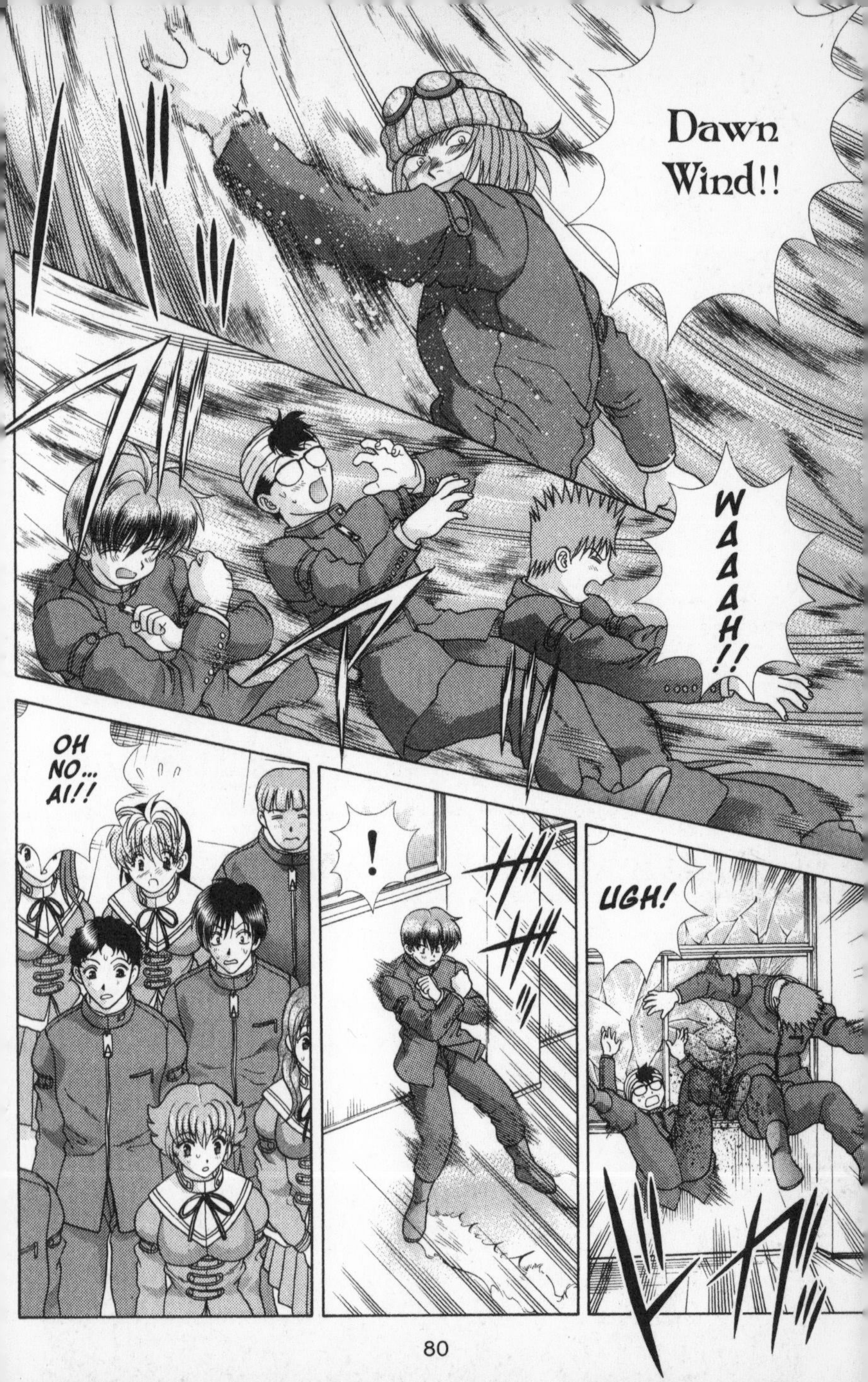
Dawn Wind!!
WAAAAH!!
OH NO... AI!!
!
UGH!

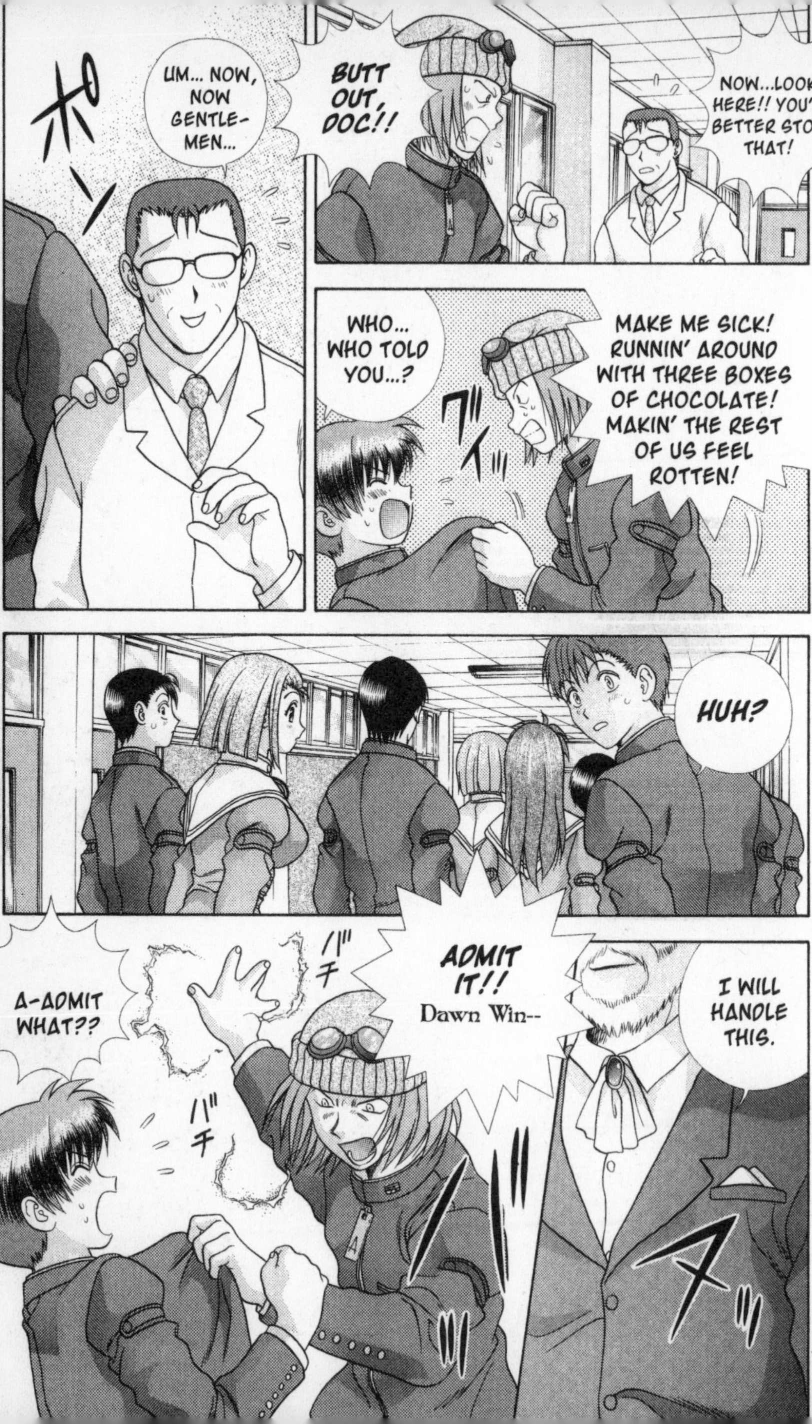
NOW...LOOK HERE!! YOU'D BETTER STOP THAT!
BUTT OUT, DOC!!
UM... NOW, NOW GENTLE-MEN...
MAKE ME SICK! RUNNIN' AROUND WITH THREE BOXES OF CHOCOLATE! MAKIN' THE REST OF US FEEL ROTTEN!
WHO... WHO TOLD YOU...?
HUH?
I WILL HANDLE THIS.
ADMIT IT!! Dawn Win--
A-ADMIT WHAT??

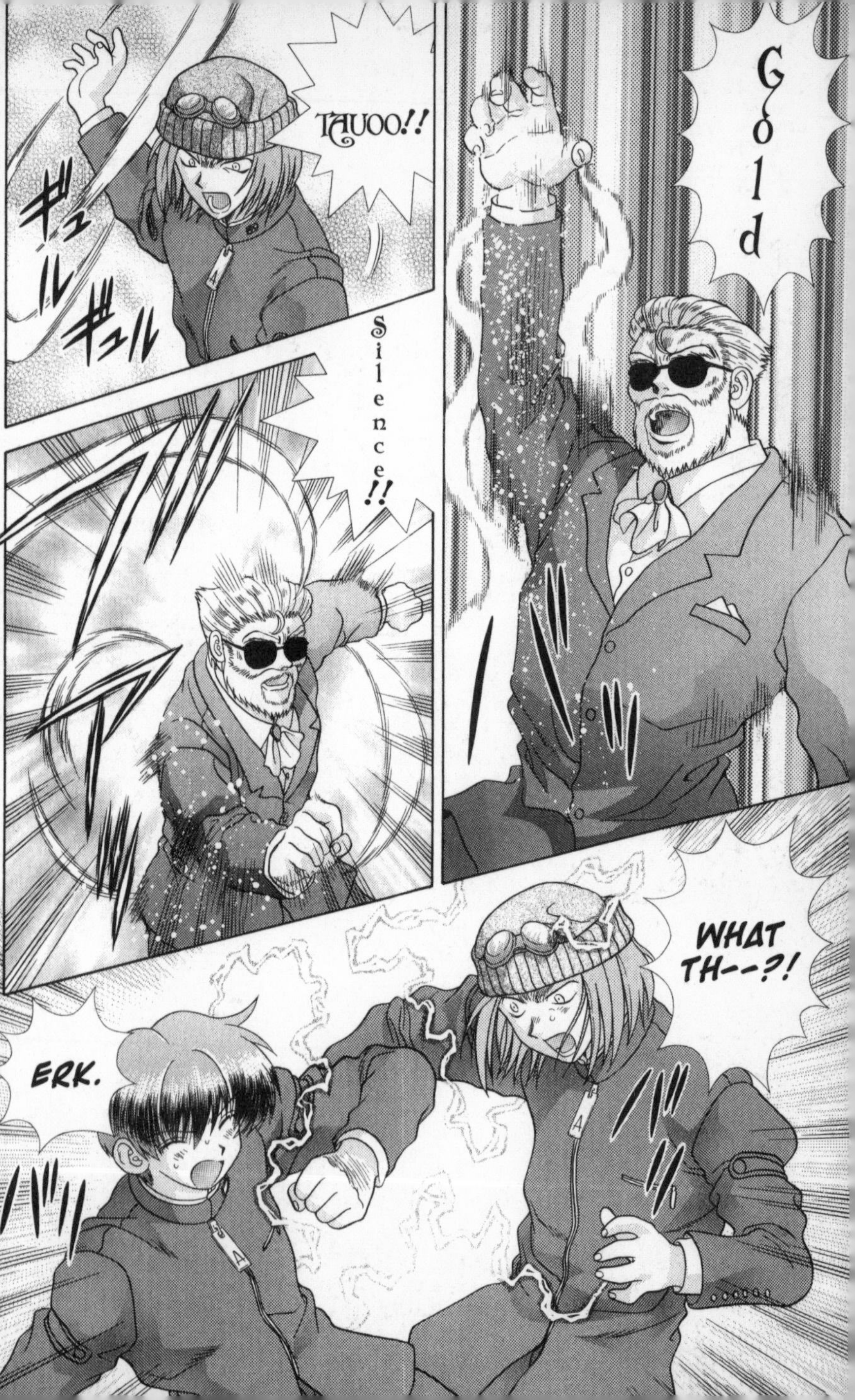
Gold
TAUOO!!
ギュル ギュル
Silence!!
WHAT TH--?!
ERK.

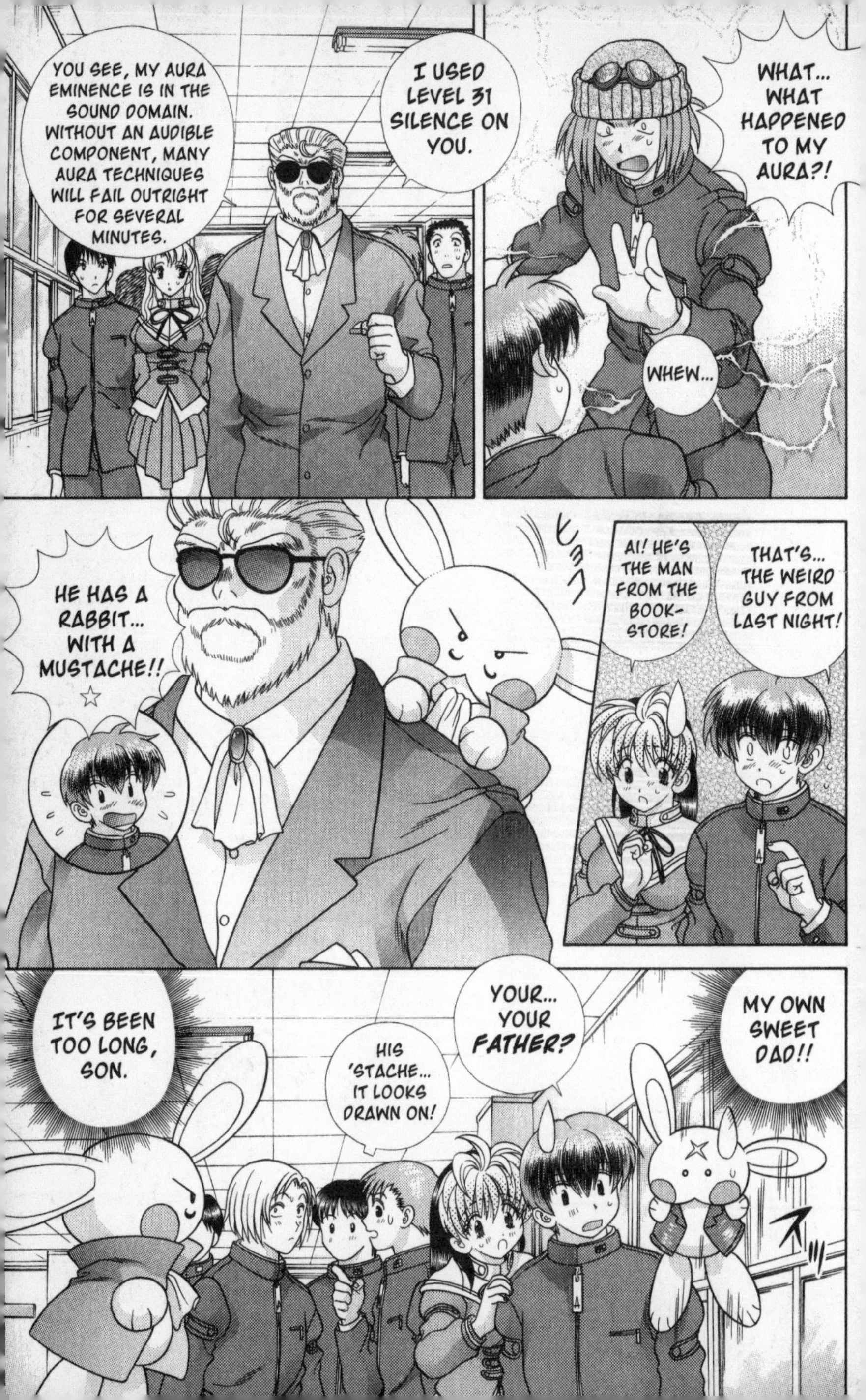
WHAT... WHAT HAPPENED TO MY AURA?!
WHEW...
I USED LEVEL 31 SILENCE ON YOU.
YOU SEE, MY AURA EMINENCE IS IN THE SOUND DOMAIN. WITHOUT AN AUDIBLE COMPONENT, MANY AURA TECHNIQUES WILL FAIL OUTRIGHT FOR SEVERAL MINUTES.
THAT'S... THE WEIRD GUY FROM LAST NIGHT!
AI! HE'S THE MAN FROM THE BOOK-STORE!
ヒョコ
HE HAS A RABBIT... WITH A MUSTACHE!! ☆
MY OWN SWEET DAD!!
YOUR... YOUR FATHER?
HIS 'STACHE... IT LOOKS DRAWN ON!
IT'S BEEN TOO LONG, SON.

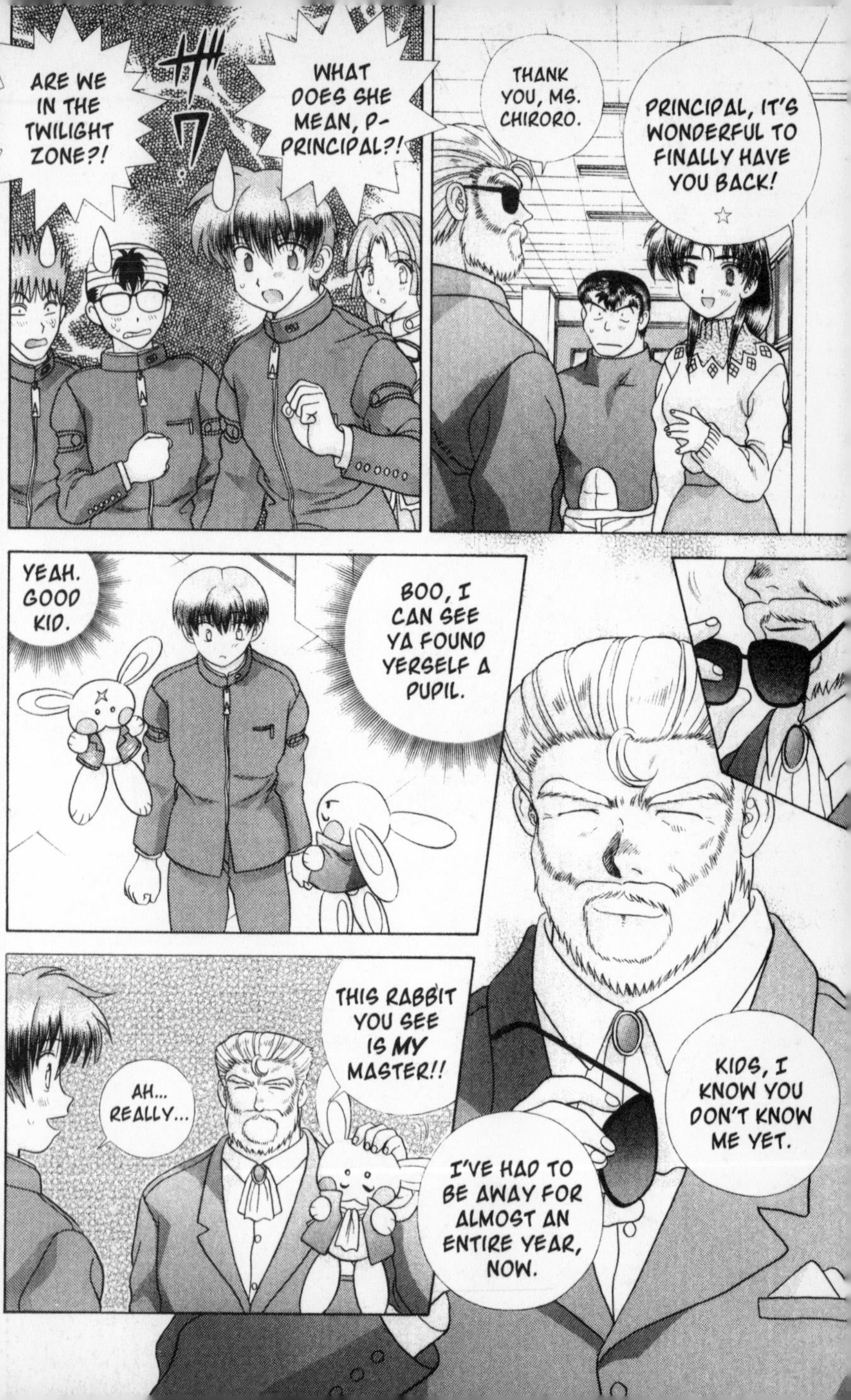

PRINCIPAL, IT'S WONDERFUL TO FINALLY HAVE YOU BACK! ☆
THANK YOU, MS. CHIRORO.
WHAT DOES SHE MEAN, P-PRINCIPAL?!
ARE WE IN THE TWILIGHT ZONE?!
KIDS, I KNOW YOU DON'T KNOW ME YET.
I'VE HAD TO BE AWAY FOR ALMOST AN ENTIRE YEAR, NOW.
BOO, I CAN SEE YA FOUND YERSELF A PUPIL.
YEAH. GOOD KID.
THIS RABBIT YOU SEE IS MY MASTER!!
AH... REALLY...

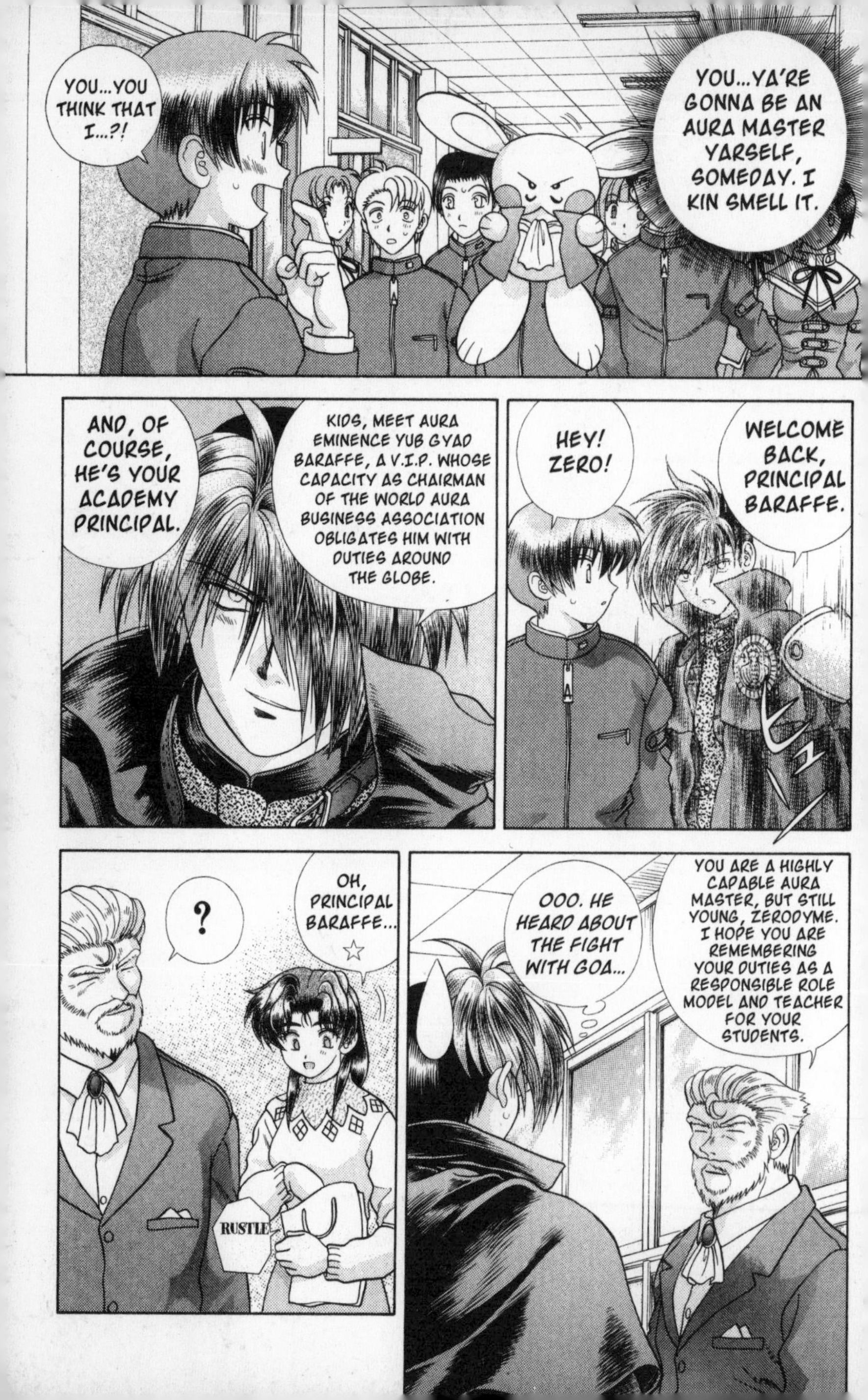
YOU...YA'RE GONNA BE AN AURA MASTER YARSELF, SOMEDAY. I KIN SMELL IT.
YOU...YOU THINK THAT I...?!
WELCOME BACK, PRINCIPAL BARAFFE.
HEY! ZERO!
KIDS, MEET AURA EMINENCE YUB GYAD BARAFFE, A V.I.P. WHOSE CAPACITY AS CHAIRMAN OF THE WORLD AURA BUSINESS ASSOCIATION OBLIGATES HIM WITH DUTIES AROUND THE GLOBE.
AND, OF COURSE, HE'S YOUR ACADEMY PRINCIPAL.
YOU ARE A HIGHLY CAPABLE AURA MASTER, BUT STILL YOUNG, ZERODYME. I HOPE YOU ARE REMEMBERING YOUR DUTIES AS A RESPONSIBLE ROLE MODEL AND TEACHER FOR YOUR STUDENTS.
OOO. HE HEARD ABOUT THE FIGHT WITH GOA...
OH, PRINCIPAL BARAFFE...☆
?
RUSTLE

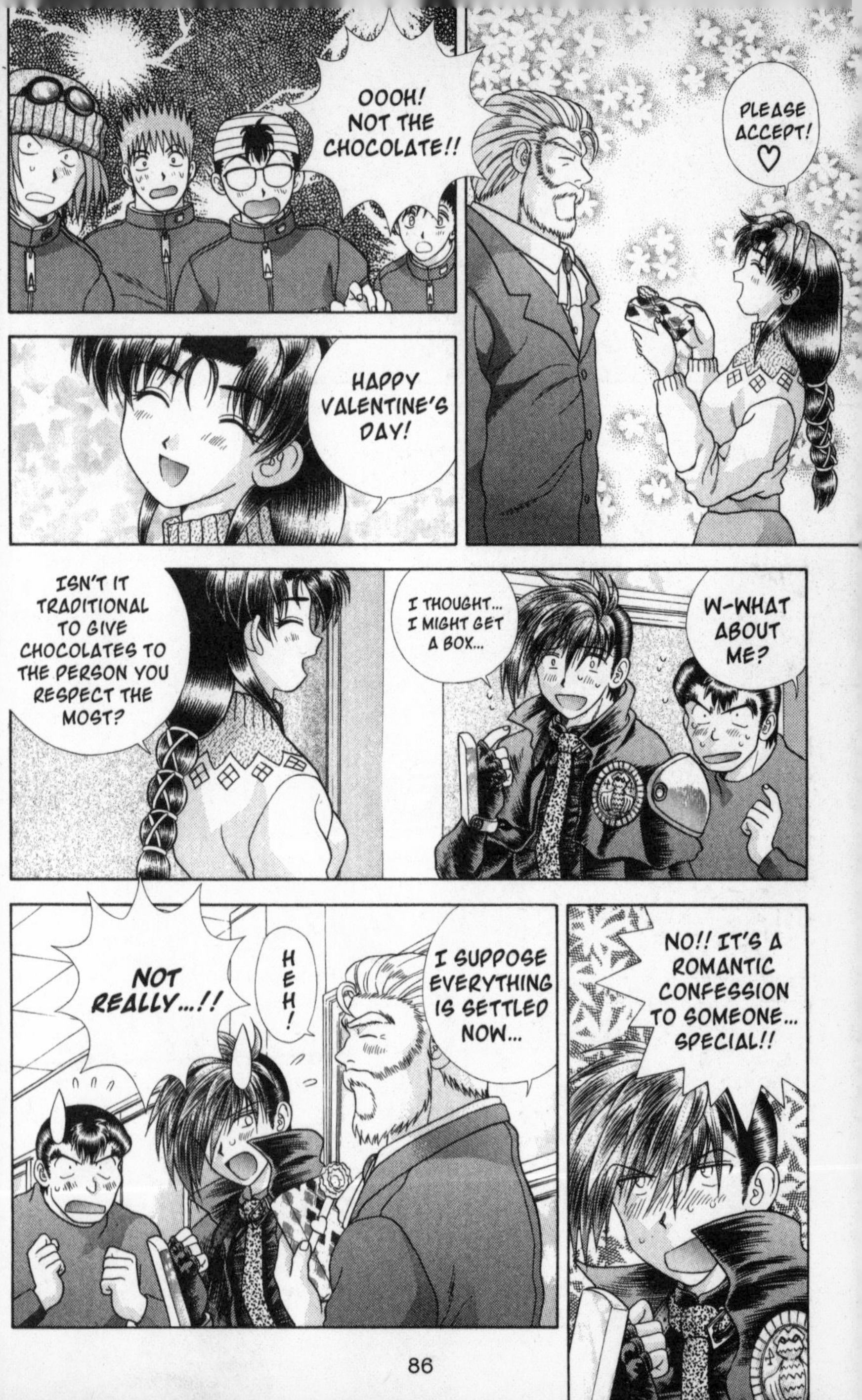
PLEASE ACCEPT! ♡
OOOH! NOT THE CHOCOLATE!!
HAPPY VALENTINE'S DAY!
W-WHAT ABOUT ME?
I THOUGHT... I MIGHT GET A BOX...
ISN'T IT TRADITIONAL TO GIVE CHOCOLATES TO THE PERSON YOU RESPECT THE MOST?
NO!! IT'S A ROMANTIC CONFESSION TO SOMEONE... SPECIAL!!
I SUPPOSE EVERYTHING IS SETTLED NOW...
HEH!
NOT REALLY...!!

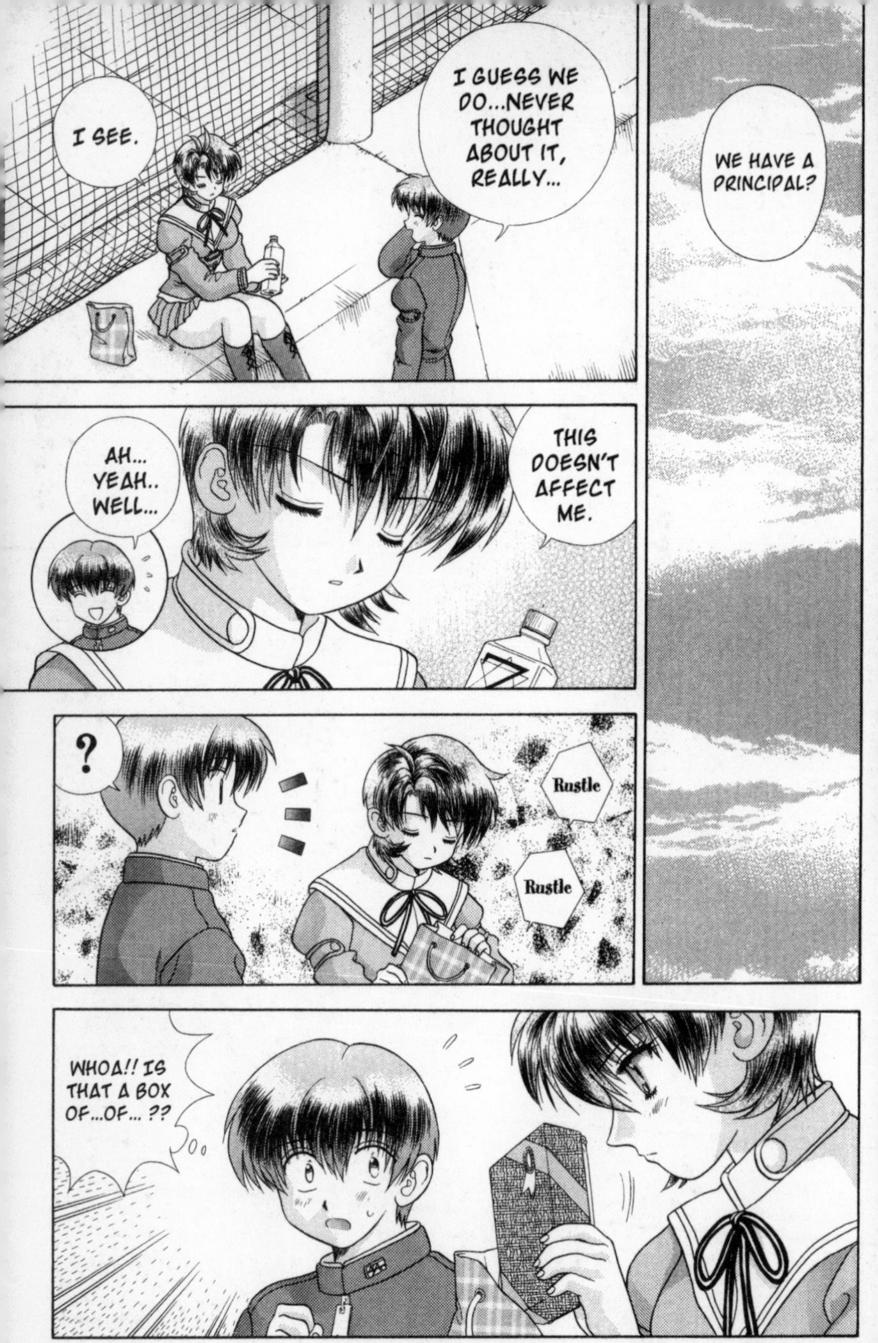
WE HAVE A PRINCIPAL?
I GUESS WE DO...NEVER THOUGHT ABOUT IT, REALLY...
I SEE.
THIS DOESN'T AFFECT ME.
AH... YEAH.. WELL...
Rustle
Rustle
?
WHOA!! IS THAT A BOX OF...OF... ??

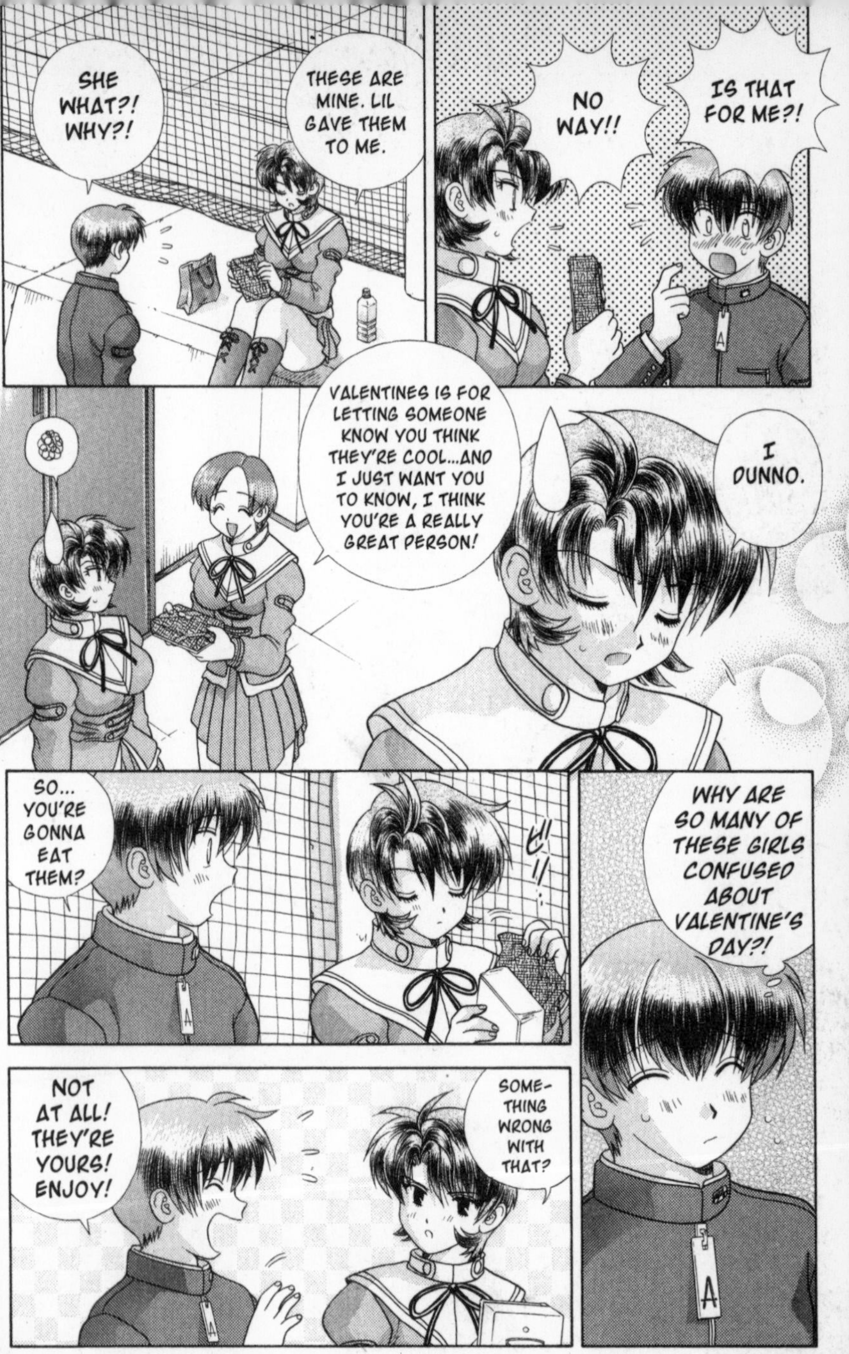
IS THAT FOR ME?!
NO WAY!!
THESE ARE MINE. LIL GAVE THEM TO ME.
SHE WHAT?! WHY?!
I DUNNO.
VALENTINES IS FOR LETTING SOMEONE KNOW YOU THINK THEY'RE COOL...AND I JUST WANT YOU TO KNOW, I THINK YOU'RE A REALLY GREAT PERSON!
SO... YOU'RE GONNA EAT THEM?
SOME-THING WRONG WITH THAT?
NOT AT ALL! THEY'RE YOURS! ENJOY!
WHY ARE SO MANY OF THESE GIRLS CONFUSED ABOUT VALENTINE'S DAY?!

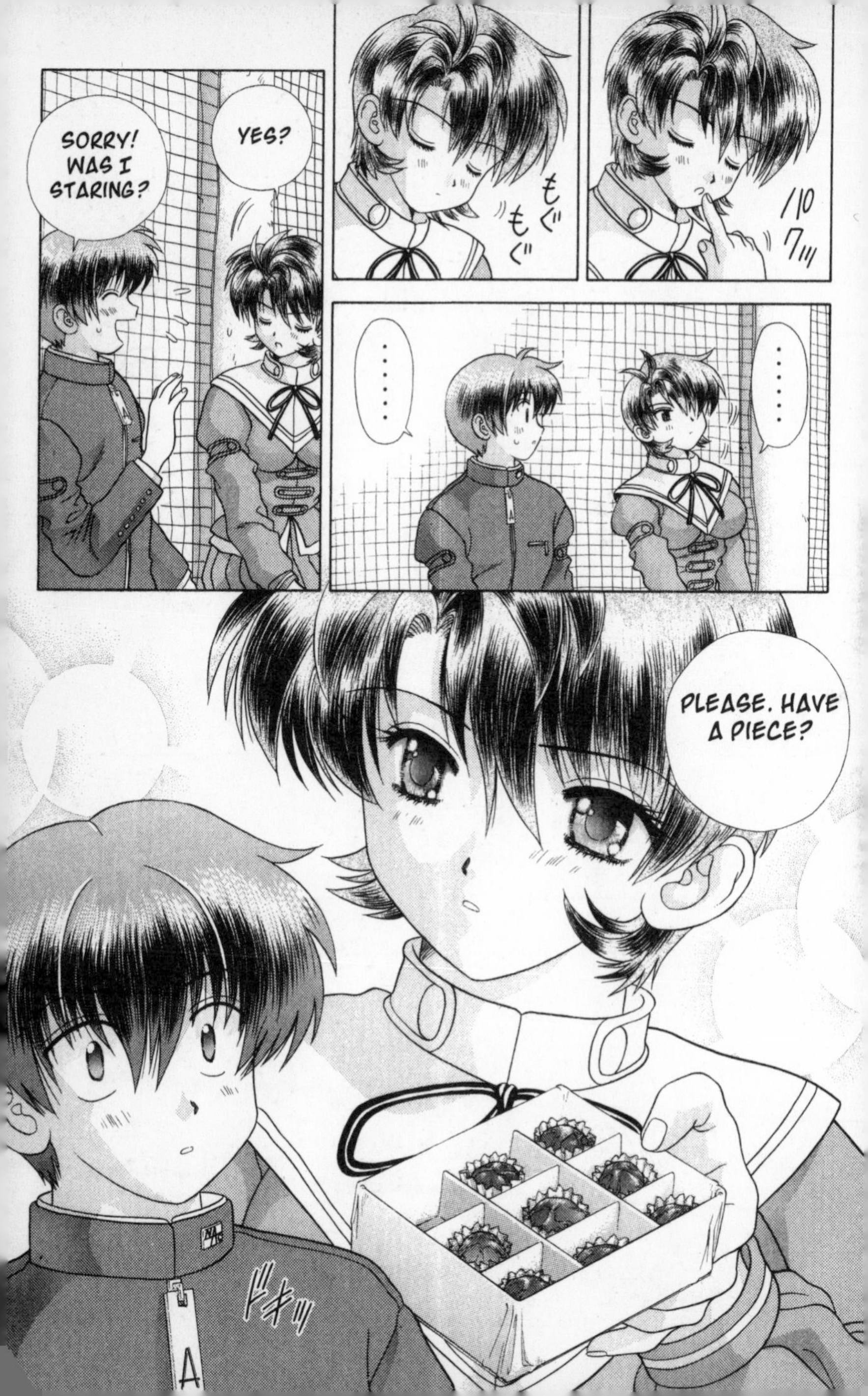

パクッ
もぐもぐ
......
......
YES?
SORRY! WAS I STARING?
PLEASE. HAVE A PIECE?
ドキッ

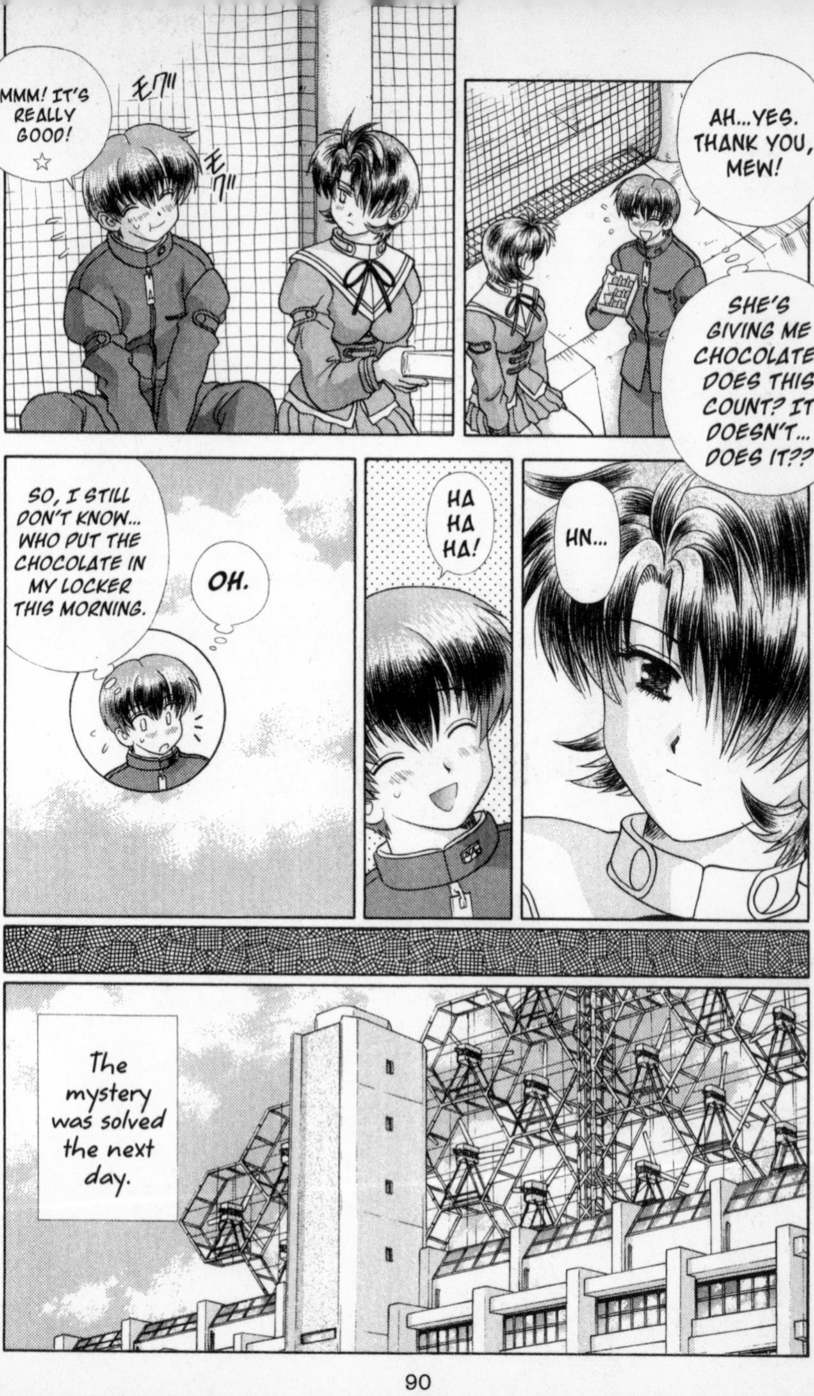
AH...YES. THANK YOU, MEW!
SHE'S GIVING ME CHOCOLATE! DOES THIS COUNT? IT DOESN'T... DOES IT??
MMM! IT'S REALLY GOOD! ☆
HN...
HA HA HA!
SO, I STILL DON'T KNOW... WHO PUT THE CHOCOLATE IN MY LOCKER THIS MORNING.
OH.
The mystery was solved the next day.

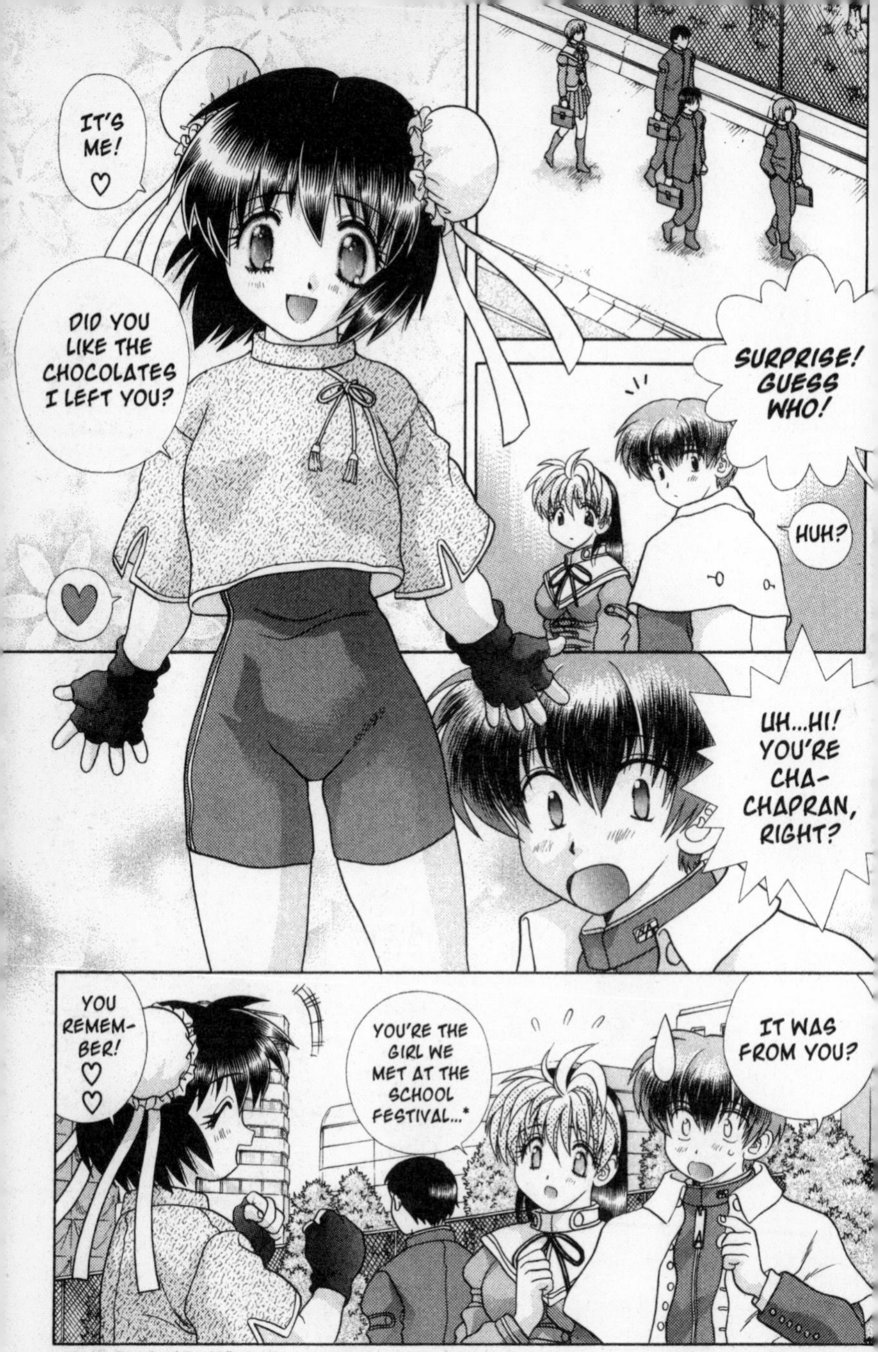
SURPRISE! GUESS WHO!
HUH?
IT'S ME! ♡
DID YOU LIKE THE CHOCOLATES I LEFT YOU?
UH...HI! YOU'RE CHA-CHAPRAN, RIGHT?
IT WAS FROM YOU?
YOU'RE THE GIRL WE MET AT THE SCHOOL FESTIVAL...*
YOU REMEMBER! ♡ ♡

*Vol 6, "A School For Us"

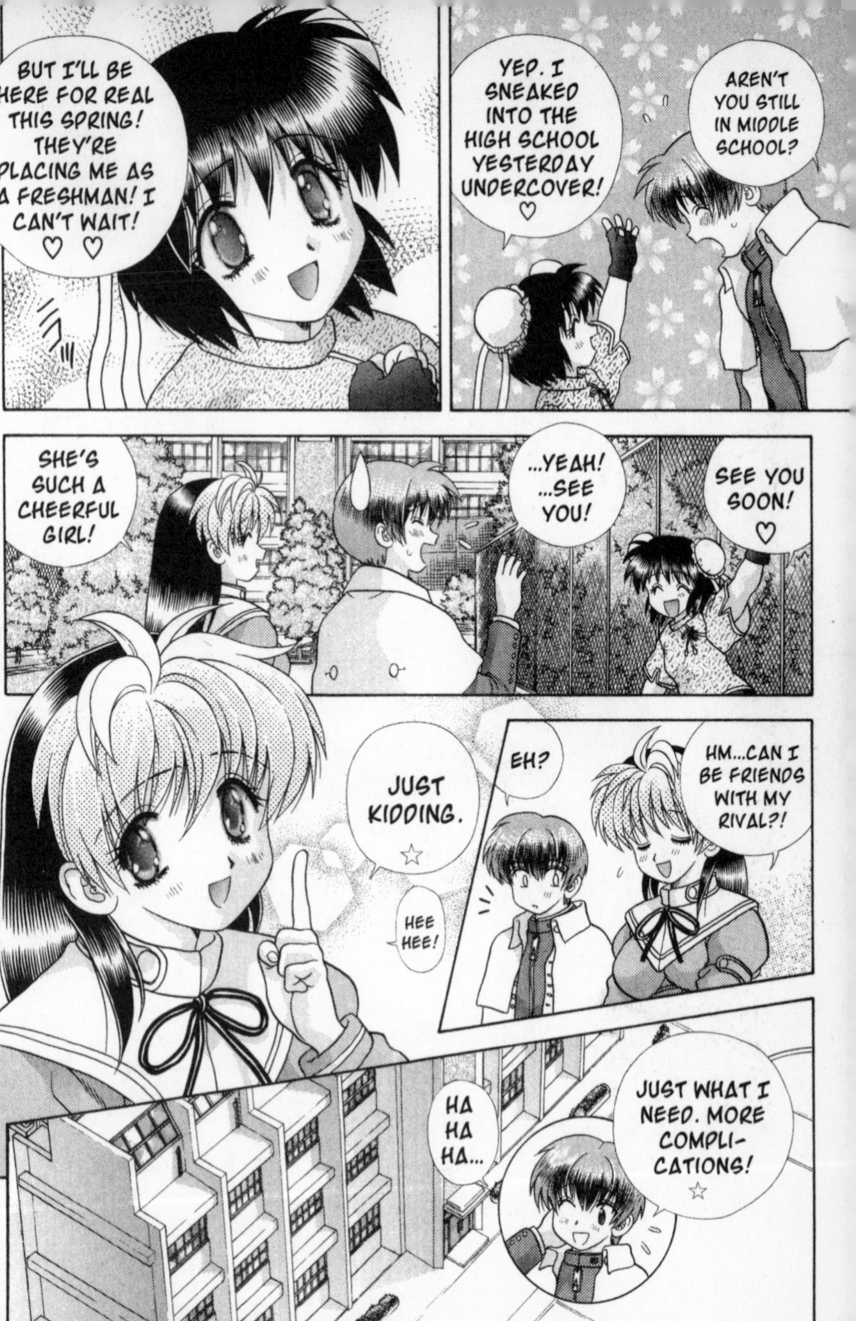
AREN'T YOU STILL IN MIDDLE SCHOOL?
YEP. I SNEAKED INTO THE HIGH SCHOOL YESTERDAY UNDERCOVER! ♡
BUT I'LL BE HERE FOR REAL THIS SPRING! THEY'RE PLACING ME AS A FRESHMAN! I CAN'T WAIT! ♡ ♡
SEE YOU SOON! ♡
...YEAH! ...SEE YOU!
SHE'S SUCH A CHEERFUL GIRL!
HM...CAN I BE FRIENDS WITH MY RIVAL?!
EH?
JUST KIDDING. ☆
HEE HEE!
JUST WHAT I NEED. MORE COMPLI-CATIONS! ☆
HA HA HA...

Chocoholism END

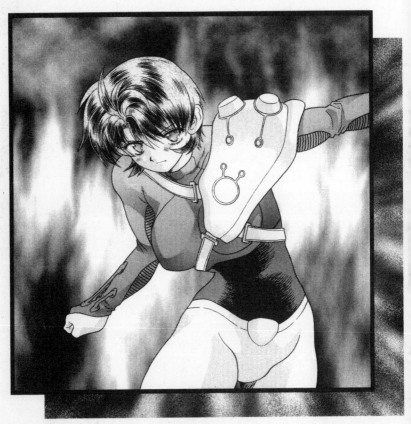

Chapter 30: The Skills Test

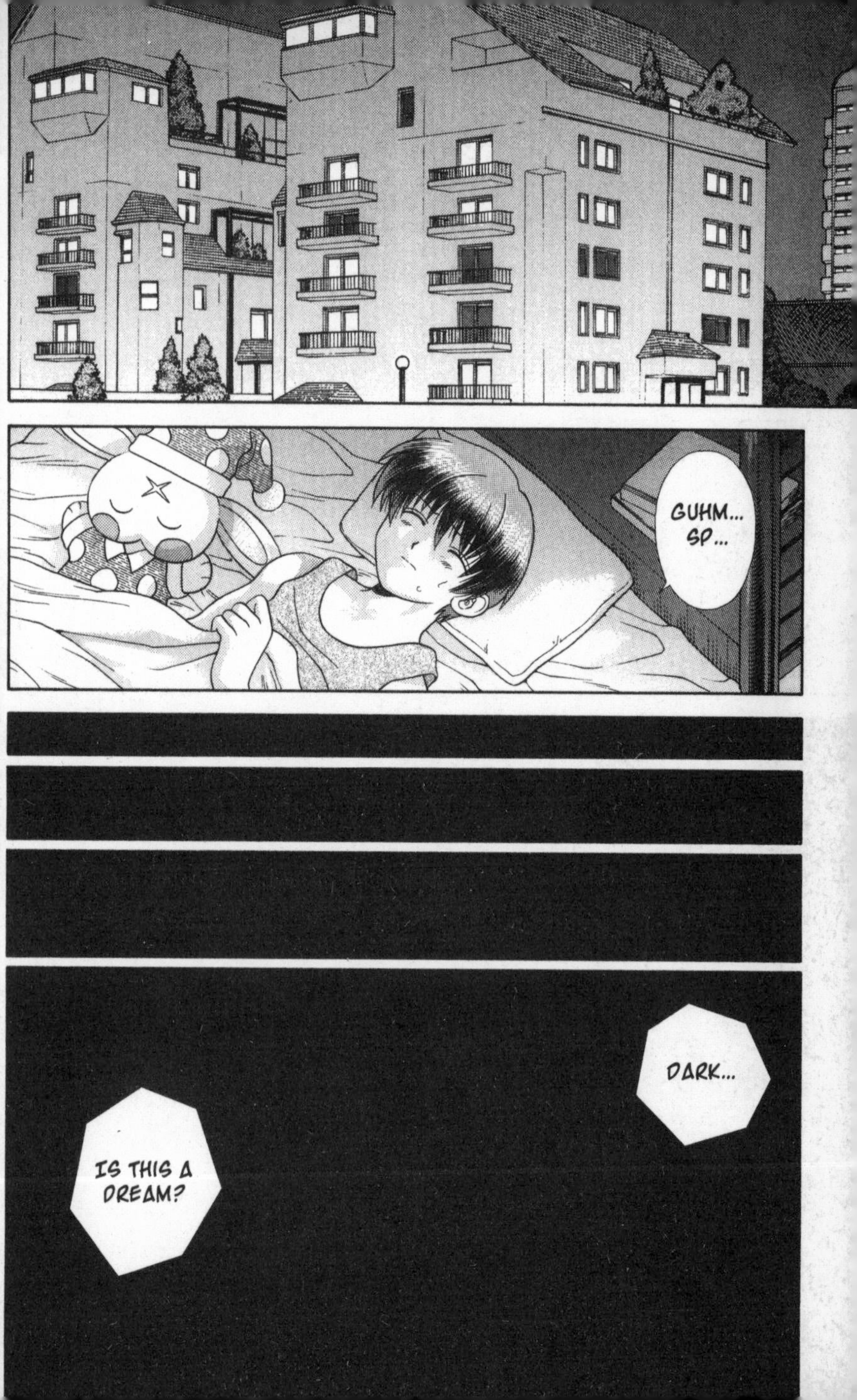
GUHM... SP...
DARK...
IS THIS A DREAM?

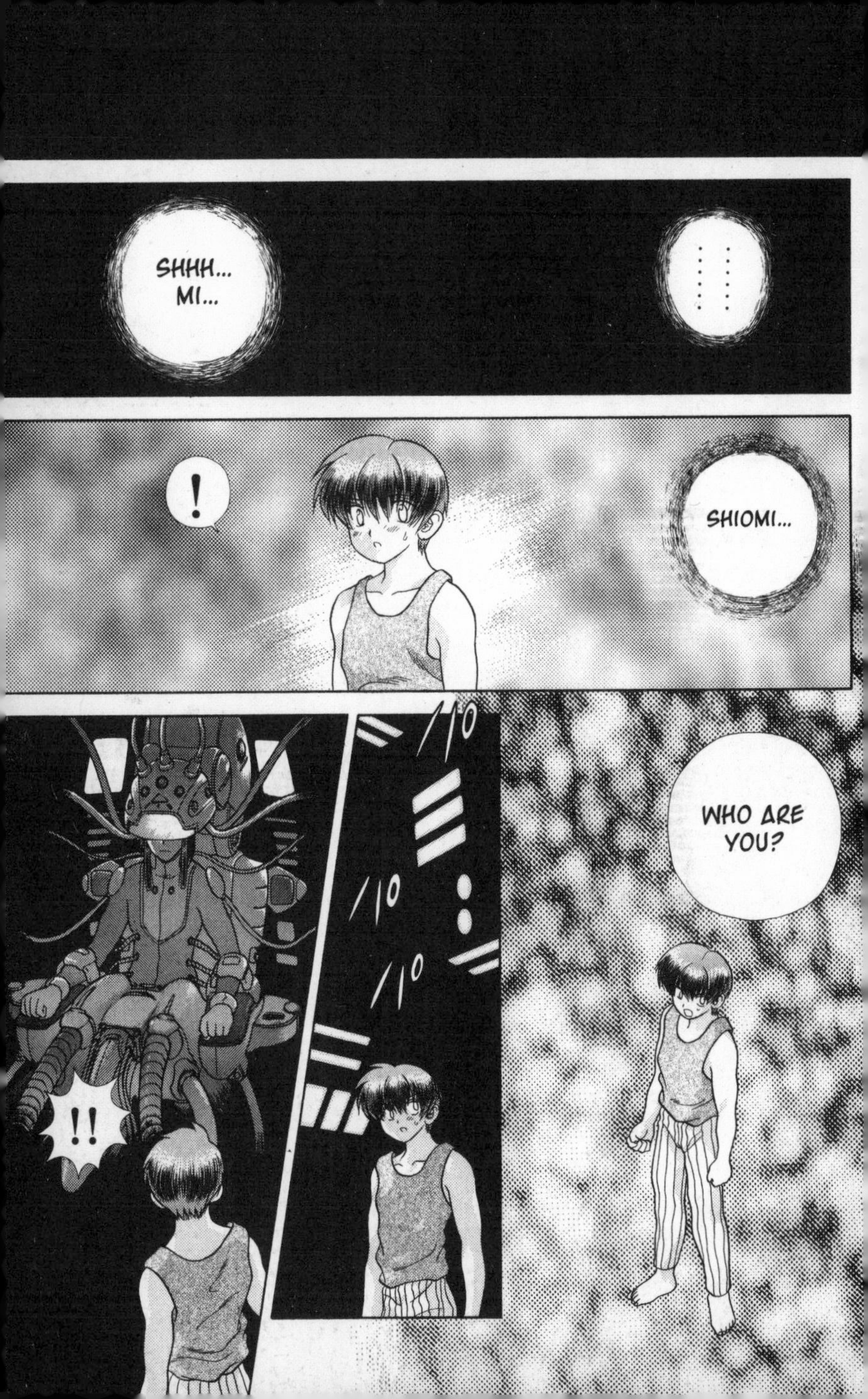

......
SHHH... MI...
SHIOMI...
!
WHO ARE YOU?
!!

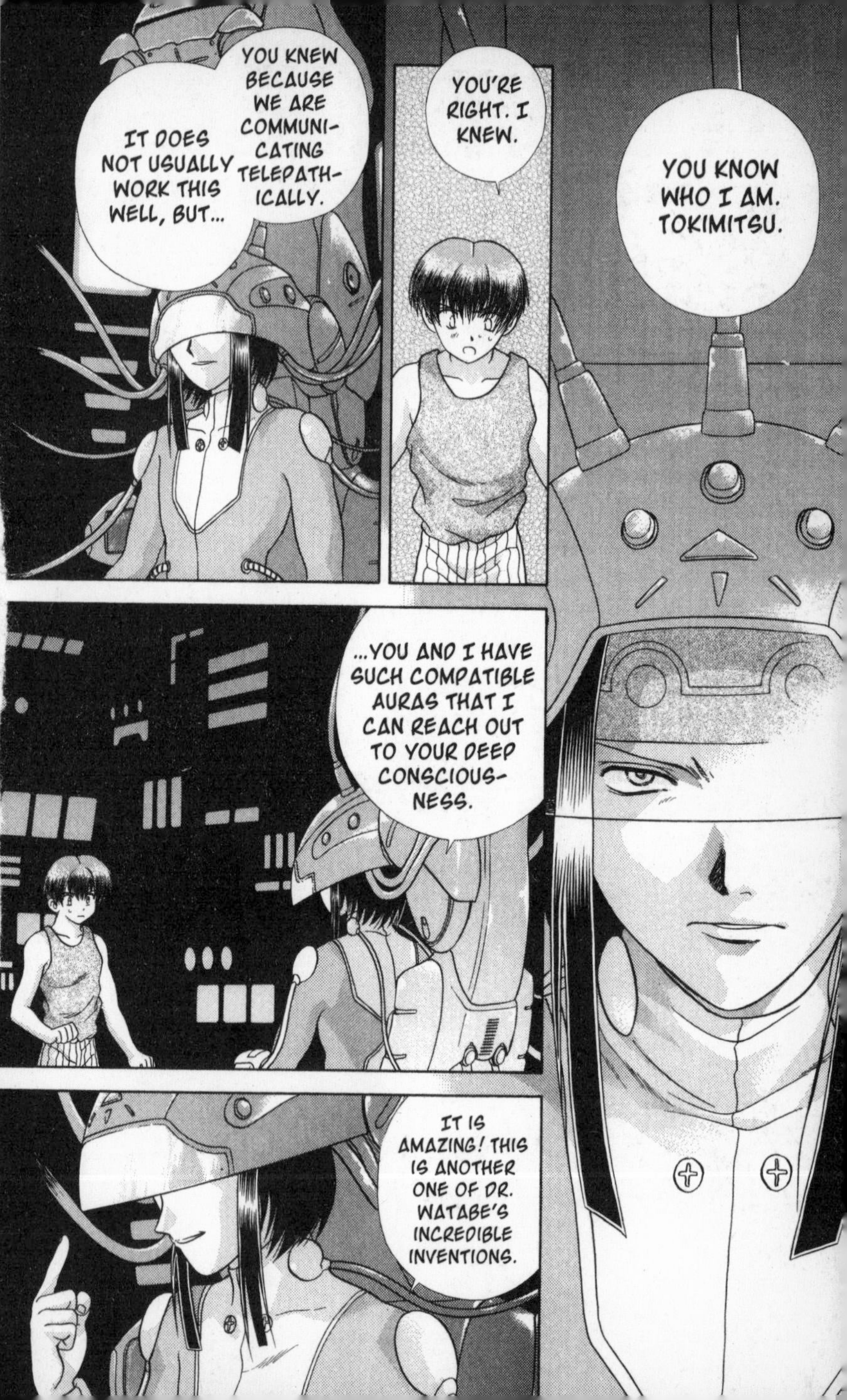
YOU KNOW WHO I AM. TOKIMITSU.
YOU'RE RIGHT. I KNEW.
YOU KNEW BECAUSE WE ARE COMMUNICATING TELEPATHICALLY.
IT DOES NOT USUALLY WORK THIS WELL, BUT...
...YOU AND I HAVE SUCH COMPATIBLE AURAS THAT I CAN REACH OUT TO YOUR DEEP CONSCIOUSNESS.
IT IS AMAZING! THIS IS ANOTHER ONE OF DR. WATABE'S INCREDIBLE INVENTIONS.

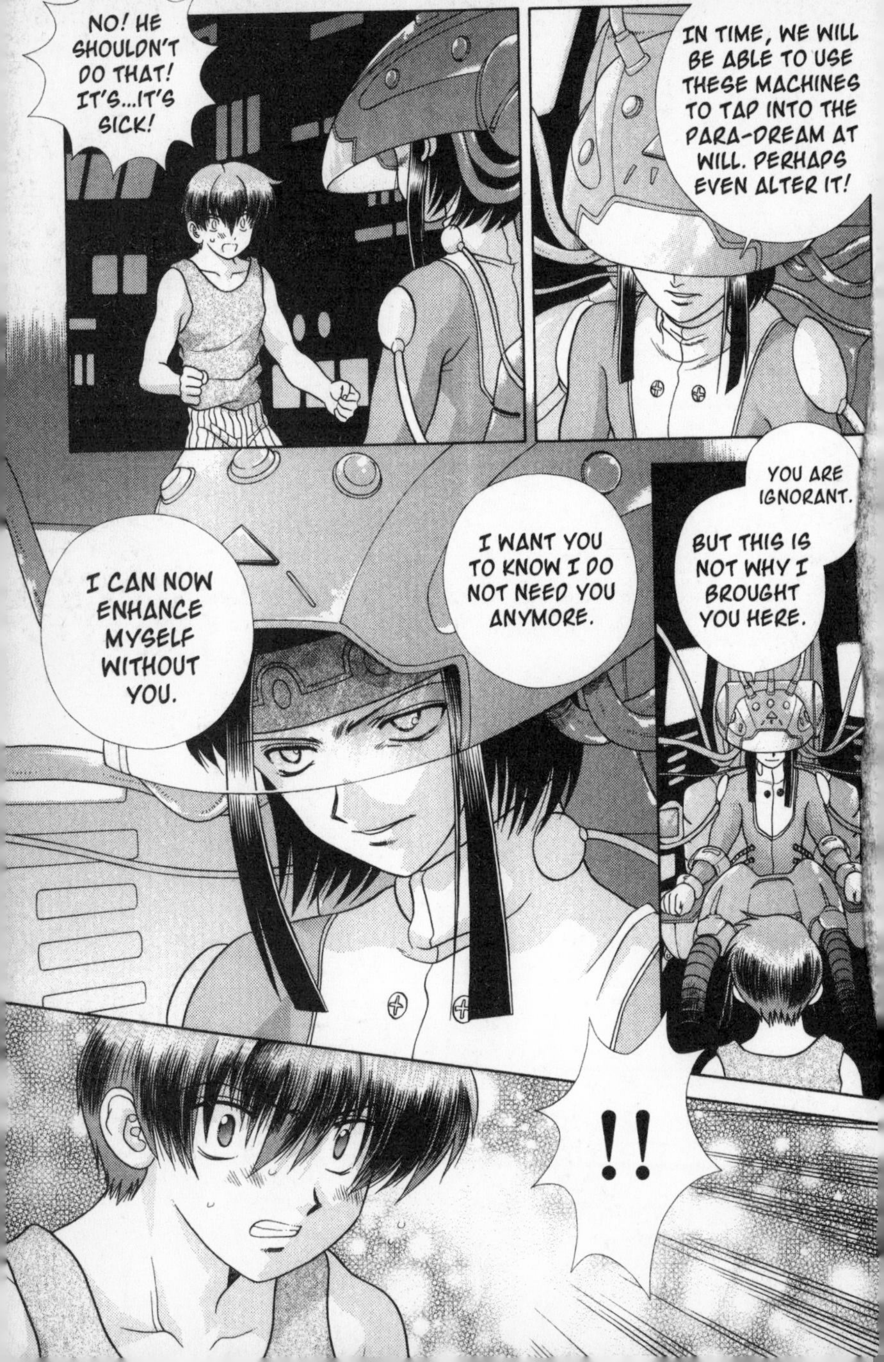
NO! HE SHOULDN'T DO THAT! IT'S...IT'S SICK!
IN TIME, WE WILL BE ABLE TO USE THESE MACHINES TO TAP INTO THE PARA-DREAM AT WILL. PERHAPS EVEN ALTER IT!
YOU ARE IGNORANT.
BUT THIS IS NOT WHY I BROUGHT YOU HERE.
I WANT YOU TO KNOW I DO NOT NEED YOU ANYMORE.
I CAN NOW ENHANCE MYSELF WITHOUT YOU.
!!

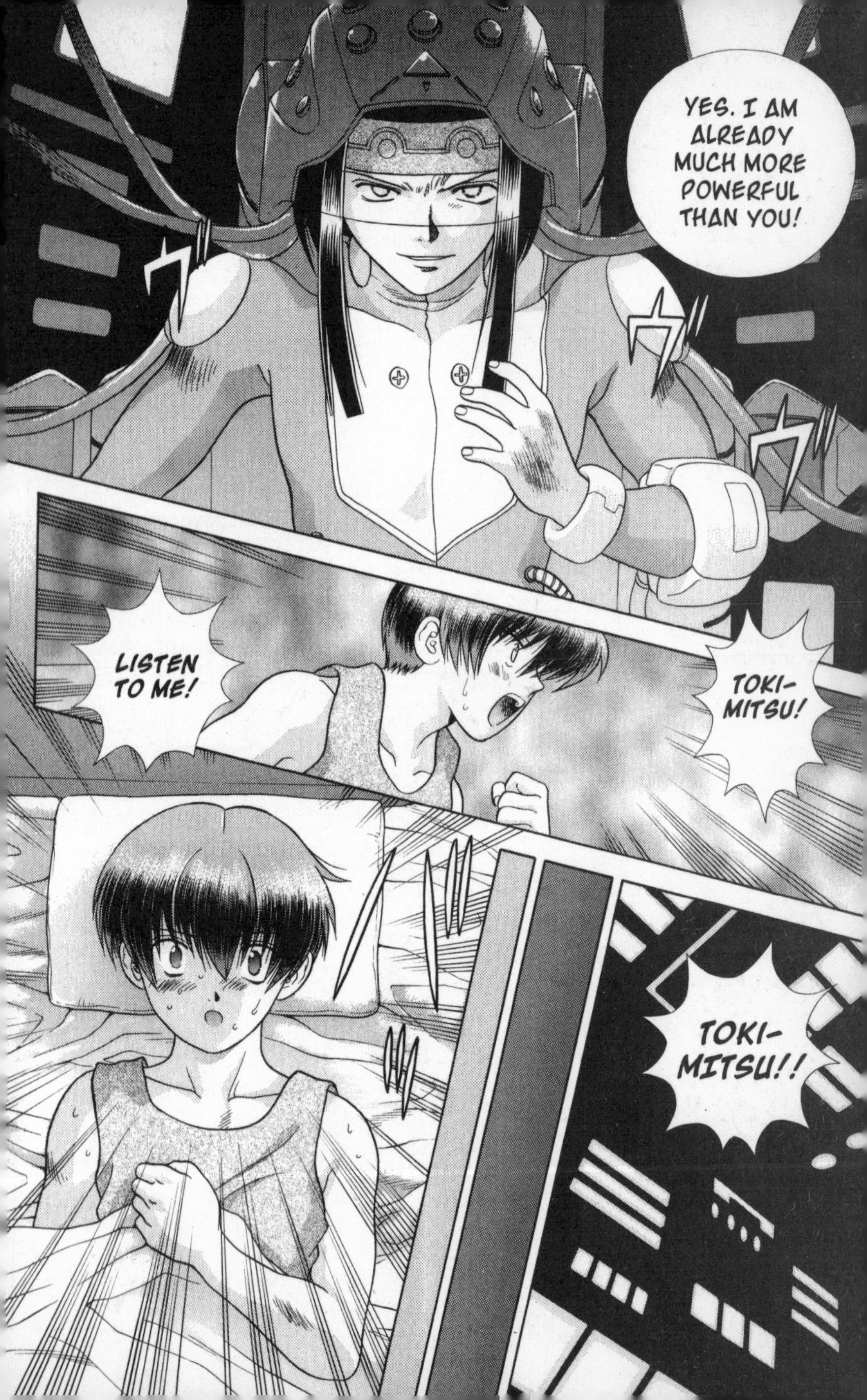
YES. I AM ALREADY MUCH MORE POWERFUL THAN YOU!
TOKI-MITSU!
LISTEN TO ME!
TOKI-MITSU!!

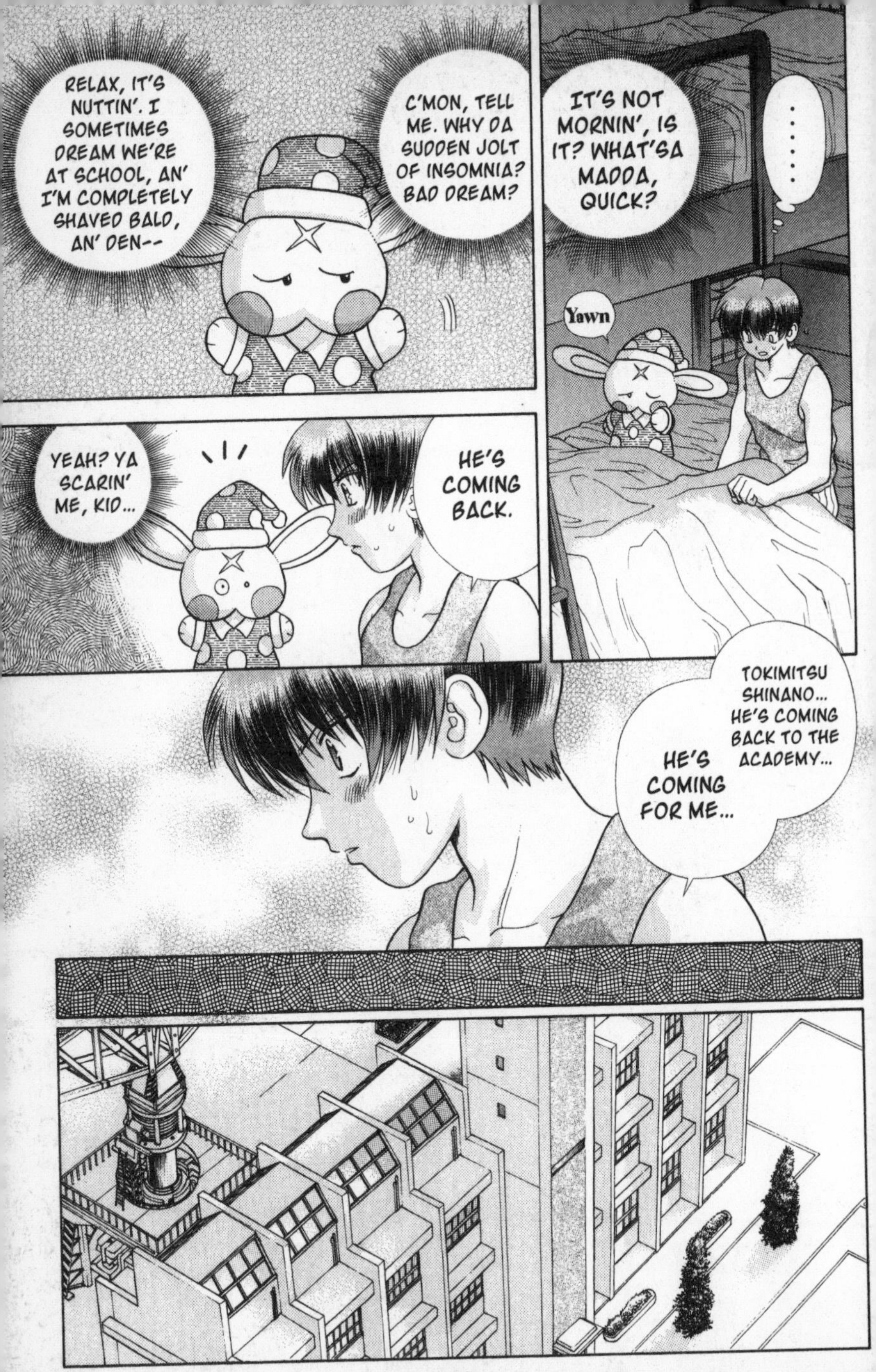
......
IT'S NOT MORNIN', IS IT? WHAT'SA MADDA, QUICK?
Yawn
C'MON, TELL ME. WHY DA SUDDEN JOLT OF INSOMNIA? BAD DREAM?
RELAX, IT'S NUTTIN'. I SOMETIMES DREAM WE'RE AT SCHOOL, AN' I'M COMPLETELY SHAVED BALD, AN' DEN--
HE'S COMING BACK.
YEAH? YA SCARIN' ME, KID...
TOKIMITSU SHINANO... HE'S COMING BACK TO THE ACADEMY...
HE'S COMING FOR ME...

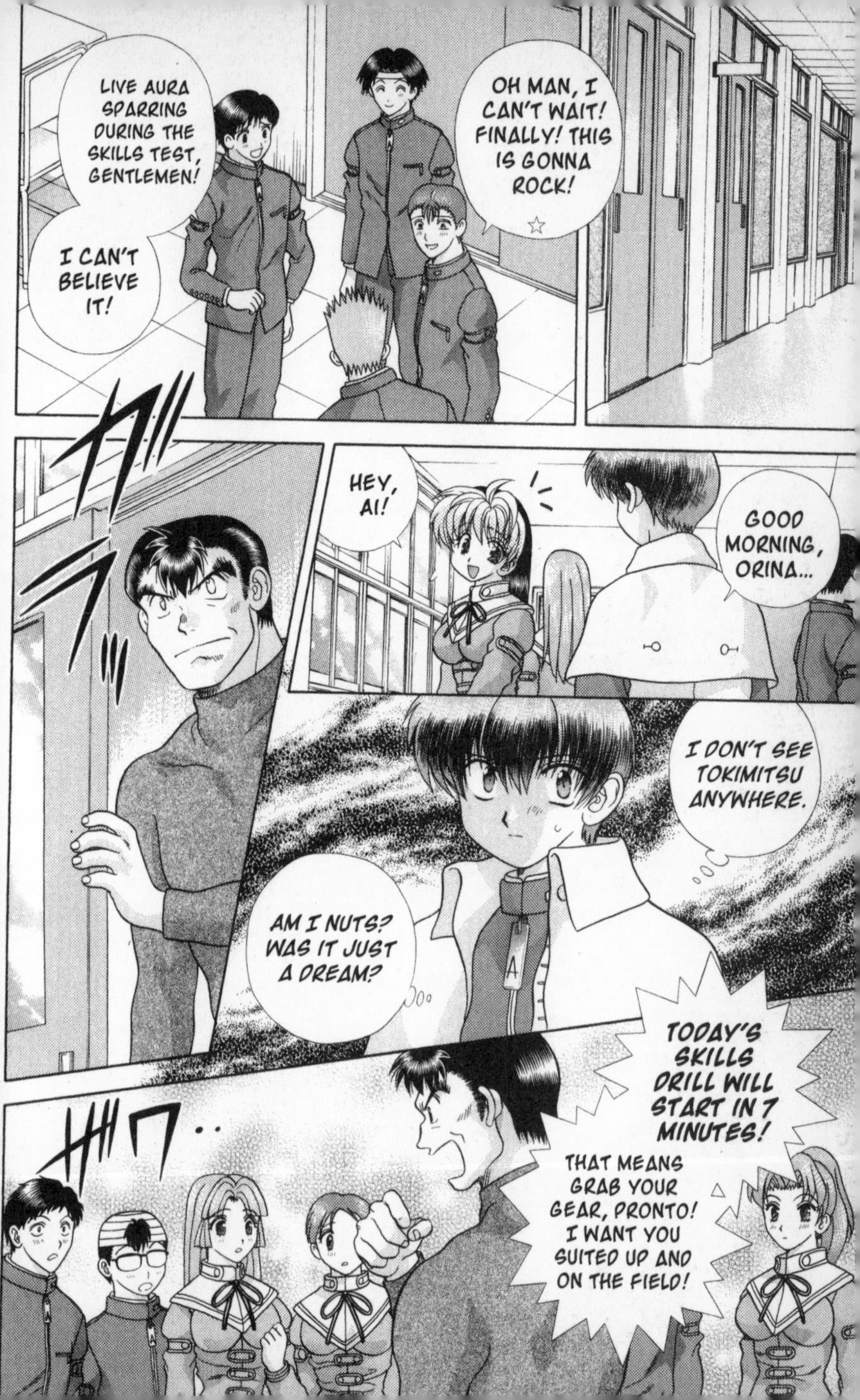
LIVE AURA SPARRING DURING THE SKILLS TEST, GENTLEMEN!
I CAN'T BELIEVE IT!
OH MAN, I CAN'T WAIT! FINALLY! THIS IS GONNA ROCK!
HEY, AI!
GOOD MORNING, ORINA...
I DON'T SEE TOKIMITSU ANYWHERE.
AM I NUTS? WAS IT JUST A DREAM?
TODAY'S SKILLS DRILL WILL START IN 7 MINUTES!
THAT MEANS GRAB YOUR GEAR, PRONTO! I WANT YOU SUITED UP AND ON THE FIELD!

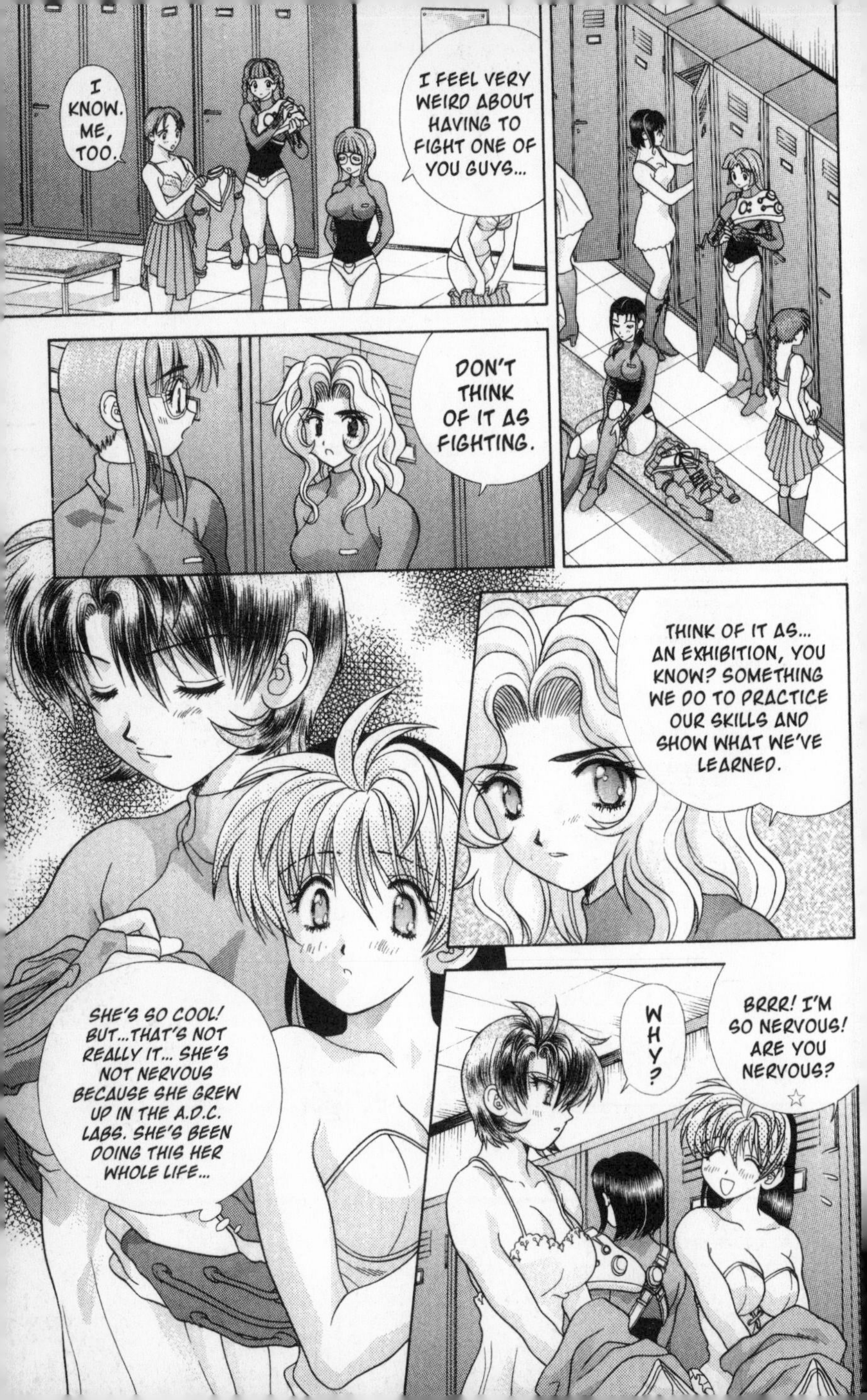
I FEEL VERY WEIRD ABOUT HAVING TO FIGHT ONE OF YOU GUYS...
I KNOW. ME, TOO.
DON'T THINK OF IT AS FIGHTING.
THINK OF IT AS... AN EXHIBITION, YOU KNOW? SOMETHING WE DO TO PRACTICE OUR SKILLS AND SHOW WHAT WE'VE LEARNED.
BRRR! I'M SO NERVOUS! ARE YOU NERVOUS? ☆
WHY?
SHE'S SO COOL! BUT...THAT'S NOT REALLY IT... SHE'S NOT NERVOUS BECAUSE SHE GREW UP IN THE A.D.C. LABS. SHE'S BEEN DOING THIS HER WHOLE LIFE...

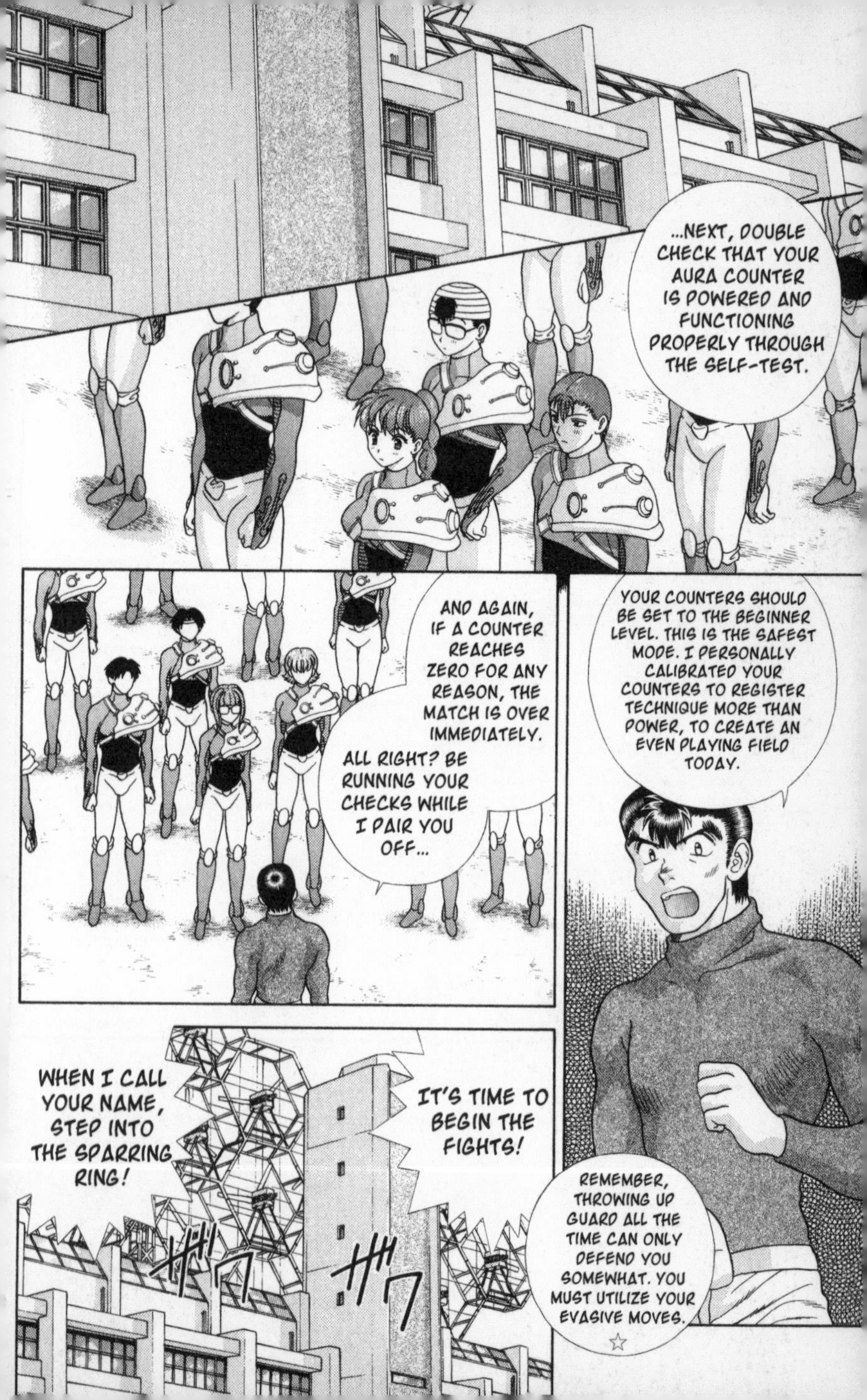
...NEXT, DOUBLE CHECK THAT YOUR AURA COUNTER IS POWERED AND FUNCTIONING PROPERLY THROUGH THE SELF-TEST.
YOUR COUNTERS SHOULD BE SET TO THE BEGINNER LEVEL. THIS IS THE SAFEST MODE. I PERSONALLY CALIBRATED YOUR COUNTERS TO REGISTER TECHNIQUE MORE THAN POWER, TO CREATE AN EVEN PLAYING FIELD TODAY.
REMEMBER, THROWING UP GUARD ALL THE TIME CAN ONLY DEFEND YOU SOMEWHAT. YOU MUST UTILIZE YOUR EVASIVE MOVES. ☆
AND AGAIN, IF A COUNTER REACHES ZERO FOR ANY REASON, THE MATCH IS OVER IMMEDIATELY.
ALL RIGHT? BE RUNNING YOUR CHECKS WHILE I PAIR YOU OFF...
IT'S TIME TO BEGIN THE FIGHTS!
WHEN I CALL YOUR NAME, STEP INTO THE SPARRING RING!
ザワ
ザワ

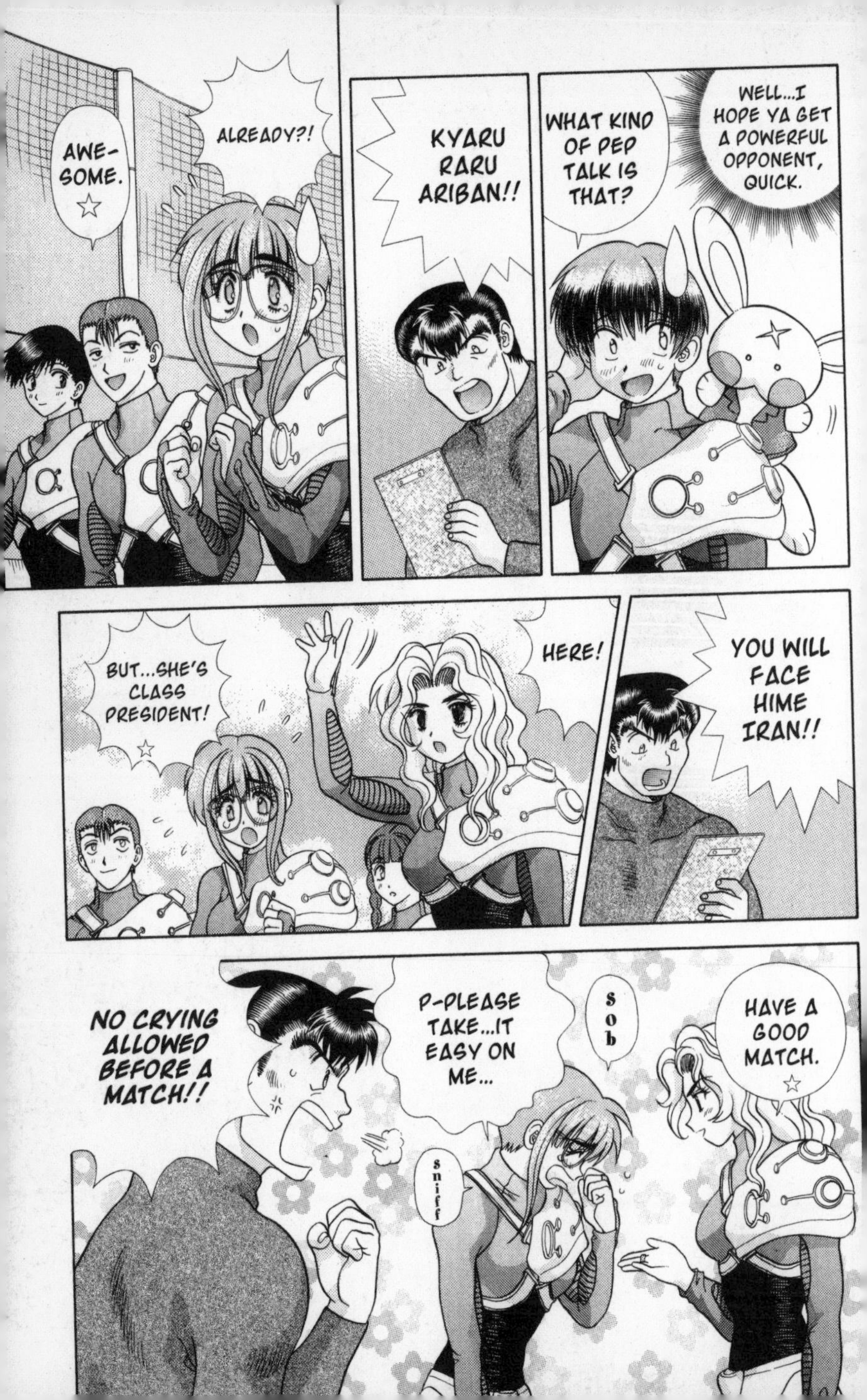
WELL...I HOPE YA GET A POWERFUL OPPONENT, QUICK.
WHAT KIND OF PEP TALK IS THAT?
KYARU RARU ARIBAN!!
ALREADY?!
AWE-SOME. ☆
YOU WILL FACE HIME IRAN!!
HERE!
BUT...SHE'S CLASS PRESIDENT! ☆
HAVE A GOOD MATCH. ☆
sob
P-PLEASE TAKE...IT EASY ON ME...
sniff
NO CRYING ALLOWED BEFORE A MATCH!!

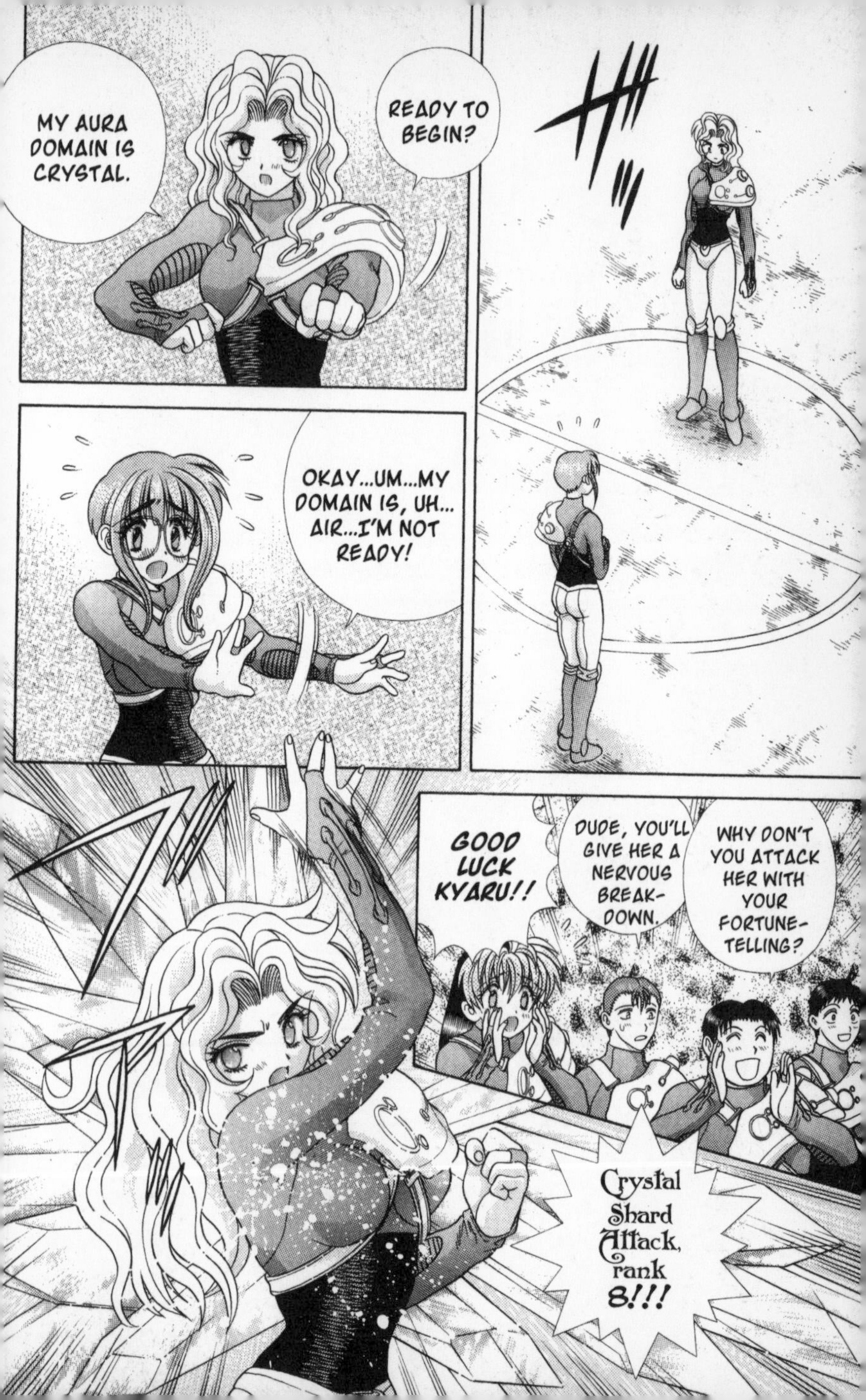
MY AURA DOMAIN IS CRYSTAL.
READY TO BEGIN?
OKAY...UM...MY DOMAIN IS, UH... AIR...I'M NOT READY!
GOOD LUCK KYARU!!
DUDE, YOU'LL GIVE HER A NERVOUS BREAK-DOWN.
WHY DON'T YOU ATTACK HER WITH YOUR FORTUNE-TELLING?
Crystal Shard Attack, rank 8!!!

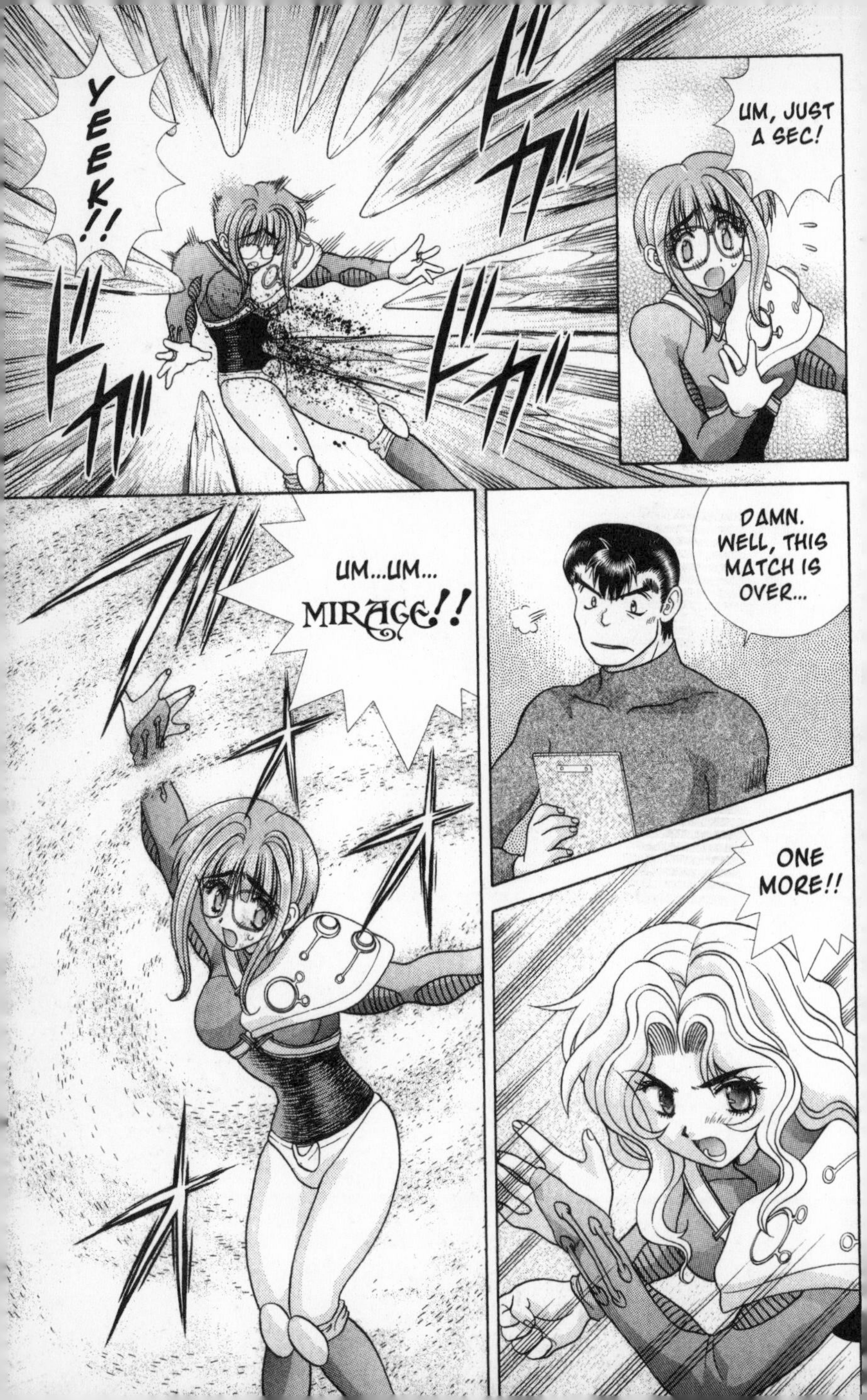
UM, JUST A SEC!
YEEEK!!
DAMN. WELL, THIS MATCH IS OVER...
ONE MORE!!
UM...UM...
MIRAGE!!

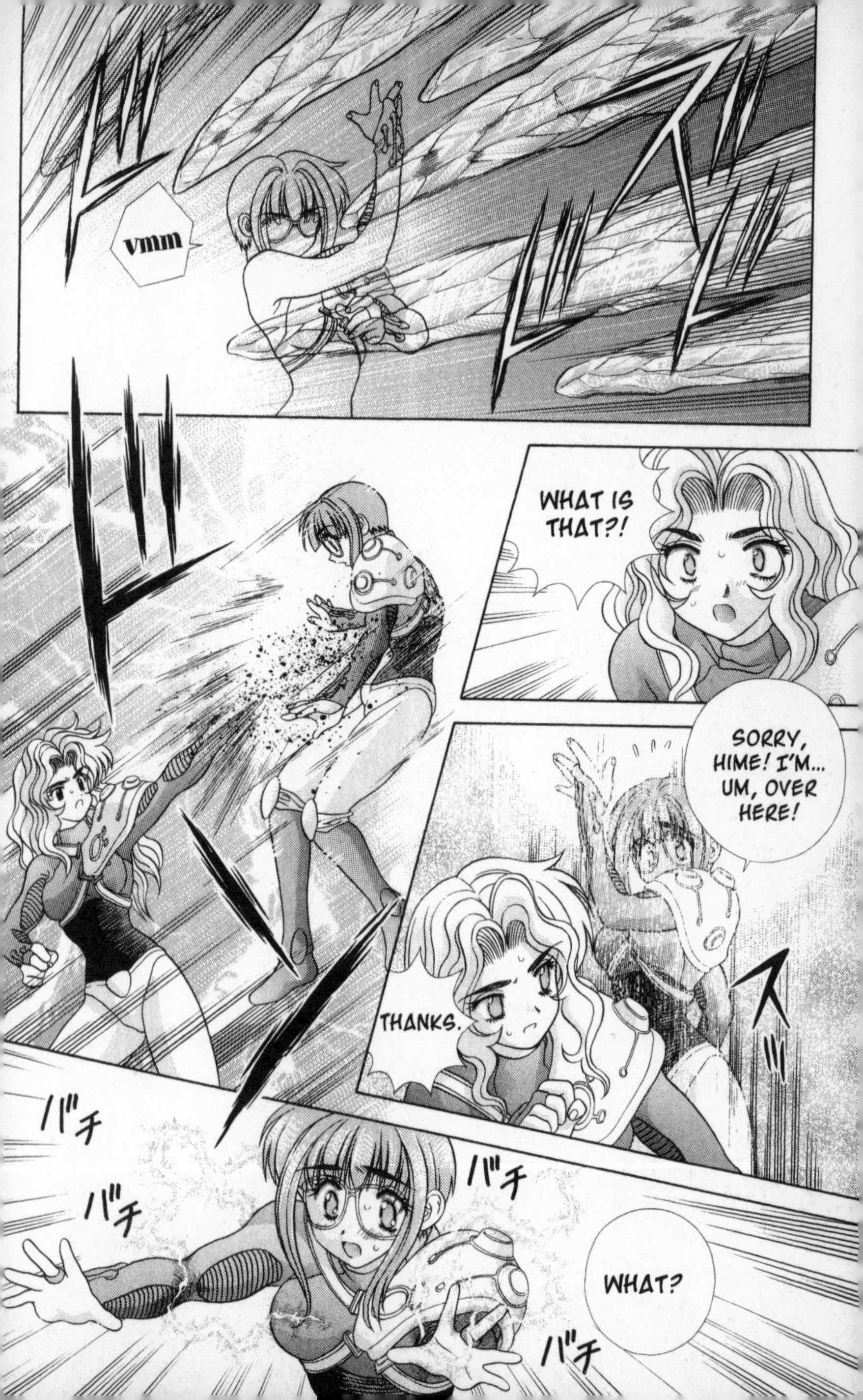

vmm
WHAT IS THAT?!
SORRY, HIME! I'M... UM, OVER HERE!
THANKS.
バチ
バチ
バチ
WHAT?
バチ

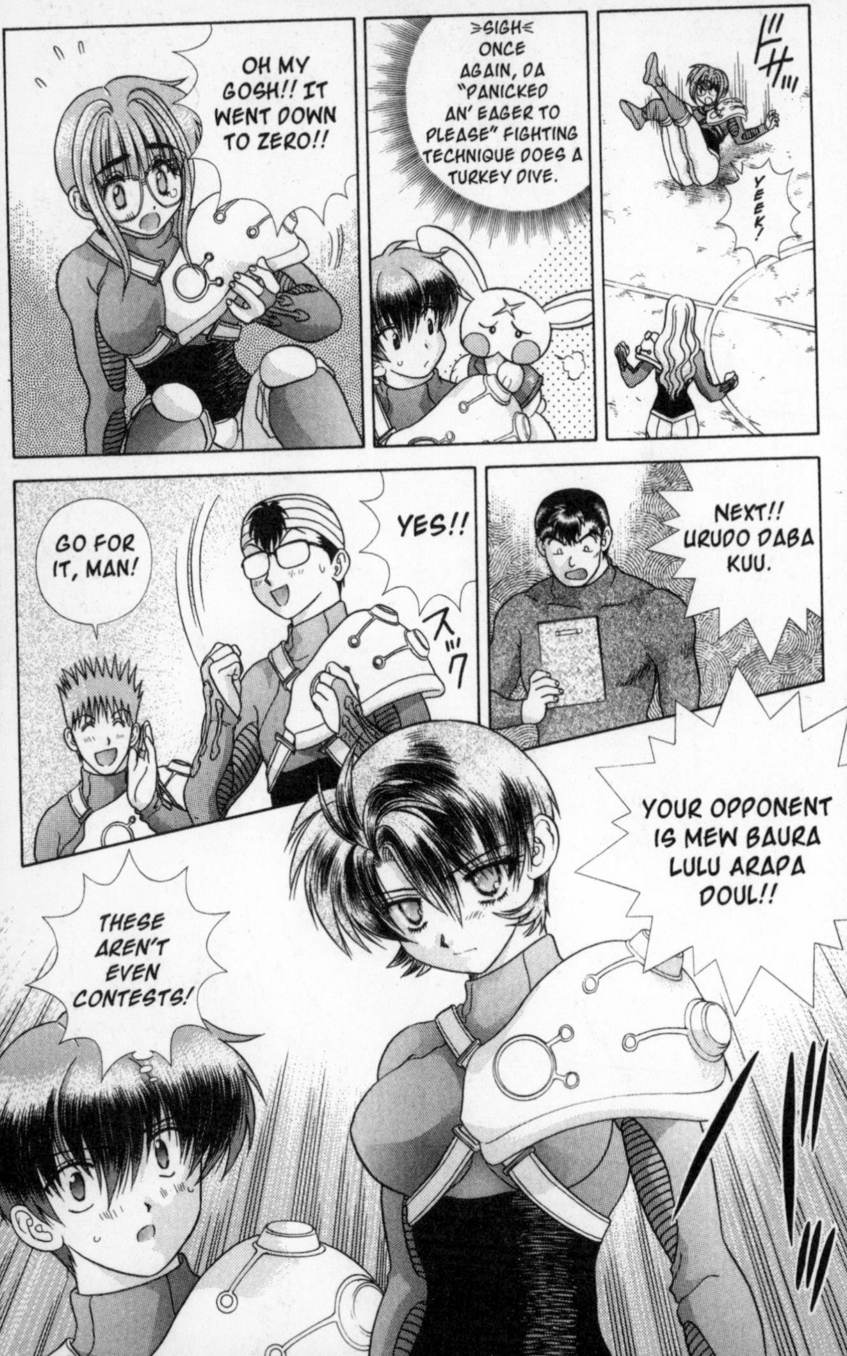
ドサッ
YEEK!
≥SIGH≤ ONCE AGAIN, DA "PANICKED AN' EAGER TO PLEASE" FIGHTING TECHNIQUE DOES A TURKEY DIVE.
OH MY GOSH!! IT WENT DOWN TO ZERO!!
NEXT!! URUDO DABA KUU.
YES!!
スク
GO FOR IT, MAN!
YOUR OPPONENT IS MEW BAURA LULU ARAPA DOUL!!
THESE AREN'T EVEN CONTESTS!

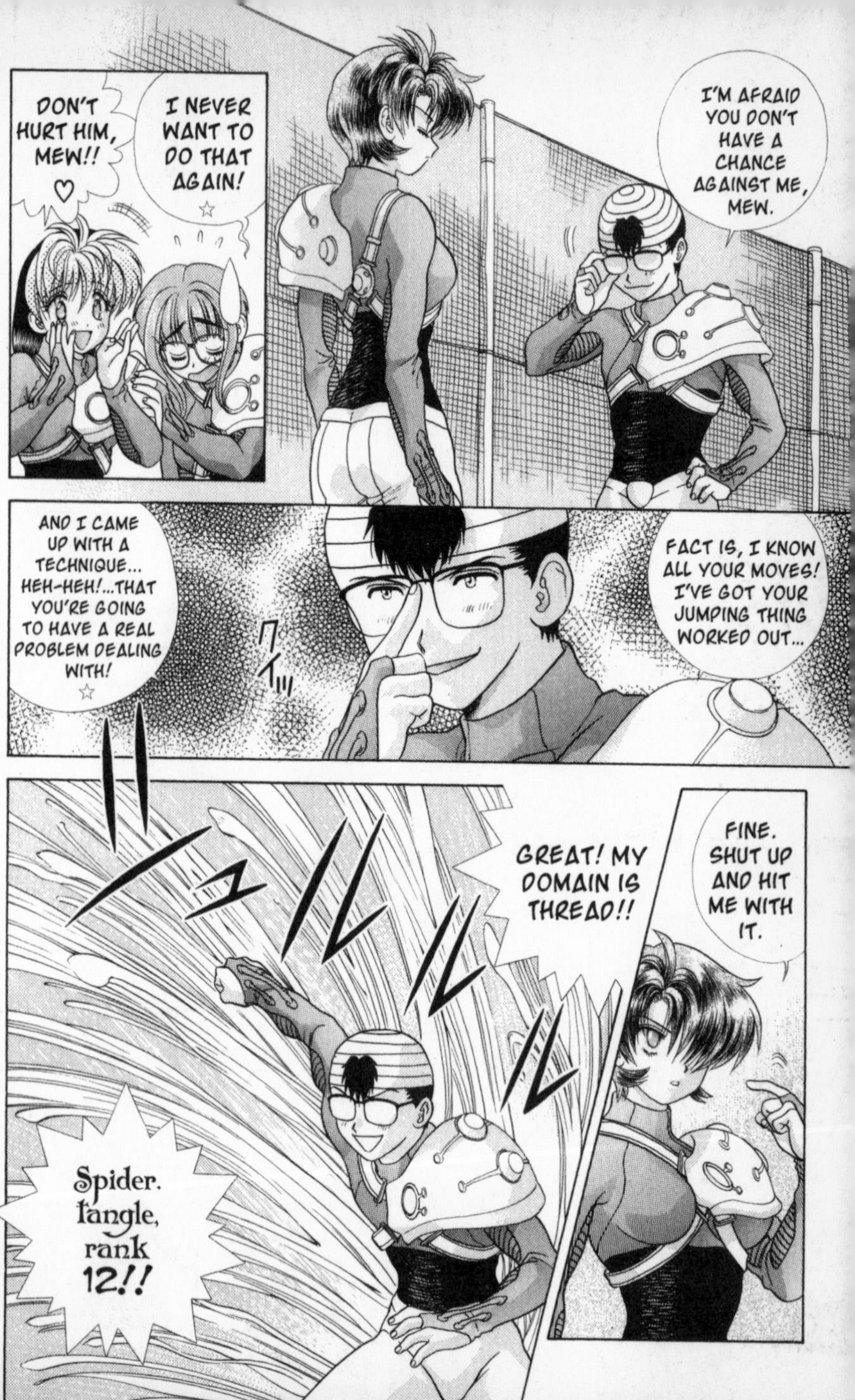
I'M AFRAID YOU DON'T HAVE A CHANCE AGAINST ME, MEW.
I NEVER WANT TO DO THAT AGAIN! ☆
DON'T HURT HIM, MEW!! ♡
FACT IS, I KNOW ALL YOUR MOVES! I'VE GOT YOUR JUMPING THING WORKED OUT...
AND I CAME UP WITH A TECHNIQUE... HEH-HEH!...THAT YOU'RE GOING TO HAVE A REAL PROBLEM DEALING WITH! ☆
FINE. SHUT UP AND HIT ME WITH IT.
GREAT! MY DOMAIN IS THREAD!!
Spider tangle, rank 12!!

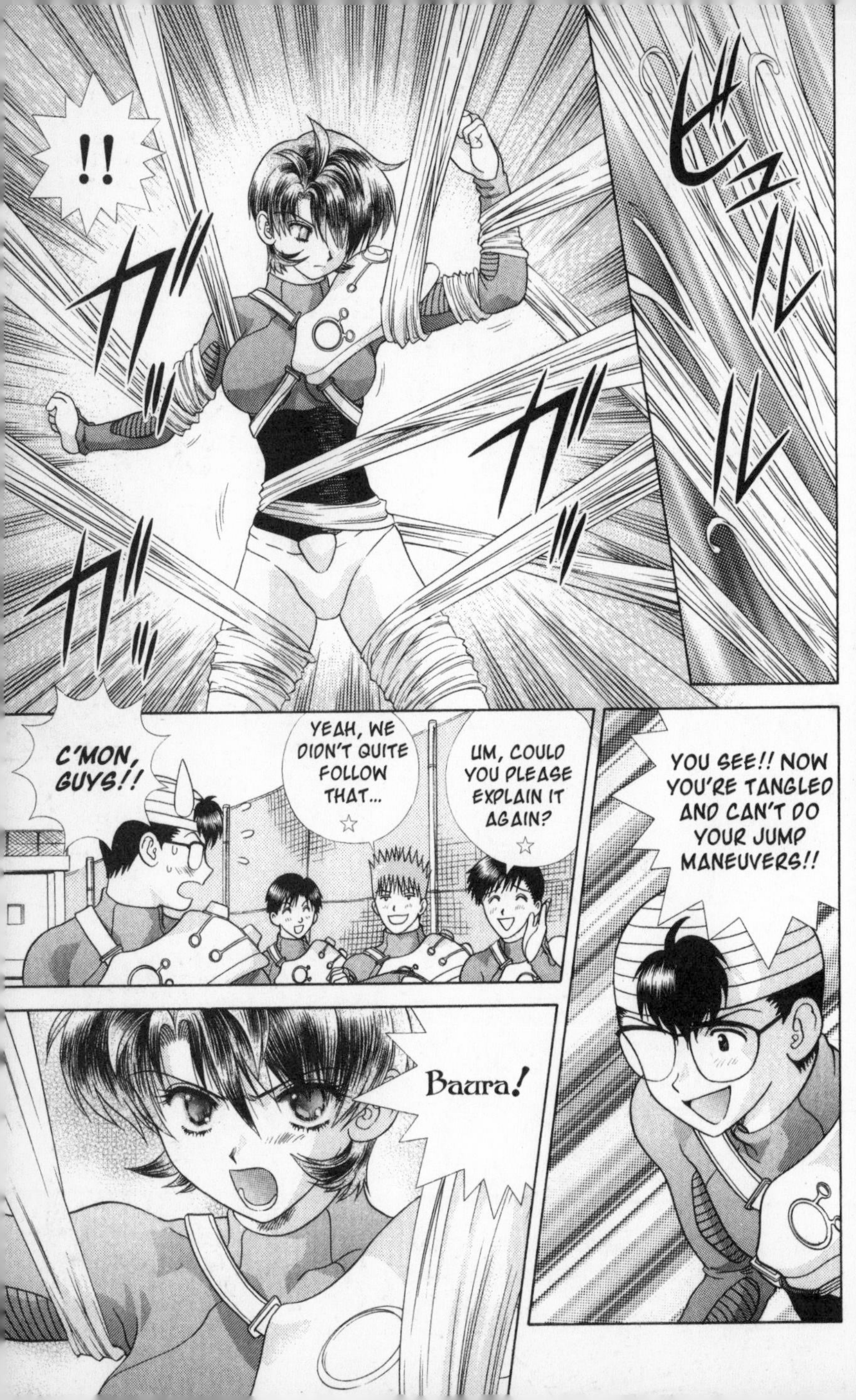
!!
YOU SEE!! NOW YOU'RE TANGLED AND CAN'T DO YOUR JUMP MANEUVERS!!
UM, COULD YOU PLEASE EXPLAIN IT AGAIN? ☆
YEAH, WE DIDN'T QUITE FOLLOW THAT... ☆
C'MON, GUYS!!
Baura!

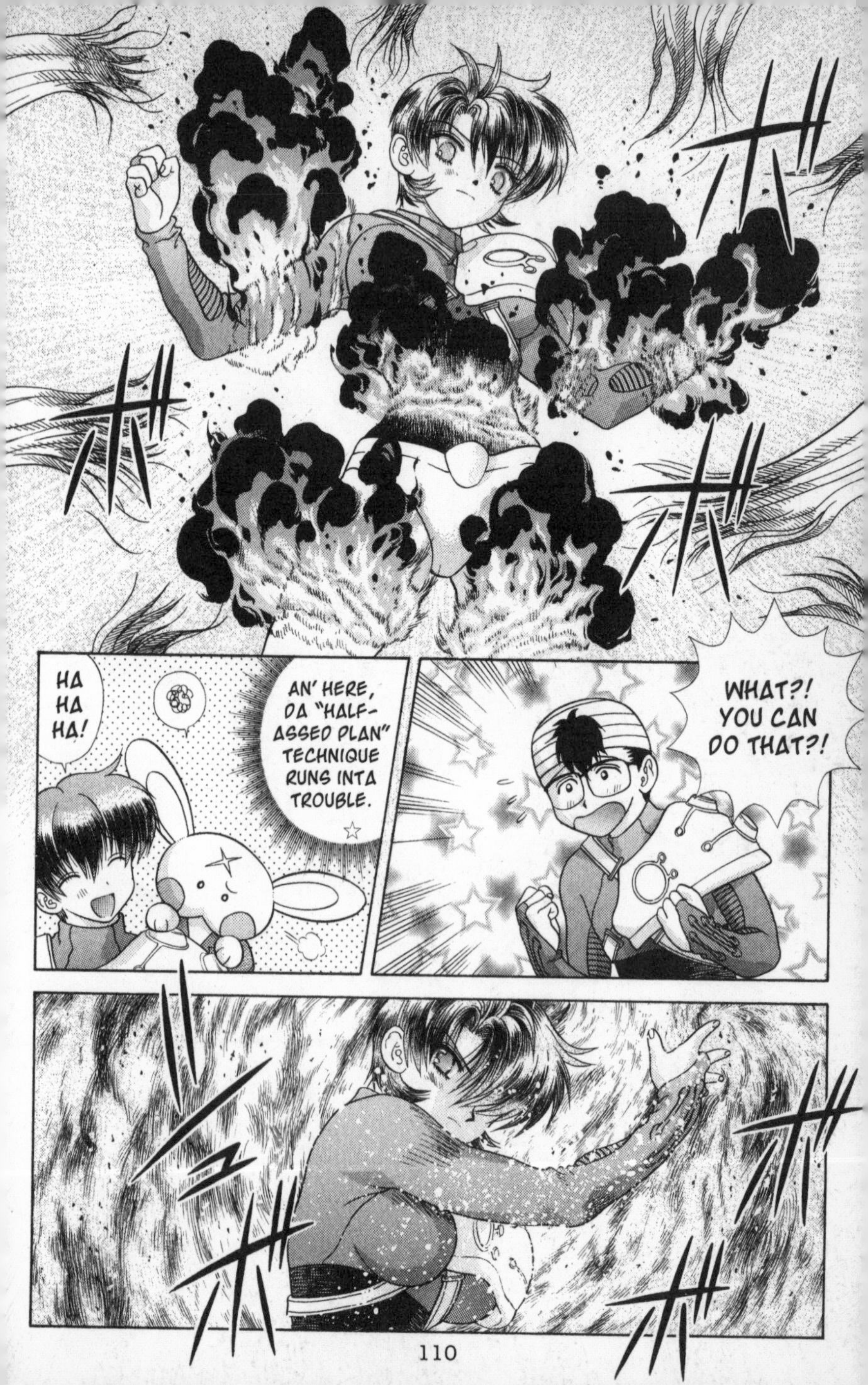
WHAT?! YOU CAN DO THAT?!
AN' HERE, DA "HALF-ASSED PLAN" TECHNIQUE RUNS INTA TROUBLE.
HA HA HA!

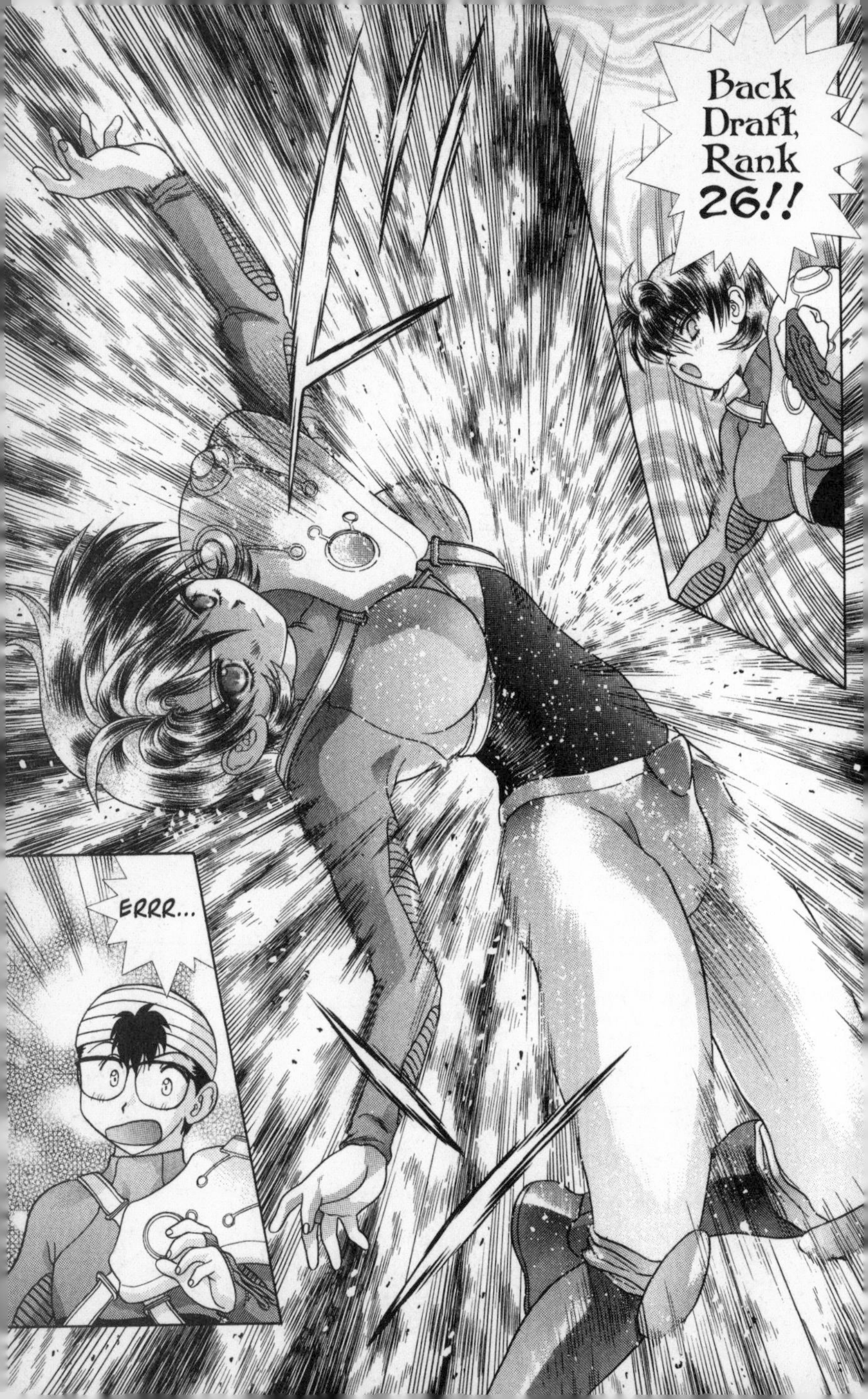
Back Draft, Rank 26!!
ERRR...

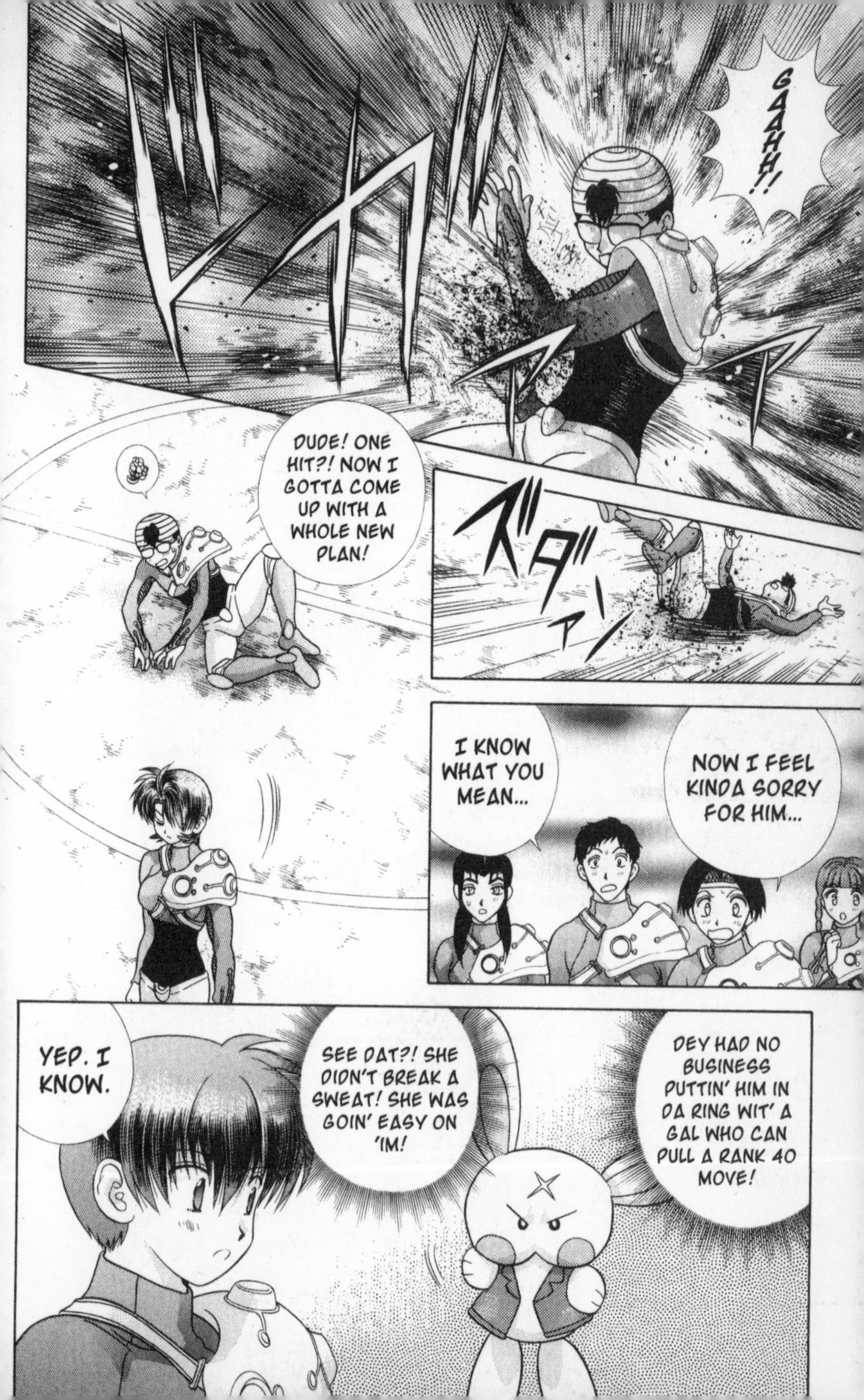
GAAHH!!
DUDE! ONE HIT?! NOW I GOTTA COME UP WITH A WHOLE NEW PLAN!
NOW I FEEL KINDA SORRY FOR HIM...
I KNOW WHAT YOU MEAN...
DEY HAD NO BUSINESS PUTTIN' HIM IN DA RING WIT' A GAL WHO CAN PULL A RANK 40 MOVE!
SEE DAT?! SHE DIDN'T BREAK A SWEAT! SHE WAS GOIN' EASY ON 'IM!
YEP. I KNOW.

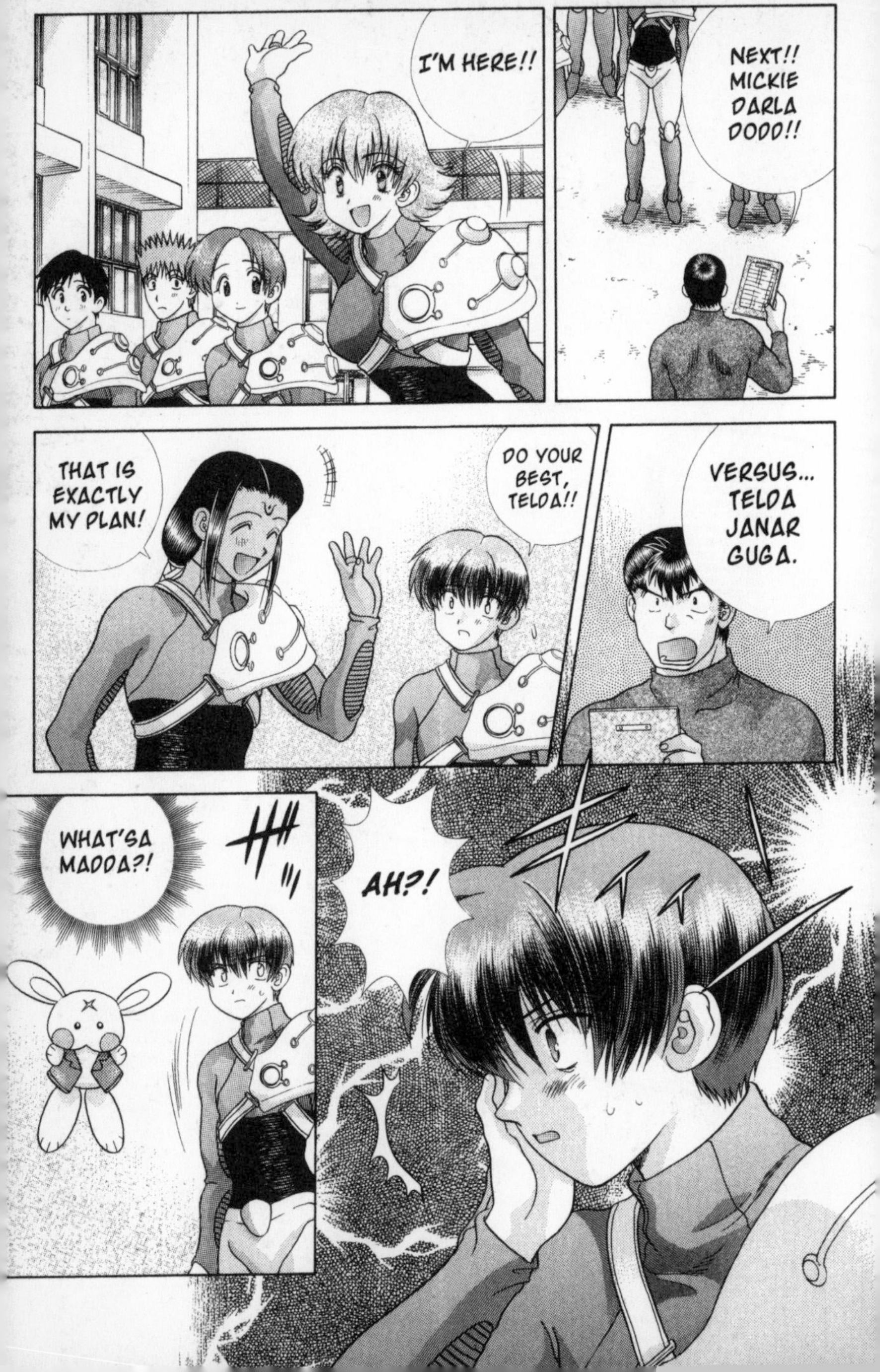
I'M HERE!!
NEXT!! MICKIE DARLA DODO!!
THAT IS EXACTLY MY PLAN!
DO YOUR BEST, TELDA!!
VERSUS... TELDA JANAR GUGA.
WHAT'SA MADDA?!
AH?!

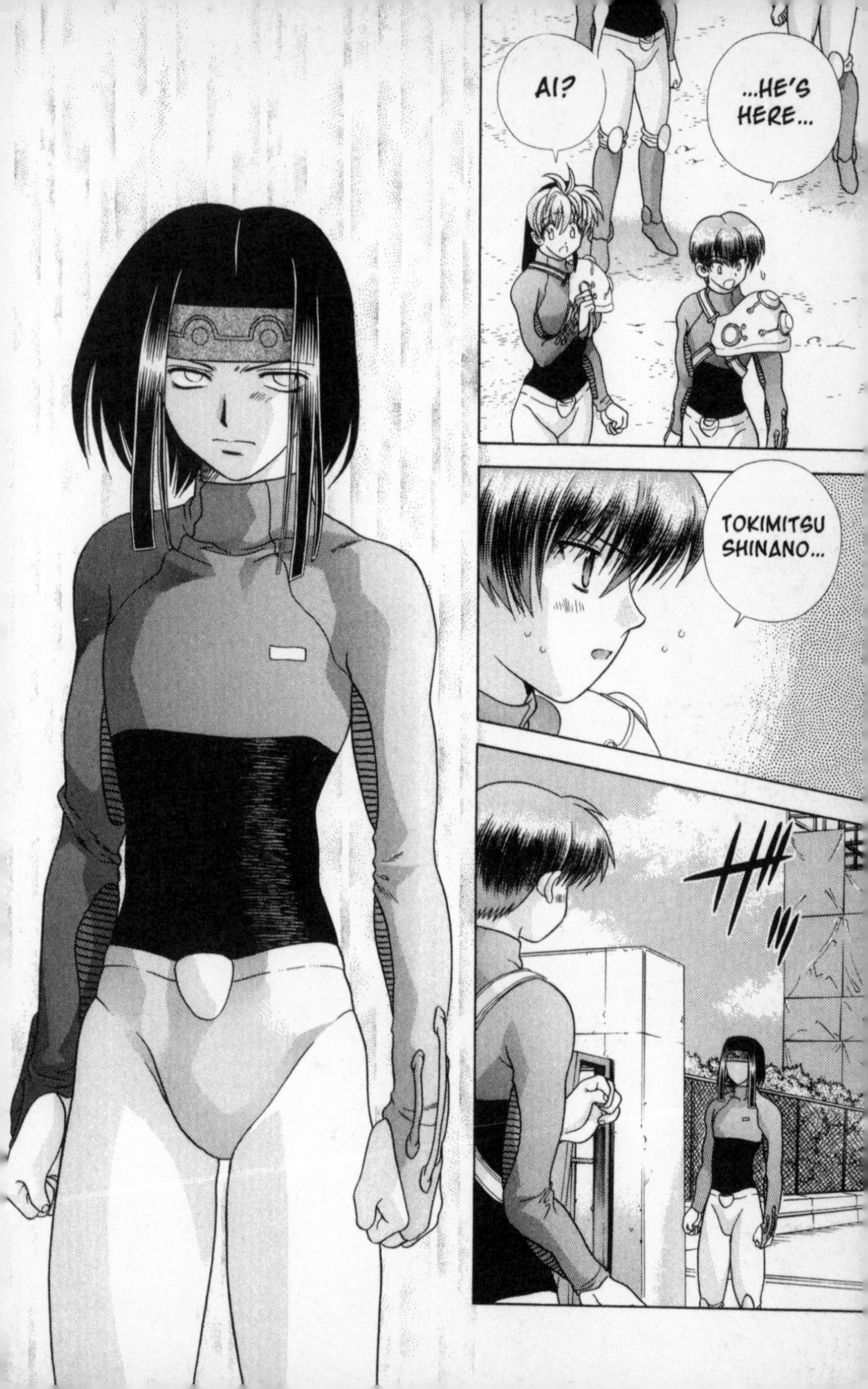
...HE'S HERE...
AI?
TOKIMITSU SHINANO...

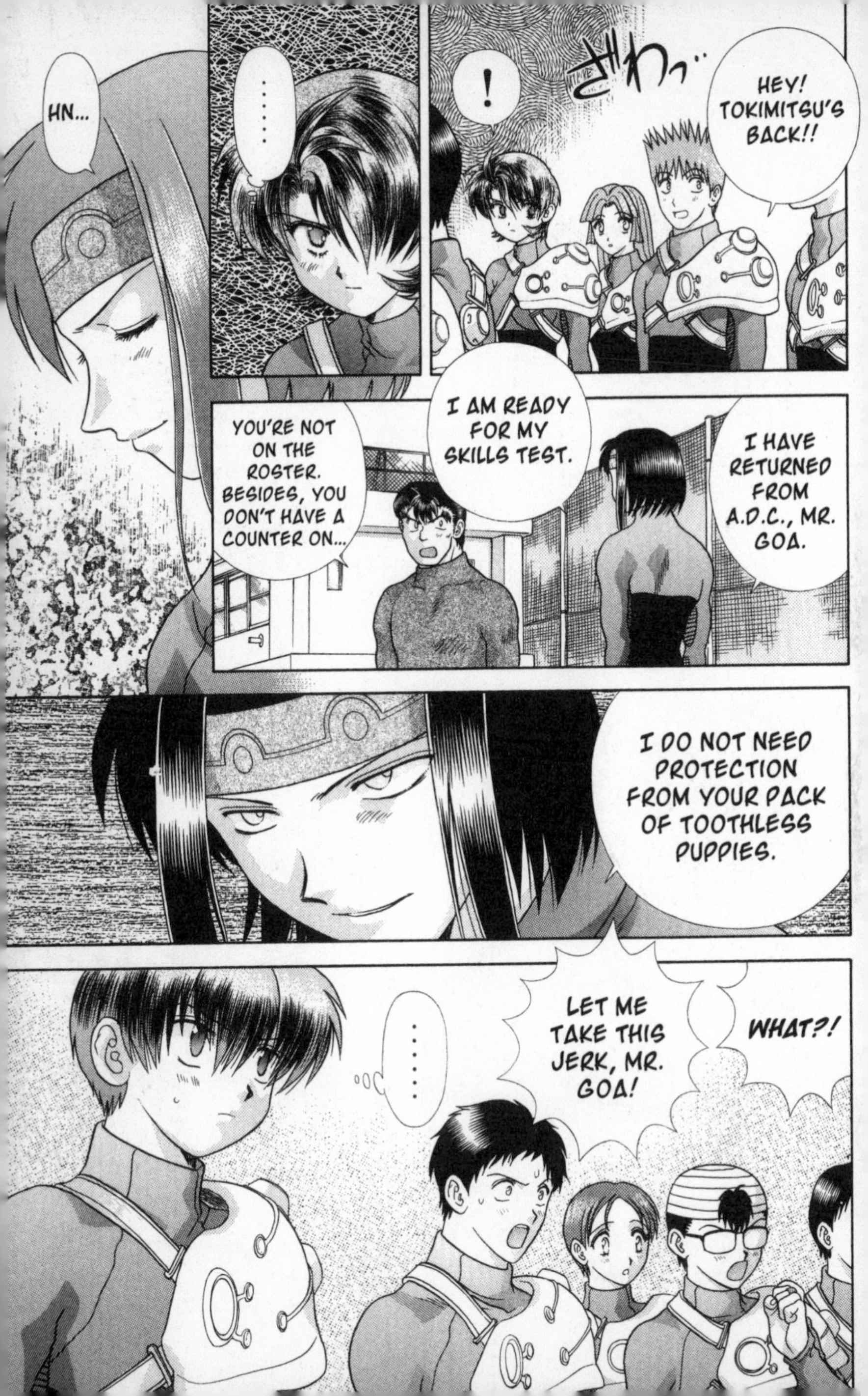
HEY! TOKIMITSU'S BACK!!
ざわっ…
!
......
HN...
I HAVE RETURNED FROM A.D.C., MR. GOA.
I AM READY FOR MY SKILLS TEST.
YOU'RE NOT ON THE ROSTER. BESIDES, YOU DON'T HAVE A COUNTER ON...
I DO NOT NEED PROTECTION FROM YOUR PACK OF TOOTHLESS PUPPIES.
WHAT?!
LET ME TAKE THIS JERK, MR. GOA!
......

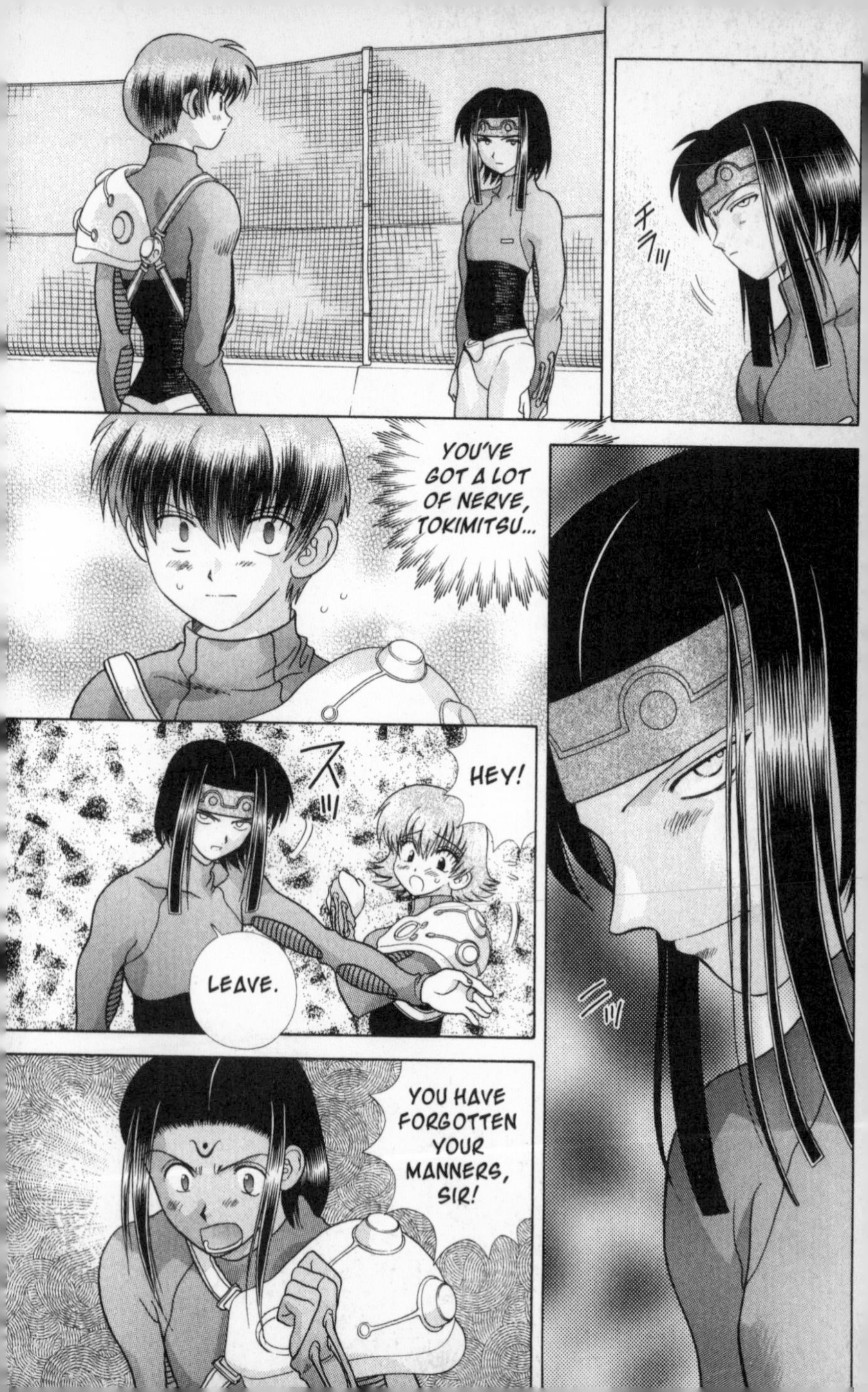

チラッ
YOU'VE GOT A LOT OF NERVE, TOKIMITSU...
HEY!
スッ
LEAVE.
YOU HAVE FORGOTTEN YOUR MANNERS, SIR!

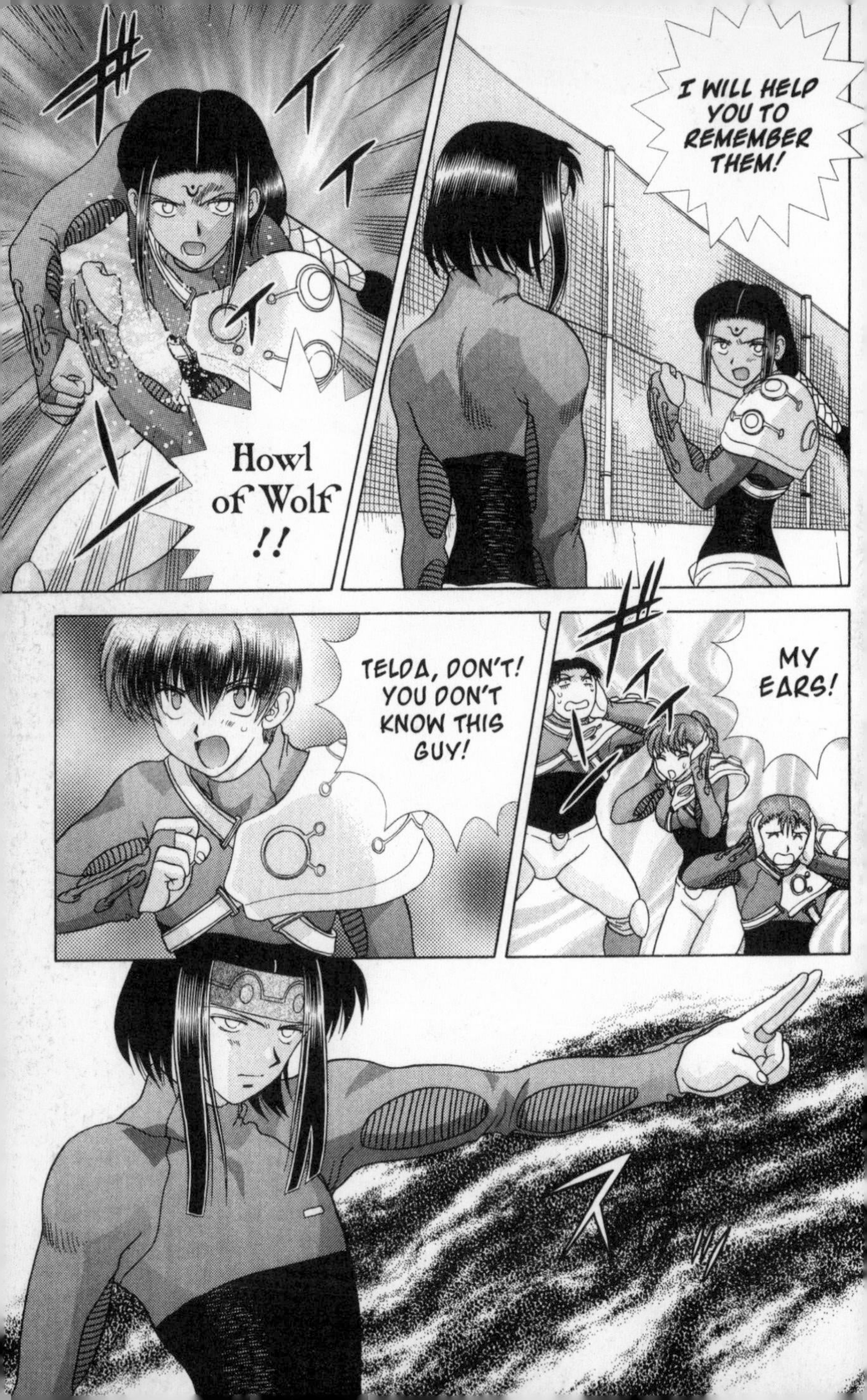
I WILL HELP YOU TO REMEMBER THEM!
Howl of Wolf !!
MY EARS!
TELDA, DON'T! YOU DON'T KNOW THIS GUY!

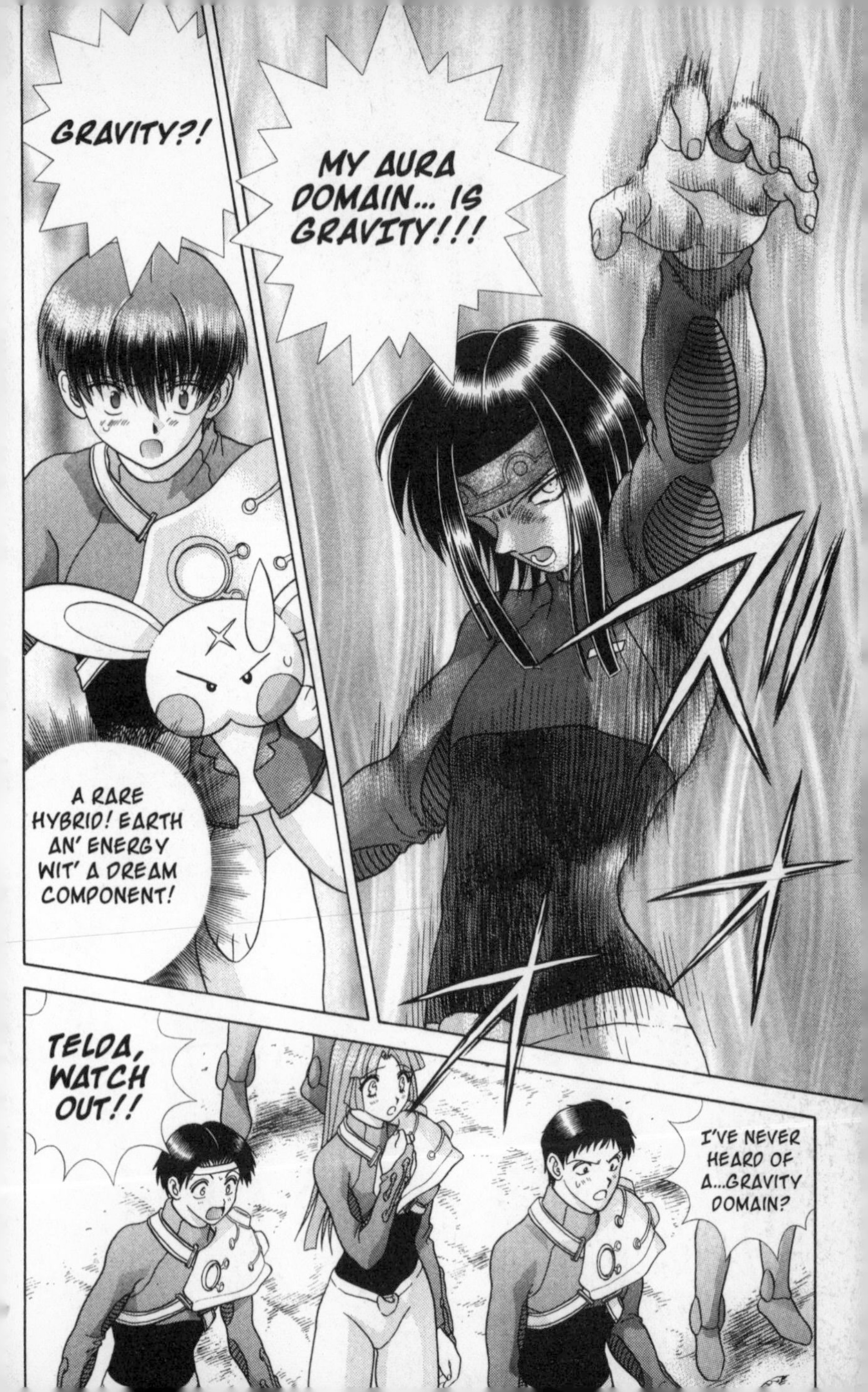
MY AURA DOMAIN... IS GRAVITY!!!
GRAVITY?!
A RARE HYBRID! EARTH AN' ENERGY WIT' A DREAM COMPONENT!
I'VE NEVER HEARD OF A...GRAVITY DOMAIN?
TELDA, WATCH OUT!!

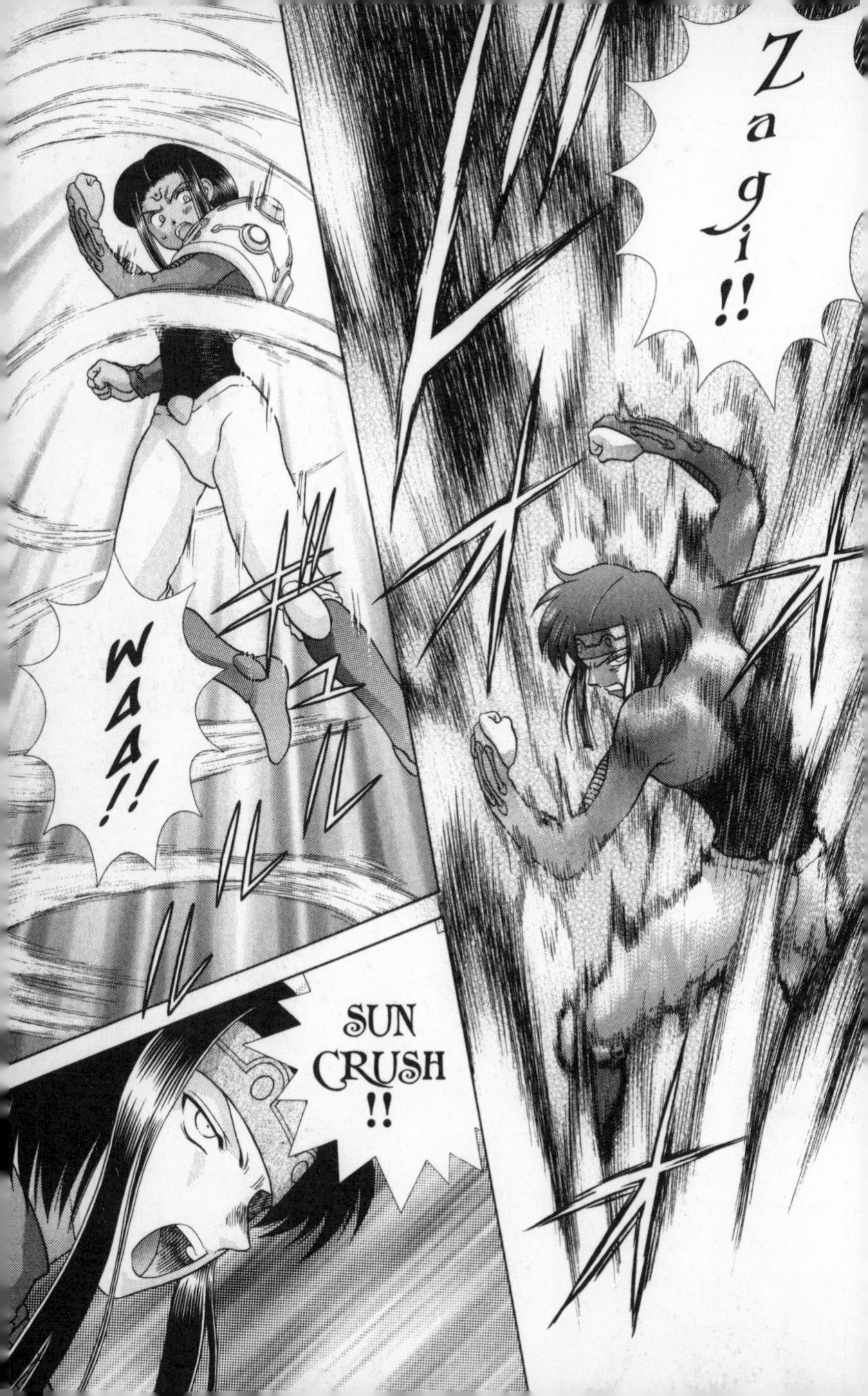
Zagi!!
WAAA!!
SUN CRUSH!!

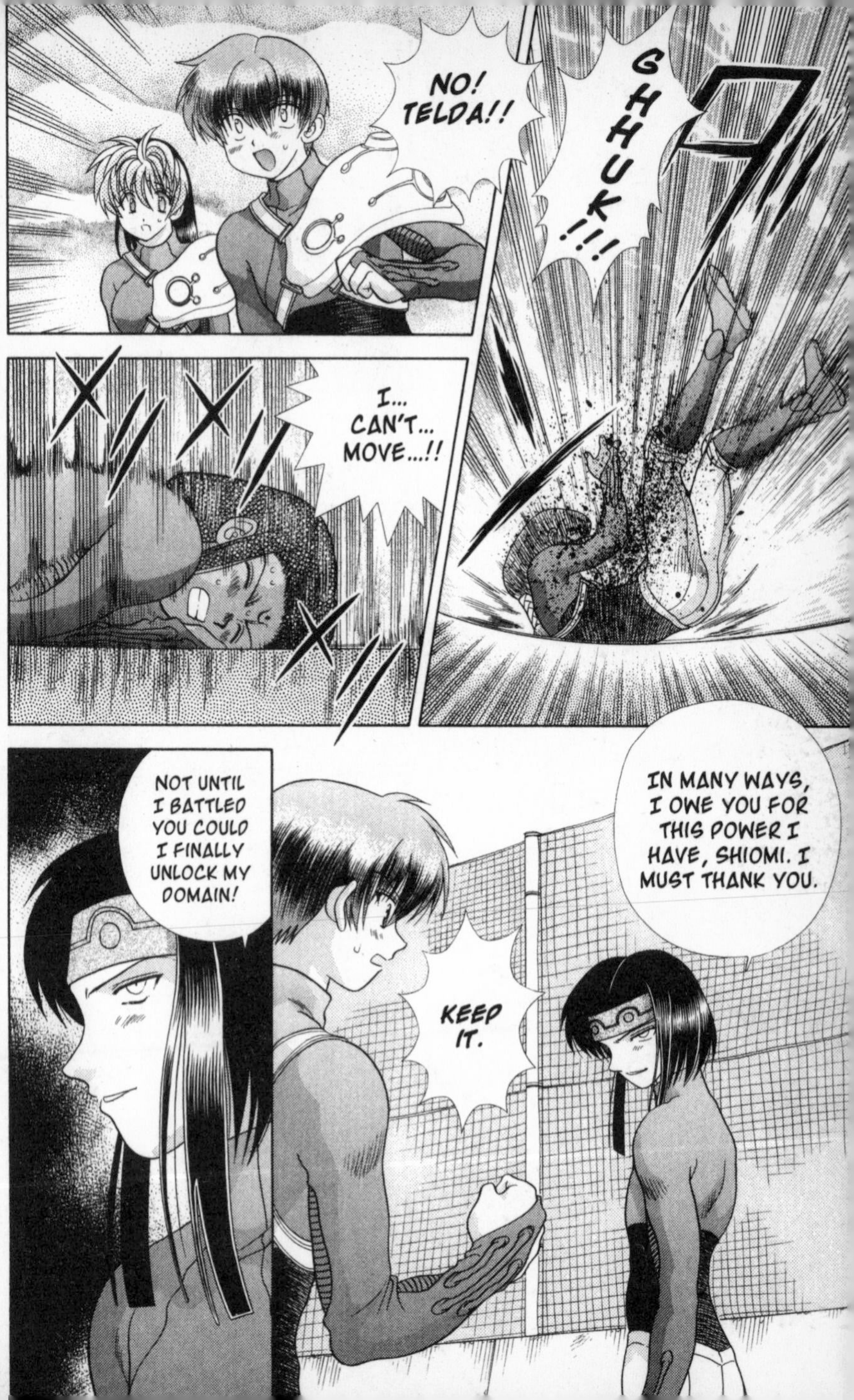
GHHUK!!!!
NO! TELDA!!
I... CAN'T... MOVE...!!
IN MANY WAYS, I OWE YOU FOR THIS POWER I HAVE, SHIOMI. I MUST THANK YOU.
NOT UNTIL I BATTLED YOU COULD I FINALLY UNLOCK MY DOMAIN!
KEEP IT.

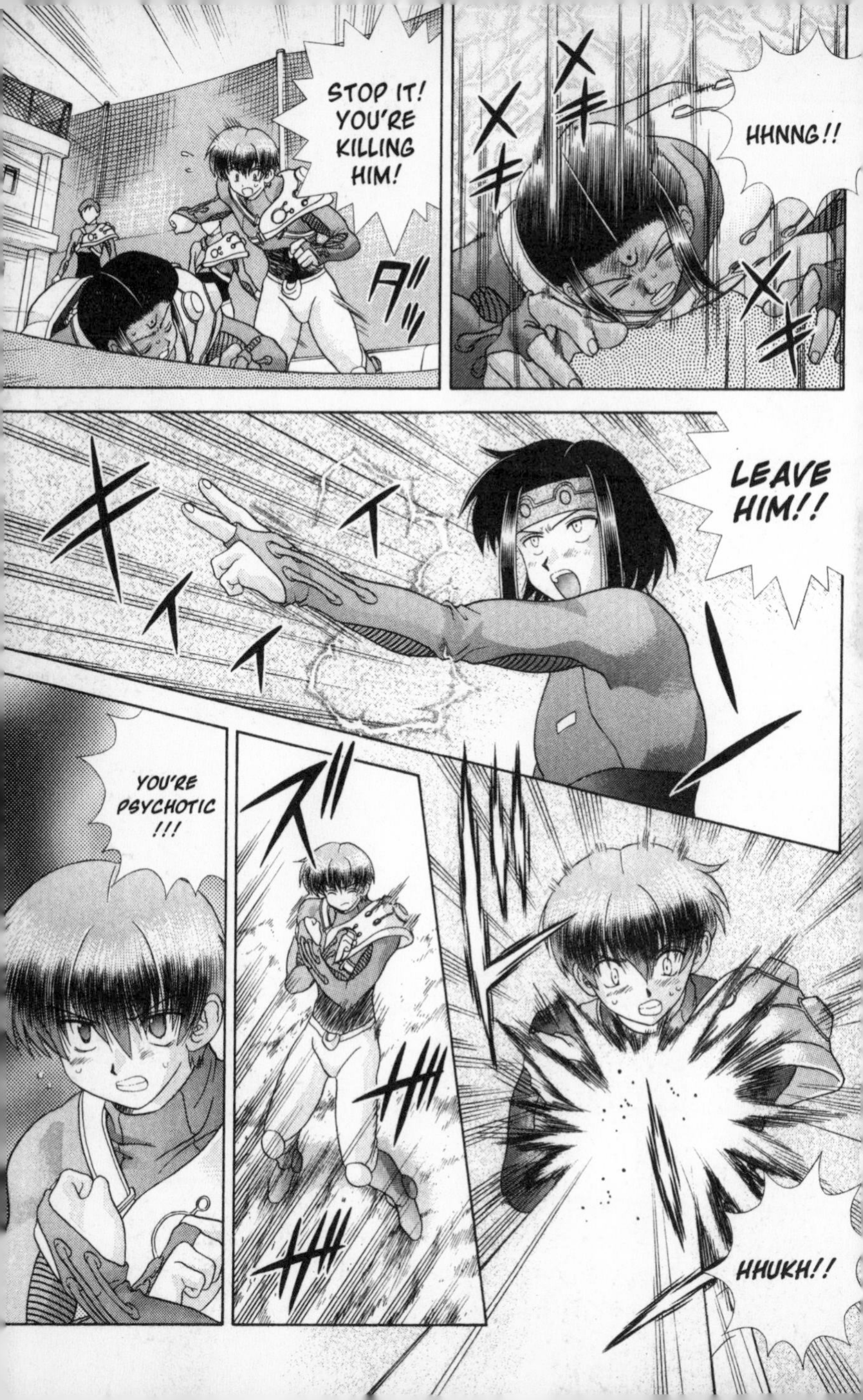
HHNNG!!
STOP IT! YOU'RE KILLING HIM!
LEAVE HIM!!
HHUKH!!
YOU'RE PSYCHOTIC!!!

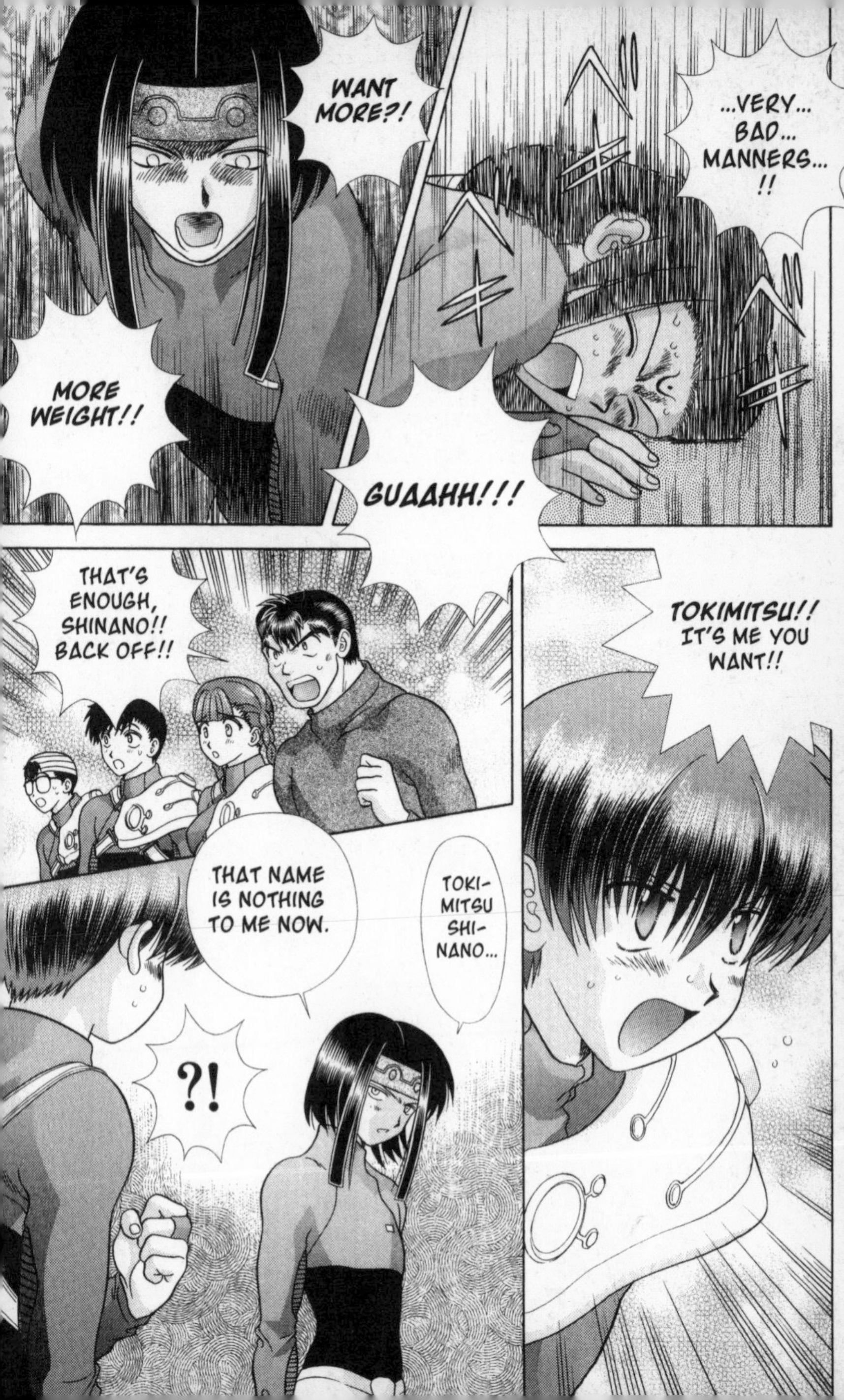
...VERY... BAD... MANNERS... !!
WANT MORE?!
MORE WEIGHT!!
GUAAHH!!!
TOKIMITSU!! IT'S ME YOU WANT!!
THAT'S ENOUGH, SHINANO!! BACK OFF!!
TOKI-MITSU SHI-NANO...
THAT NAME IS NOTHING TO ME NOW.
?!

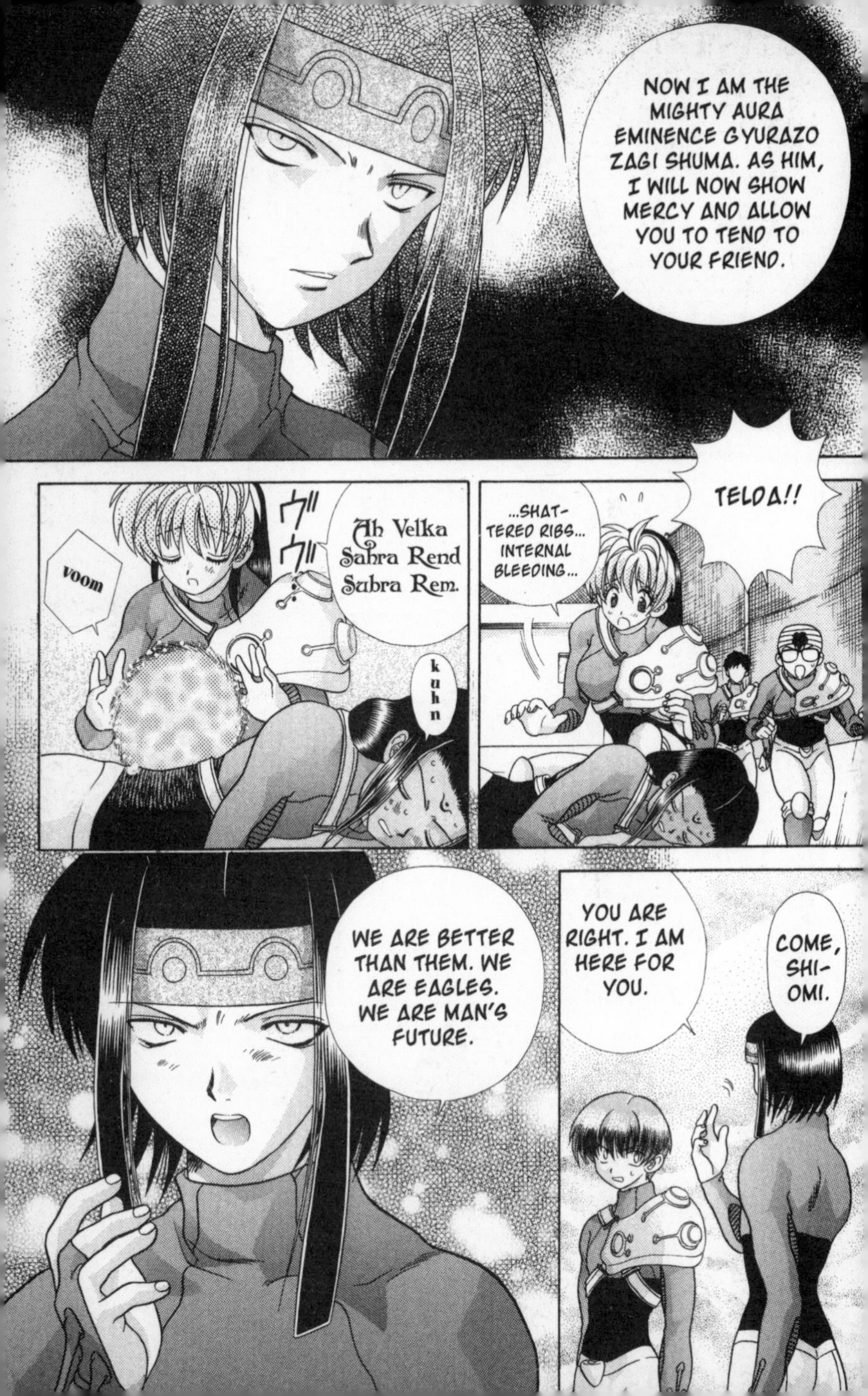
NOW I AM THE MIGHTY AURA EMINENCE GYURAZO ZAGI SHUMA. AS HIM, I WILL NOW SHOW MERCY AND ALLOW YOU TO TEND TO YOUR FRIEND.
TELDA!!
...SHATTERED RIBS... INTERNAL BLEEDING...
Ah Velka Sahra Rend Subra Rem.
voom
kuhn
WE ARE BETTER THAN THEM. WE ARE EAGLES. WE ARE MAN'S FUTURE.
COME, SHI-OMI.
YOU ARE RIGHT. I AM HERE FOR YOU.

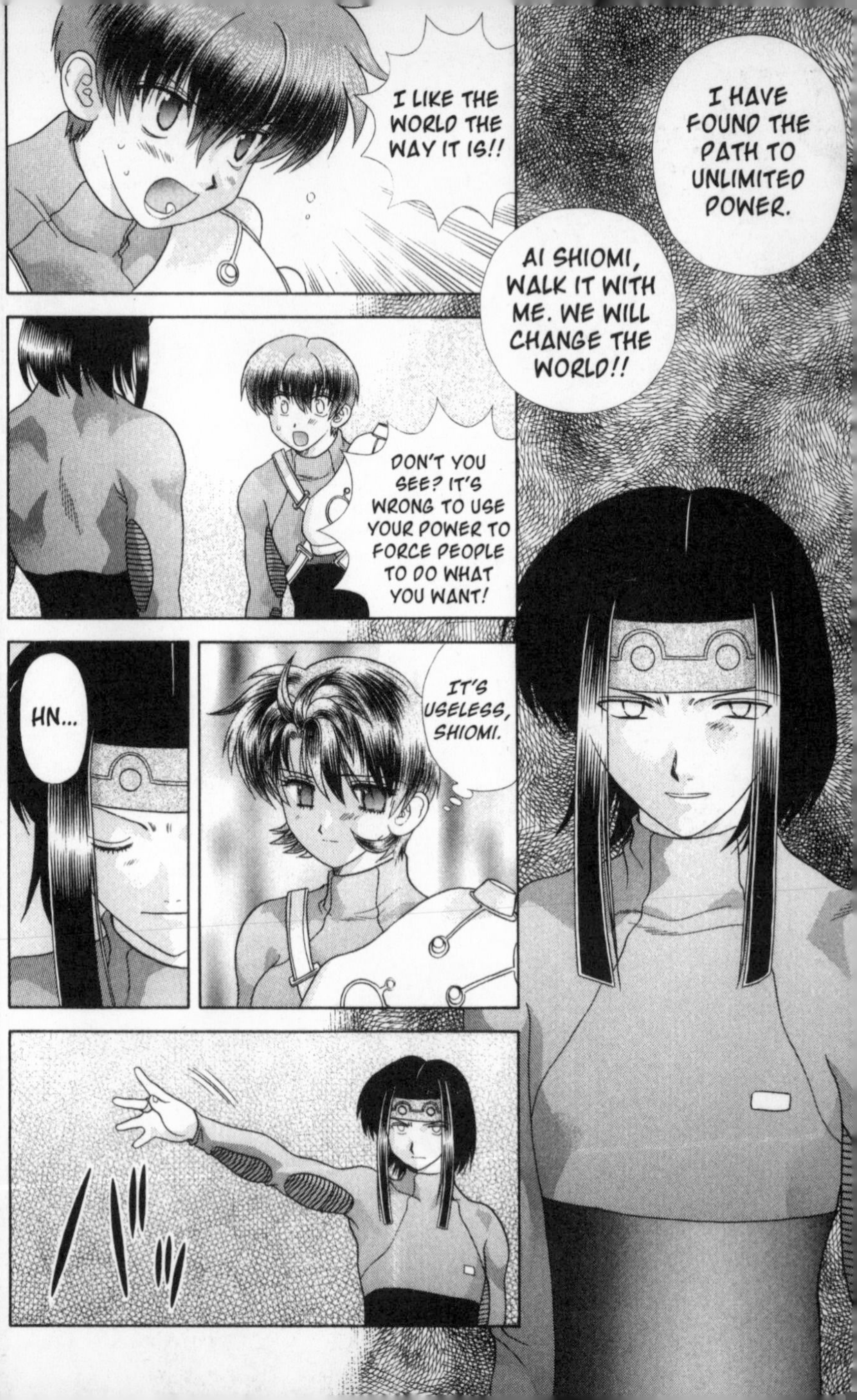
I HAVE FOUND THE PATH TO UNLIMITED POWER.
AI SHIOMI, WALK IT WITH ME. WE WILL CHANGE THE WORLD!!
I LIKE THE WORLD THE WAY IT IS!!
DON'T YOU SEE? IT'S WRONG TO USE YOUR POWER TO FORCE PEOPLE TO DO WHAT YOU WANT!
IT'S USELESS, SHIOMI.
HN...

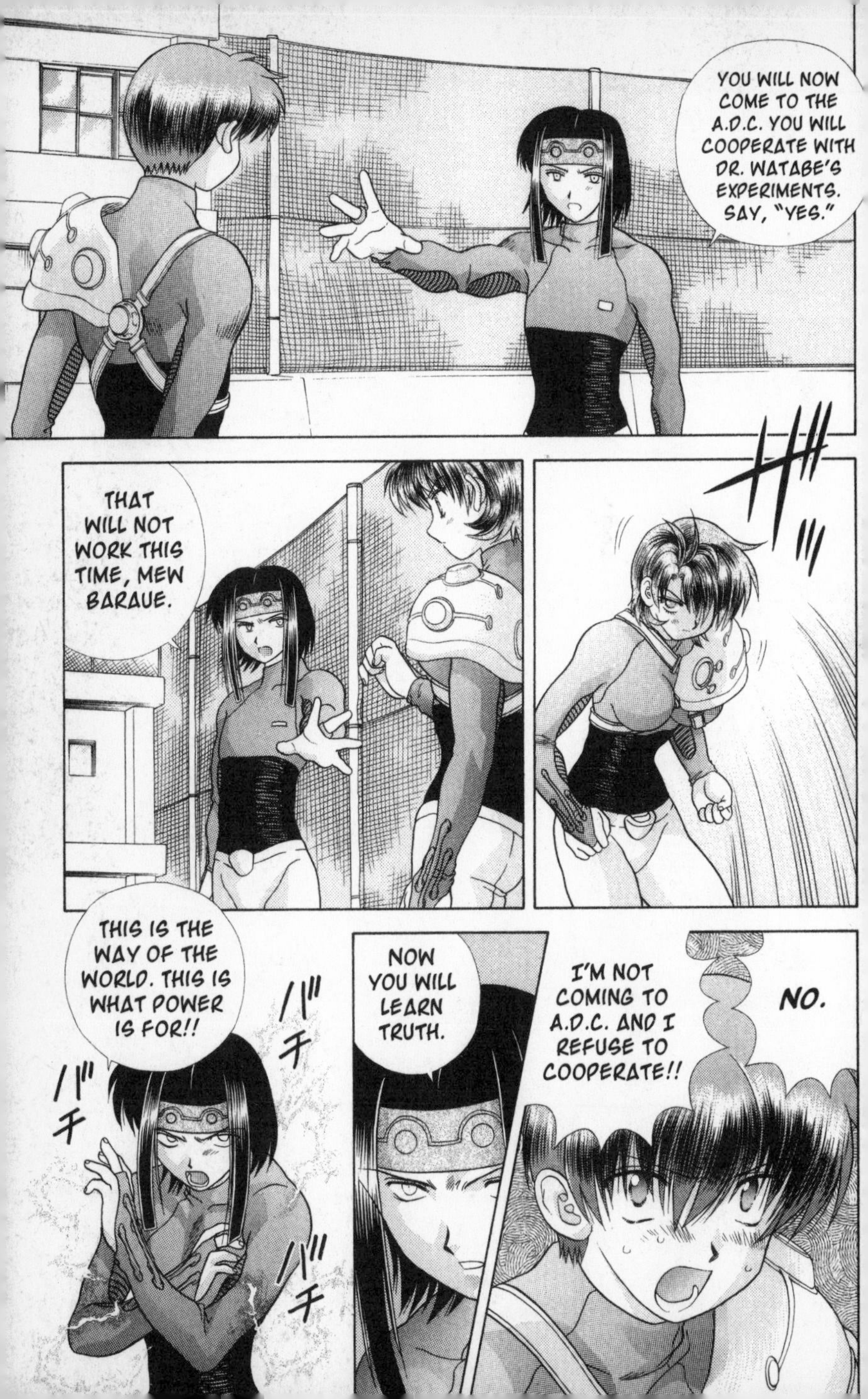
YOU WILL NOW COME TO THE A.D.C. YOU WILL COOPERATE WITH DR. WATABE'S EXPERIMENTS. SAY, "YES."
THAT WILL NOT WORK THIS TIME, MEW BARAUE.
NO.
I'M NOT COMING TO A.D.C. AND I REFUSE TO COOPERATE!!
NOW YOU WILL LEARN TRUTH.
バチ
バチ
THIS IS THE WAY OF THE WORLD. THIS IS WHAT POWER IS FOR!!
バチ

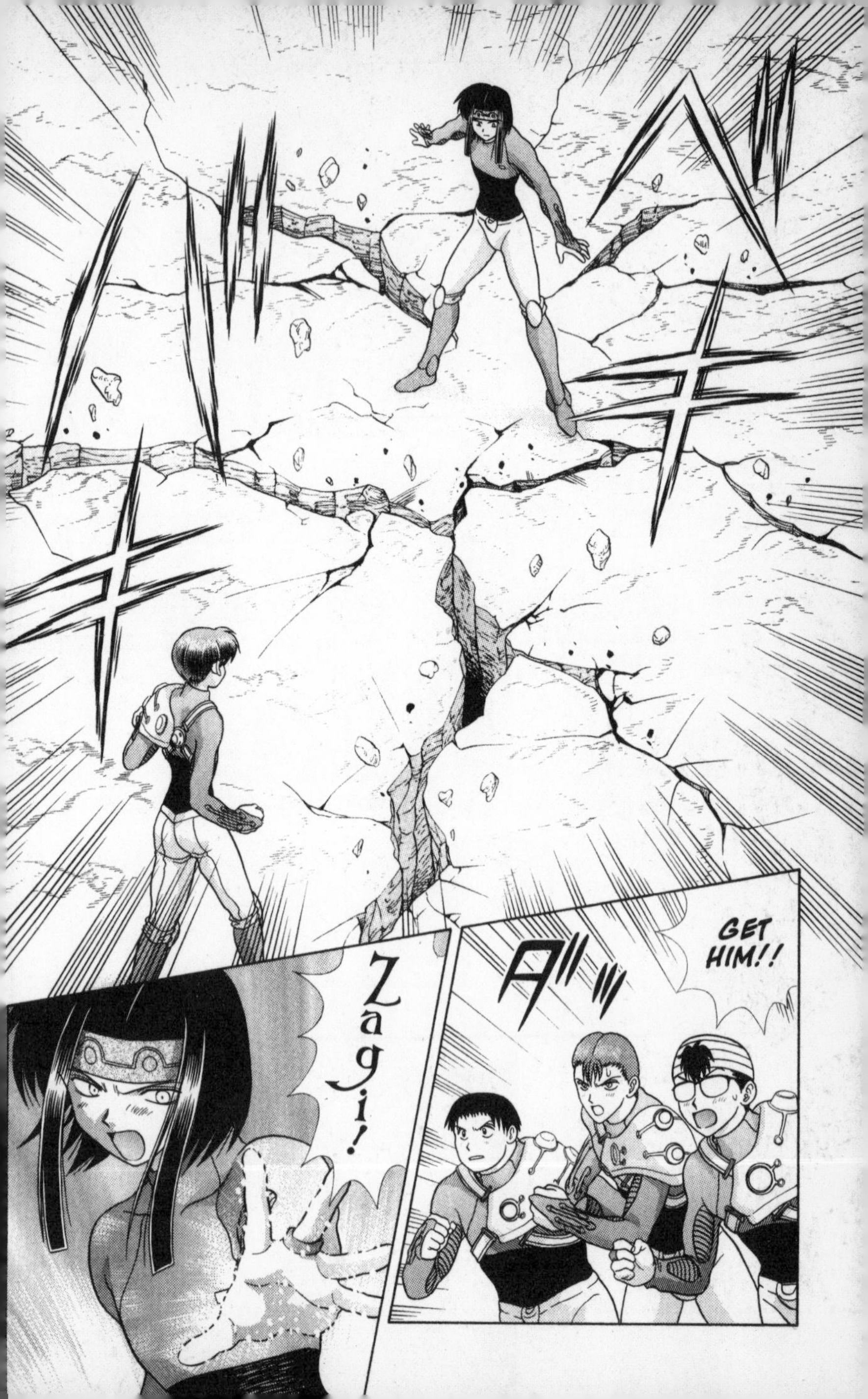
GET HIM!!
Zagi!

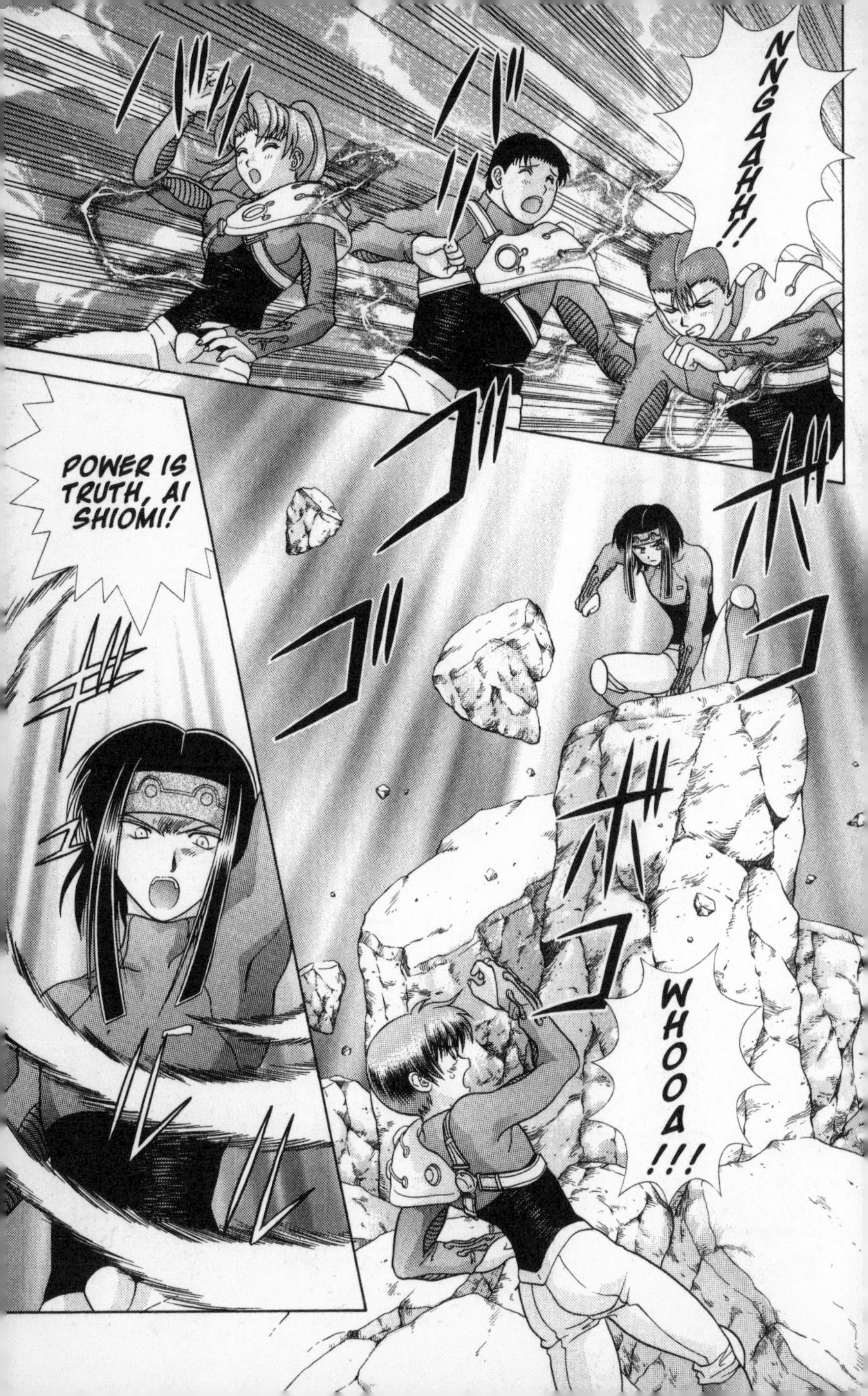
NNGAAAHH!!
POWER IS TRUTH, AI SHIOMI!
WHOOAA!!!

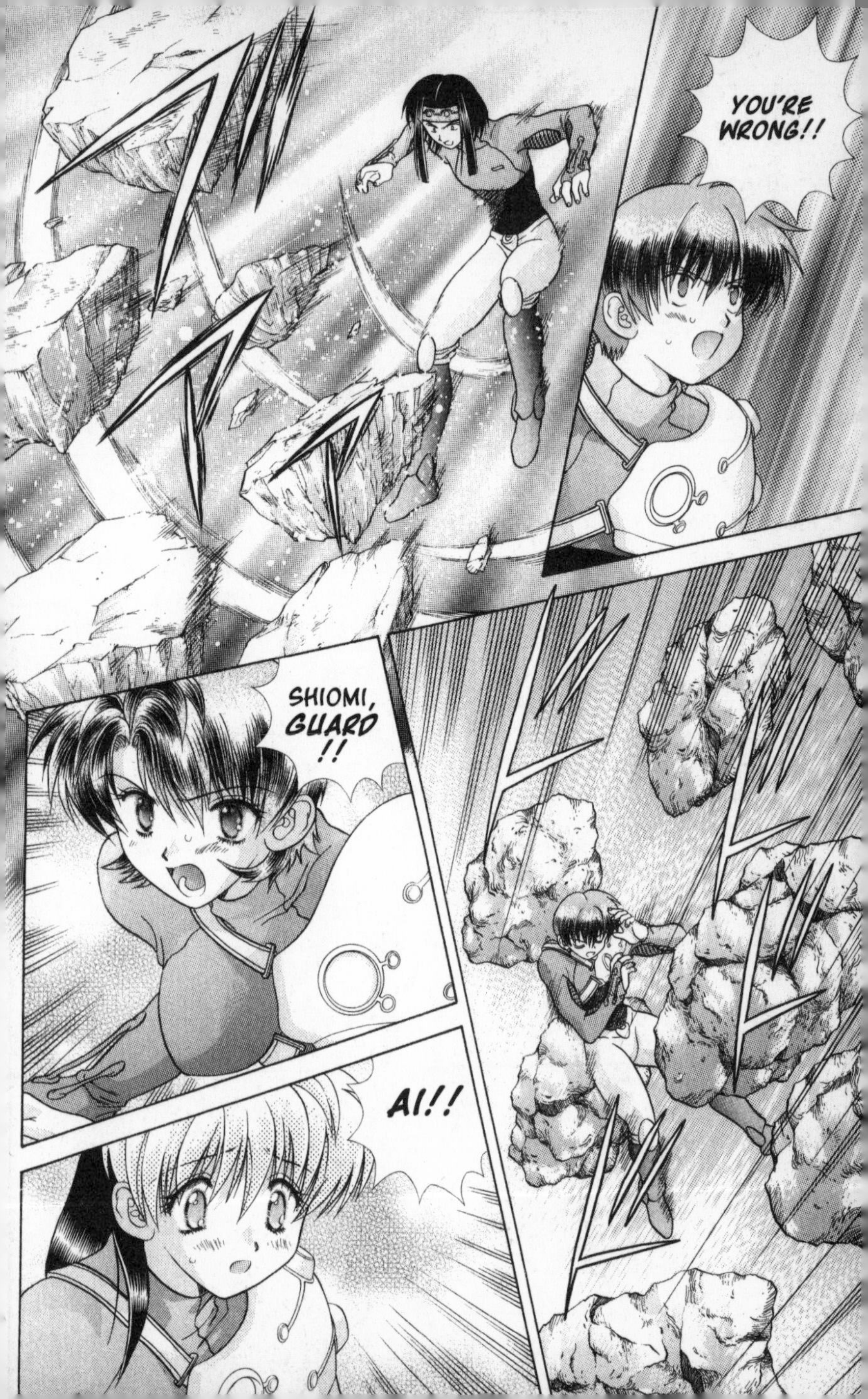
YOU'RE WRONG!!
SHIOMI, GUARD !!
AI!!

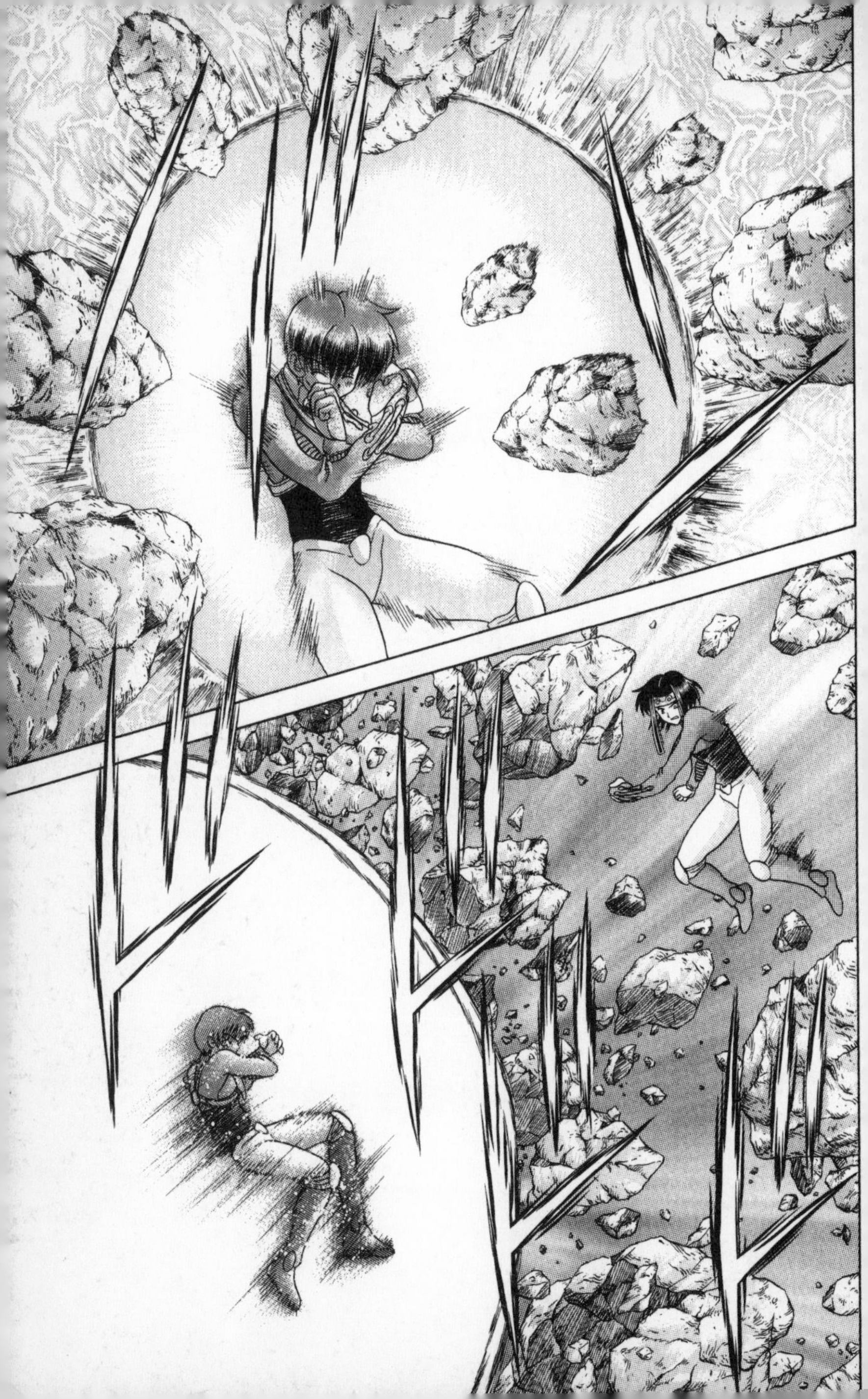

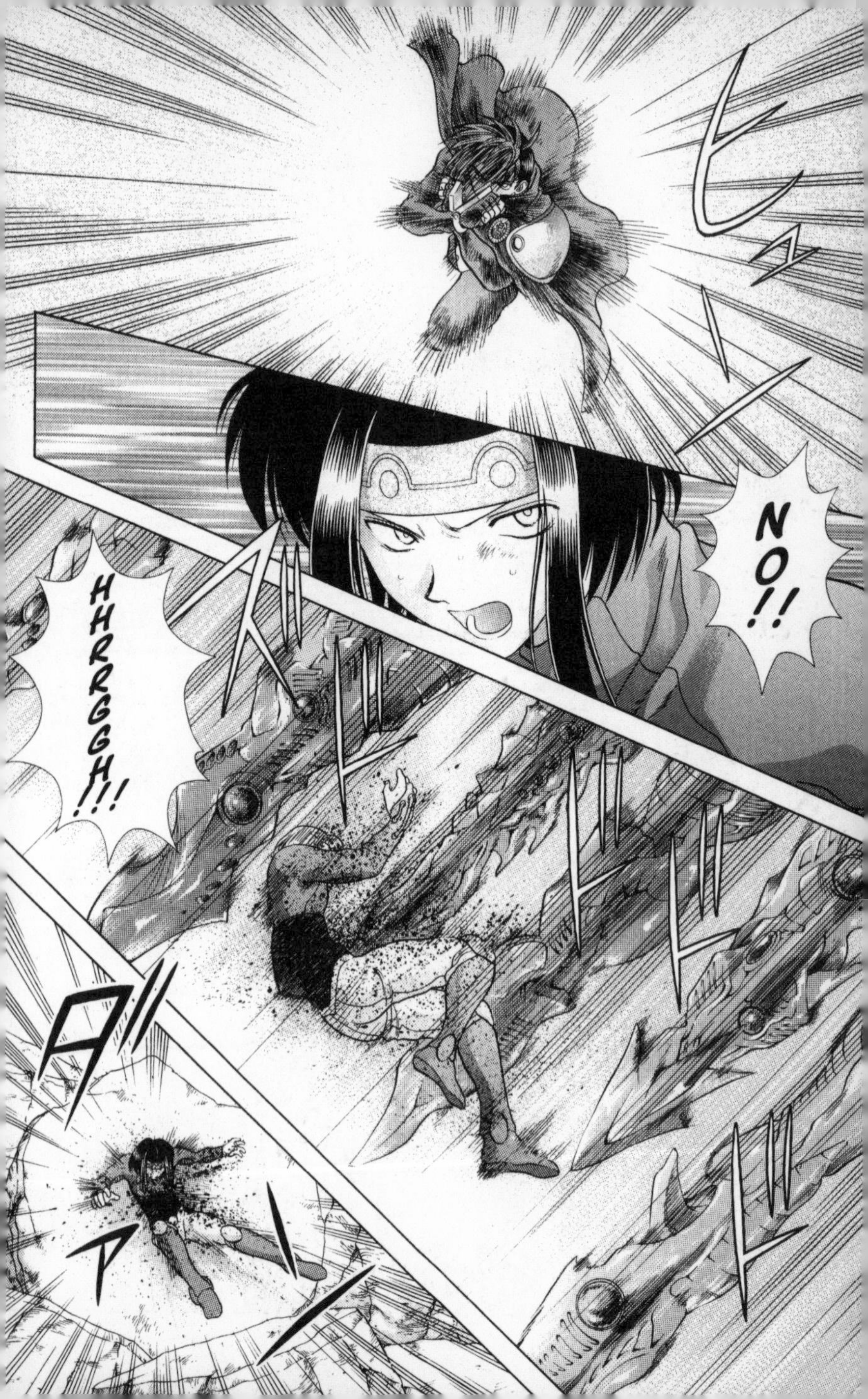
NO!!
HHRRGGH!!!

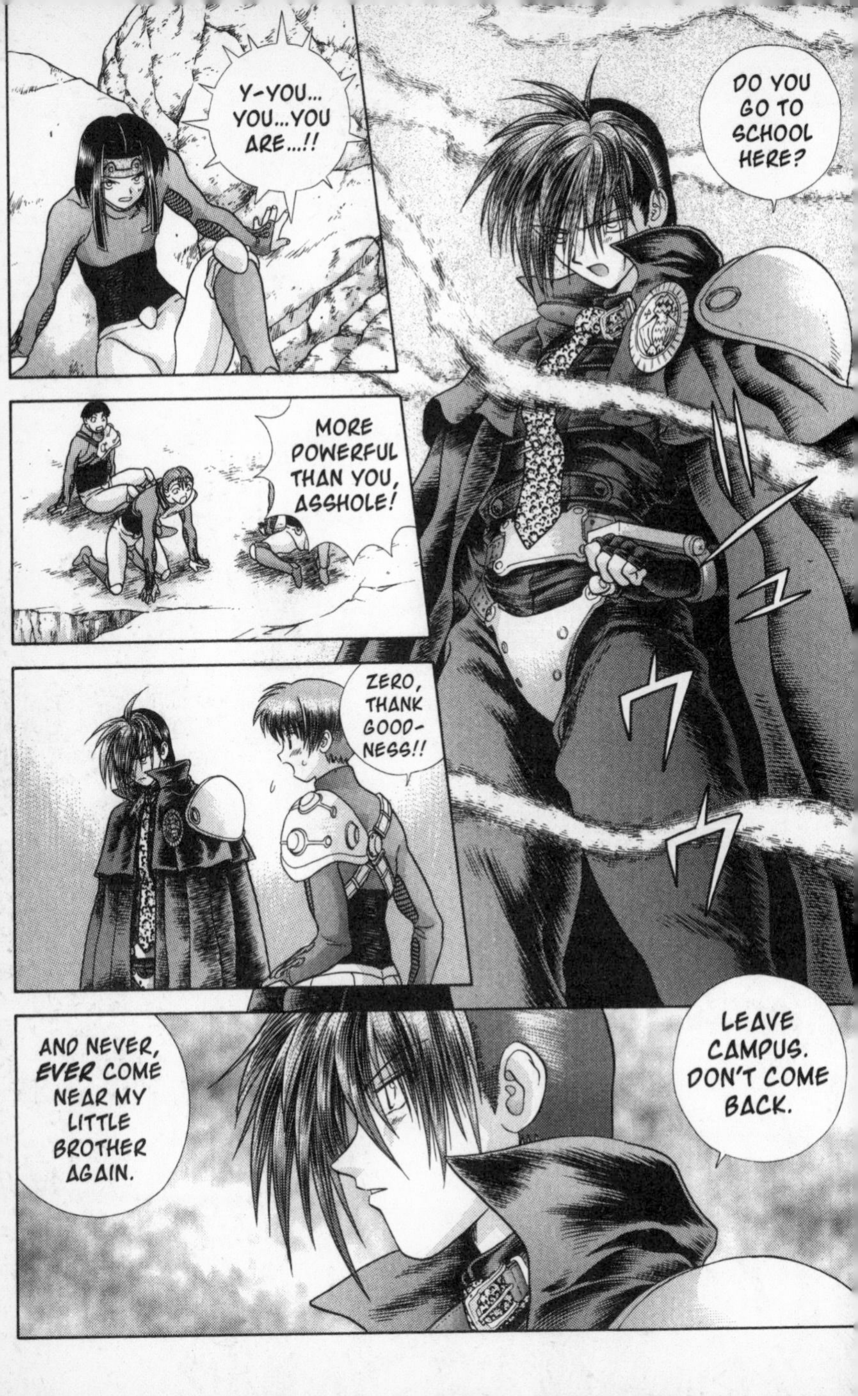
DO YOU GO TO SCHOOL HERE?
Y-YOU... YOU...YOU ARE...!!
MORE POWERFUL THAN YOU, ASSHOLE!
ZERO, THANK GOOD-NESS!!
LEAVE CAMPUS. DON'T COME BACK.
AND NEVER, EVER COME NEAR MY LITTLE BROTHER AGAIN.

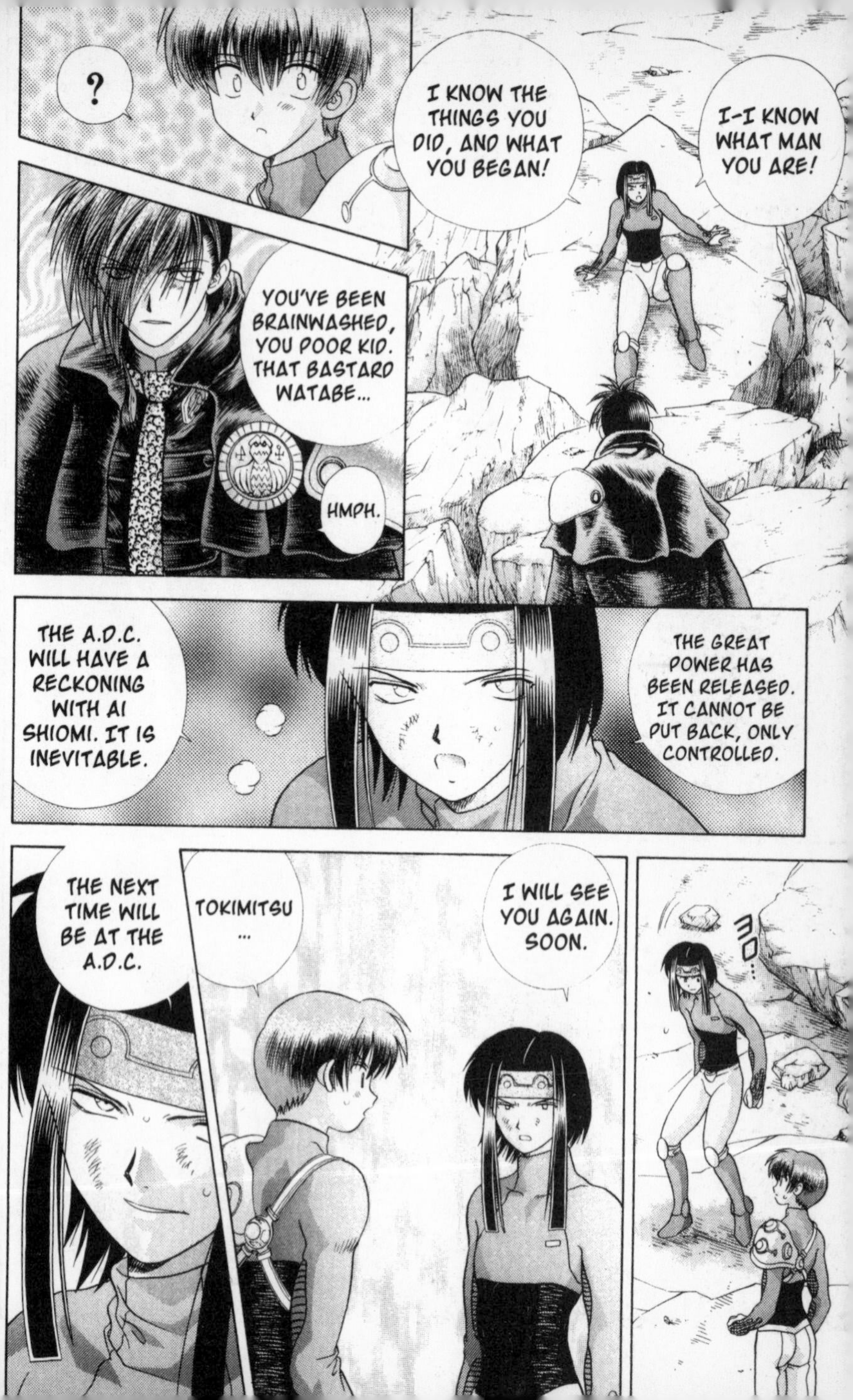

I-I KNOW WHAT MAN YOU ARE!
I KNOW THE THINGS YOU DID, AND WHAT YOU BEGAN!
?
YOU'VE BEEN BRAINWASHED, YOU POOR KID. THAT BASTARD WATABE...
HMPH.
THE GREAT POWER HAS BEEN RELEASED. IT CANNOT BE PUT BACK, ONLY CONTROLLED.
THE A.D.C. WILL HAVE A RECKONING WITH AI SHIOMI. IT IS INEVITABLE.
ヨロ...
I WILL SEE YOU AGAIN. SOON.
TOKIMITSU ...
THE NEXT TIME WILL BE AT THE A.D.C.

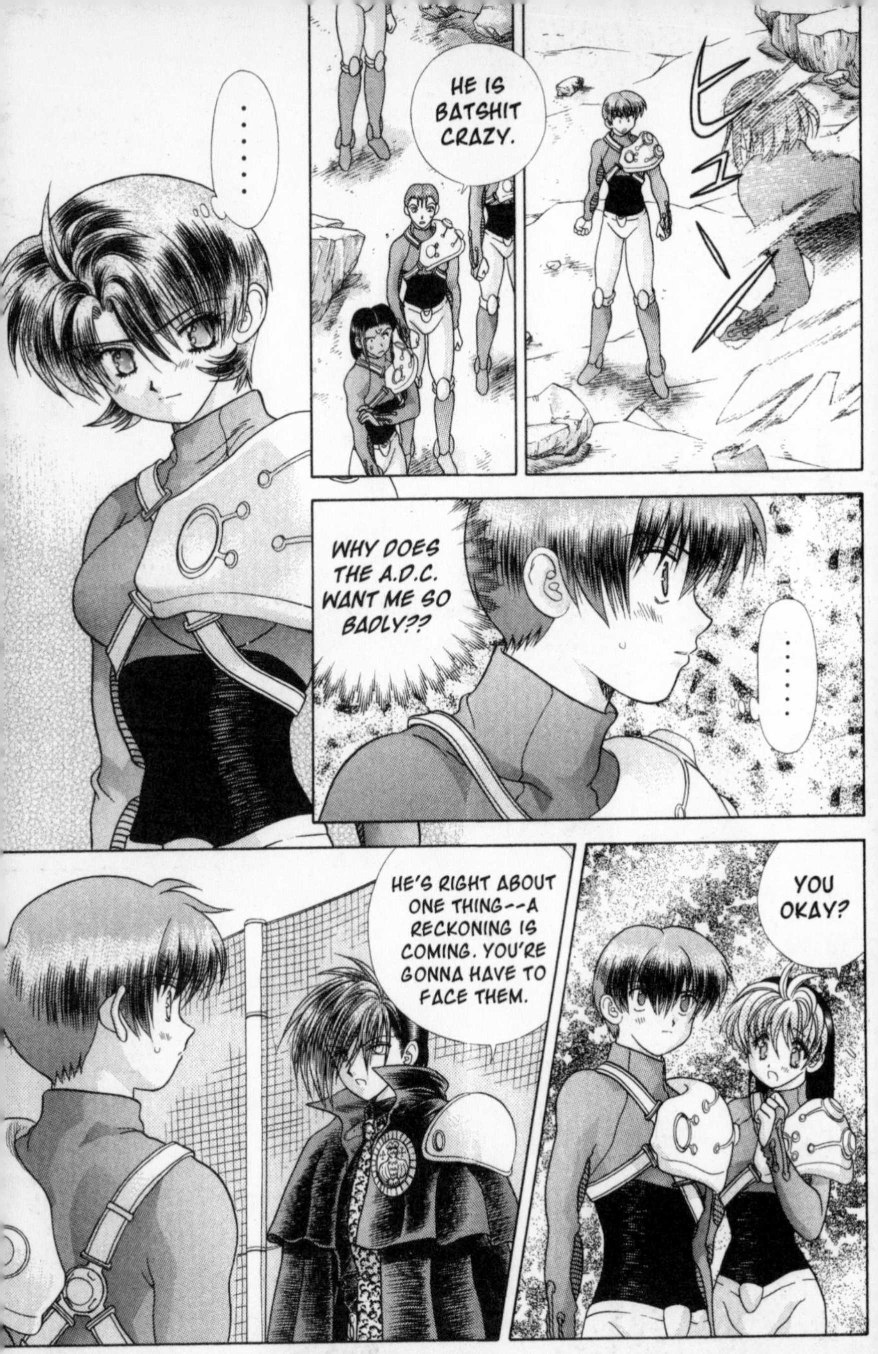
HE IS BATSHIT CRAZY.
......
......
WHY DOES THE A.D.C. WANT ME SO BADLY??
YOU OKAY?
HE'S RIGHT ABOUT ONE THING--A RECKONING IS COMING. YOU'RE GONNA HAVE TO FACE THEM.

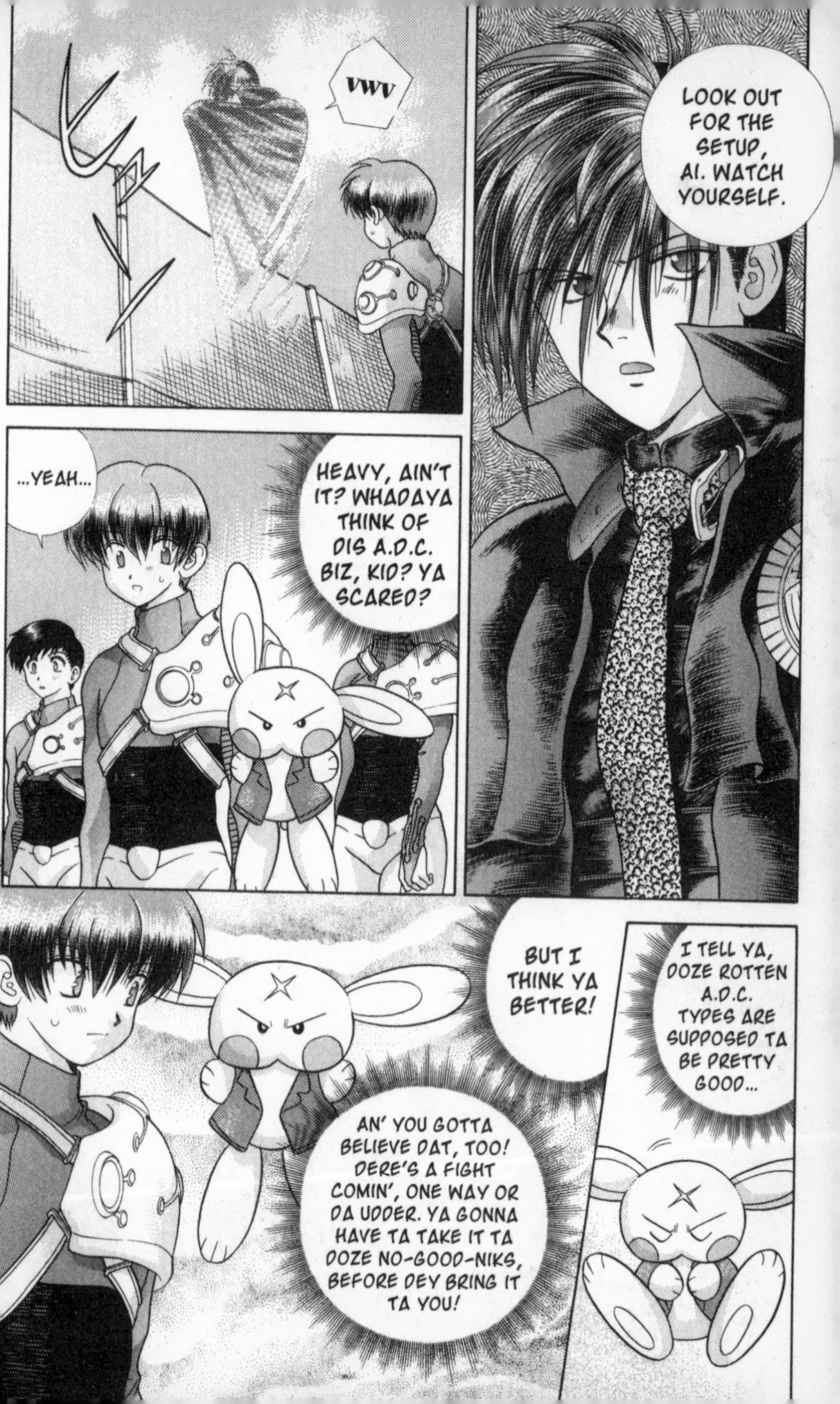
LOOK OUT FOR THE SETUP, AI. WATCH YOURSELF.
VWV
HEAVY, AIN'T IT? WHADAYA THINK OF DIS A.D.C. BIZ, KID? YA SCARED?
...YEAH...
I TELL YA, DOZE ROTTEN A.D.C. TYPES ARE SUPPOSED TA BE PRETTY GOOD...
BUT I THINK YA BETTER!
AN' YOU GOTTA BELIEVE DAT, TOO! DERE'S A FIGHT COMIN', ONE WAY OR DA UDDER. YA GONNA HAVE TA TAKE IT TA DOZE NO-GOOD-NIKS, BEFORE DEY BRING IT TA YOU!

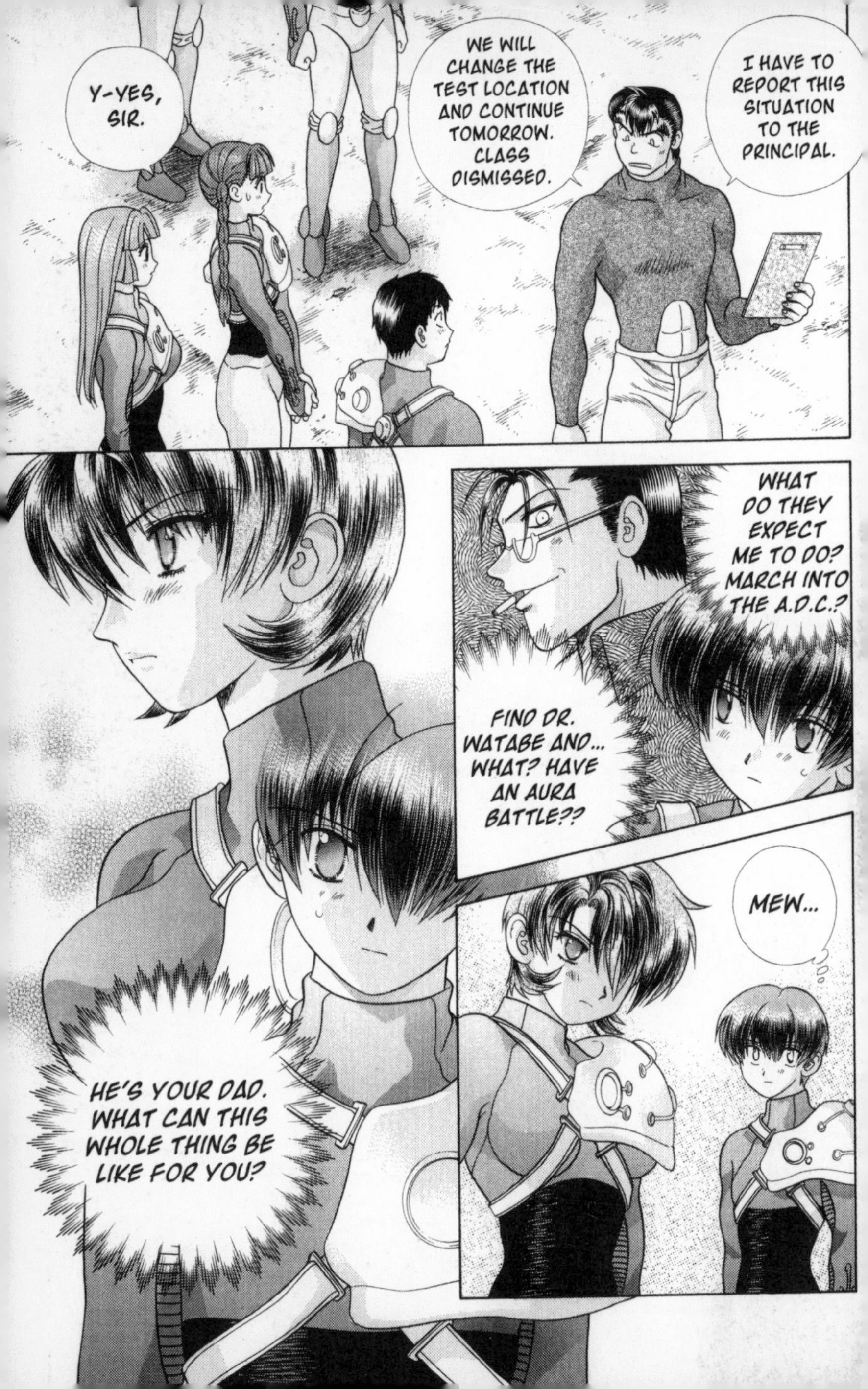
I HAVE TO REPORT THIS SITUATION TO THE PRINCIPAL.
WE WILL CHANGE THE TEST LOCATION AND CONTINUE TOMORROW. CLASS DISMISSED.
Y-YES, SIR.
WHAT DO THEY EXPECT ME TO DO? MARCH INTO THE A.D.C.?
FIND DR. WATABE AND... WHAT? HAVE AN AURA BATTLE??
MEW...
HE'S YOUR DAD. WHAT CAN THIS WHOLE THING BE LIKE FOR YOU?

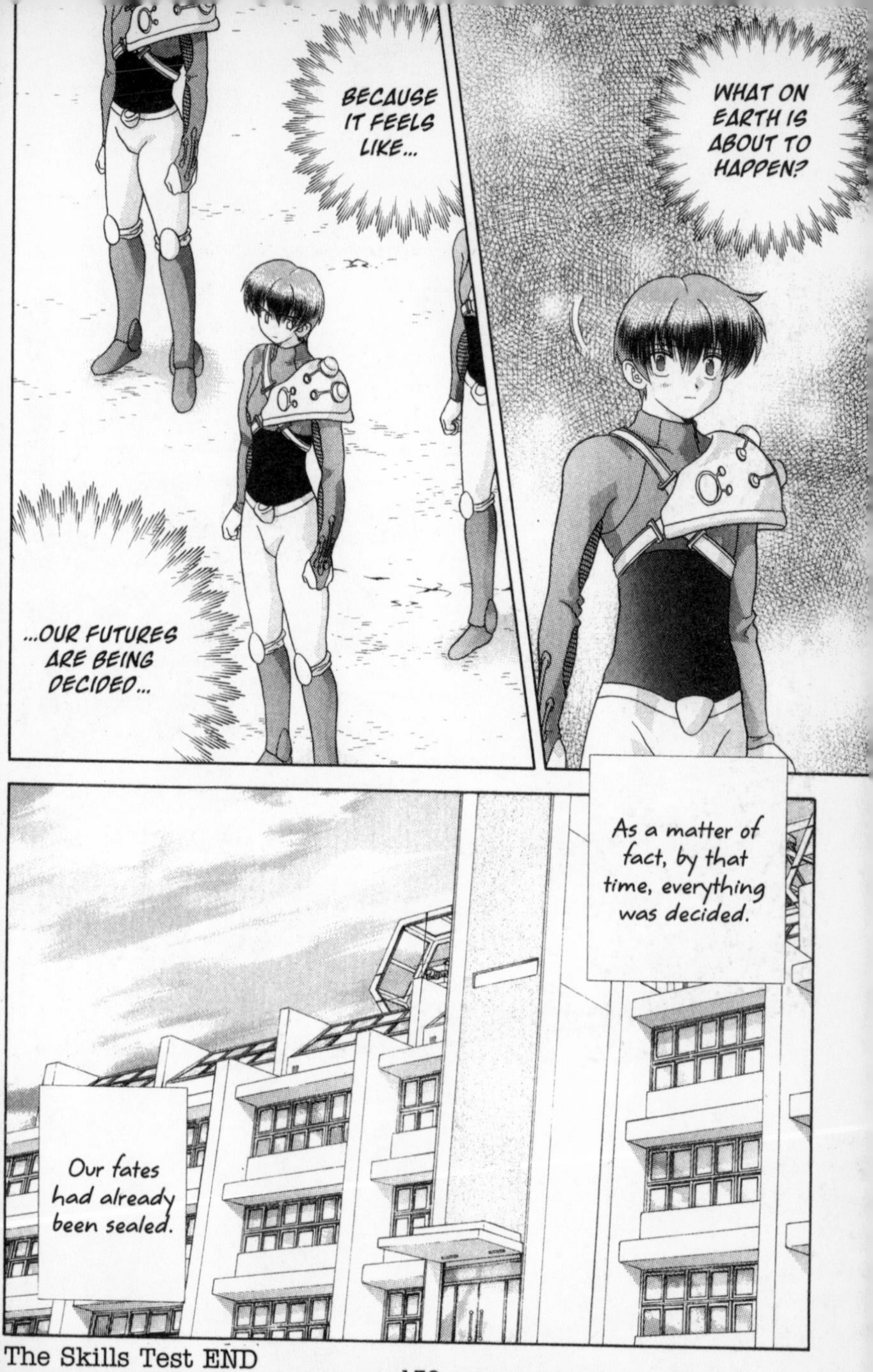
WHAT ON EARTH IS ABOUT TO HAPPEN?
BECAUSE IT FEELS LIKE...
...OUR FUTURES ARE BEING DECIDED...
As a matter of fact, by that time, everything was decided.
Our fates had already been sealed.

The Skills Test END

Chapter 31: Mystery Punch II

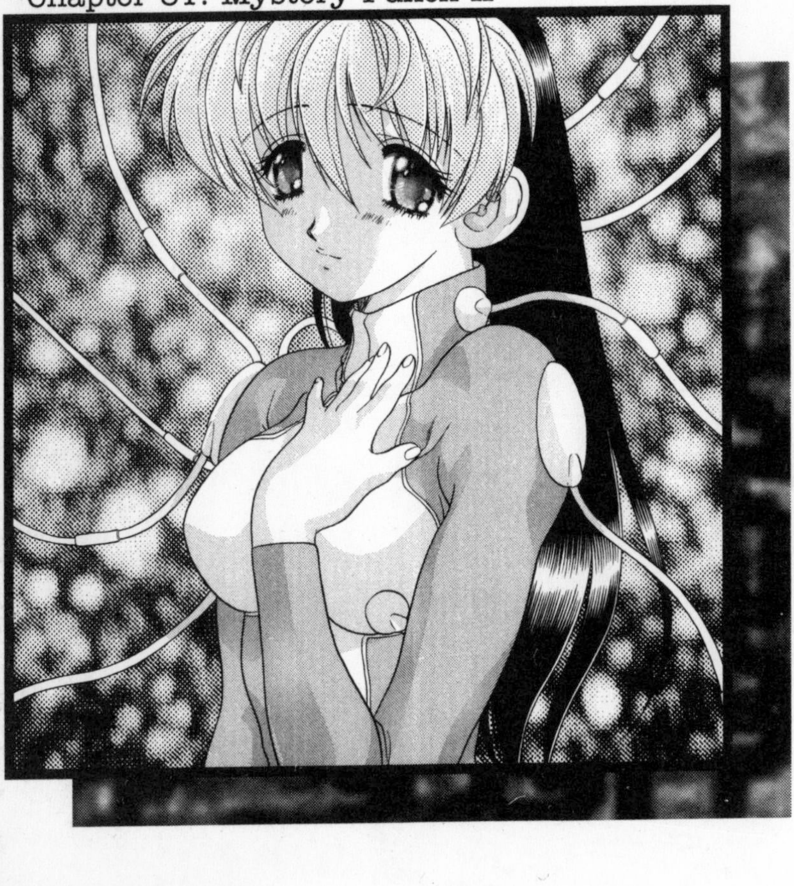

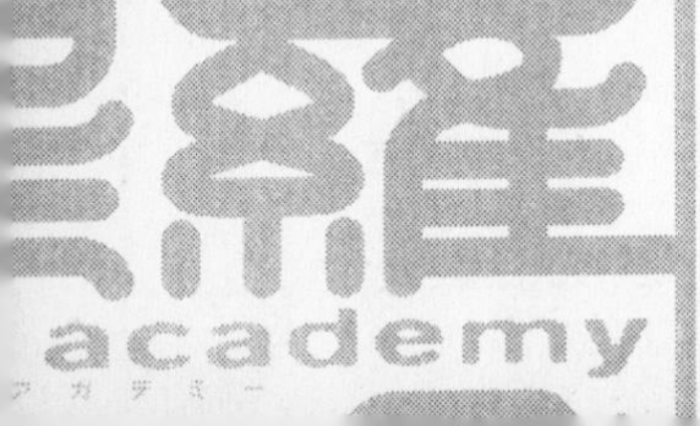
academy

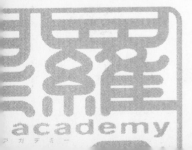

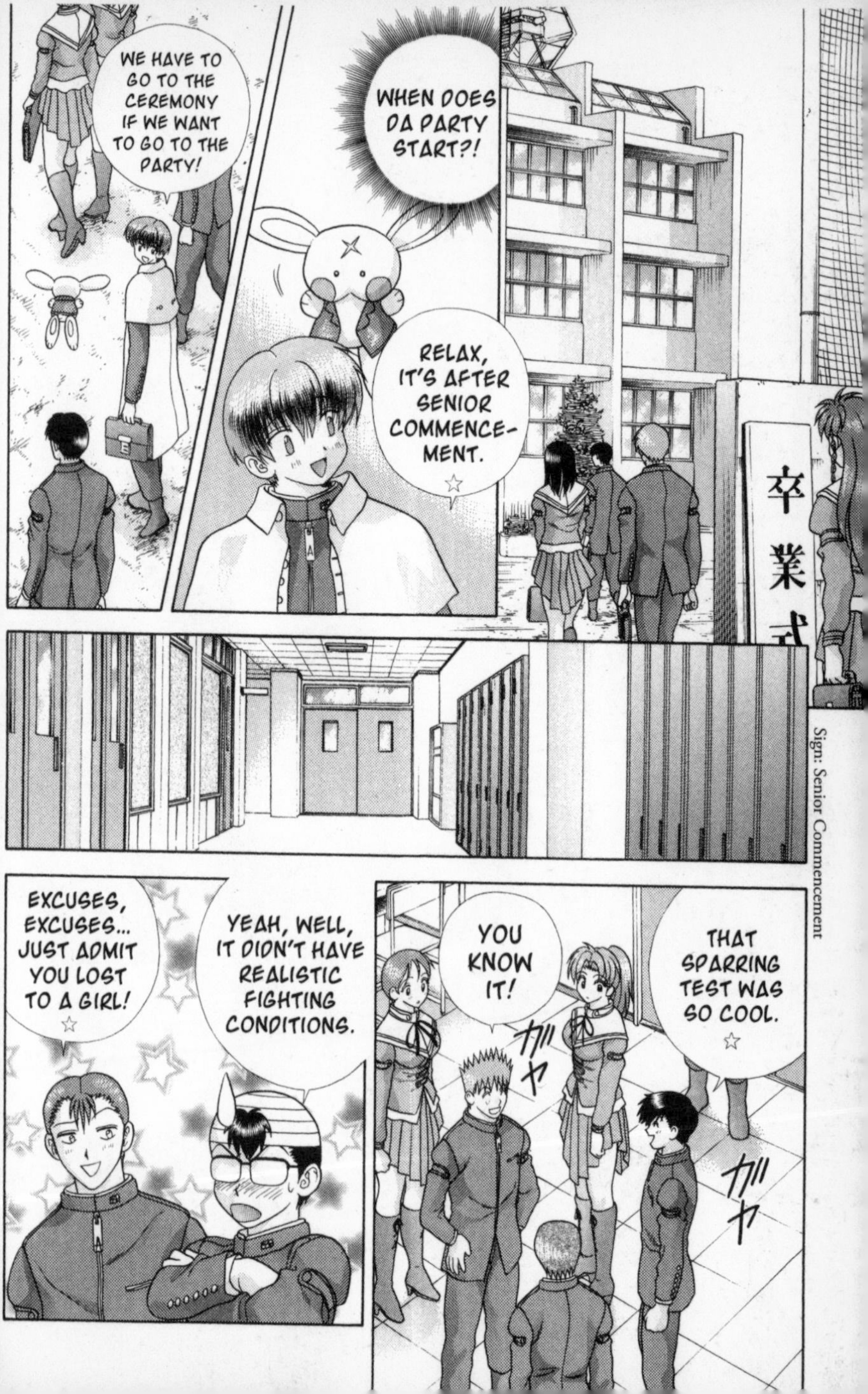

卒業式
WHEN DOES DA PARTY START?!
RELAX, IT'S AFTER SENIOR COMMENCE-MENT. ☆
WE HAVE TO GO TO THE CEREMONY IF WE WANT TO GO TO THE PARTY!
THAT SPARRING TEST WAS SO COOL. ☆
YOU KNOW IT!
ガヤ
ガヤ
YEAH, WELL, IT DIDN'T HAVE REALISTIC FIGHTING CONDITIONS.
EXCUSES, EXCUSES... JUST ADMIT YOU LOST TO A GIRL! ☆

Sign: Senior Commencement

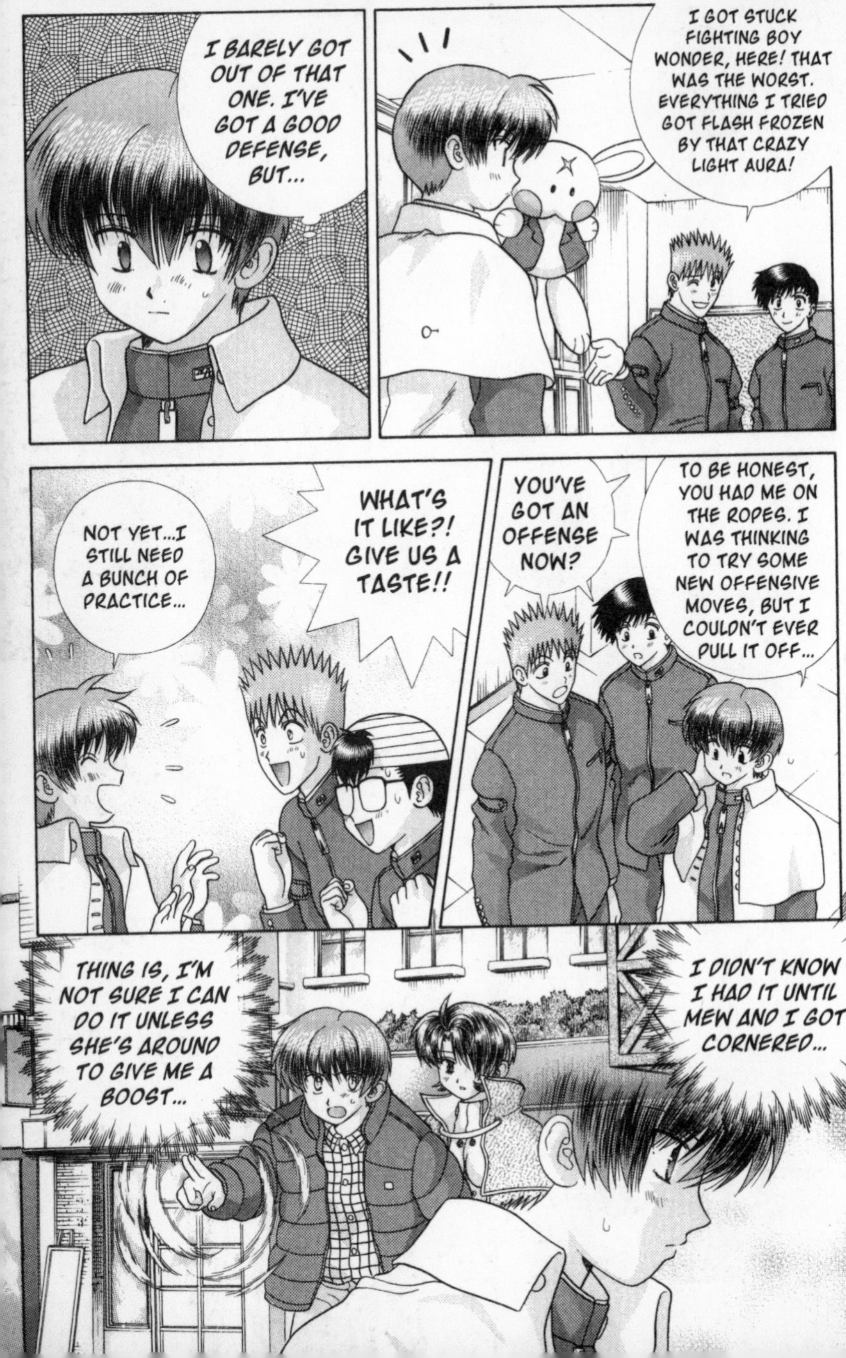
I BARELY GOT OUT OF THAT ONE. I'VE GOT A GOOD DEFENSE, BUT...
I GOT STUCK FIGHTING BOY WONDER, HERE! THAT WAS THE WORST. EVERYTHING I TRIED GOT FLASH FROZEN BY THAT CRAZY LIGHT AURA!
TO BE HONEST, YOU HAD ME ON THE ROPES. I WAS THINKING TO TRY SOME NEW OFFENSIVE MOVES, BUT I COULDN'T EVER PULL IT OFF...
YOU'VE GOT AN OFFENSE NOW?
WHAT'S IT LIKE?! GIVE US A TASTE!!
NOT YET...I STILL NEED A BUNCH OF PRACTICE...
I DIDN'T KNOW I HAD IT UNTIL MEW AND I GOT CORNERED...
THING IS, I'M NOT SURE I CAN DO IT UNLESS SHE'S AROUND TO GIVE ME A BOOST...

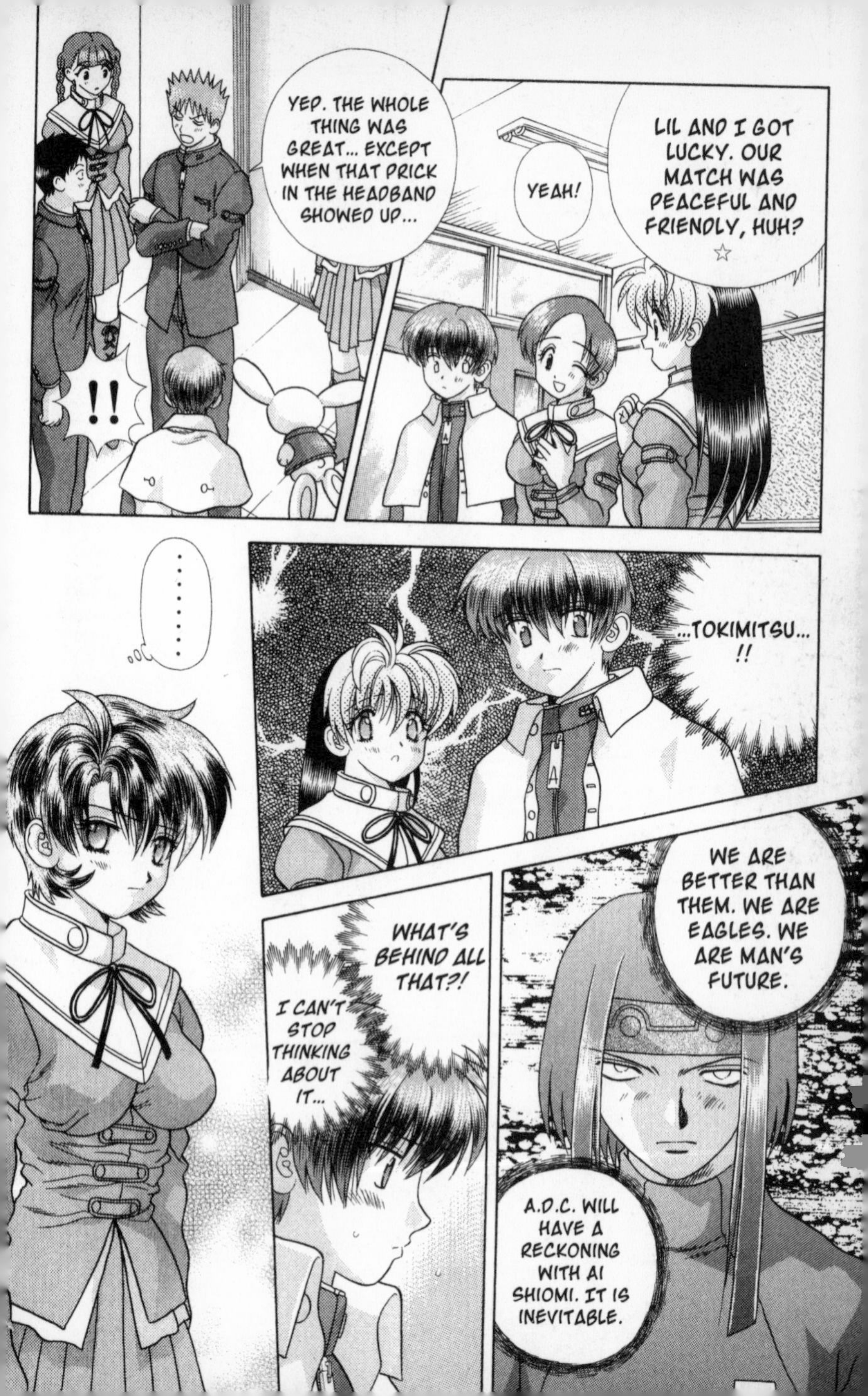
LIL AND I GOT LUCKY. OUR MATCH WAS PEACEFUL AND FRIENDLY, HUH? ☆
YEAH!
YEP. THE WHOLE THING WAS GREAT... EXCEPT WHEN THAT PRICK IN THE HEADBAND SHOWED UP...
!!
...TOKIMITSU... !!
....
WE ARE BETTER THAN THEM. WE ARE EAGLES. WE ARE MAN'S FUTURE.
A.D.C. WILL HAVE A RECKONING WITH AI SHIOMI. IT IS INEVITABLE.
WHAT'S BEHIND ALL THAT?!
I CAN'T STOP THINKING ABOUT IT...

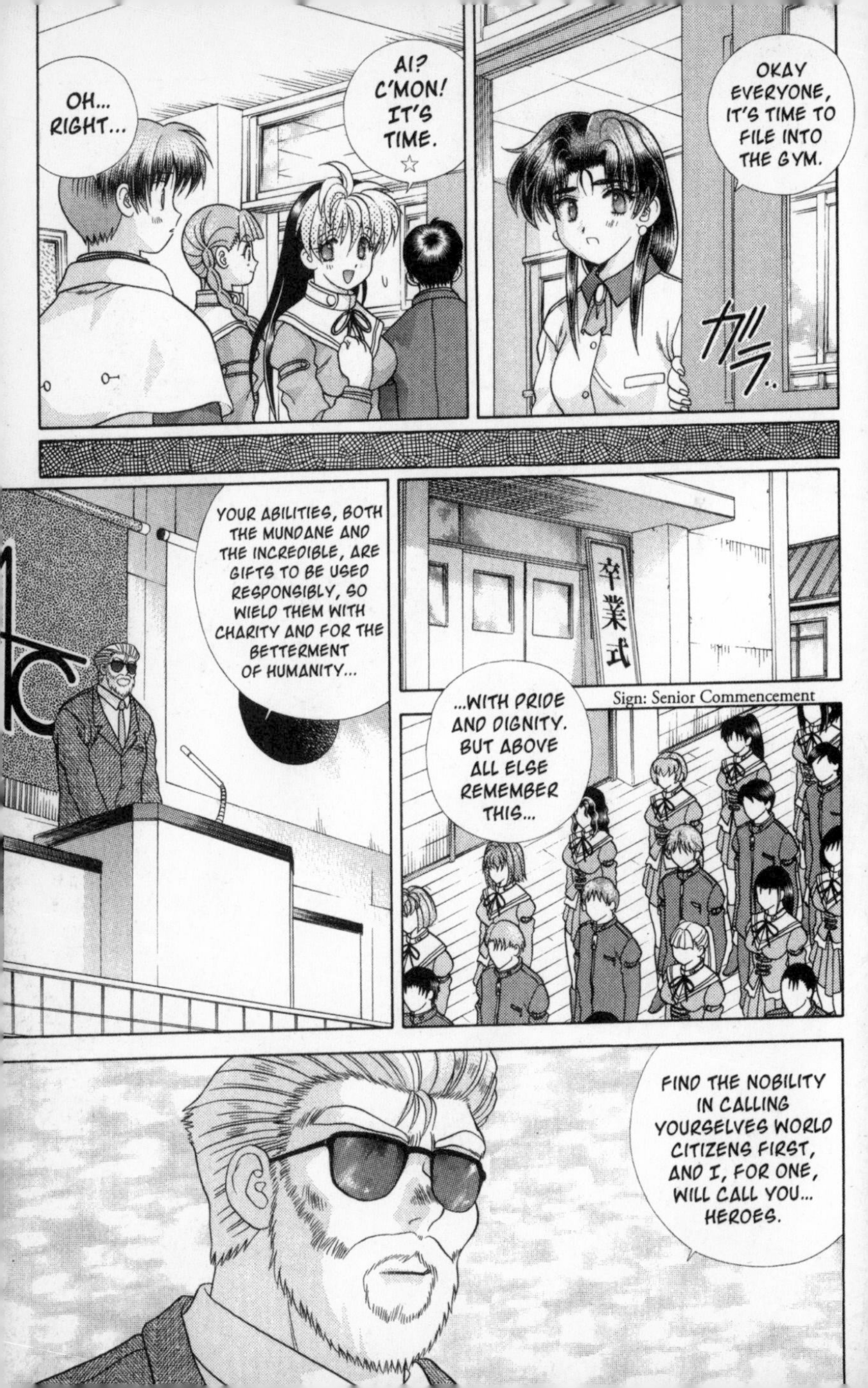
OKAY EVERYONE, IT'S TIME TO FILE INTO THE GYM.
ガラ..
AI? C'MON! IT'S TIME. ☆
OH... RIGHT...
卒業式
Sign: Senior Commencement
YOUR ABILITIES, BOTH THE MUNDANE AND THE INCREDIBLE, ARE GIFTS TO BE USED RESPONSIBLY, SO WIELD THEM WITH CHARITY AND FOR THE BETTERMENT OF HUMANITY...
...WITH PRIDE AND DIGNITY. BUT ABOVE ALL ELSE REMEMBER THIS...
FIND THE NOBILITY IN CALLING YOURSELVES WORLD CITIZENS FIRST, AND I, FOR ONE, WILL CALL YOU... HEROES.

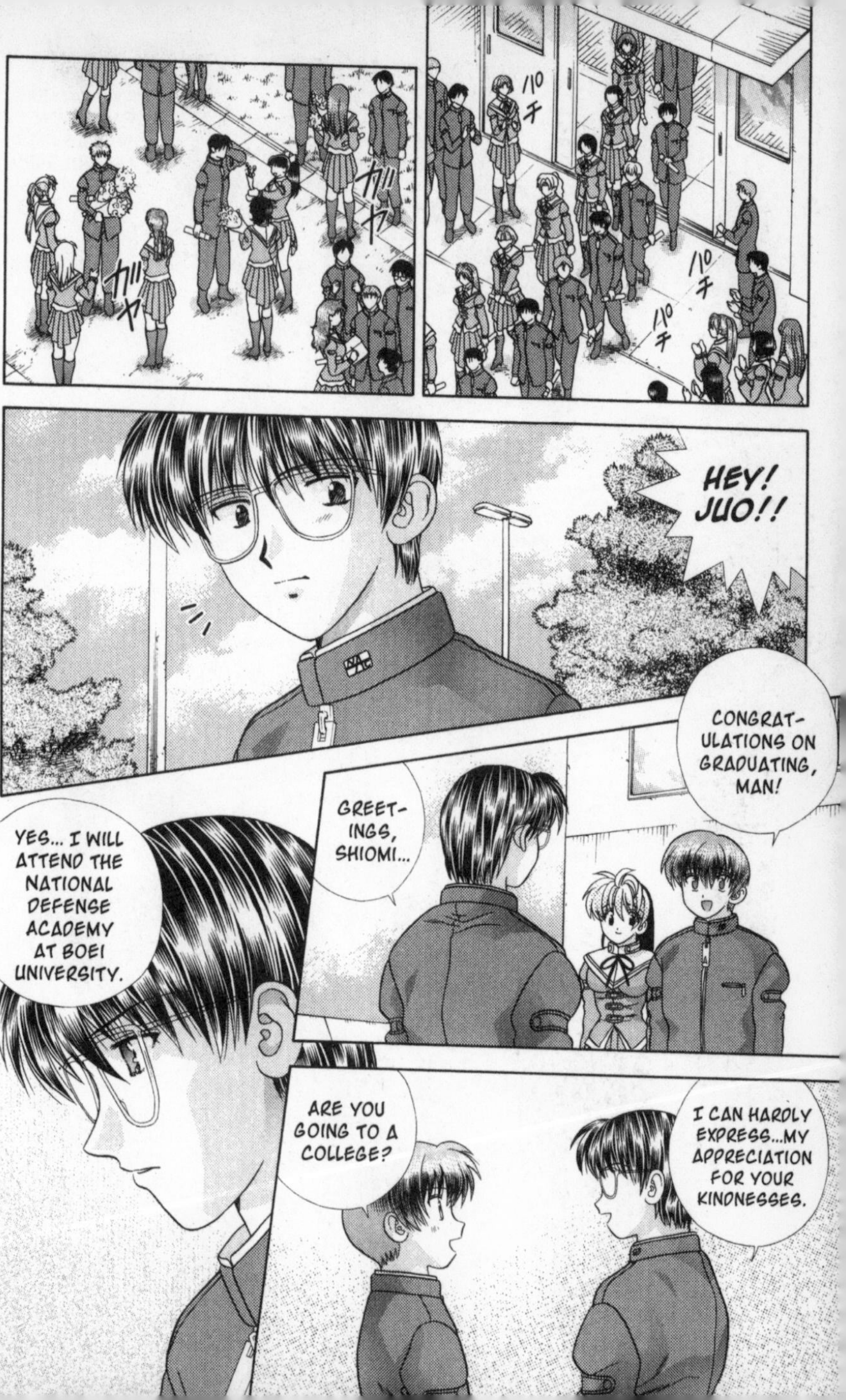
パチ
パチ
パチ
ガヤ
ガヤ
HEY! JUO!!
CONGRAT-ULATIONS ON GRADUATING, MAN!
GREET-INGS, SHIOMI...
I CAN HARDLY EXPRESS...MY APPRECIATION FOR YOUR KINDNESSES.
ARE YOU GOING TO A COLLEGE?
YES... I WILL ATTEND THE NATIONAL DEFENSE ACADEMY AT BOEI UNIVERSITY.

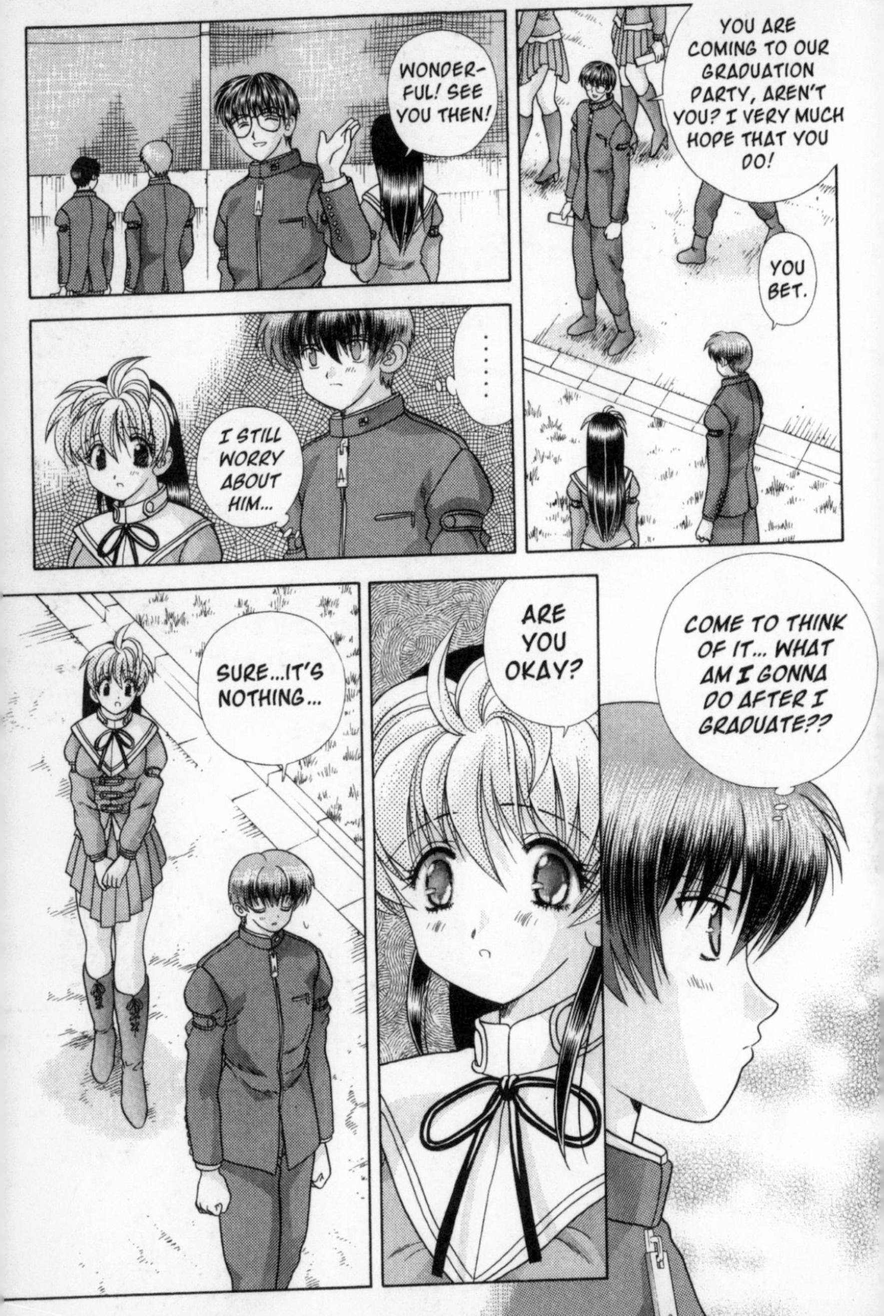
YOU ARE COMING TO OUR GRADUATION PARTY, AREN'T YOU? I VERY MUCH HOPE THAT YOU DO!
YOU BET.
WONDER-FUL! SEE YOU THEN!
......
I STILL WORRY ABOUT HIM...
COME TO THINK OF IT... WHAT AM I GONNA DO AFTER I GRADUATE??
ARE YOU OKAY?
SURE...IT'S NOTHING...

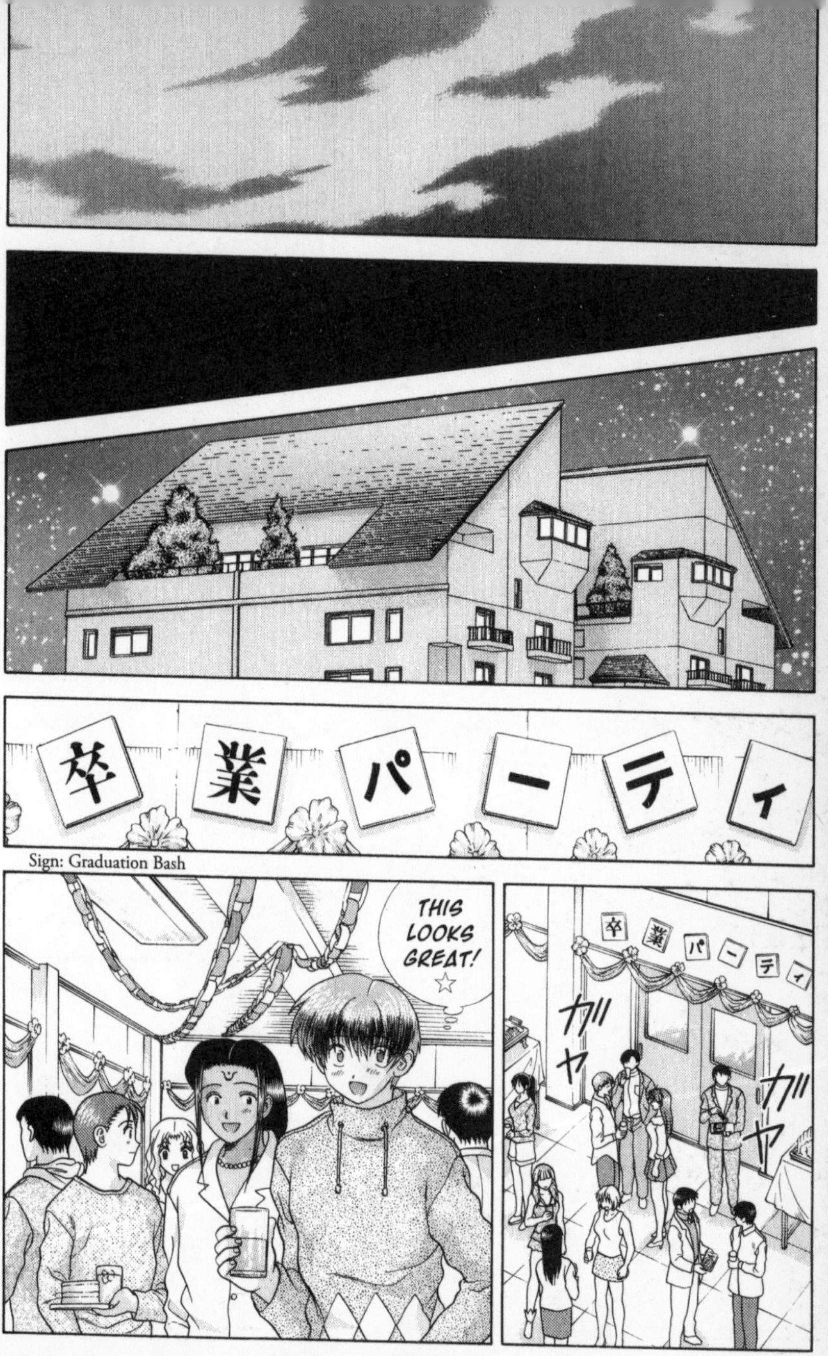
卒業パーティ
THIS LOOKS GREAT! ☆
ガヤ
ガヤ
卒業パーティ
Sign: Graduation Bash

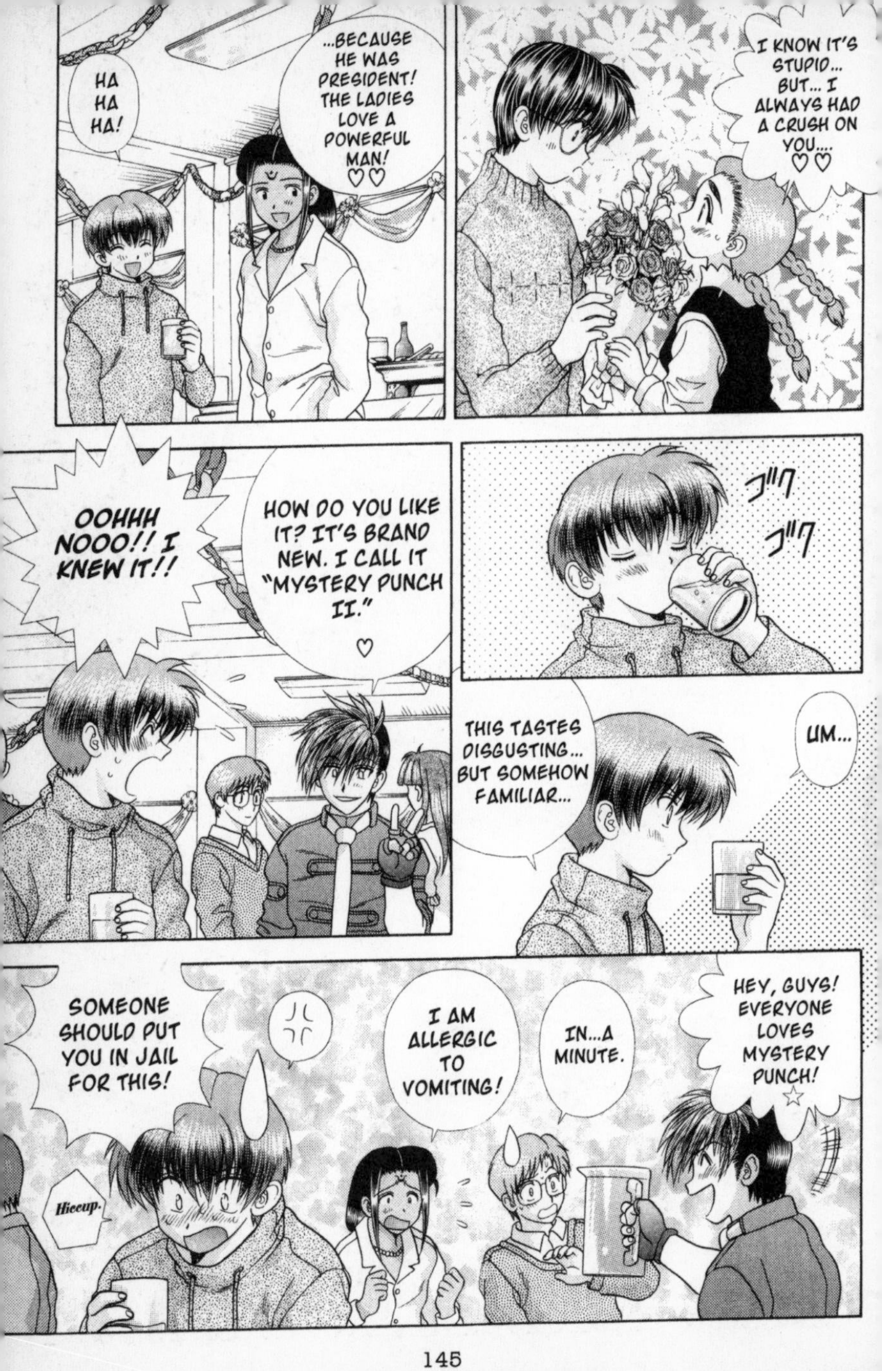
I KNOW IT'S STUPID... BUT... I ALWAYS HAD A CRUSH ON YOU.... ♡♡
...BECAUSE HE WAS PRESIDENT! THE LADIES LOVE A POWERFUL MAN! ♡♡
HA HA HA!
ゴク
ゴク
UM...
THIS TASTES DISGUSTING... BUT SOMEHOW FAMILIAR...
HOW DO YOU LIKE IT? IT'S BRAND NEW. I CALL IT "MYSTERY PUNCH II." ♡
OOHHH NOOO!! I KNEW IT!!
HEY, GUYS! EVERYONE LOVES MYSTERY PUNCH! ☆
IN...A MINUTE.
I AM ALLERGIC TO VOMITING!
SOMEONE SHOULD PUT YOU IN JAIL FOR THIS!
Hiccup.

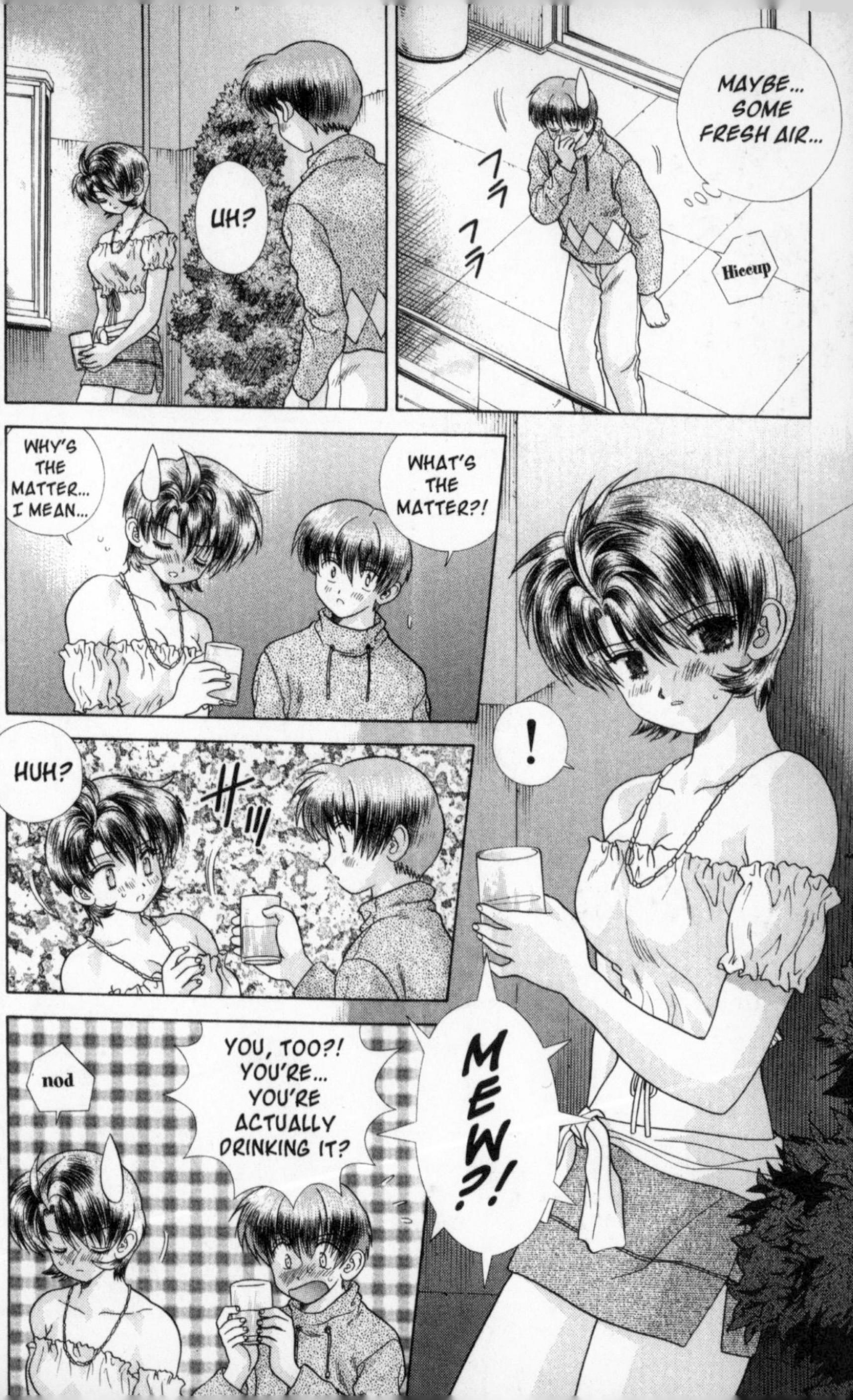
MAYBE... SOME FRESH AIR...
フラ
フラ
Hiccup
UH?
!
MEW?!
WHAT'S THE MATTER?!
WHY'S THE MATTER... I MEAN...
HUH?
YOU, TOO?! YOU'RE... YOU'RE ACTUALLY DRINKING IT?
nod

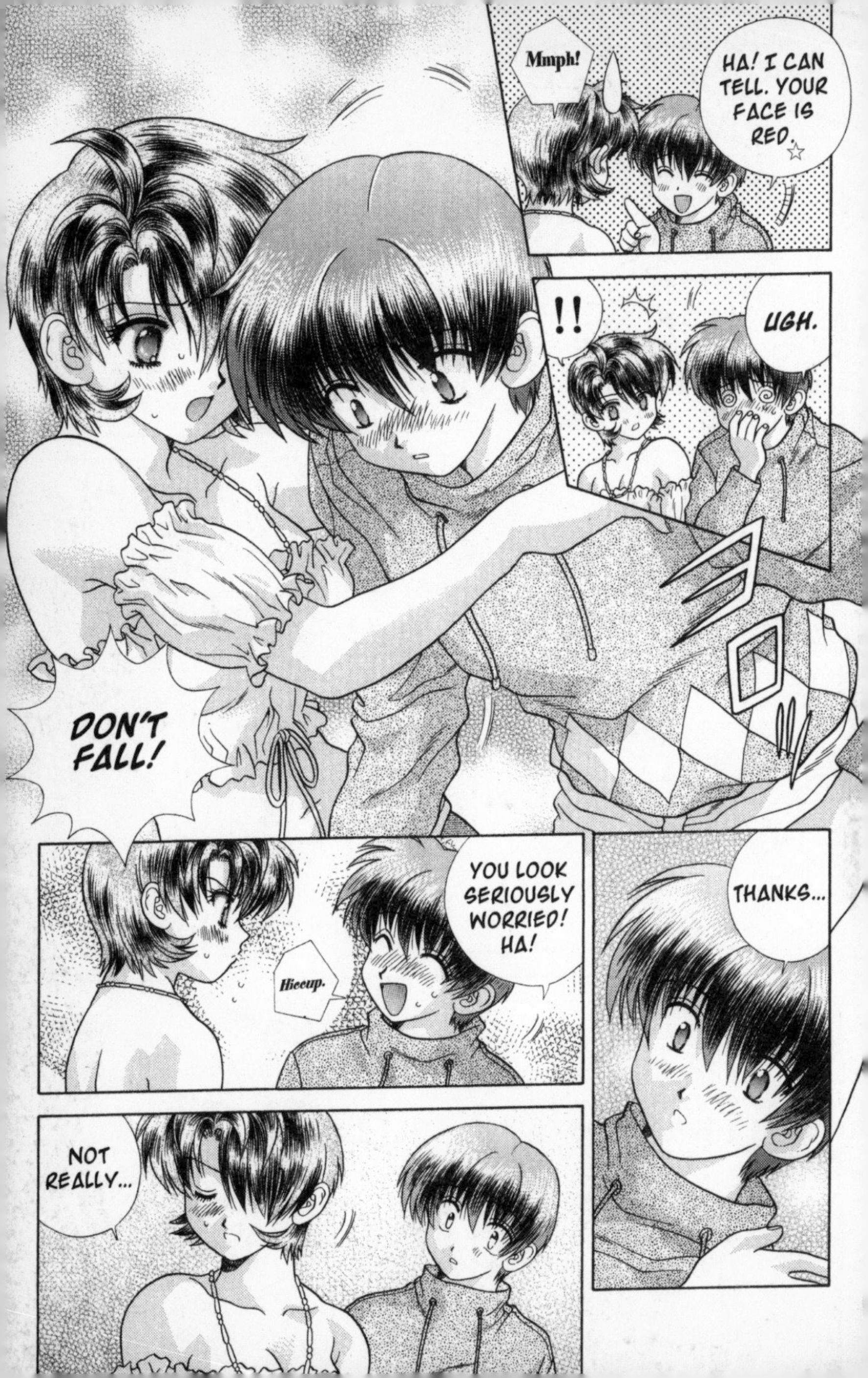
HA! I CAN TELL. YOUR FACE IS RED. ☆
Mmph!
UGH.
!!
DON'T FALL!
THANKS...
YOU LOOK SERIOUSLY WORRIED! HA!
Hiccup.
NOT REALLY...

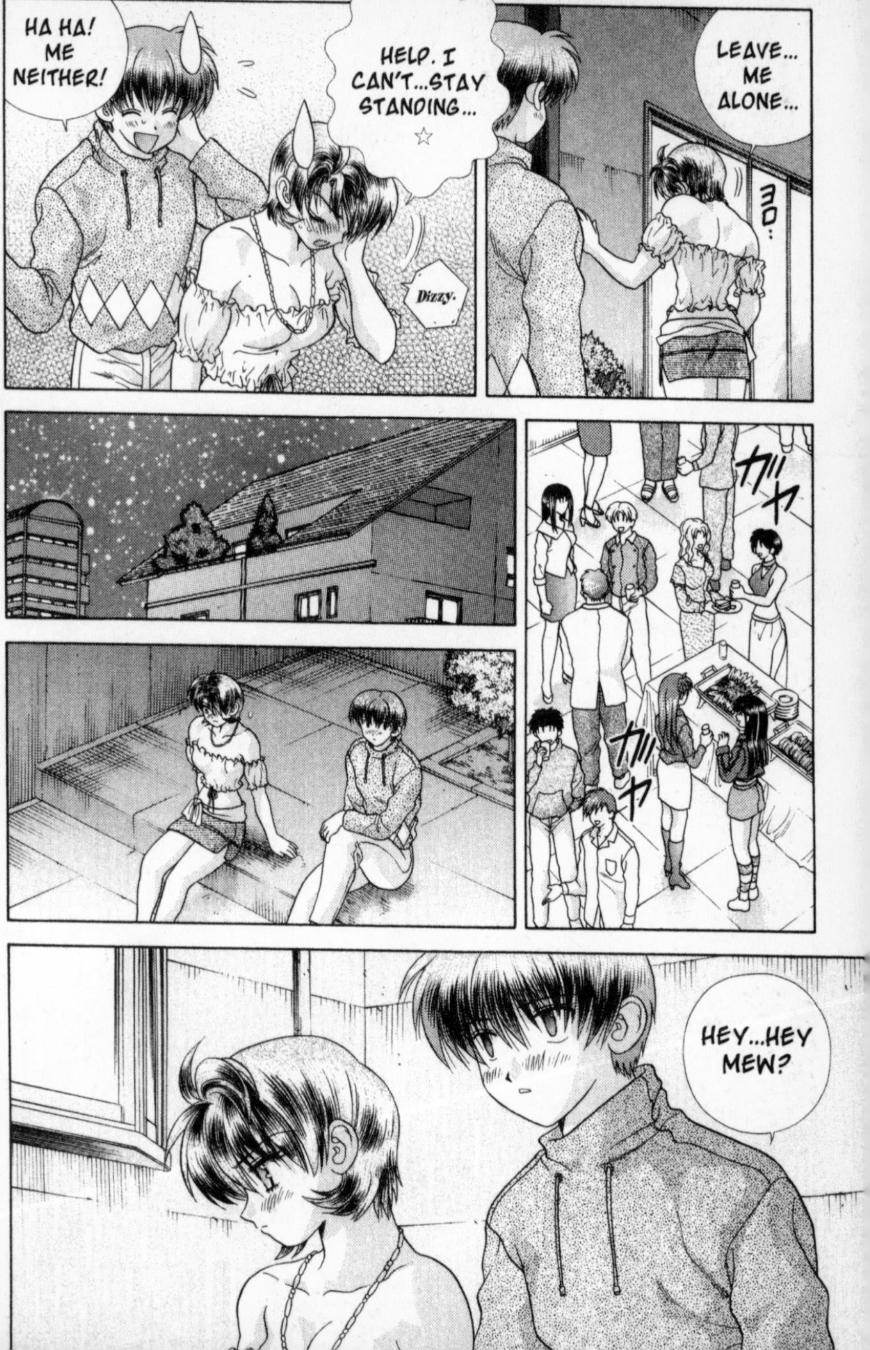
LEAVE... ME ALONE...
ヨロ...
HELP. I CAN'T...STAY STANDING... ☆
Dizzy.
HA HA! ME NEITHER!
ガヤ
ガヤ
HEY...HEY MEW?

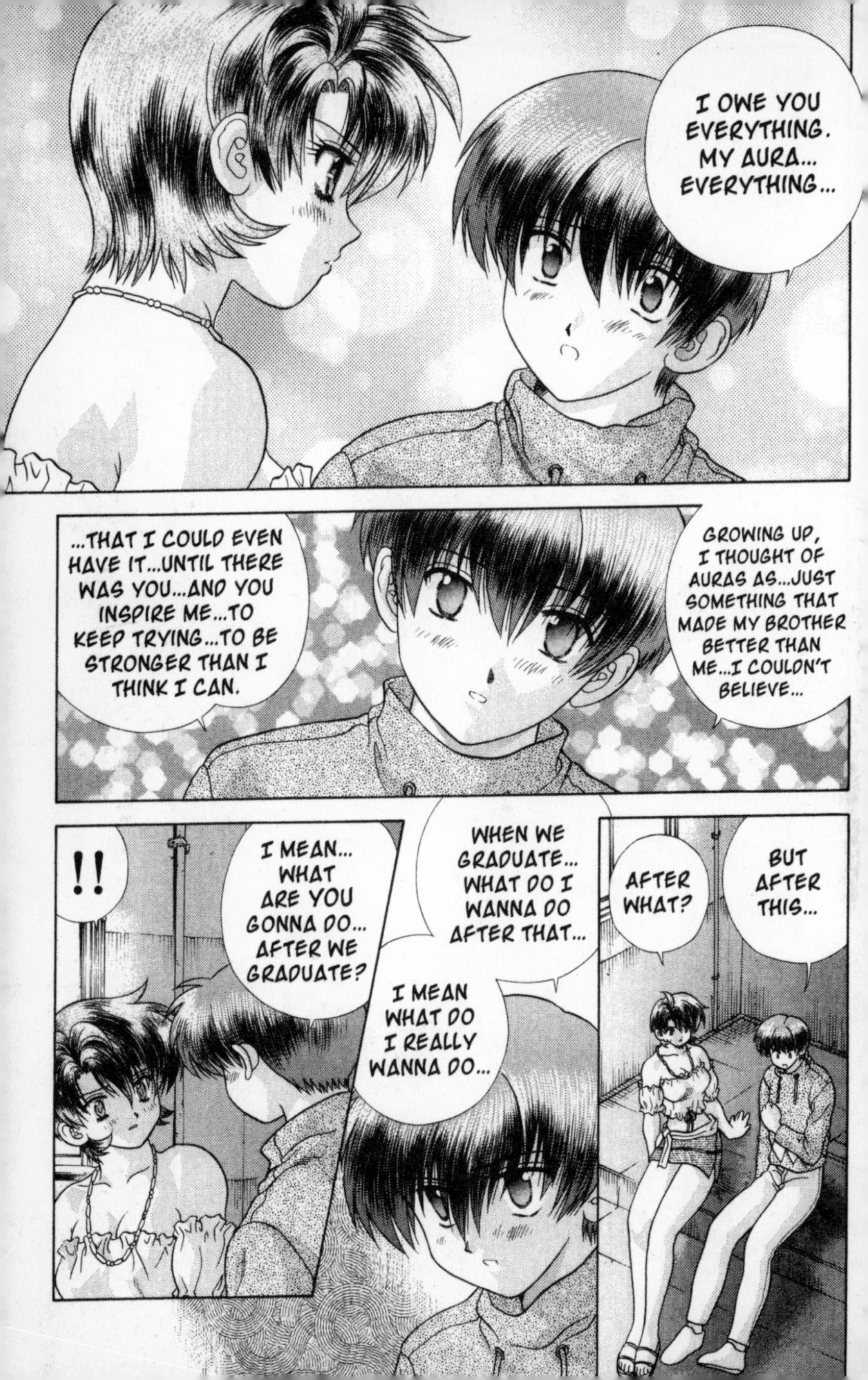
I OWE YOU EVERYTHING. MY AURA... EVERYTHING...
GROWING UP, I THOUGHT OF AURAS AS...JUST SOMETHING THAT MADE MY BROTHER BETTER THAN ME...I COULDN'T BELIEVE...
...THAT I COULD EVEN HAVE IT...UNTIL THERE WAS YOU...AND YOU INSPIRE ME...TO KEEP TRYING...TO BE STRONGER THAN I THINK I CAN.
BUT AFTER THIS...
AFTER WHAT?
WHEN WE GRADUATE... WHAT DO I WANNA DO AFTER THAT...
I MEAN WHAT DO I REALLY WANNA DO...
I MEAN... WHAT ARE YOU GONNA DO... AFTER WE GRADUATE?
!!

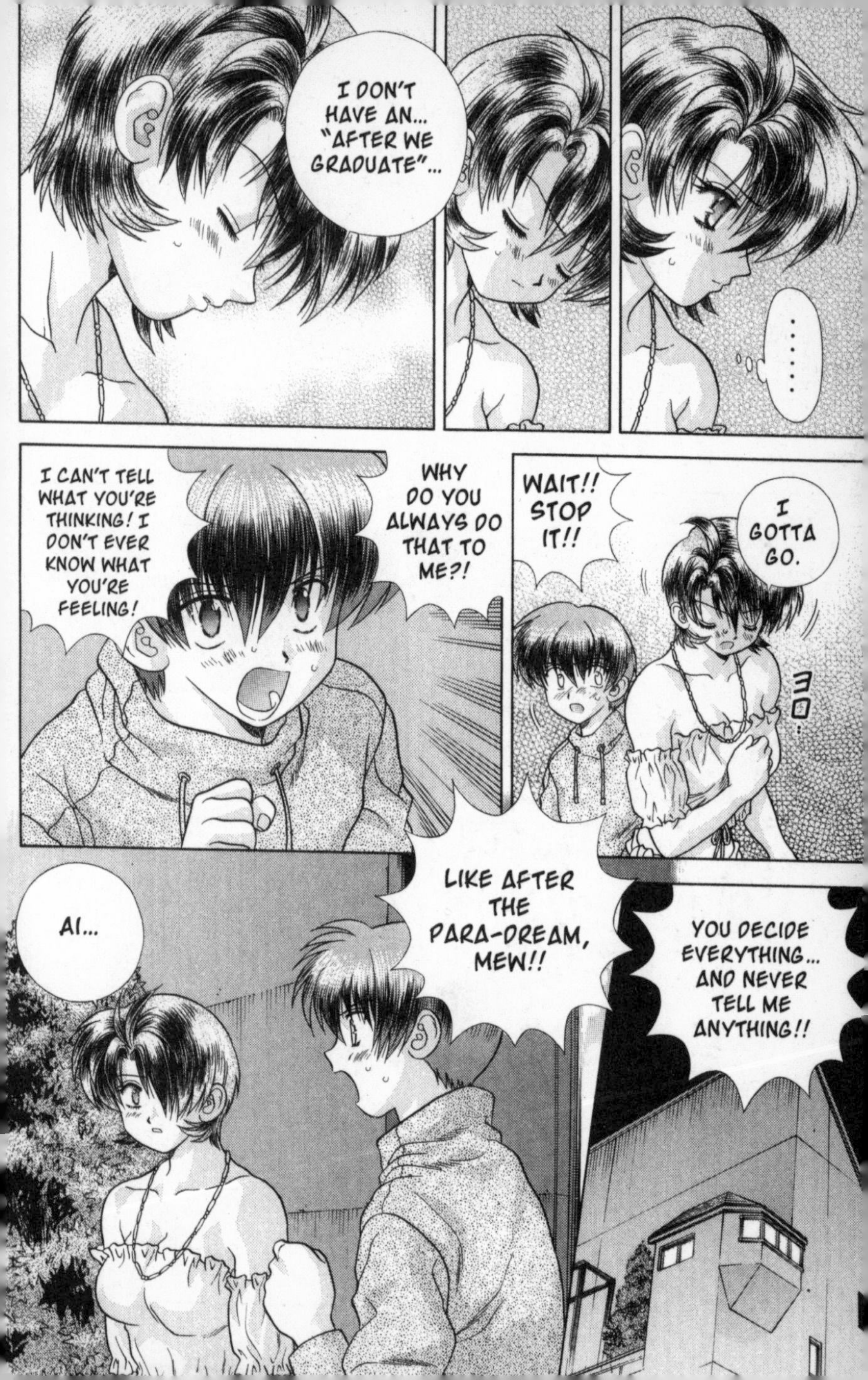
......
I DON'T HAVE AN... "AFTER WE GRADUATE"...
I GOTTA GO.
WAIT!! STOP IT!!
WHY DO YOU ALWAYS DO THAT TO ME?!
I CAN'T TELL WHAT YOU'RE THINKING! I DON'T EVER KNOW WHAT YOU'RE FEELING!
YOU DECIDE EVERYTHING... AND NEVER TELL ME ANYTHING!!
LIKE AFTER THE PARA-DREAM, MEW!!
AI...

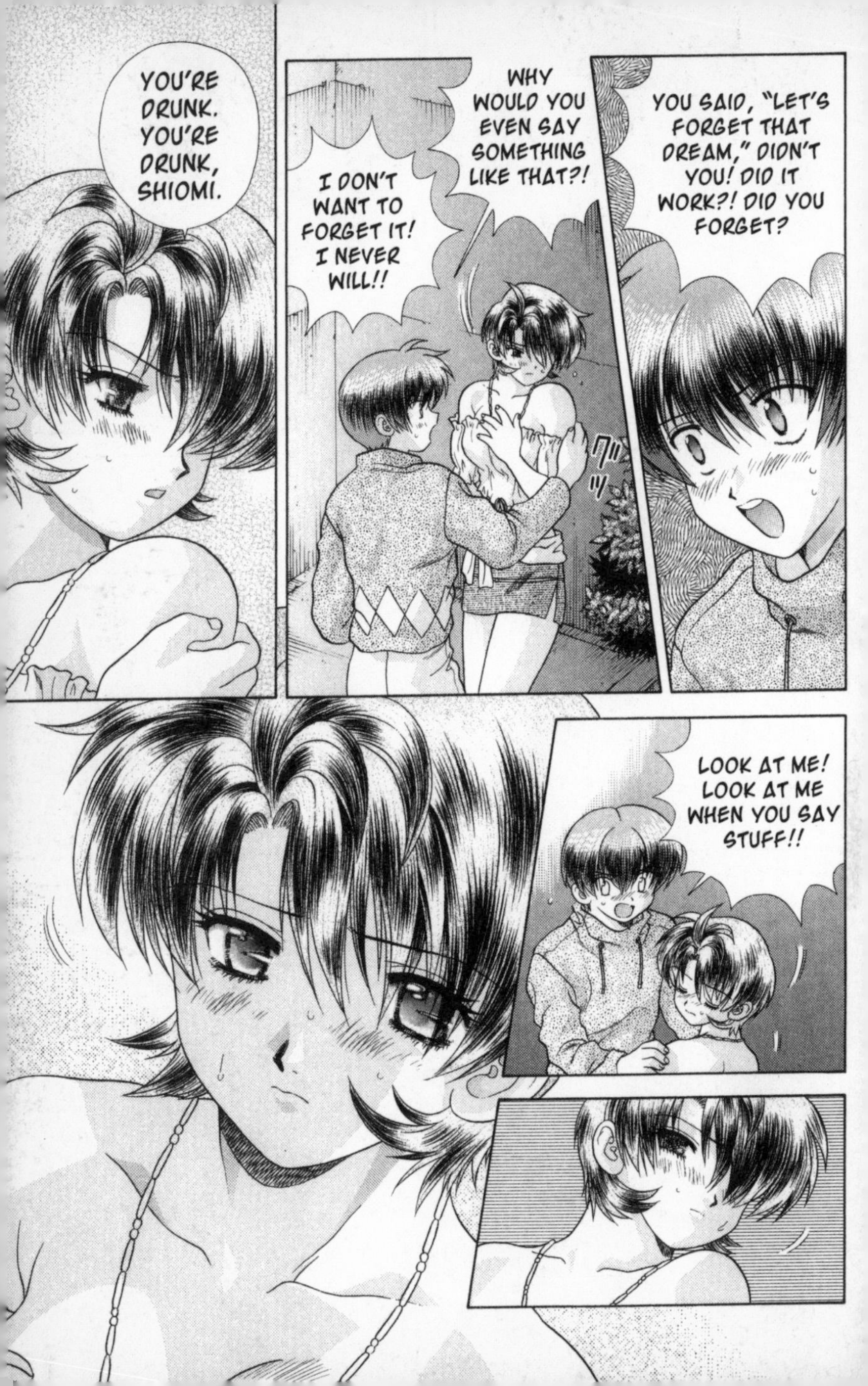
YOU SAID, "LET'S FORGET THAT DREAM," DIDN'T YOU! DID IT WORK?! DID YOU FORGET?
WHY WOULD YOU EVEN SAY SOMETHING LIKE THAT?!
I DON'T WANT TO FORGET IT! I NEVER WILL!!
グッ
YOU'RE DRUNK. YOU'RE DRUNK, SHIOMI.
LOOK AT ME! LOOK AT ME WHEN YOU SAY STUFF!!

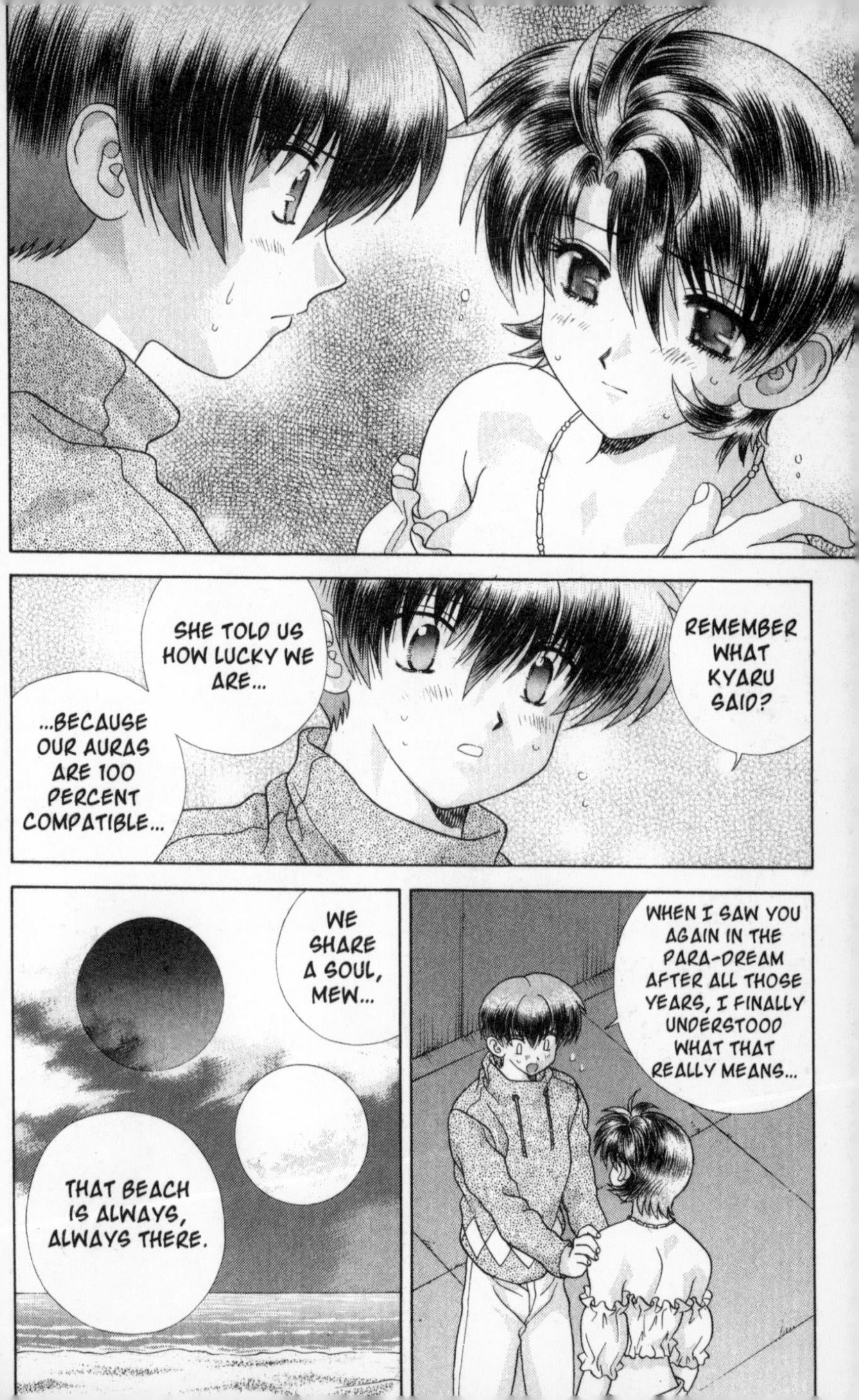
REMEMBER WHAT KYARU SAID?
SHE TOLD US HOW LUCKY WE ARE...
...BECAUSE OUR AURAS ARE 100 PERCENT COMPATIBLE...
WHEN I SAW YOU AGAIN IN THE PARA-DREAM AFTER ALL THOSE YEARS, I FINALLY UNDERSTOOD WHAT THAT REALLY MEANS...
WE SHARE A SOUL, MEW...
THAT BEACH IS ALWAYS, ALWAYS THERE.

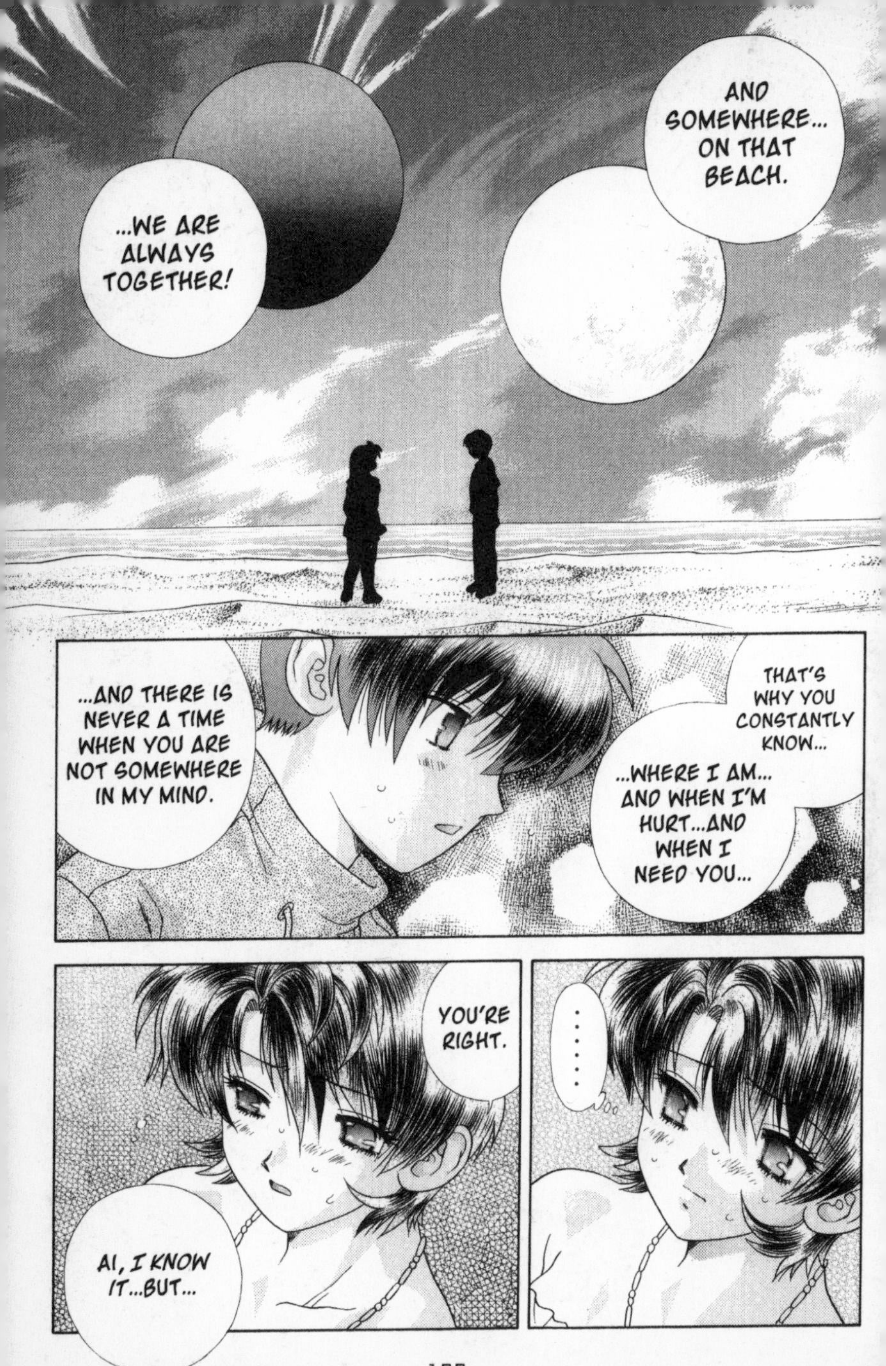
AND SOMEWHERE... ON THAT BEACH.
...WE ARE ALWAYS TOGETHER!
THAT'S WHY YOU CONSTANTLY KNOW...
...WHERE I AM... AND WHEN I'M HURT...AND WHEN I NEED YOU...
...AND THERE IS NEVER A TIME WHEN YOU ARE NOT SOMEWHERE IN MY MIND.
......
YOU'RE RIGHT.
AI, I KNOW IT...BUT...

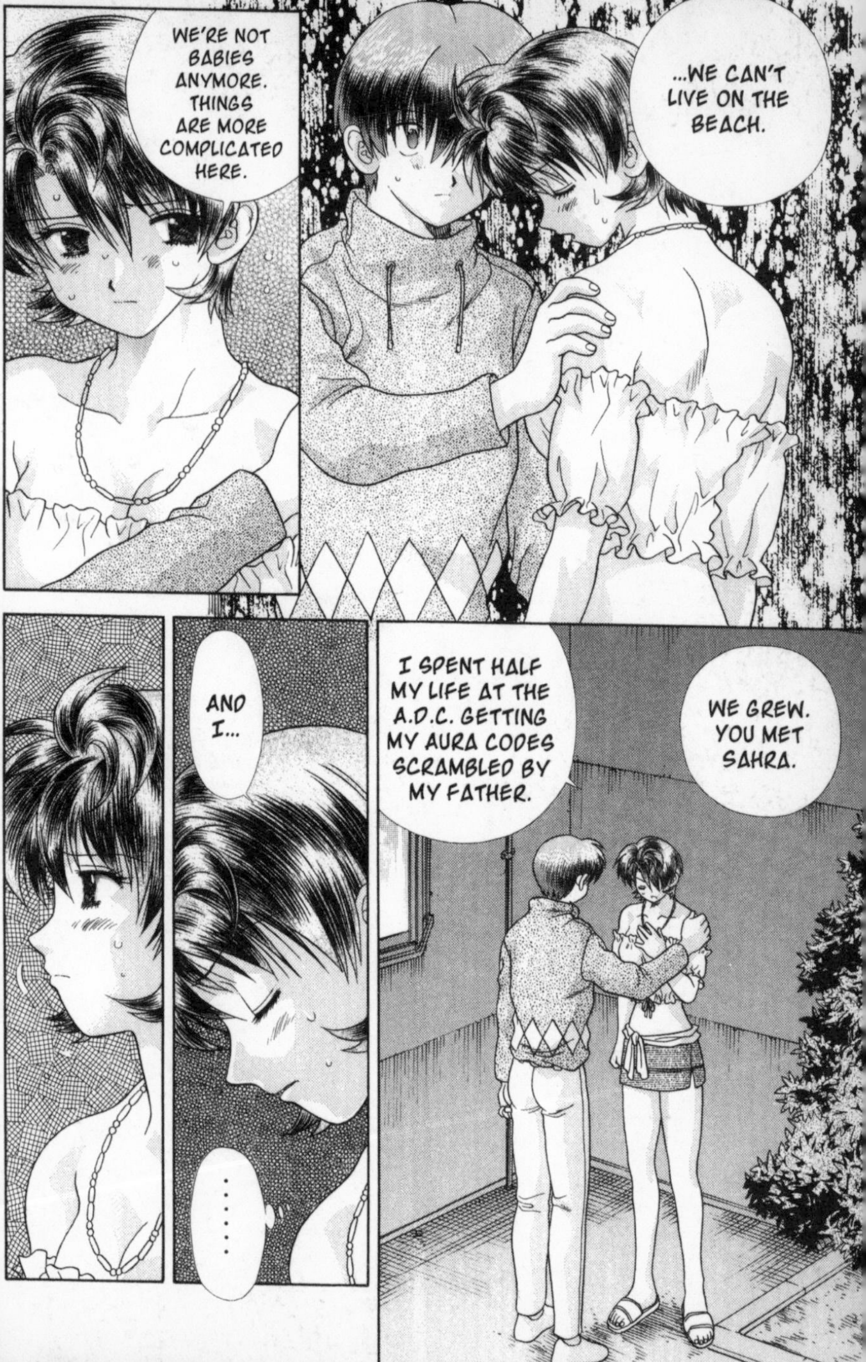
...WE CAN'T LIVE ON THE BEACH.
WE'RE NOT BABIES ANYMORE. THINGS ARE MORE COMPLICATED HERE.
WE GREW. YOU MET SAHRA.
I SPENT HALF MY LIFE AT THE A.D.C. GETTING MY AURA CODES SCRAMBLED BY MY FATHER.
AND I...
......

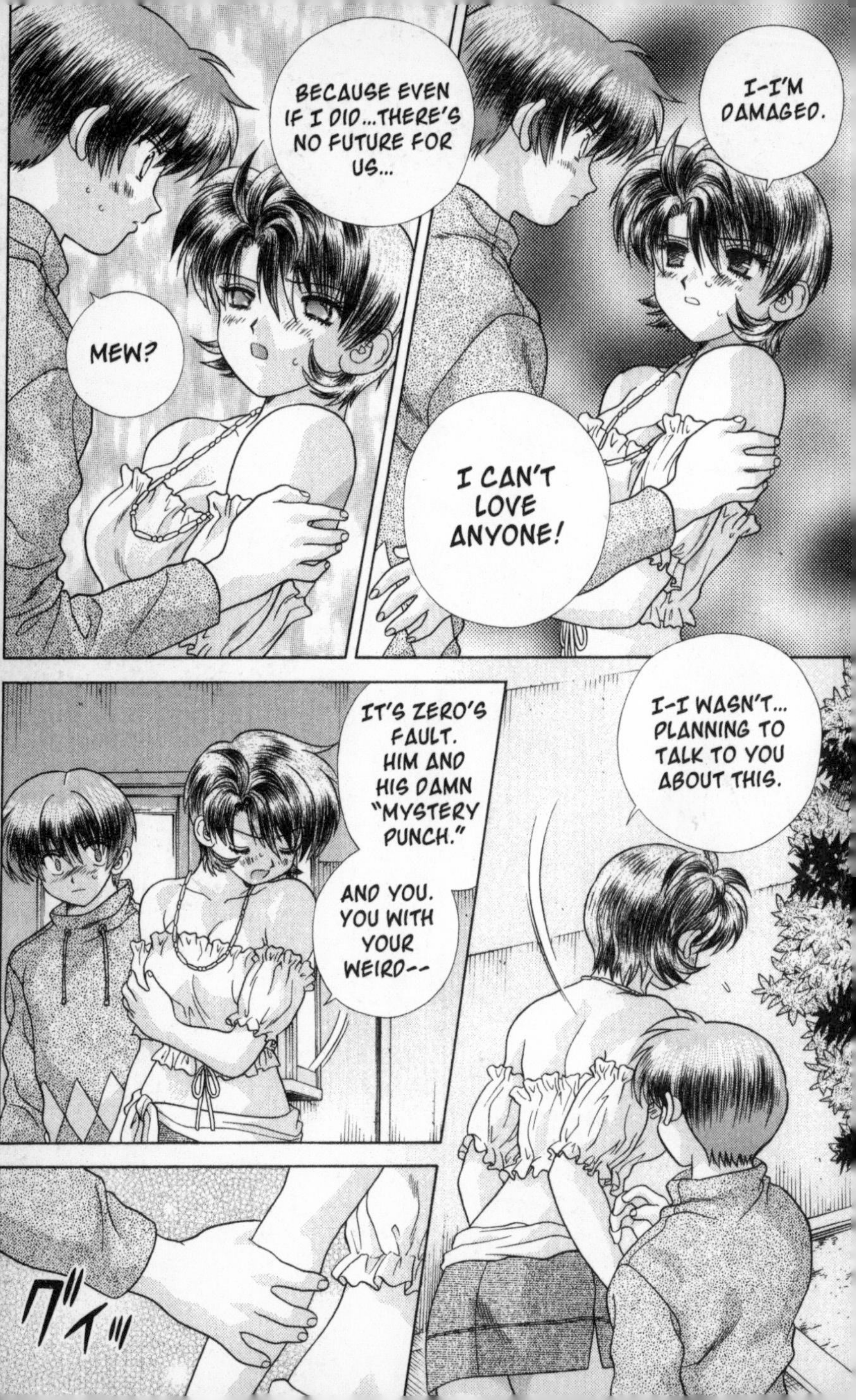
I-I'M DAMAGED.
I CAN'T LOVE ANYONE!
BECAUSE EVEN IF I DID...THERE'S NO FUTURE FOR US...
MEW?
I-I WASN'T... PLANNING TO TALK TO YOU ABOUT THIS.
IT'S ZERO'S FAULT. HIM AND HIS DAMN "MYSTERY PUNCH."
AND YOU. YOU WITH YOUR WEIRD--
グイッ

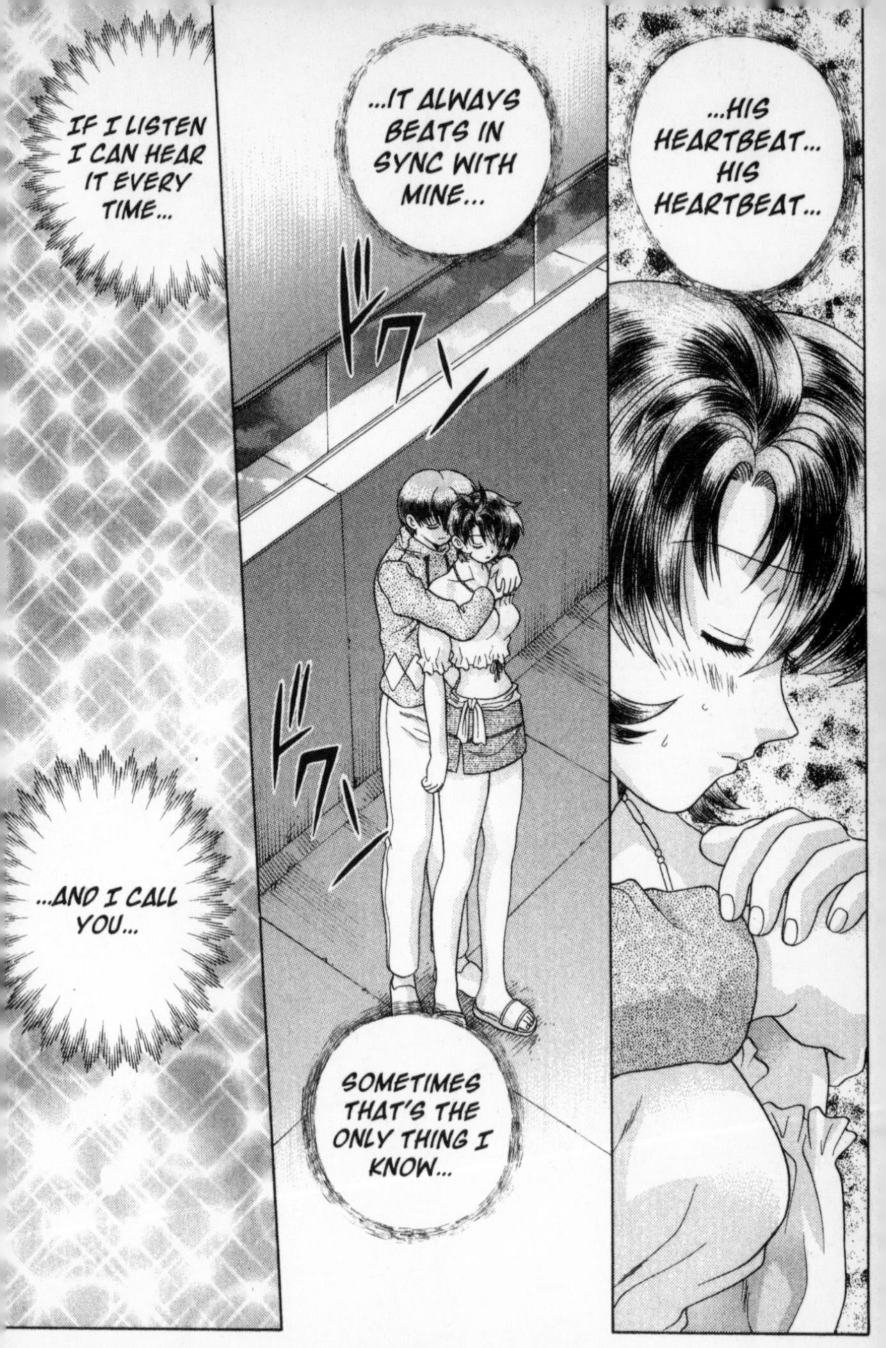
...HIS HEARTBEAT... HIS HEARTBEAT...
...IT ALWAYS BEATS IN SYNC WITH MINE...
ドクン
ドクン
SOMETIMES THAT'S THE ONLY THING I KNOW...
IF I LISTEN I CAN HEAR IT EVERY TIME...
...AND I CALL YOU...

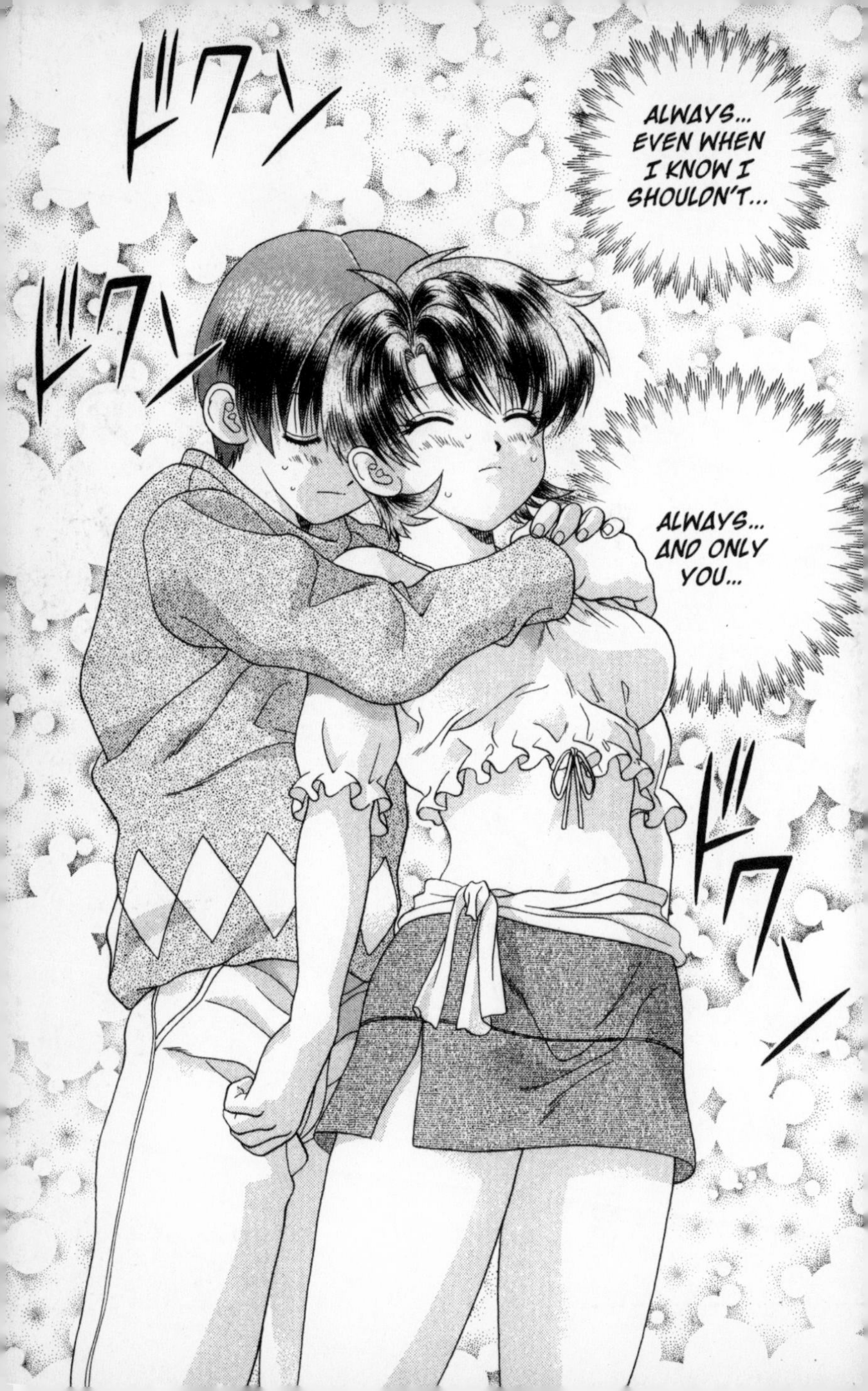
ALWAYS... EVEN WHEN I KNOW I SHOULDN'T...
ALWAYS... AND ONLY YOU...
ドクン
ドクン
ドクン

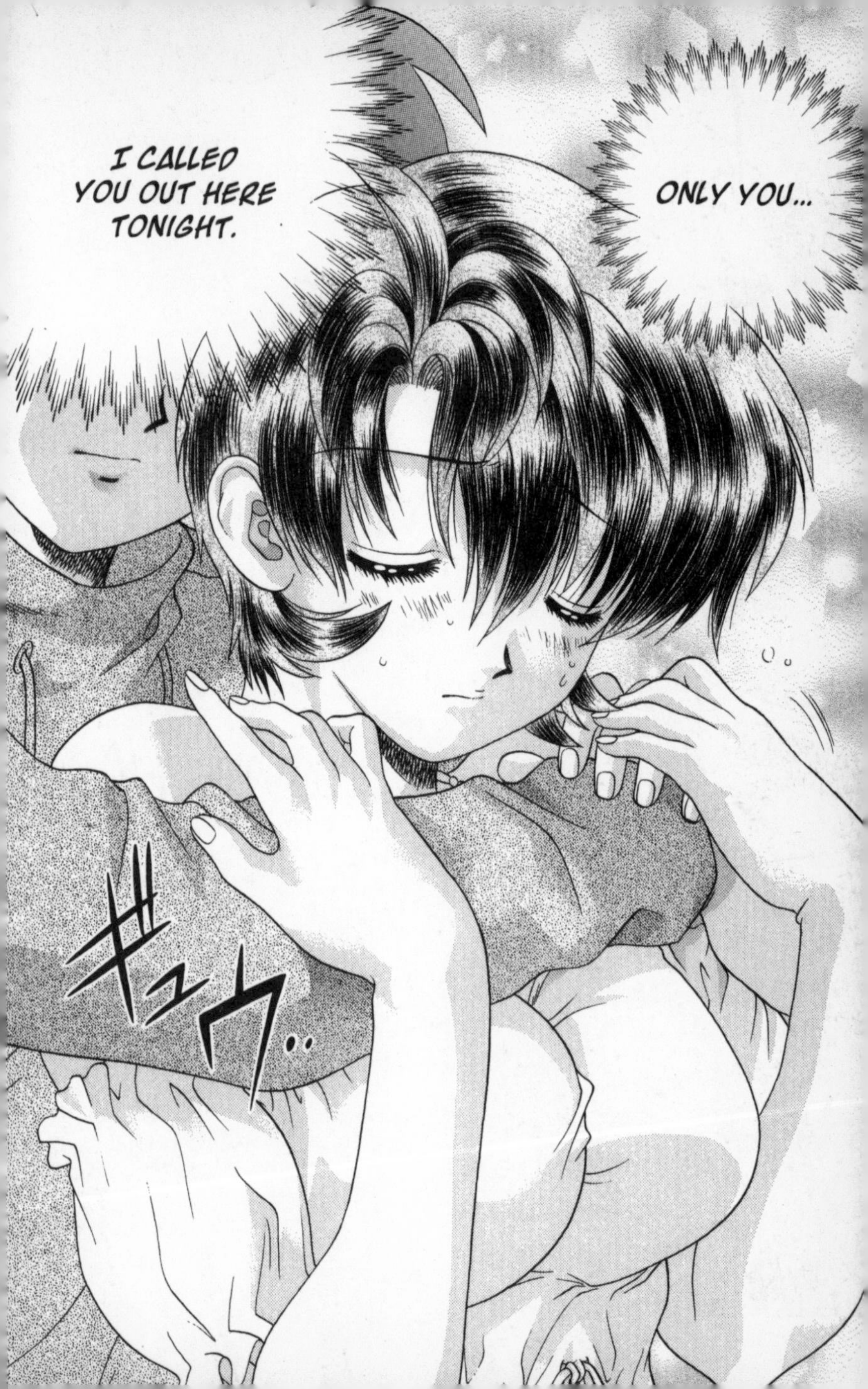
ONLY YOU...
I CALLED YOU OUT HERE TONIGHT.
ギュウ..

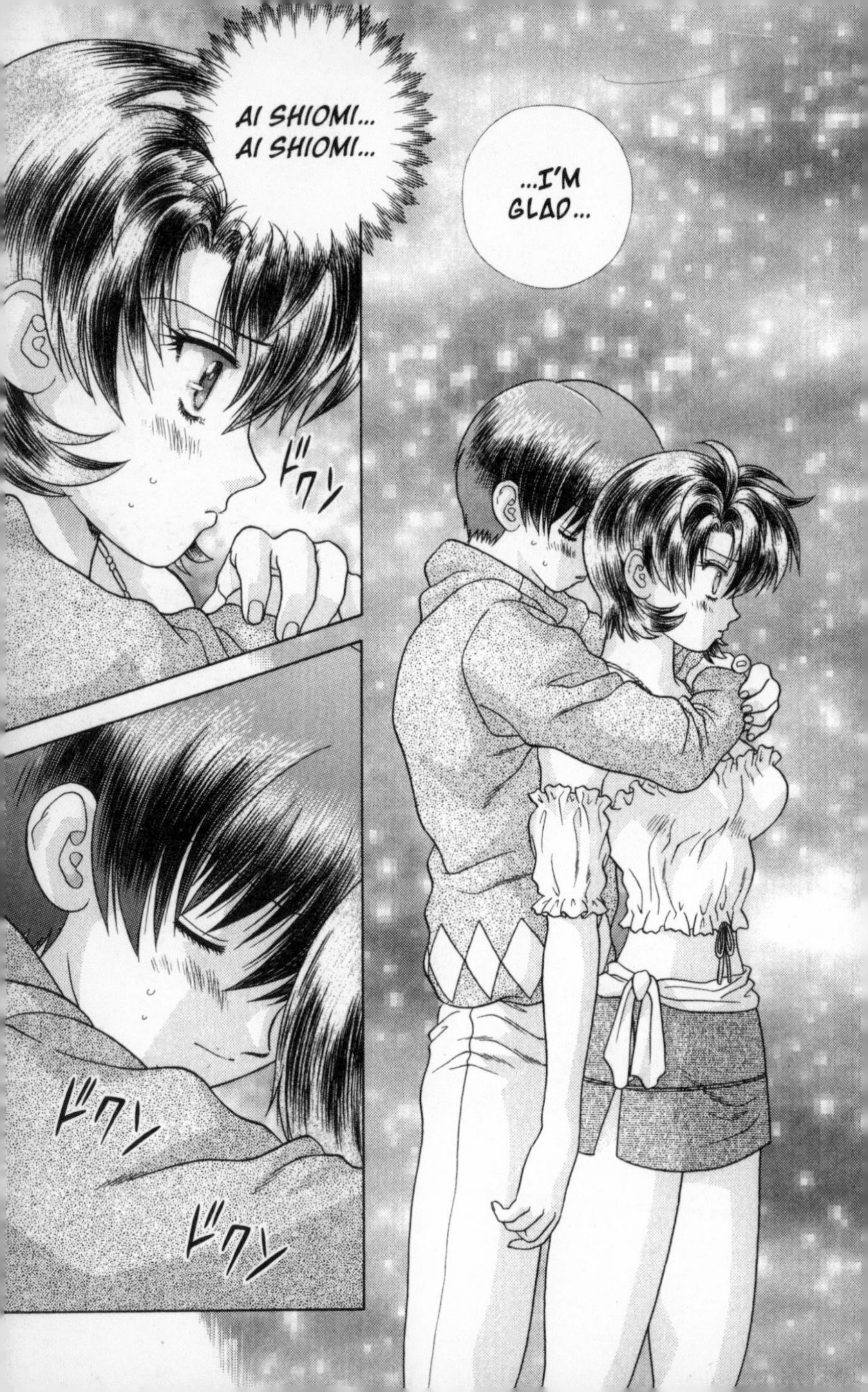
...I'M GLAD...
AI SHIOMI... AI SHIOMI...
ドクン
ドクン
ドクン

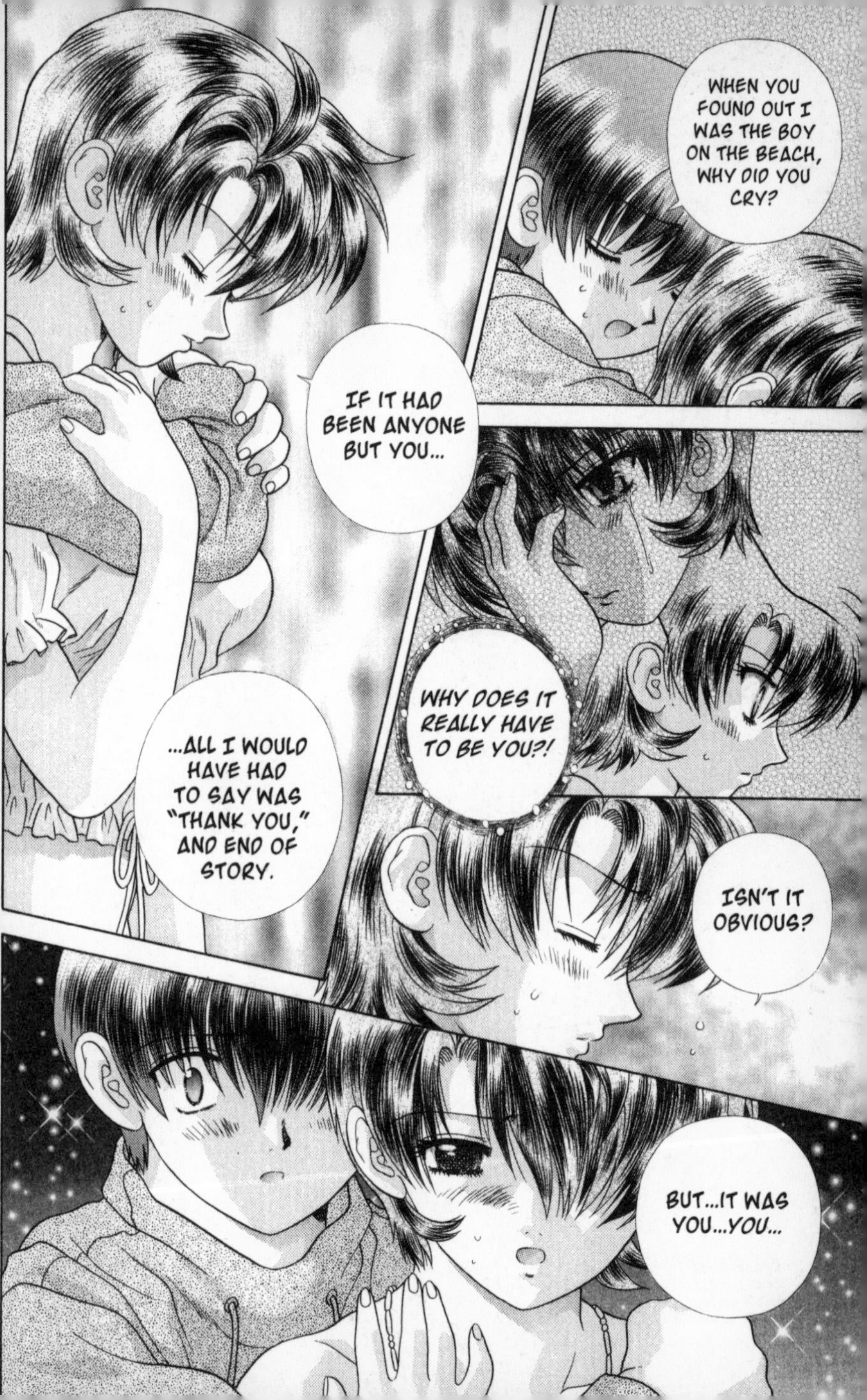
WHEN YOU FOUND OUT I WAS THE BOY ON THE BEACH, WHY DID YOU CRY?
IF IT HAD BEEN ANYONE BUT YOU...
...ALL I WOULD HAVE HAD TO SAY WAS "THANK YOU," AND END OF STORY.
WHY DOES IT REALLY HAVE TO BE YOU?!
ISN'T IT OBVIOUS?
BUT...IT WAS YOU...YOU...

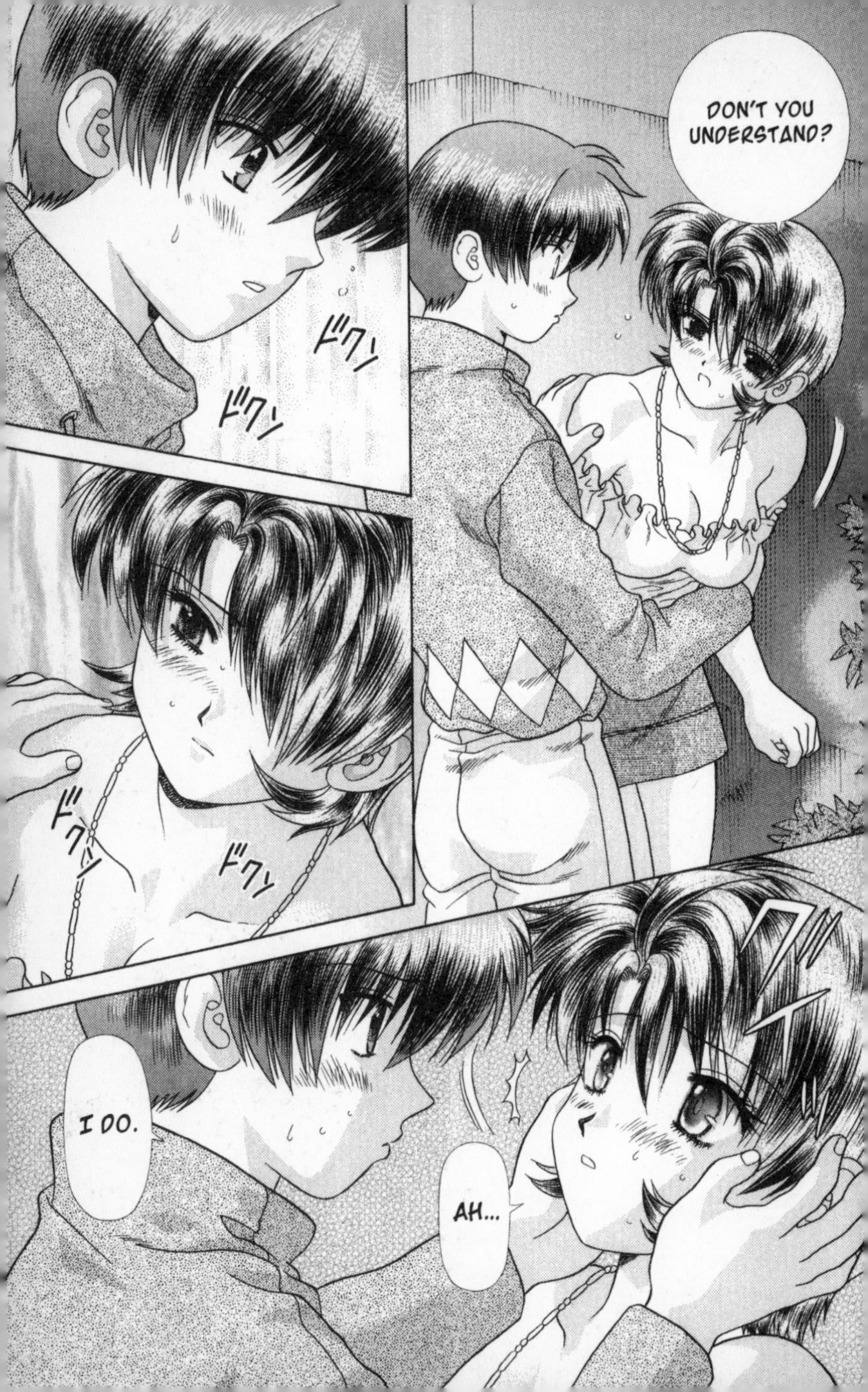

DON'T YOU UNDERSTAND?
ドクン
ドクン
ドクン
ドクン
AH...
I DO.

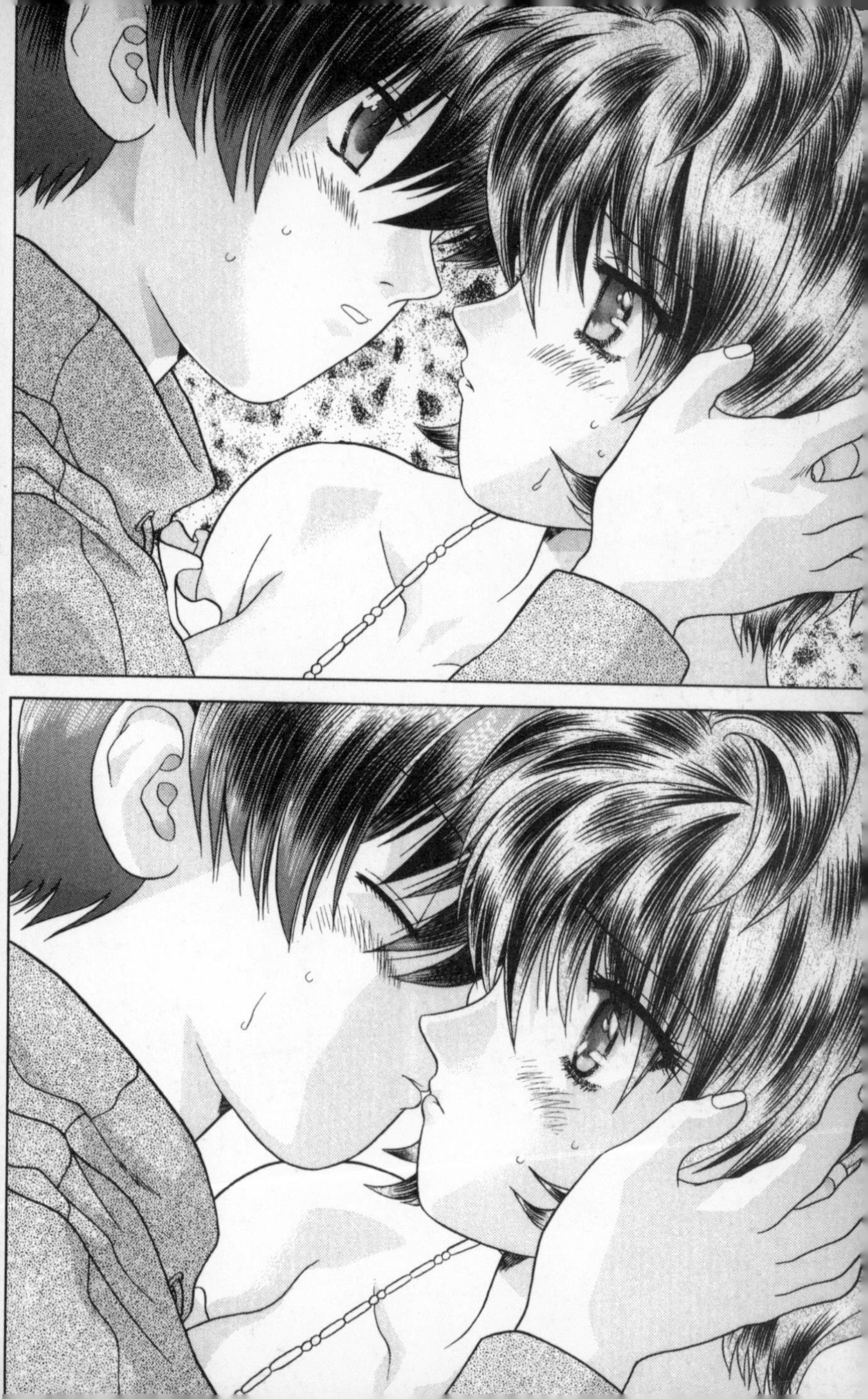

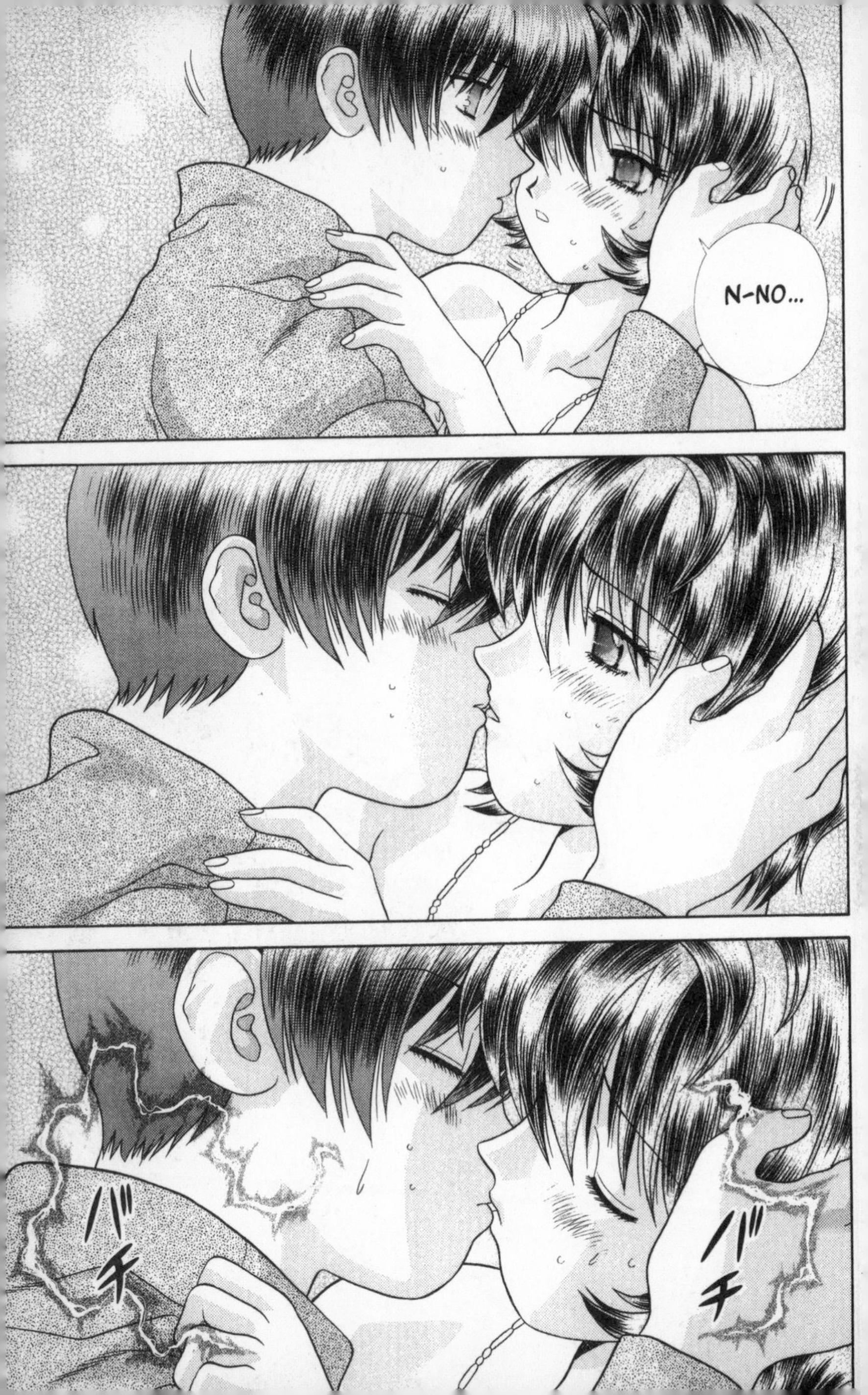
N-NO...
バチ
バチ

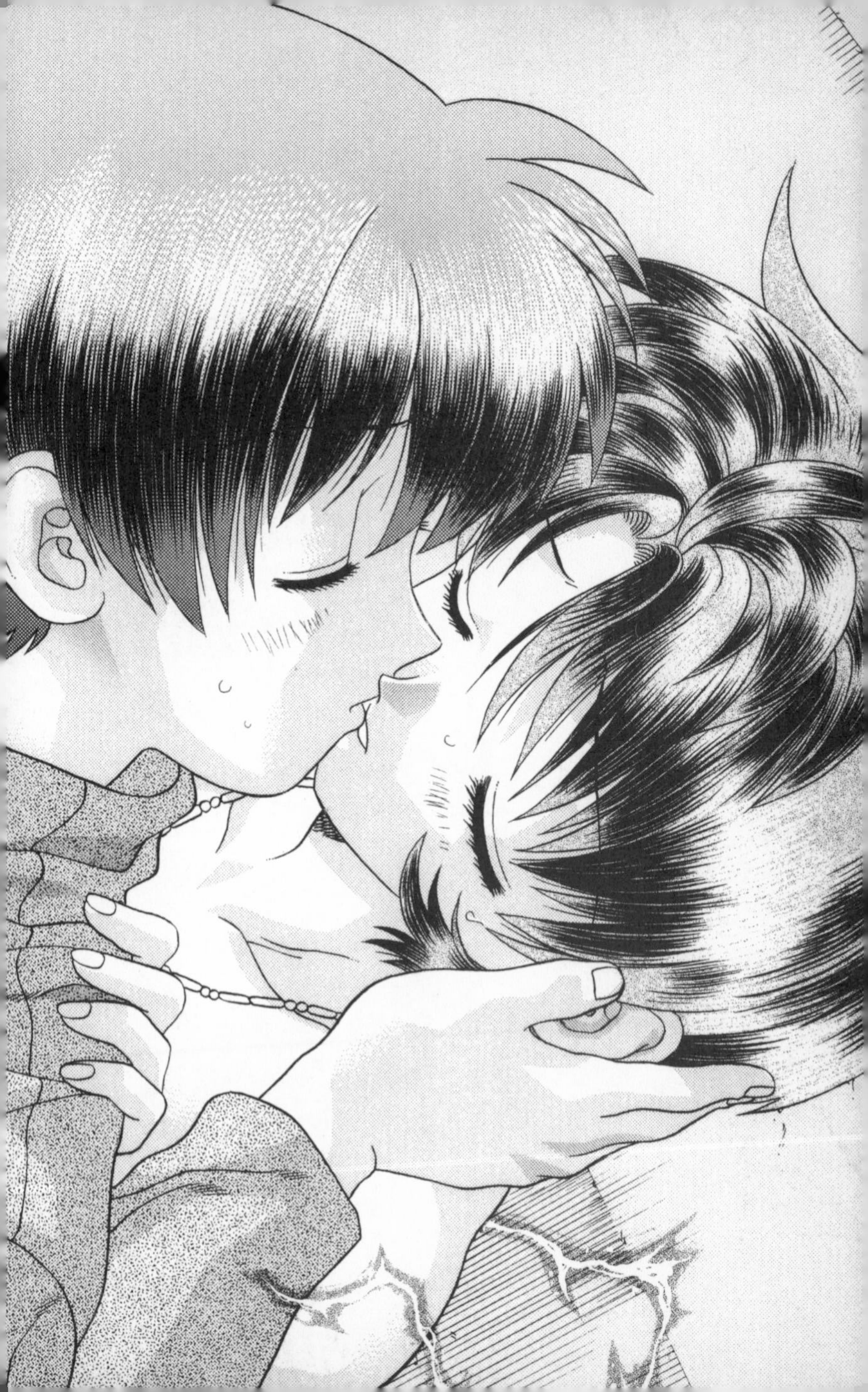

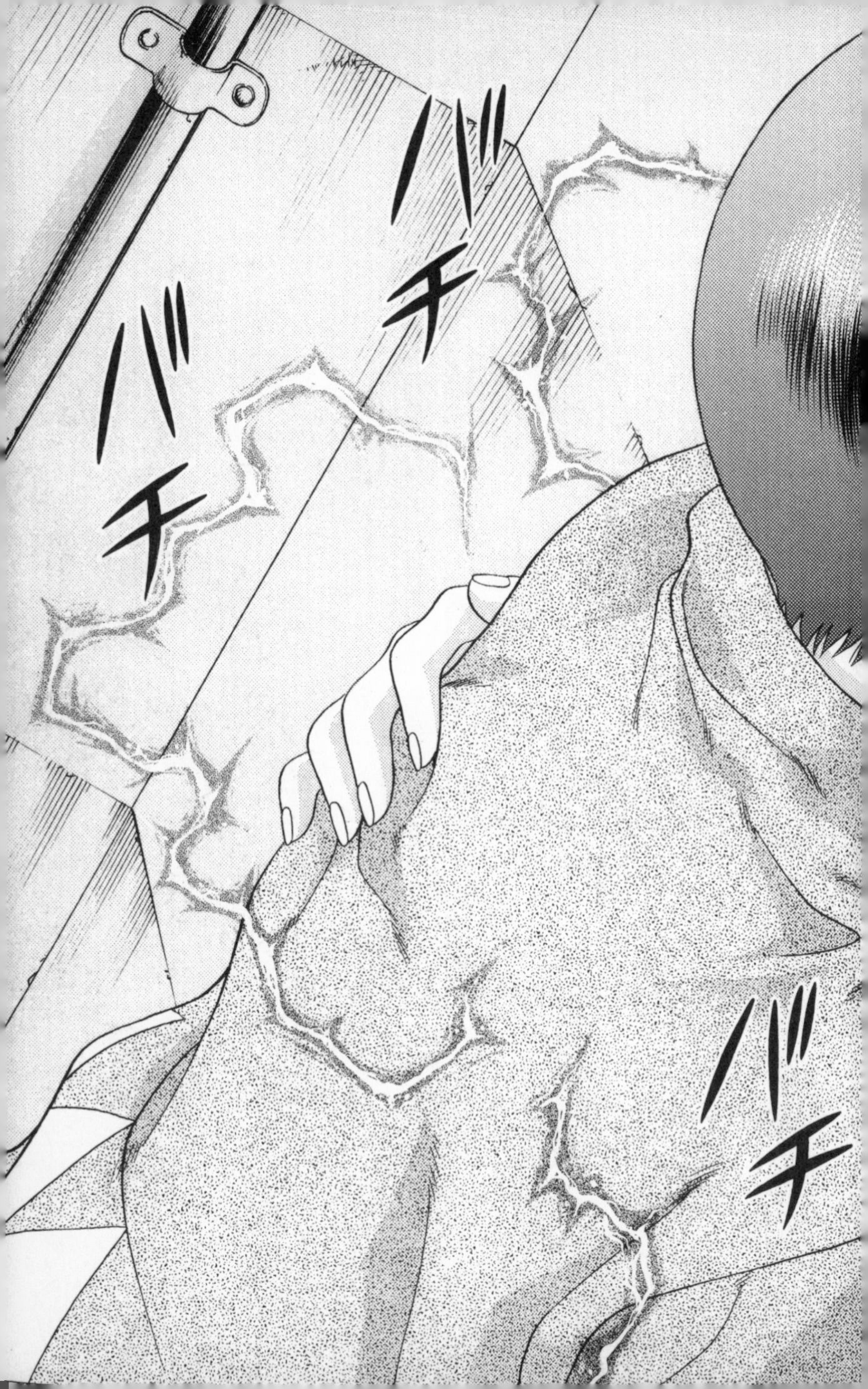
バヂチ
バヂチ
バヂチ

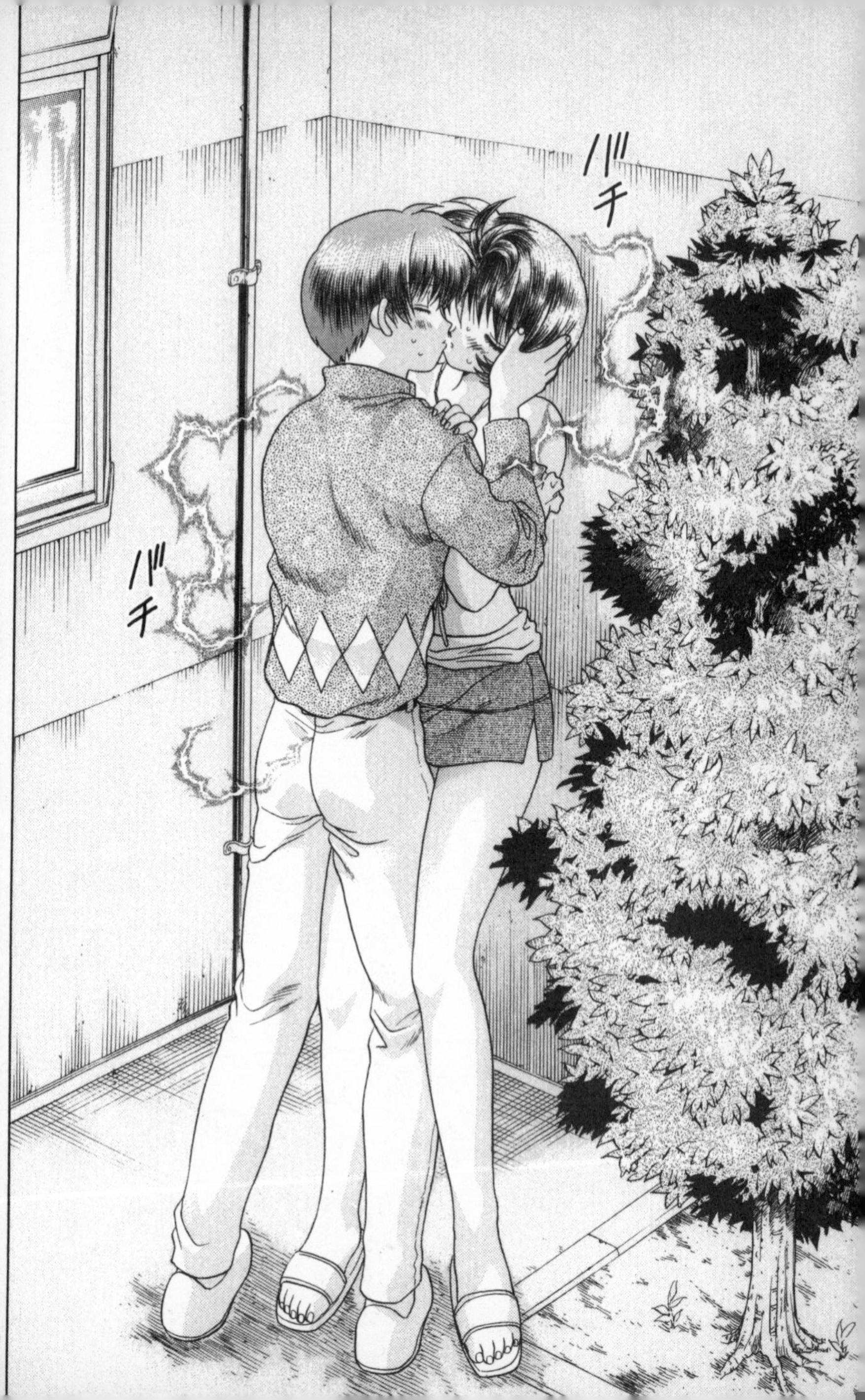
バチ
バチ

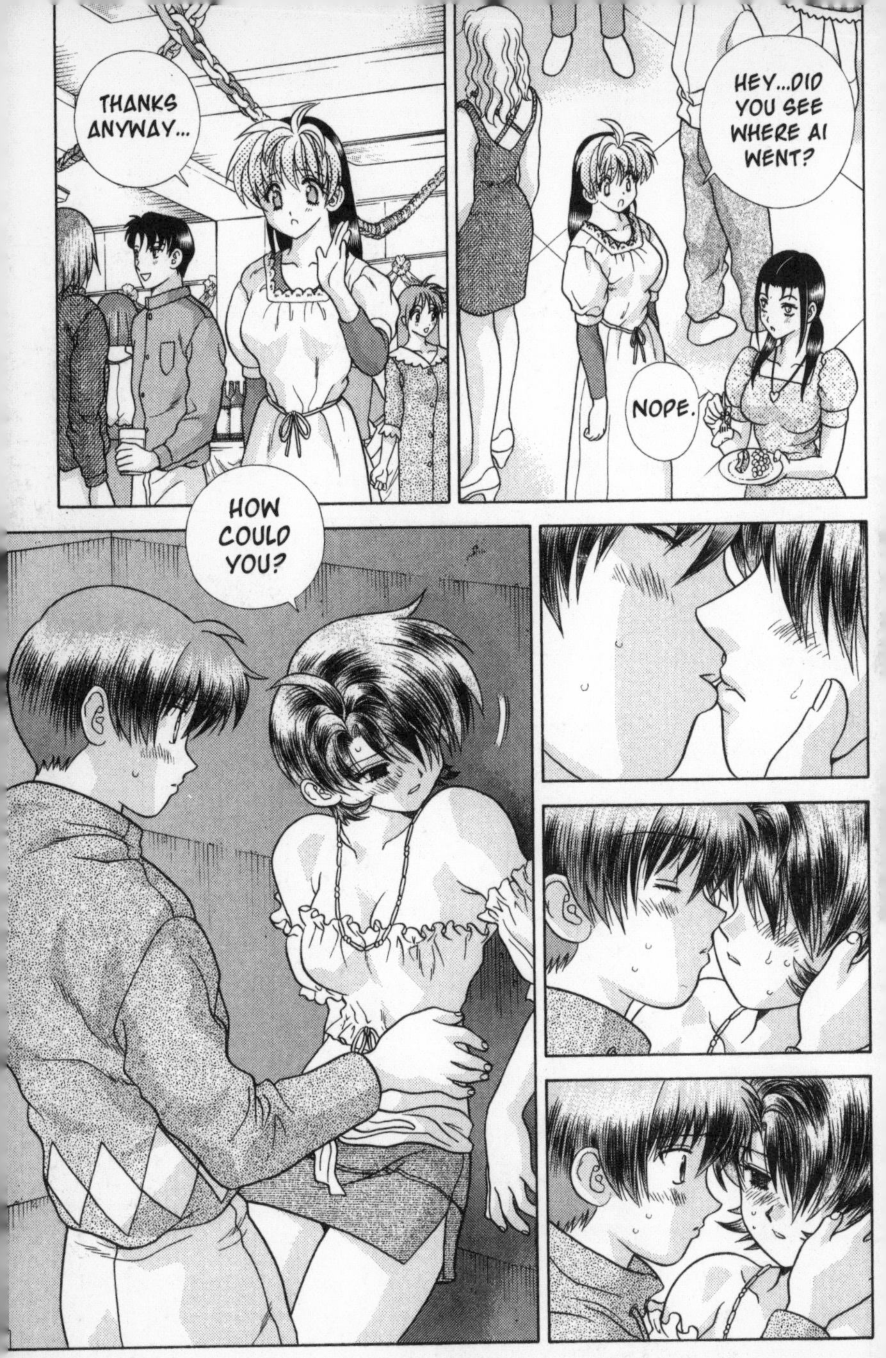
HEY...DID YOU SEE WHERE AI WENT?
NOPE.
THANKS ANYWAY...
HOW COULD YOU?

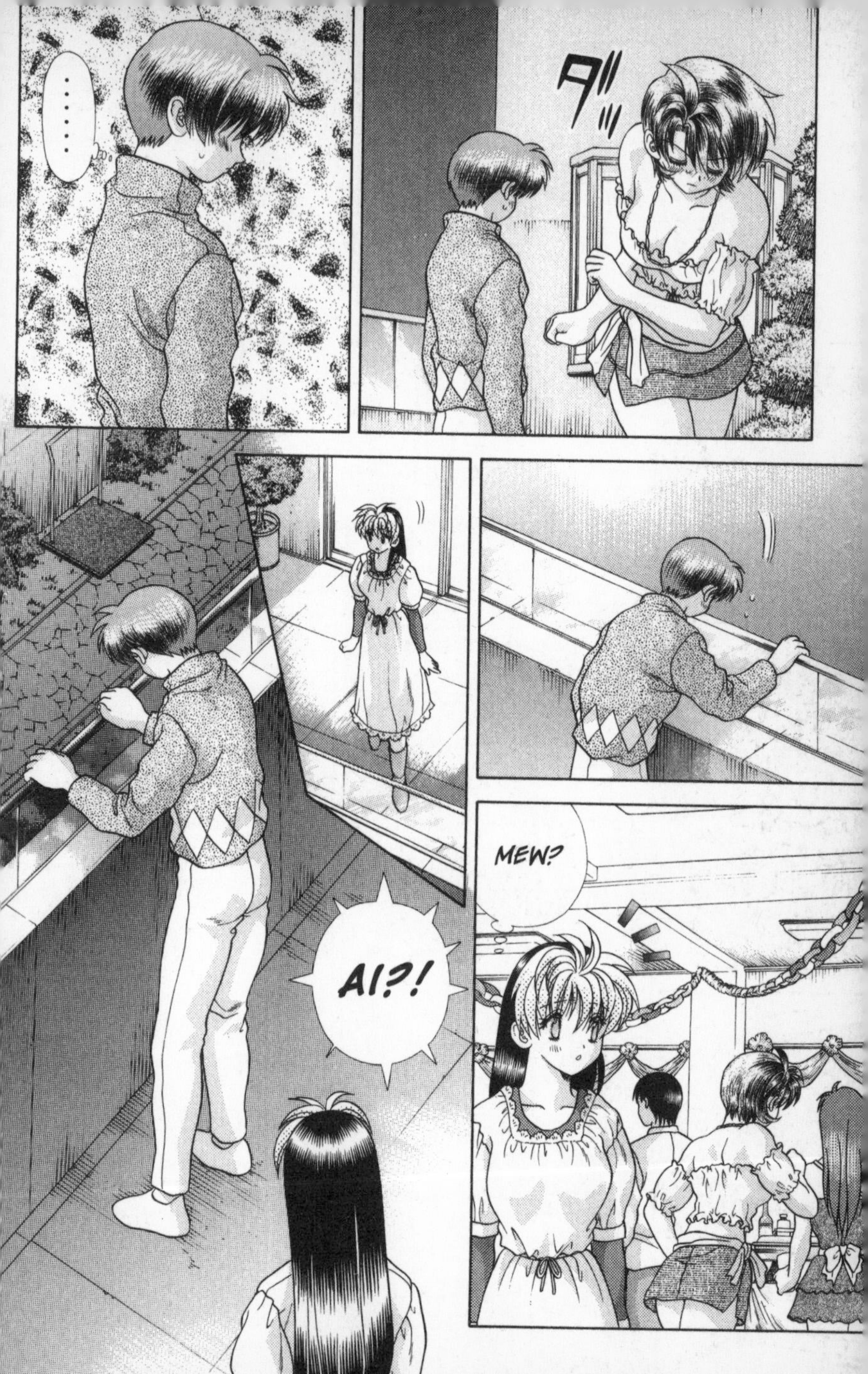
......
ﾀﾞｯ
MEW?
AI?!

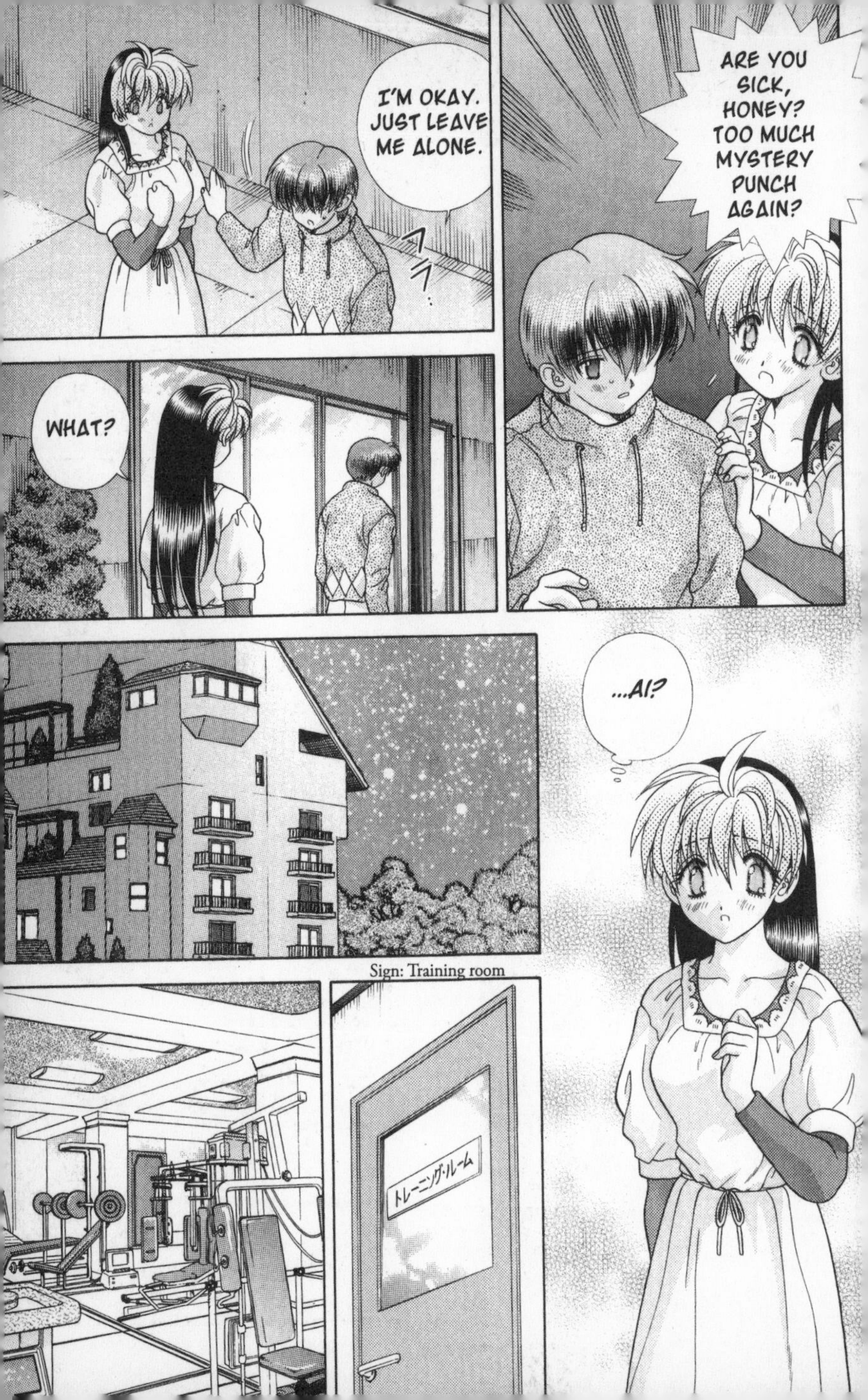
ARE YOU SICK, HONEY? TOO MUCH MYSTERY PUNCH AGAIN?
I'M OKAY. JUST LEAVE ME ALONE.
WHAT?
...AI?
Sign: Training room
トレーニング・ルーム

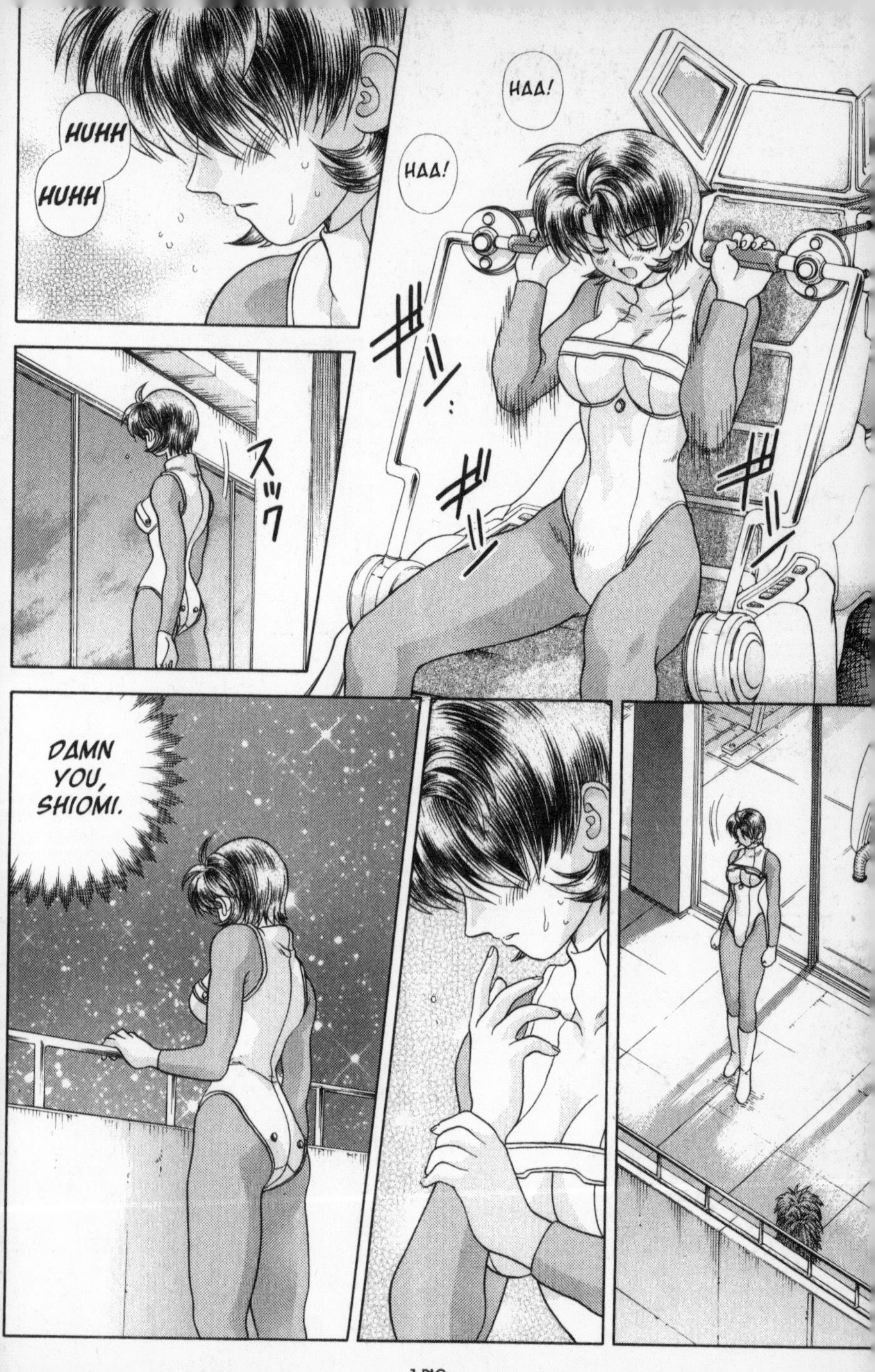
HAA!
HAA!
HUHH
HUHH
スック
DAMN YOU, SHIOMI.

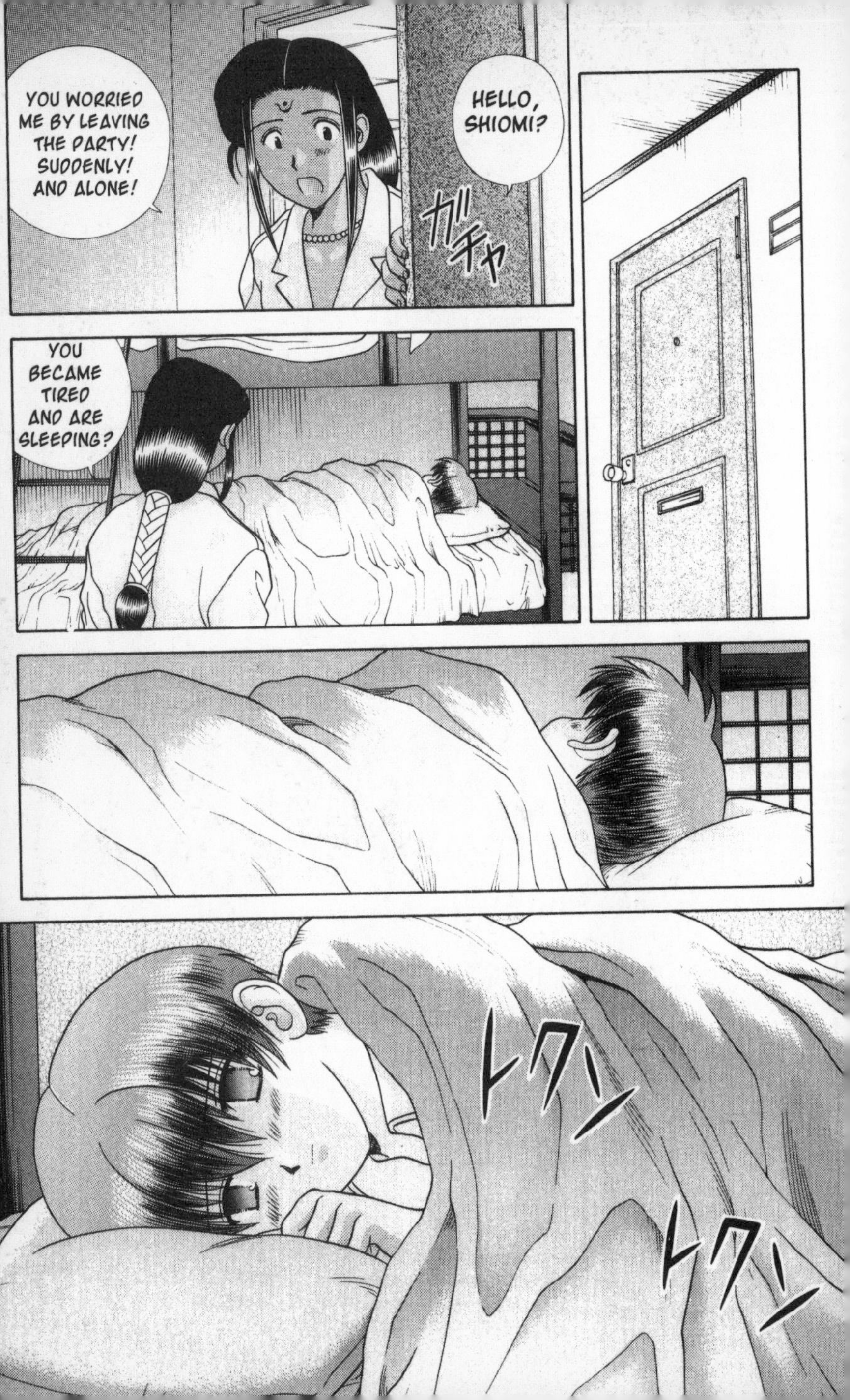
HELLO, SHIOMI?
ガチャ
YOU WORRIED ME BY LEAVING THE PARTY! SUDDENLY! AND ALONE!
YOU BECAME TIRED AND ARE SLEEPING?
トクン
トクン

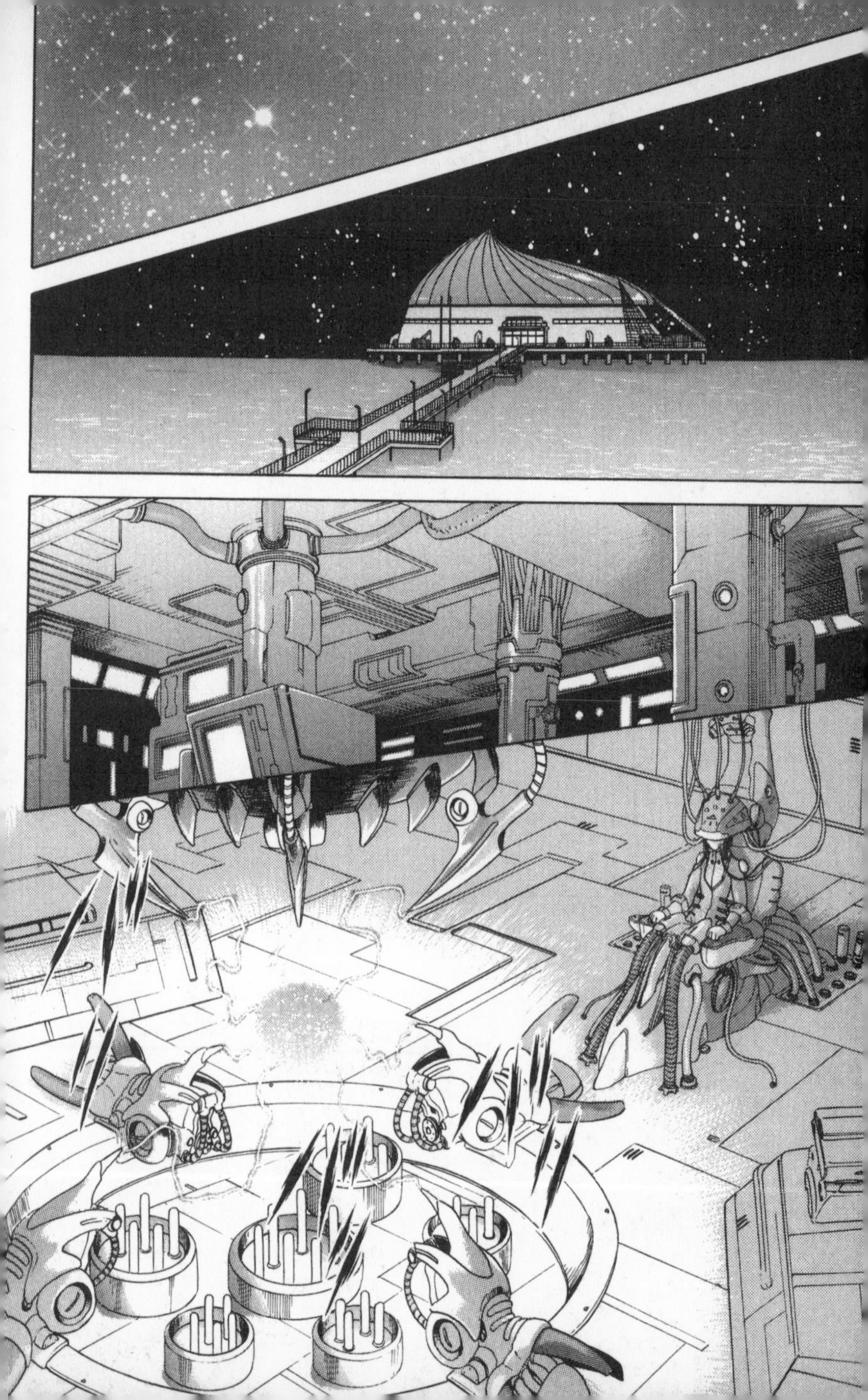

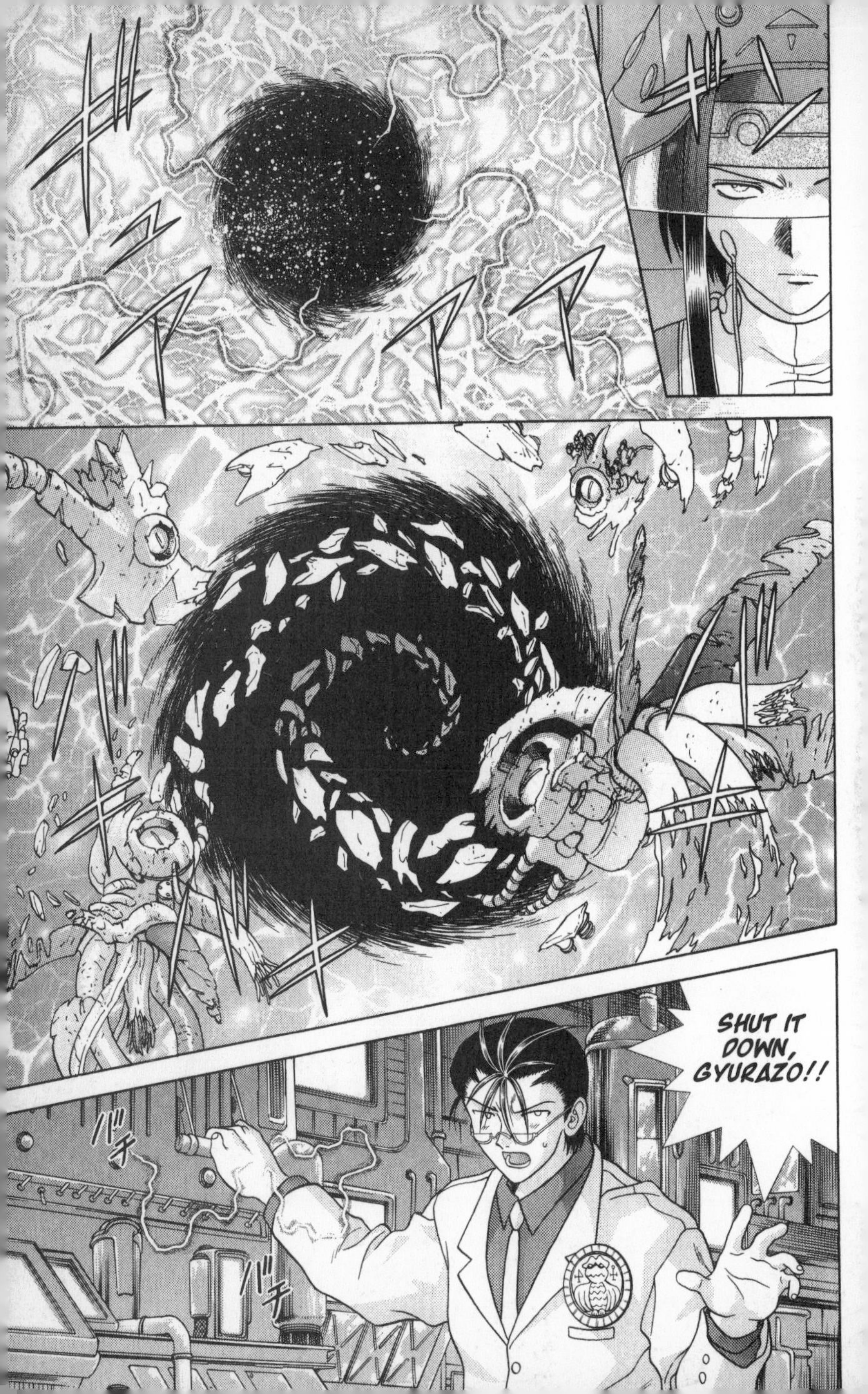
SHUT IT DOWN, GYURAZO!!

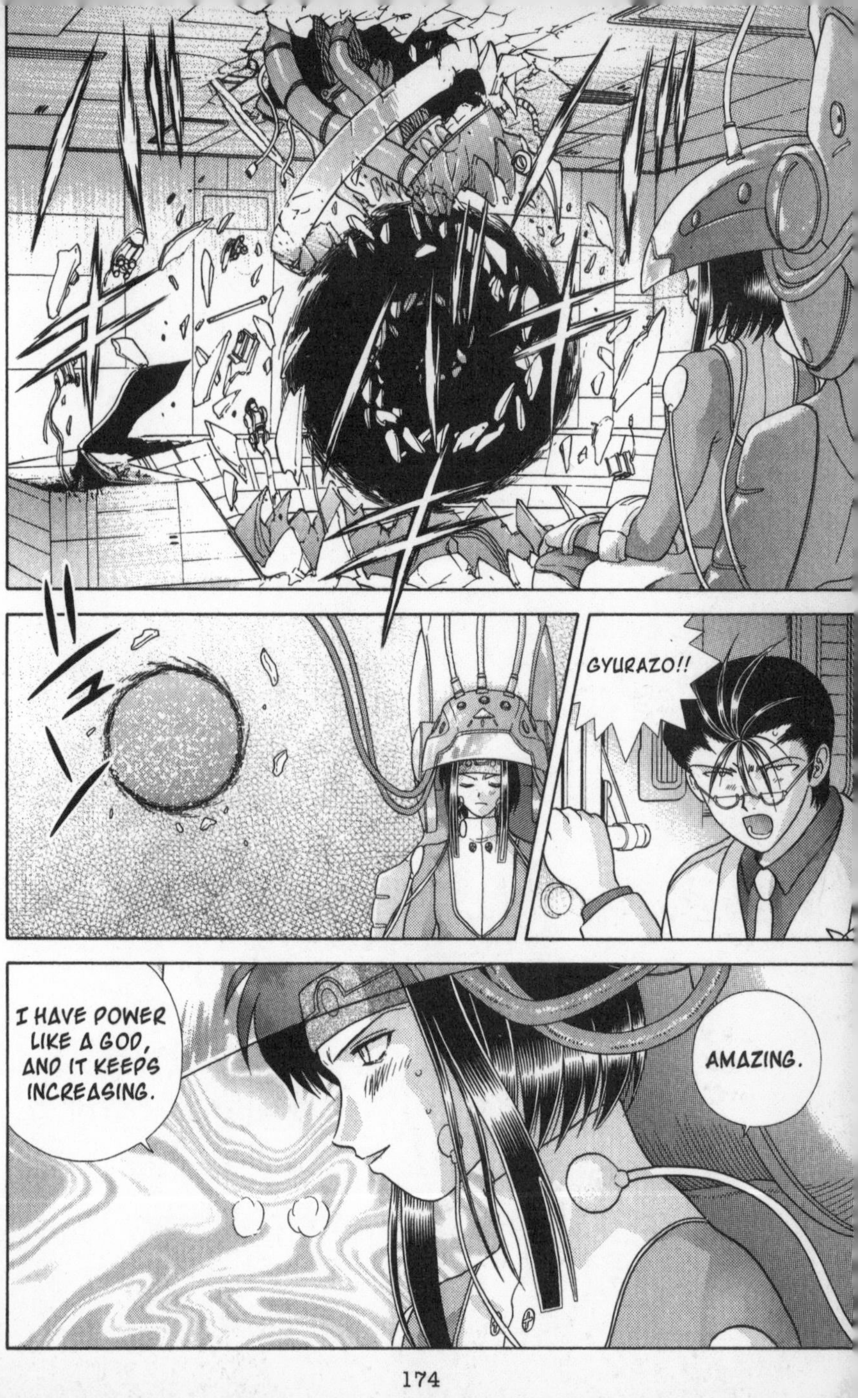
GYURAZO!!
I HAVE POWER LIKE A GOD, AND IT KEEPS INCREASING.
AMAZING.

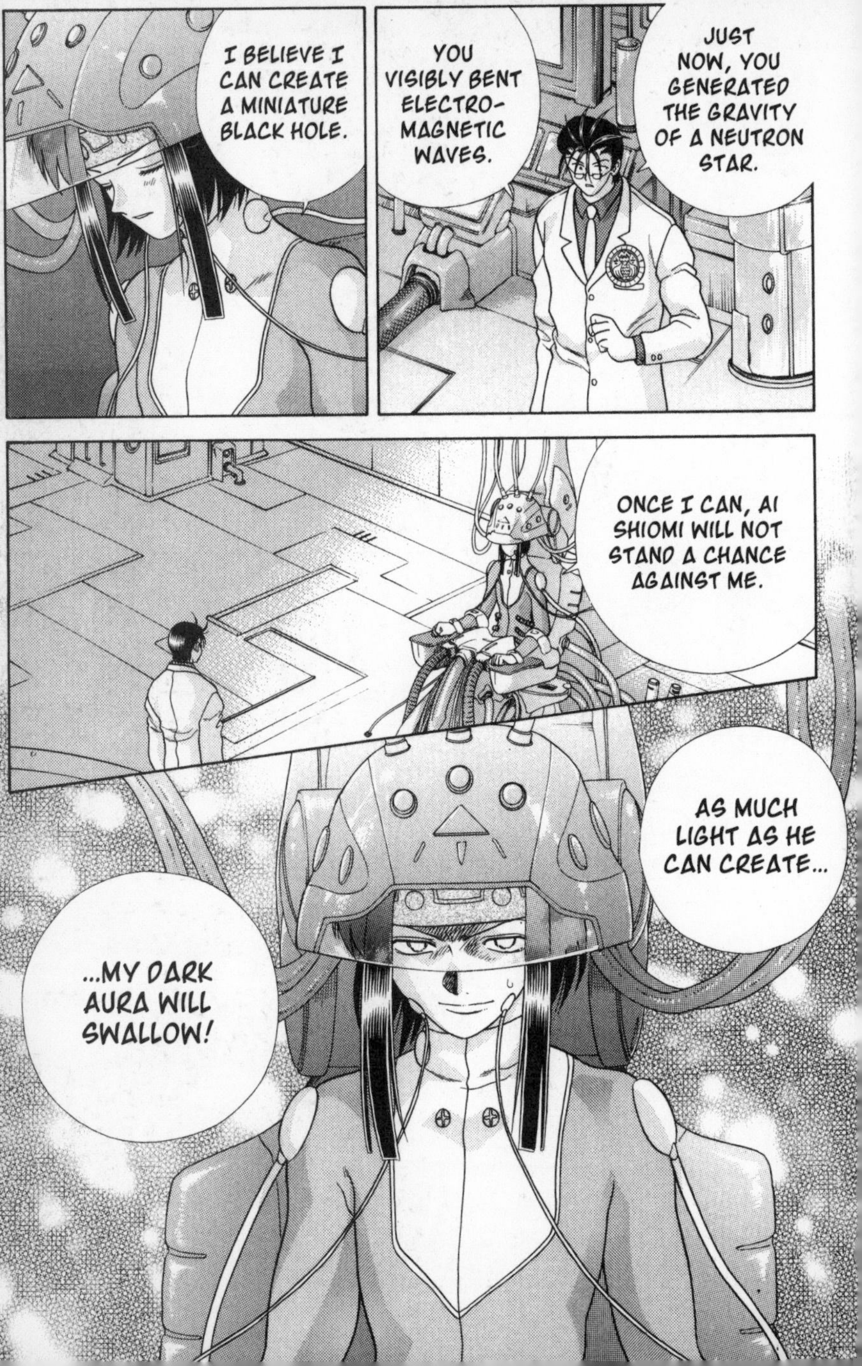
JUST NOW, YOU GENERATED THE GRAVITY OF A NEUTRON STAR.
YOU VISIBLY BENT ELECTRO-MAGNETIC WAVES.
I BELIEVE I CAN CREATE A MINIATURE BLACK HOLE.
ONCE I CAN, AI SHIOMI WILL NOT STAND A CHANCE AGAINST ME.
AS MUCH LIGHT AS HE CAN CREATE...
...MY DARK AURA WILL SWALLOW!

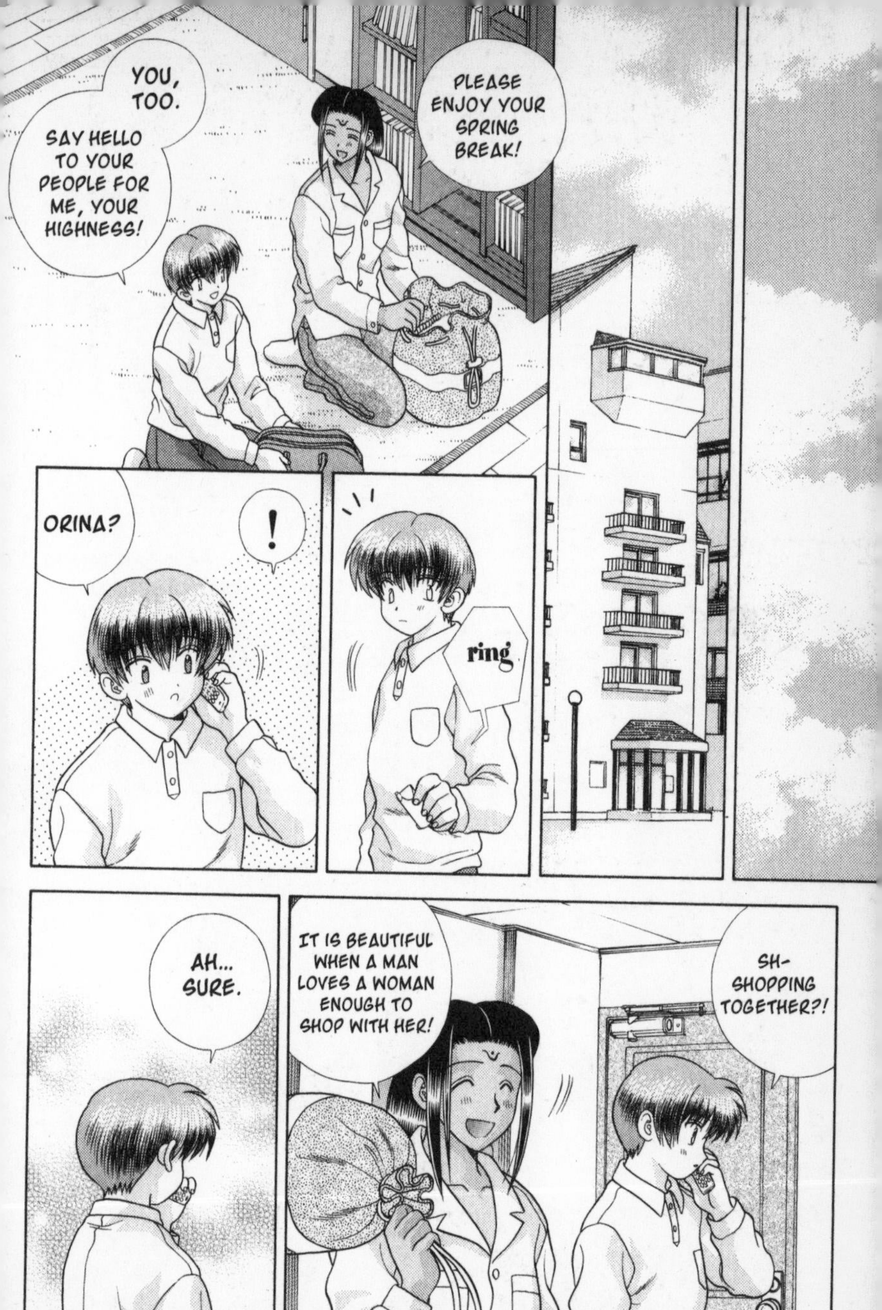

PLEASE ENJOY YOUR SPRING BREAK!
YOU, TOO.
SAY HELLO TO YOUR PEOPLE FOR ME, YOUR HIGHNESS!
ring
!
ORINA?
SH-SHOPPING TOGETHER?!
IT IS BEAUTIFUL WHEN A MAN LOVES A WOMAN ENOUGH TO SHOP WITH HER!
AH... SURE.

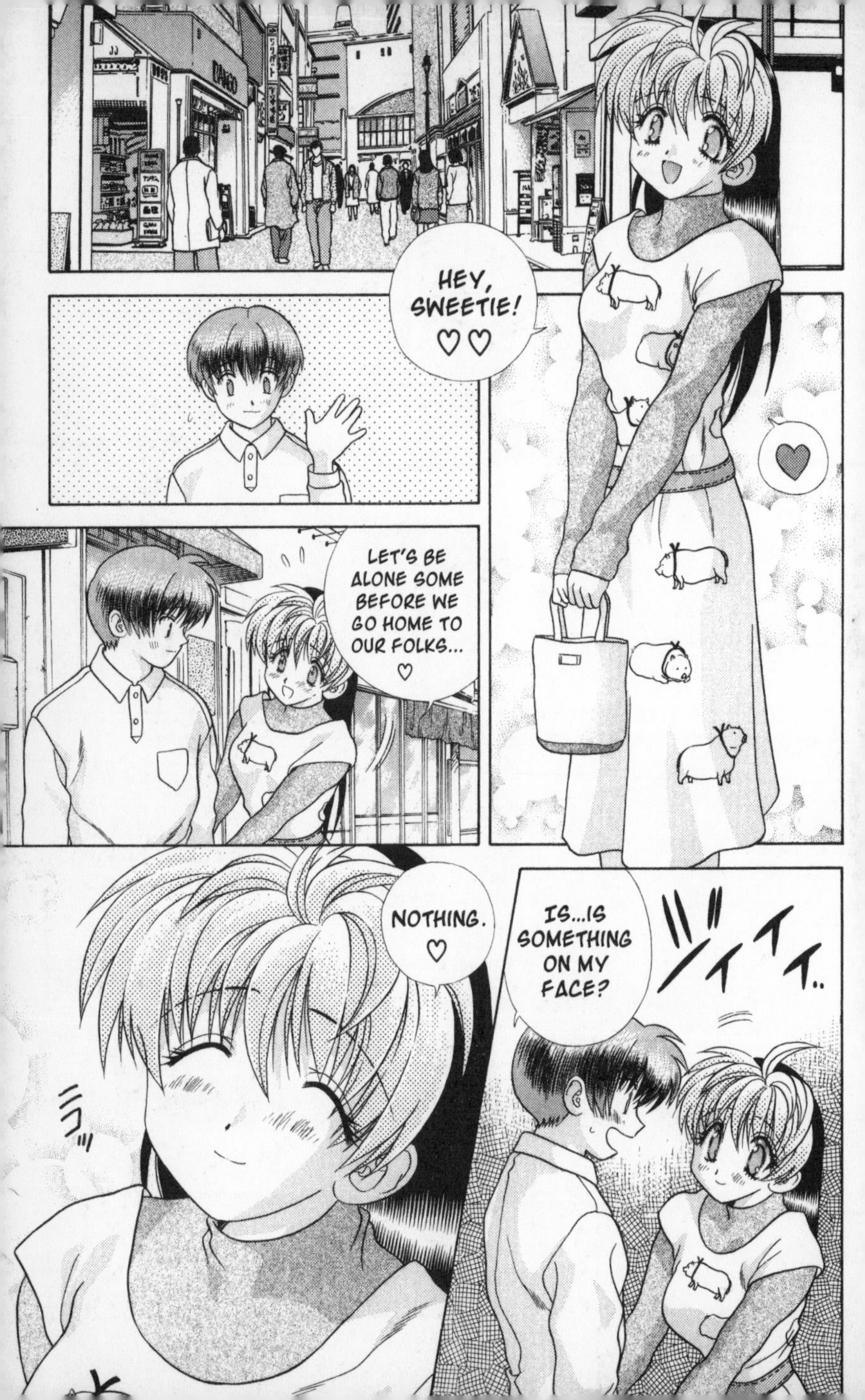
HEY, SWEETIE! ♡♡
♡
LET'S BE ALONE SOME BEFORE WE GO HOME TO OUR FOLKS... ♡
IS...IS SOMETHING ON MY FACE?
NOTHING. ♡

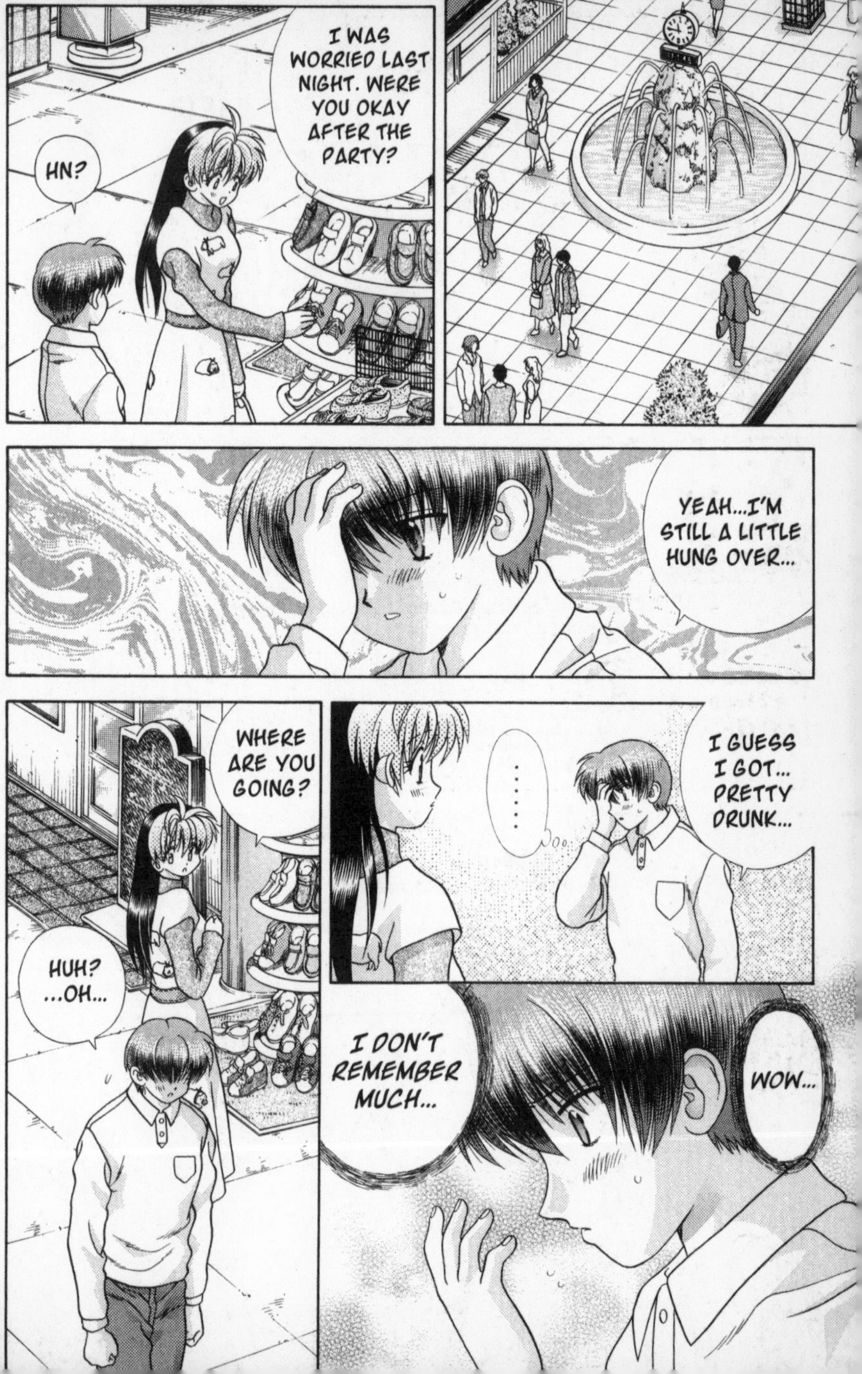
I WAS WORRIED LAST NIGHT. WERE YOU OKAY AFTER THE PARTY?
HN?
YEAH...I'M STILL A LITTLE HUNG OVER...
I GUESS I GOT... PRETTY DRUNK...
......
WOW...
I DON'T REMEMBER MUCH...
WHERE ARE YOU GOING?
HUH? ...OH...

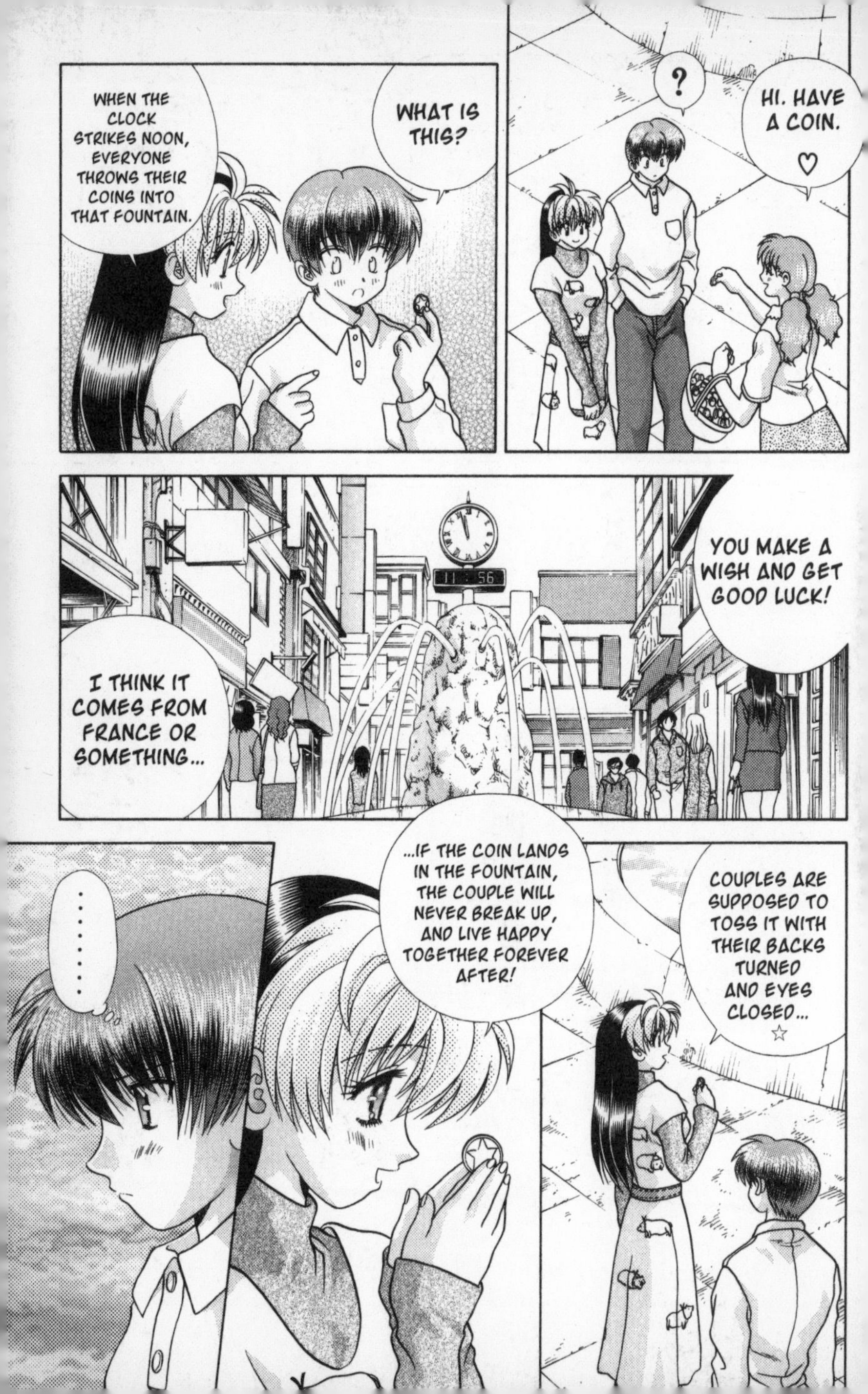
?
HI. HAVE A COIN. ♡
WHAT IS THIS?
WHEN THE CLOCK STRIKES NOON, EVERYONE THROWS THEIR COINS INTO THAT FOUNTAIN.
11:56
YOU MAKE A WISH AND GET GOOD LUCK!
I THINK IT COMES FROM FRANCE OR SOMETHING...
COUPLES ARE SUPPOSED TO TOSS IT WITH THEIR BACKS TURNED AND EYES CLOSED... ☆
...IF THE COIN LANDS IN THE FOUNTAIN, THE COUPLE WILL NEVER BREAK UP, AND LIVE HAPPY TOGETHER FOREVER AFTER!
....

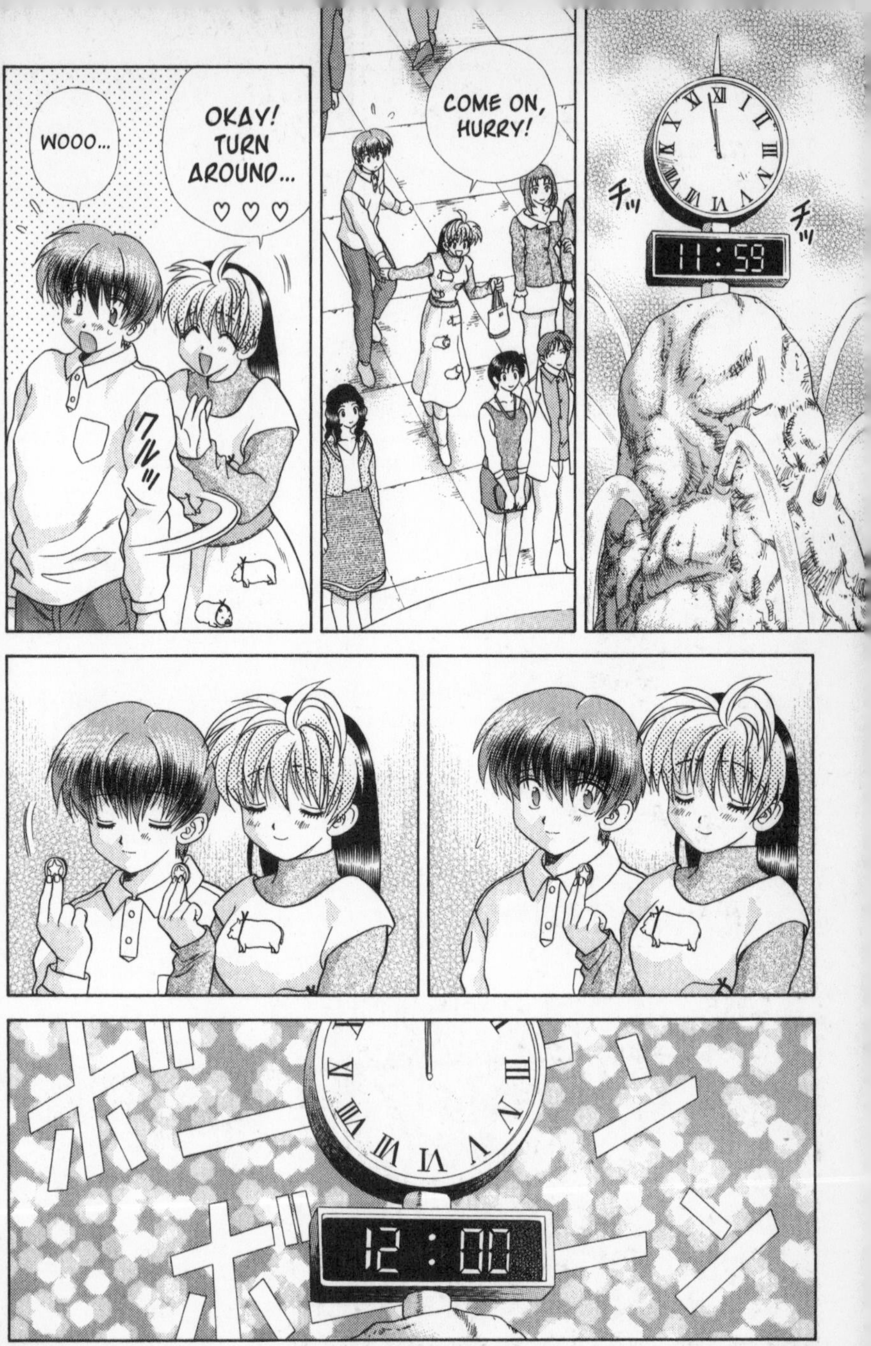
チッ
チッ
11:59
COME ON, HURRY!
OKAY! TURN AROUND... ♡ ♡ ♡
WOOO...
クルッ
ボーン
ボーン
12:00

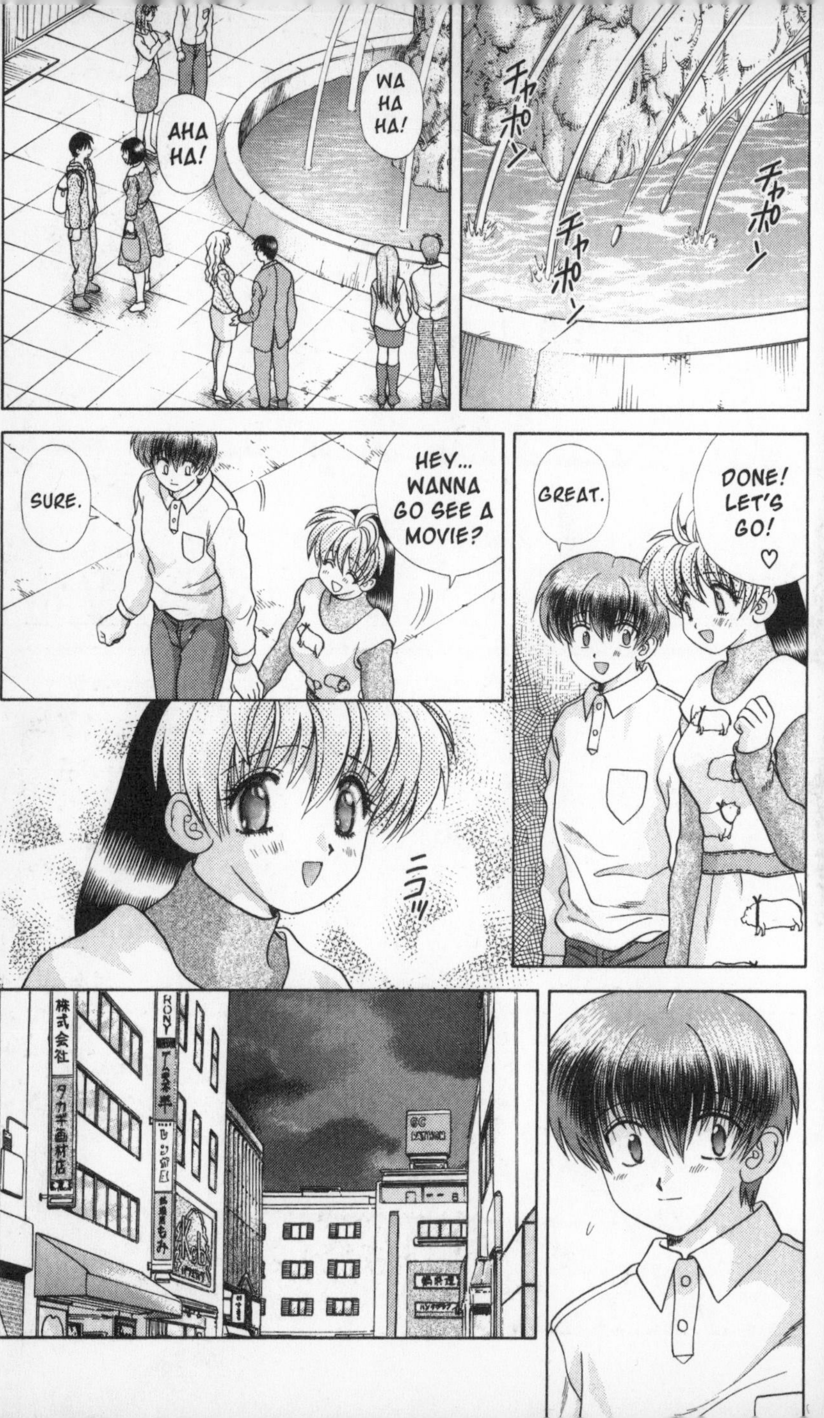
チャポン
チャポーン
チャポーン
WA HA HA!
AHA HA!
DONE! LET'S GO! ♥
GREAT.
HEY... WANNA GO SEE A MOVIE?
SURE.
ニコッ
株式会社
RONY

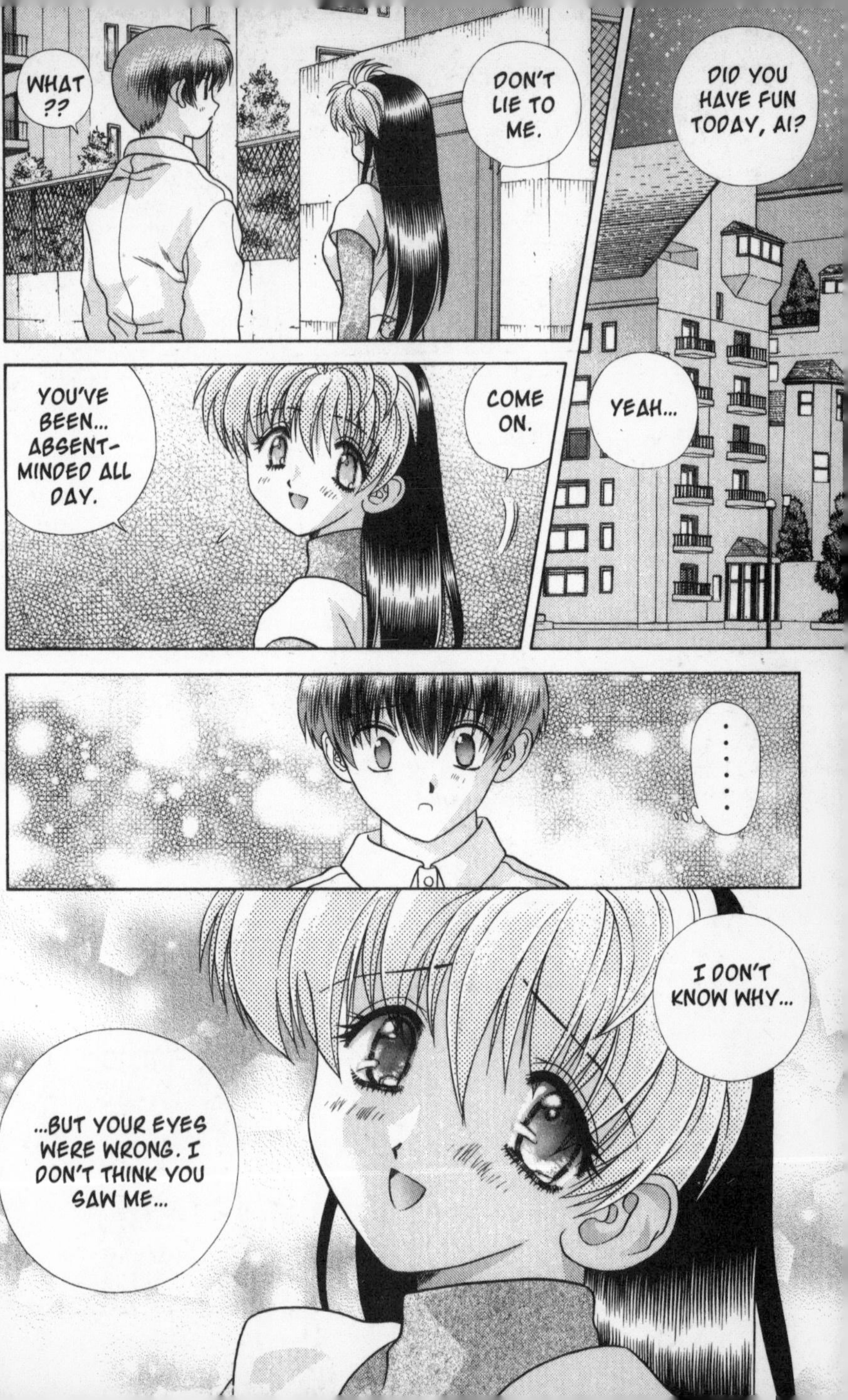
DID YOU HAVE FUN TODAY, AI?
YEAH...
DON'T LIE TO ME.
WHAT ??
COME ON.
YOU'VE BEEN... ABSENT-MINDED ALL DAY.
......
I DON'T KNOW WHY...
...BUT YOUR EYES WERE WRONG. I DON'T THINK YOU SAW ME...

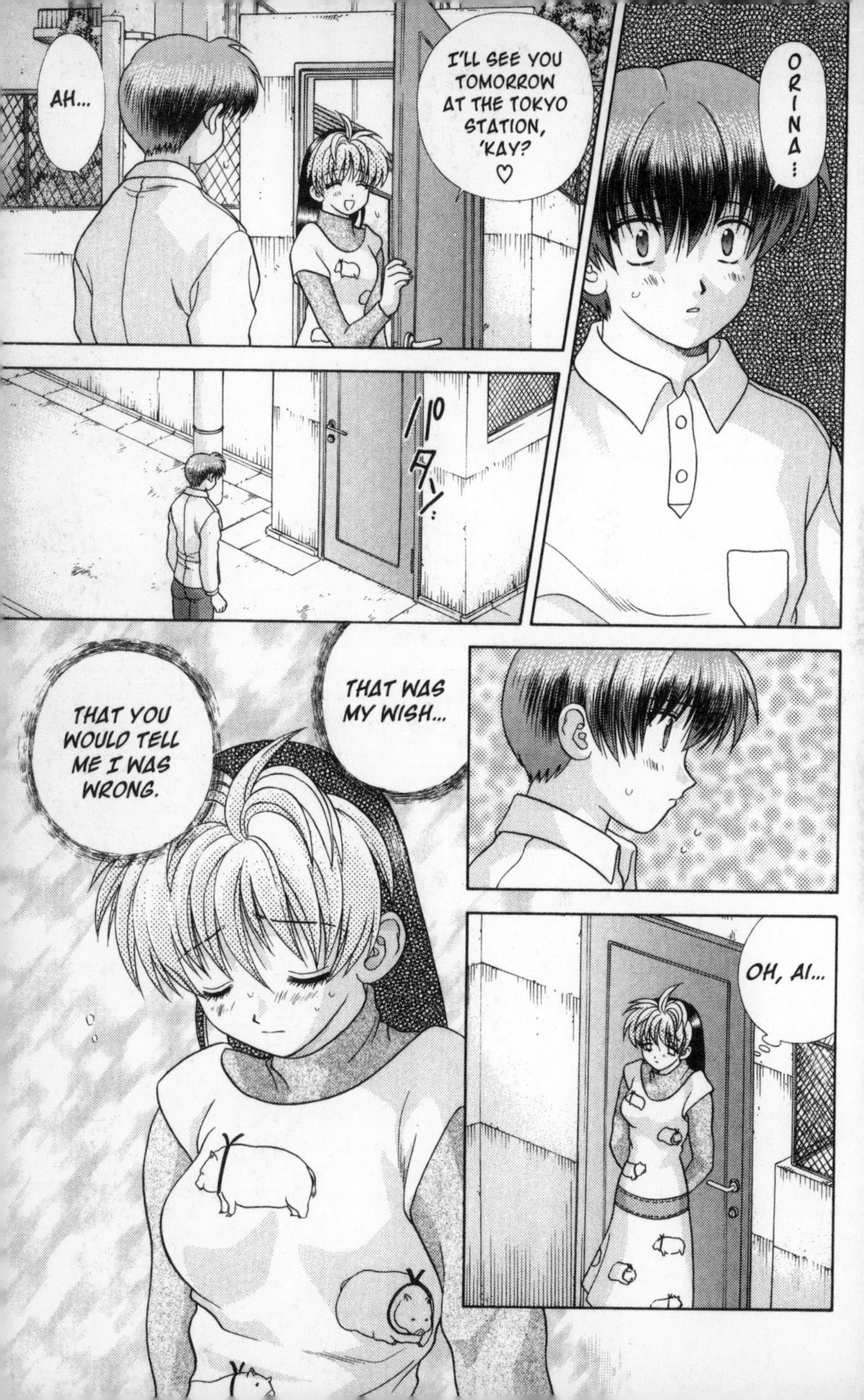
I'LL SEE YOU TOMORROW AT THE TOKYO STATION, 'KAY? ♡
AH...
パタン
ORINA...
THAT WAS MY WISH...
THAT YOU WOULD TELL ME I WAS WRONG.
OH, AI...

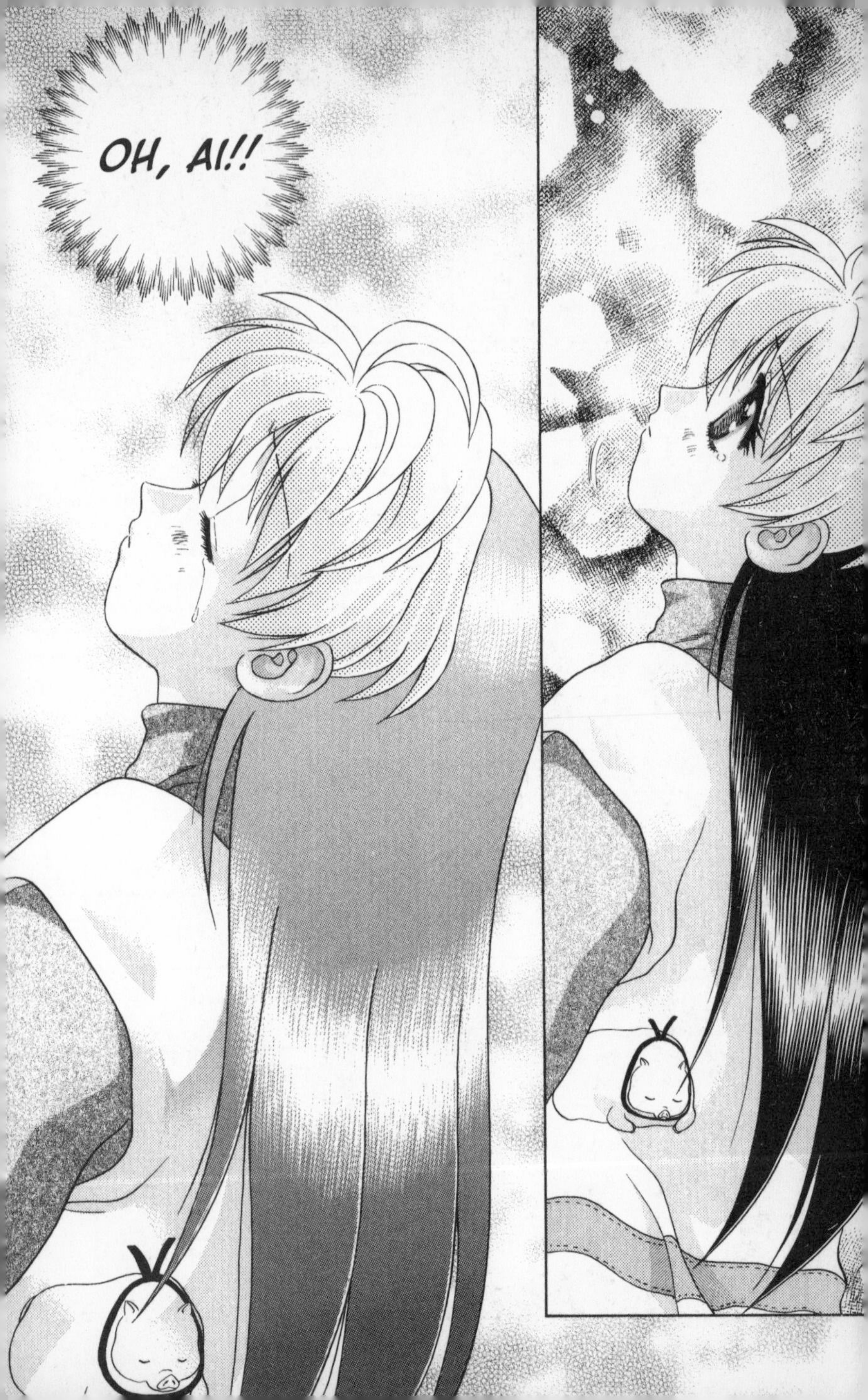
OH, AI!!

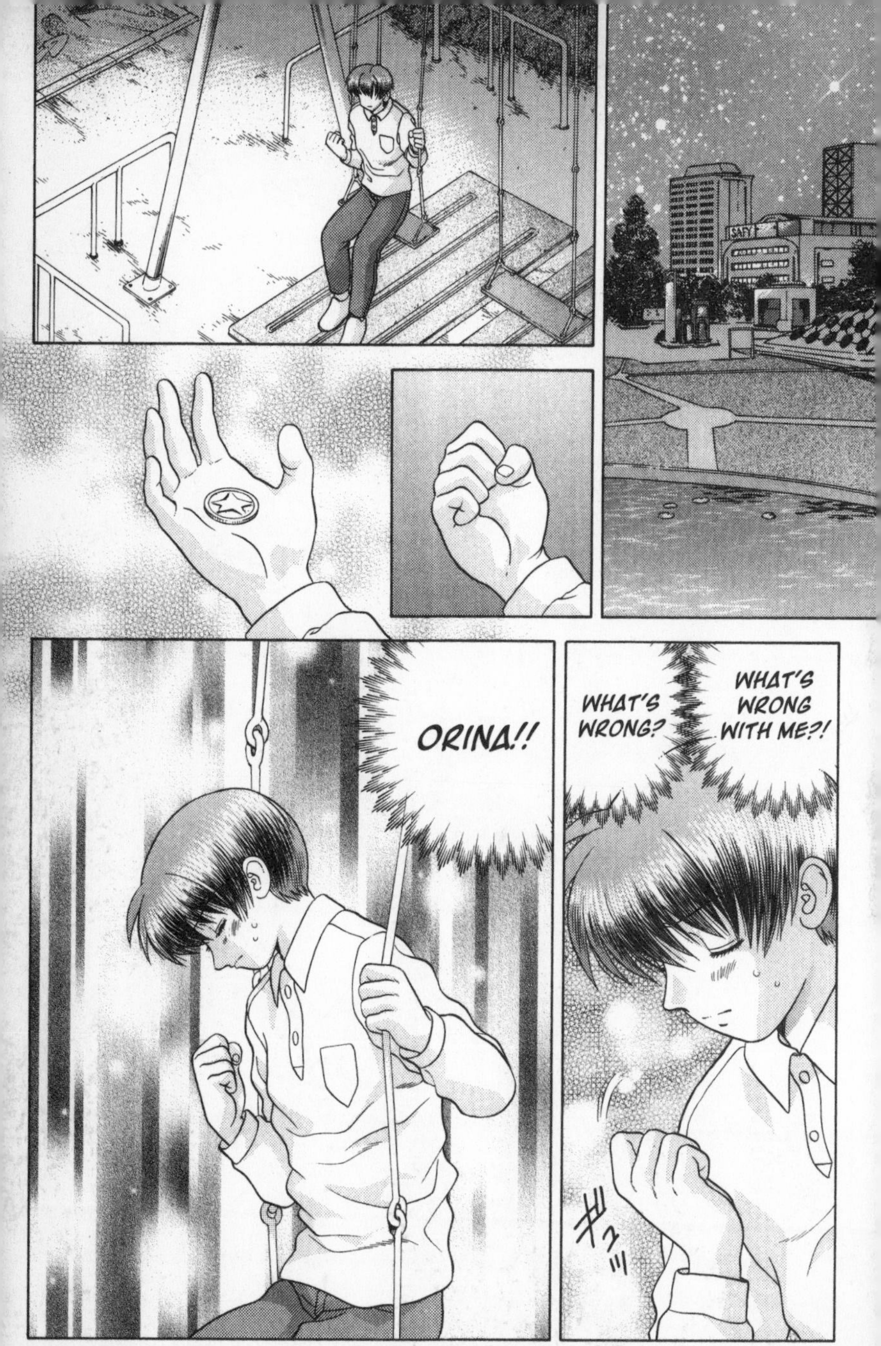
ORINA!!
WHAT'S WRONG?
WHAT'S WRONG WITH ME?!

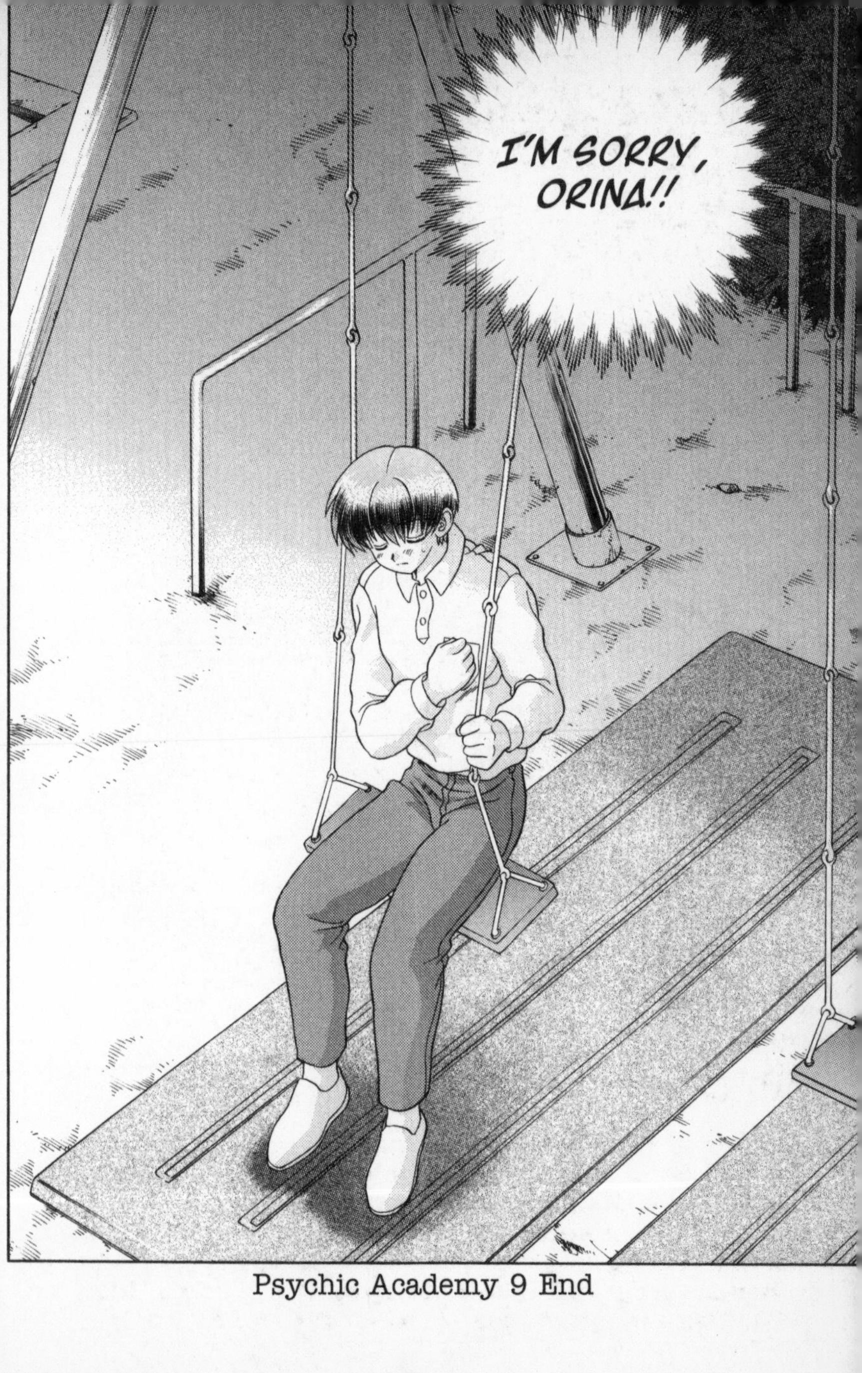
I'M SORRY, ORINA!!

Psychic Academy 9 End

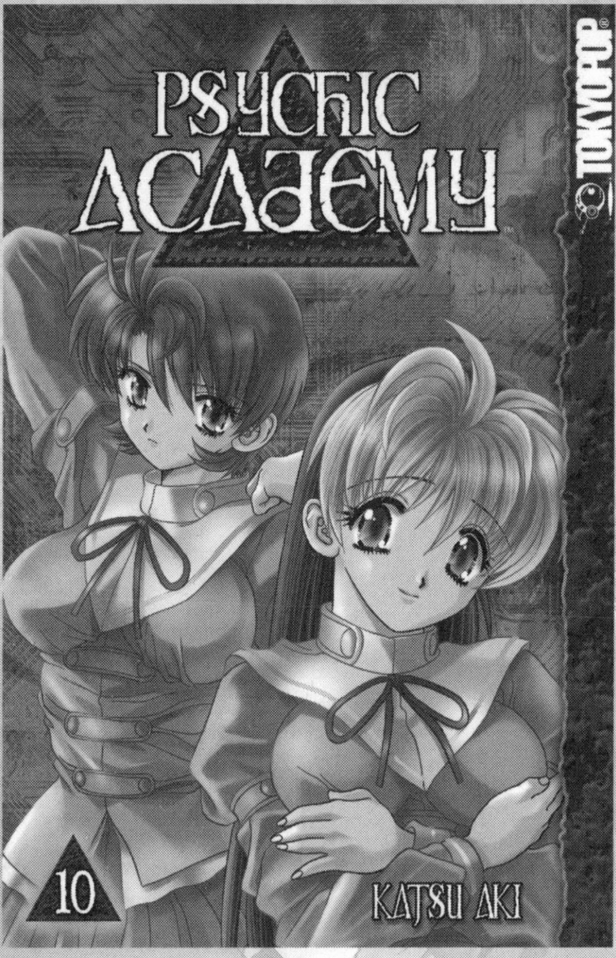
PSYCHIC ACADEMY
TOKYOPOP
10
KATSU AKI

In the next volume...

Gabriella comes to principal Baraffe as an agent of ADC Japan to request ward-ship of Shiomi. When Baraffe refuses, Dr. Watabe orders Gabriella to take Shiomi by any means necessary! Meanwhile, Ren is still plotting to eliminate ADC, much to Fafa's dismay. When Ren appears inside ADC, Tokimitsu is ready to greet him. Will Ren's efforts be the source of his own demise?

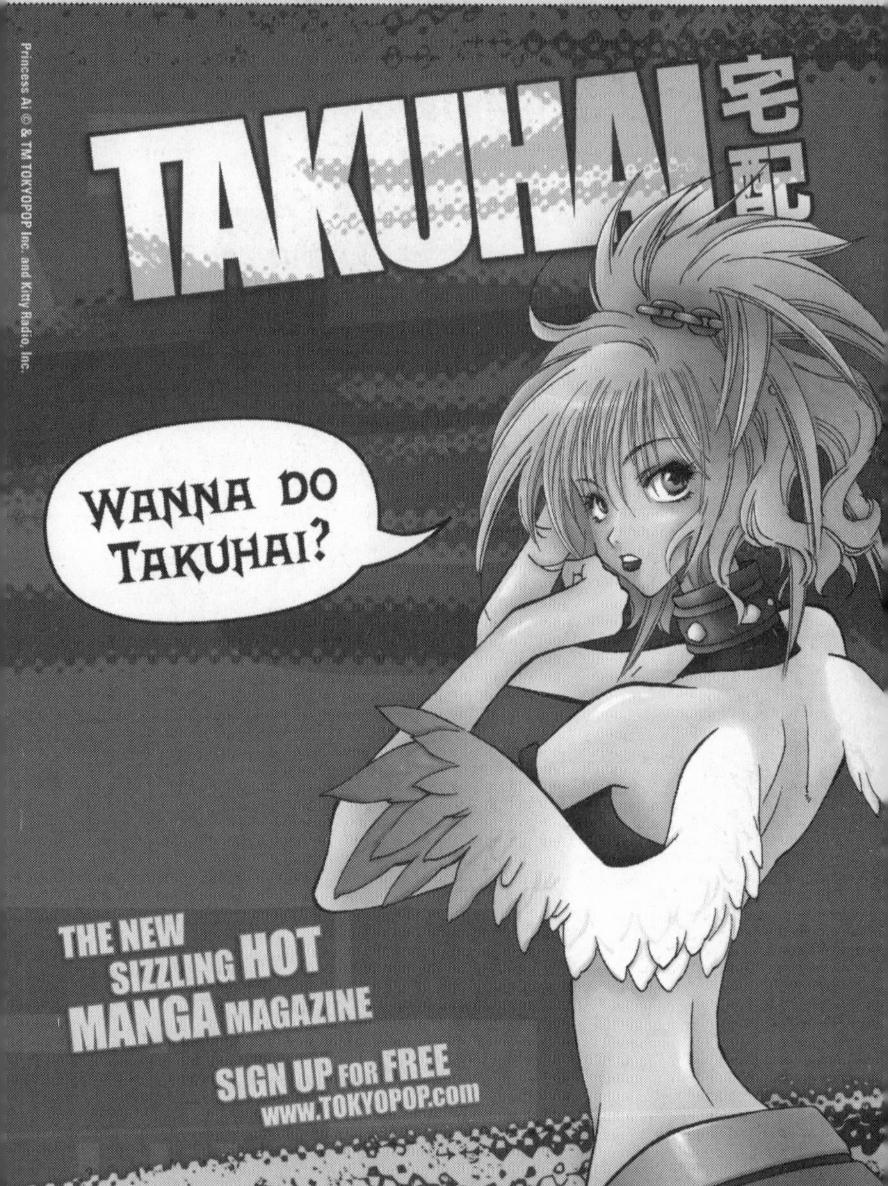
TAKUHAI 宅配
WANNA DO TAKUHAI?
THE NEW SIZZLING HOT MANGA MAGAZINE
SIGN UP FOR FREE
WWW.TOKYOPOP.com
Ai from *Princess Ai*
Princess Ai © & TM TOKYOPOP Inc. and Kitty Radio, Inc.

TOKYOPOP SHOP

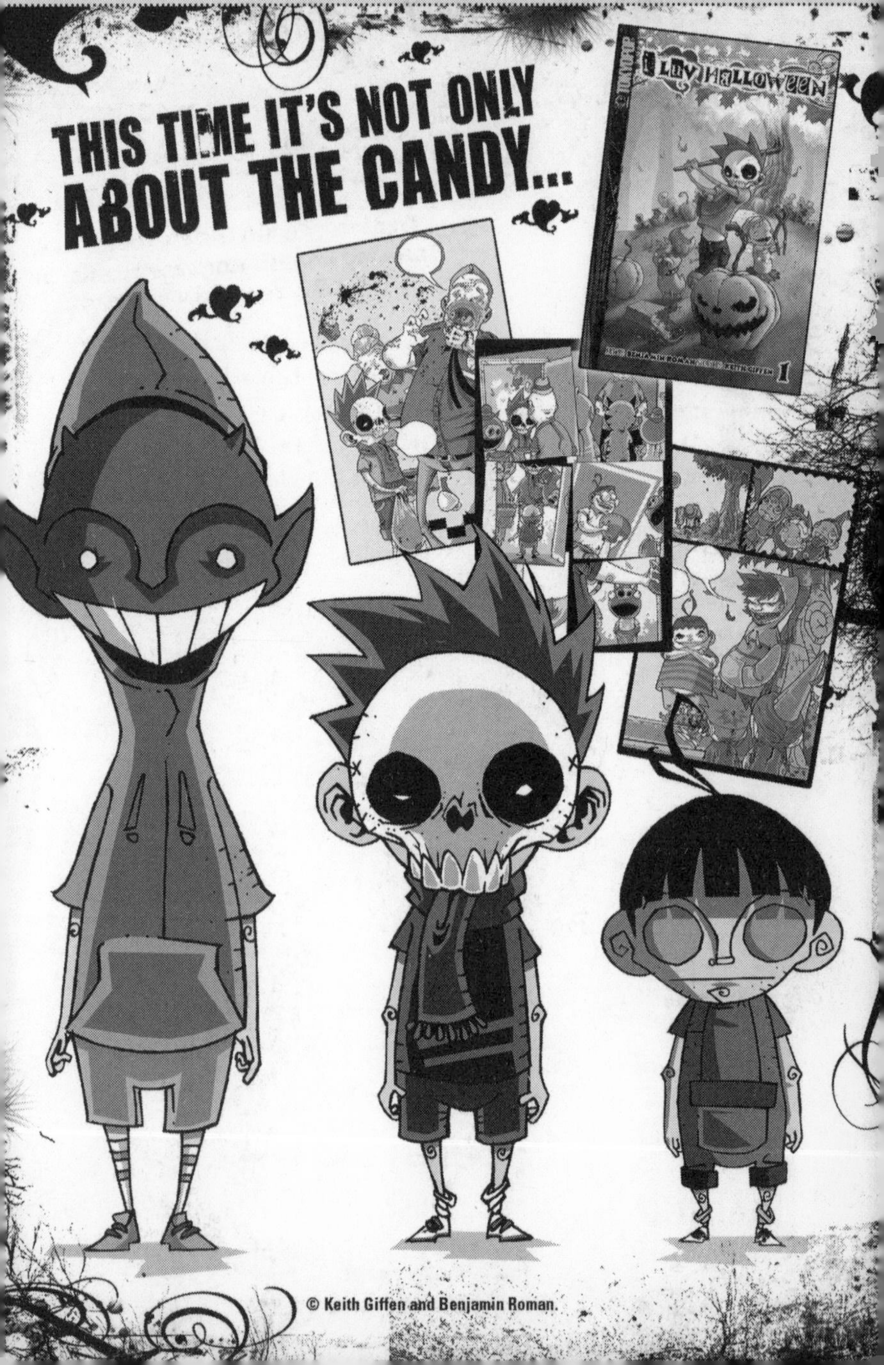
THIS TIME IT'S NOT ONLY ABOUT THE CANDY...
I LUV HALLOWEEN
1